ITALY

ITALY

EDITED BY LORRAINE MURRAY , EDITOR, GEOGRAPHY

Britannica®
Educational Publishing

IN ASSOCIATION WITH

ROSEN
EDUCATIONAL SERVICES

Published in 2014 by Britannica Educational Publishing
(a trademark of Encyclopædia Britannica, Inc.)
in association with Rosen Educational Services, LLC
29 East 21st Street, New York, NY 10010.

Distributed exclusively by Rosen Educational Services.
For a listing of additional Britannica Educational Publishing titles, call toll free (800) 237-9932.

First Edition

Britannica Educational Publishing
J.E. Luebering: Director, Core Reference Group
Adam Augustyn: Assistant Manager, Core Reference Group
Marilyn L. Barton: Senior Coordinator, Production Control
Steven Bosco: Director, Editorial Technologies
Lisa S. Braucher: Senior Producer and Data Editor
Yvette Charboneau: Senior Copy Editor
Kathy Nakamura: Manager, Media Acquisition
Edited by: Lorraine Murray, Editor, Geography

Rosen Educational Services
Jeanne Nagle: Editor
Nelson Sá: Art Director
Karen Huang: Photo Researcher
Brian Garvey: Designer, Cover Design
Introduction by Lorraine Murray

Library of Congress Cataloging-in-Publication Data

Italy/edited by Lorraine Murray.—First edition.
     pages cm.—(The Britannica guide to countries of the European Union)
"In association with Britannica Educational Publishing, Rosen Educational Services."
Includes bibliographical references and index.
ISBN 978-1-61530-966-5 (library binding)
1. Italy—Juvenile literature. 2. European Union—Italy—Juvenile literature.
I. Murray, Lorraine.
DG417.I8853 2014
945—dc23

                                                                2013000455

Manufactured in the United States of America

On the cover: Italian artist Arnaldo Pomodoro's sculpture, *Large Sphere*, decorates the fountain in front of the Palazzo della Farnesina, which houses Italy's Ministry of Foreign Affairs. *Filippo Monteforte/AFP/Getty Images*

CONTENTS

40

48

54

78

88

99

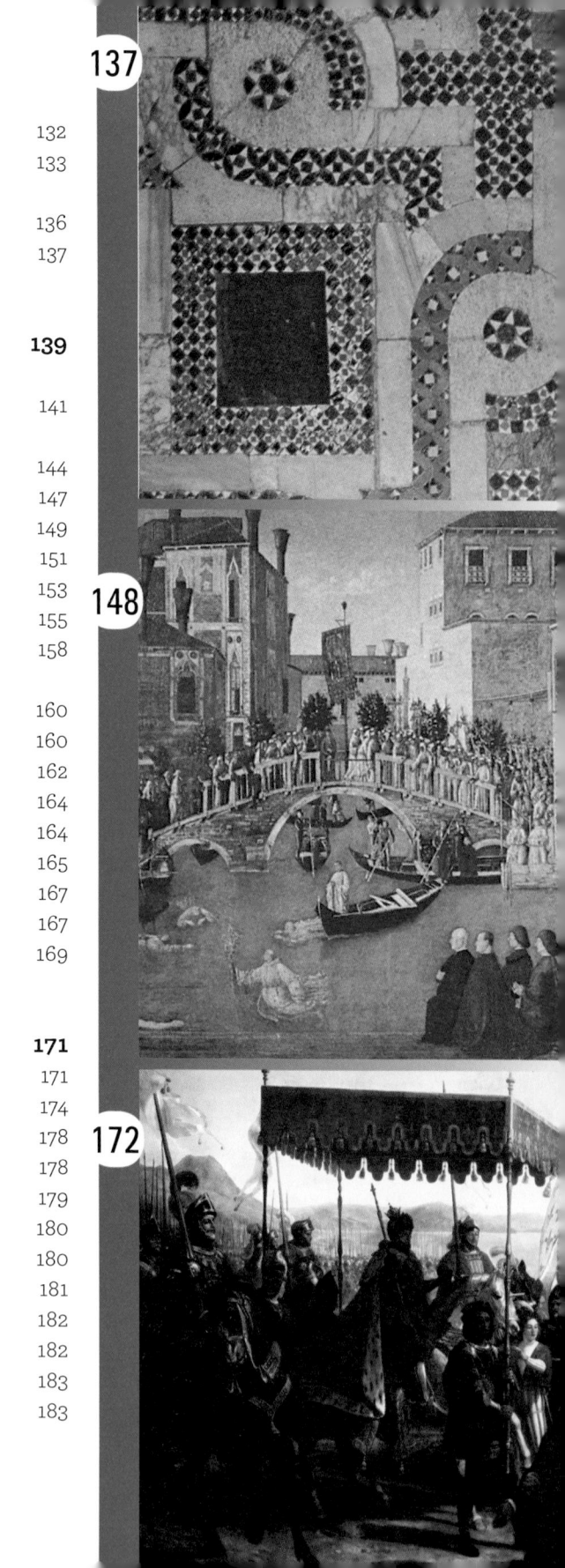

**CHAPTER 8: ITALY FROM 1870
TO THE PRESENT**

257

272

INTRODUCTION

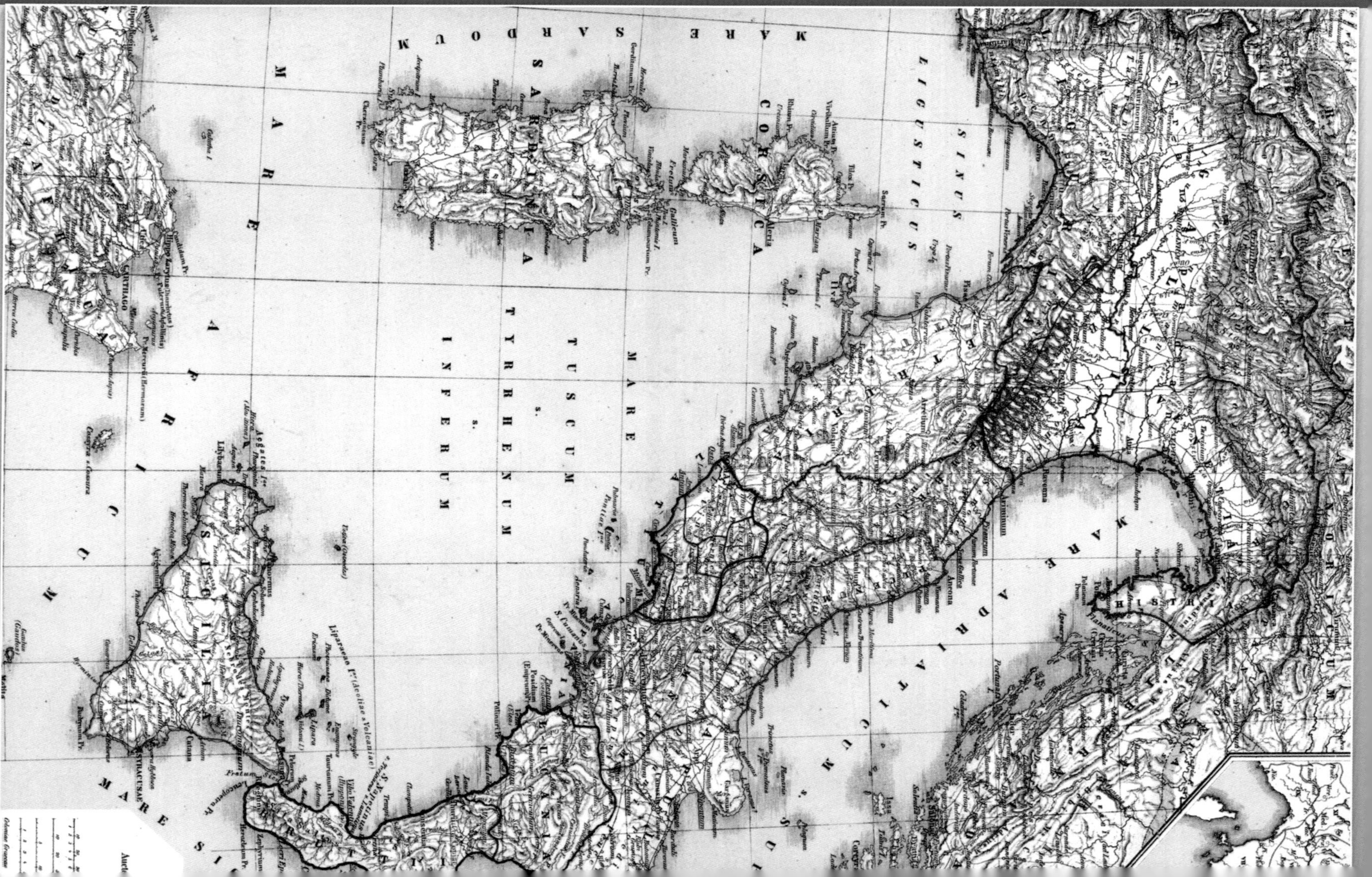

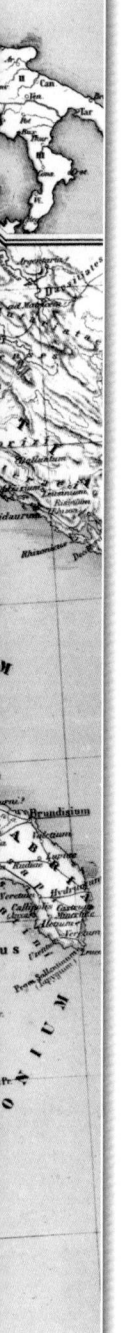

The familiar boot shape of its peninsula and its storied past as the fulcrum of a mighty empire have made Italy one of the most readily recognizable Western European countries. There is more to Italy—a founding member of the European Union (in 1952)—than geography and ancient history. This book introduces readers to the land, people, politics, economy, culture, traditions, and events that define the country as a whole. Yet one cannot help but be captivated by not only the way the country's past has shaped its present but also how the two manage to coexist so seamlessly.

Some experts have noted that despite the fact that the Italian peninsula has been long inhabited and its civilizations have had a profound impact on the Western world, Italy proper did not exist until the kingdom's unification in 1861. This is true in some meaningful sense, as the unification of Italy created a self-identified single political entity, ruled by the House of Savoy, from what had been an area that was home to loosely connected city-states, principalities, kingdoms, and republics. Throughout history these states had maintained shifting alliances, and the territory was subject to a variety of foreign influences, some of whose "foreignness" was debatable; for example, the influence of France in Italy's Piedmont region.

Yet the idea of "Italian-ness," as perceived from both within and without, was certainly not newly created at the time of the Risorgimento, the unification movement of the late 19th century. Geographical factors, most notably the natural boundaries of the Alps in the north and the Adriatic, Ionian, Tyrrhenian, and Ligurian seas surrounding the peninsula on the remaining three sides, might well have been enough to encourage the perception of Italy as a distinct region. It was the tides of history, however—including the comings and goings of tribes and conquerors—that truly put Italy on the map. The most significant and lasting impact came with the rise of ancient Rome, beginning around 700 BCE, and its growth into first a republic, then an empire stretching from Scotland to India with the city of Rome at its heart. By as early as 264 BCE, the majority of the peninsula was either part of or allied with the Roman state. By the later years of the Roman Empire (c. 300 CE), the territory known as Italia also included the islands of Sicily, Corsica, and Sardinia.

Thus it may be said that Italy actually existed millennia ago. It is this longevity that gives modern Italy what many feel is its most distinctive and haunting quality. Far from having been forgotten or left behind, the people of past eras have left bountiful physical evidence of their presence in the form of buildings, artifacts, place-names, and language. History itself persists, layer upon layer, as an almost palpable presence everywhere one turns.

This layering can be traced to ancient times. Beginning in about 750 BCE, the Greeks established colonies along the coast of what is now southern Italy and in

Sicily, known collectively as Magna Graecia (Latin: "Great Greece"), that were contemporaneous with the Etruscan civilization. These cities, the site of trade and commerce, were far from the only contact the peninsula had with Greece, but they were significant outposts of Greek culture, and they persist today as Italian cities. Tarentum (modern-day Taranto, in Puglia) was settled by Spartans and was inhabited at various times by Goths, Byzantines, Lombards, and Arabs. On the east coast of Sicily, temples to the gods Apollo, Zeus, and Athena were built in Syracuse (Siracusa), which was settled by Corinthians. Agrigento, on Sicily's southern coast, was colonized by Greeks from Gela and is rich in Greek remains, including a large, unfinished temple to Zeus and a very well preserved Doric temple that was converted to a church in the late 6th century CE. (Many churches across Italy, as well as throughout Europe and the world over, were built over pagan temples as Christianity spread.)

One of the most arresting sites in Rome is the Pantheon, in the Piazza della Rotonda. This extremely well-preserved ancient Roman structure, dating to 27 BCE (since rebuilt and renovated), dominates the piazza, not only because of its massive size but also because of the information chiseled high on the exterior. The stentorian announcement "M. AGRIPPA L. F. COS. TERTIUM FECIT" ("MARCUS AGRIPPA, SON OF LUCIUS, BUILT THIS DURING HIS THIRD CONSULATE") has proclaimed the building constructor's importance ceaselessly across the centuries. Yet, far from being a static monument, this building, like so many others in Italy, has had several incarnations. Created as a temple for all the Roman gods, it was closed and left disused by the early Christian emperors, pillaged by barbarian invaders, and eventually turned into a Christian church. It still speaks today to passersby and tourists as they walk around the dolphin fountain in the square or enjoy a slice of pizza while sitting in the square.

Such casual juxtaposition of the great and the mundane is one of Italy's most remarkable aspects. In a residential area of Rome, far from the tourist sites, one may take a walk in the fresh air, away from the apartment blocks, cafes, housewares stores, late-20th-century churches and the like, and suddenly come upon the remains of a Roman aqueduct, its arches repeating across a field as if the greatest of Western empires had just ended yesterday, or perhaps had not ended at all. Surely such daily familiarity with past eras must encourage today's Italians to have an intimate relationship with their history. One can imagine that, living among such artifacts, people might come to regard them as things some recently departed neighbors left behind, like an abandoned house or a wheelbarrow in a yard.

Rather than inspiring any of the proverbial contempt that comes with familiarity, the living history throughout Italy affords a sense of timelessness. If Marcus Agrippa's name (for example) remains before the public two millennia after his death, and if the works of past civilizations remain in use and fully within reach, the past and present combine into an eternal present. Indeed, some infrastructure left from Roman times remains functional. For example, a 2,000-year-old subterranean aqueduct that was restored during the Renaissance, 1,000 years after its destruction by the Visigoths, still provides water to a few of Rome's most famous fountains. Thus, Bernini's Fountain of the Four Rivers in Piazza Navona (finished in 1651) and the Trevi Fountain (1762) are fed by an underground conduit that dates to 19 BCE, and the people of the city still drink at public fountains similarly supplied.

Building projects in the major cities are often complicated—most fortuitously—by the propensity of Italy's construction sites to become archaeological digs. During an expansion of Naples's metro in the early 21st century, the excavations proved a treasure trove to archaeologists, not in terms of riches but in the exposition of strata encompassing the city's 2,700-hundred year history. Levels of Greco-Roman, Byzantine, and Angevin occupation were exposed and studied. Forty years earlier, Italian director Federico Fellini dramatized a similar scenario in his film *Roma* (1972). In one unforgettable sequence, the construction of Rome's first subway line leads to precious archaeological discoveries beneath the city, including that of a pristine Roman villa. Workers open a room and glimpse beautiful colored frescoes on walls unseen for 2,000 years. The

consequence of that action has an almost heart-stopping poignancy that contains a lesson about the importance of treating the past with delicacy and utmost respect.

Often, it was not through conscious historic preservation but only through luck and circumstance that these things survived. Many items lasted because they were underground or so massive that they resisted dismantling. Although there are, indeed, many ancient monuments and other works that have survived to the present day in Italy, it is stunning to consider how much has been lost. In its final years, in the early 5th century, the Roman Empire was repeatedly invaded by barbarians— Huns, Lombards, Ostrogoths, and Franks. They and subsequent invaders took down many of the great buildings of the empire, plundering their treasures and even reusing the building materials for construction elsewhere.

The Western empire's final emperor was deposed in 476 CE. The early Middle Ages saw the rise of Catholicism and its headquartering in Rome. Popes secured great temporal power during the period. Meanwhile, the cohesive rule established in Republican and imperial Rome disappeared, and the Italian lands devolved into separate regions governed by various powers. The Lombards, a Germanic people, established themselves as rulers over much of Italy before being deposed in turn by Frankish invaders in the mid-8th century, while the Byzantine Empire (the former Eastern Roman Empire) retained power in central and southern

Italy, Istria, and the islands of Sardinia and Sicily. In the 9th through 10th centuries, Sicily came under the rule of Arabs from North Africa. In time they, too, were defeated, by the Normans in 1060.

Fortunately for the world's cultural heritage, the Italian people are well-versed in the appreciation and preservation of all their country contains. Artistic preservationists and restorers practice to the height of their abilities in Italy. Witness the late-20th-century restoration of the age-darkened 15th-century fresco of Adam and Eve by Tommaso Masaccio in the Brancacci Chapel in Florence. The painstaking work to clean the painting and bring the colors back to their original brightness and vibrancy brought about such a change in the fresco that scholars found themselves revising their understanding of Masaccio's work.

Dedicated efforts are also under way to ensure that when it comes to science and technology, the past, in a manner of speaking, has a future in Italy. One of the world's greatest engineering achievements of recent decades has taken place in the northern city of Venice, which is built on more than 100 small islands. For hundreds of years the city has been inundated by floodwaters (acqua alta) several times a year, occurrences that increased in frequency during the 20th century. Not only that, but the city itself has been sinking rather quickly—11 inches over the past century. It had been clear for many years that historic Venice was in crisis and that it would take a gigantic infrastructure project to stave off the city's eventual submersion. To achieve that goal, a multifaceted project called MOSE (an acronym that recalls the Italian name of Moses, who parted the Red Sea) was conceived to protect the city from rising floodwaters. Begun in 2003, the project called for the placement of numerous inflatable floodgates at the inlets to the Venice lagoon, so as to control the incoming tides and protect the city from rising sea levels. Other components of the project were the dredging of the silted-up lagoon and the shoring up of quays and flood-prone walls and foundations. With the best efforts of the country's scientists and technicians, another priceless part of Italy's heritage is being safeguarded.

In the 21st century, Italy found itself in the unenviable position of having to safeguard, or assure, its political and economic future. The longstanding Prime Minister Silvio Berlusconi resigned from office in November 2011 amid charges of sexual misconduct and corruption and his party's loss of confidence in his leadership. At the same time the country struggled with economic instability, swept up in a looming financial crisis that threatened the ability of several countries within the European Union to refinance their national debt. The resulting turmoil and uncertainty were disruptive, yet they were not enough to tarnish the country's dynamic presence in Western Europe. Steeped in history, modern Italy has shown time and again that it is possible to honour the past while moving forward with resolve into the future.

CHAPTER 1

Italy: The Land and Its People

Italy, which comprises some of the most varied and scenic landscapes on Earth, is often described as being shaped like a boot. At its broad top stand the Alps, which are among the world's most rugged mountains. Italy's highest points are along Monte Rosa, which peaks in Switzerland, and along Mont Blanc, which peaks in France. The western Alps overlook a landscape of Alpine lakes and glacier-carved valleys that stretch down to the Po River and the Piedmont. From the central Alps, running down the length of the country, radiate the tall Apennine Mountains, which widen near Rome to cover nearly the entire width of the Italian peninsula. South of Rome the Apennines narrow and are flanked by two wide coastal plains, one facing the Tyrrhenian Sea, the other facing the Adriatic Sea. Much of the lower Apennine chain is near-wilderness, hosting a wide range of species rarely seen elsewhere in western Europe, such as wild boars, wolves, asps, and bears. The southern Apennines are tectonically unstable and feature several active volcanoes, including Vesuvius, which from time to time belches ash and steam into the air above Naples and its island-strewn bay. To the west and southwest, in the Mediterranean Sea, lie the islands of Sardinia and Sicily.

To the north the Alps separate Italy from France, Switzerland, Austria, and Slovenia. Elsewhere Italy is surrounded by the Mediterranean Sea, in particular by the Adriatic Sea to the northeast, the Ionian Sea to the southeast, the Tyrrhenian Sea to the southwest, and the Ligurian Sea to the northwest. Areas of plain, which are practically limited to the great northern triangle of the Po valley, cover only about one-fifth of the total area of the country; the remainder is roughly evenly divided between hilly and mountainous land, providing variations to the generally temperate climate.

MOUNTAIN RANGES

Mountain ranges higher than 2,300 feet (702 metres) occupy more than one-third of Italy. There are two mountain systems: the scenic Alps, parts of which lie within the neighbouring countries of France, Switzerland, Austria, and Slovenia; and the Apennines, which form the spine of the entire peninsula and of the island of Sicily. A third mountain system exists on the two large islands to the west, Italian Sardinia and French Corsica.

The Alps run in a broad west-to-east arc from the Cadibona Pass, near Savona on the Gulf of Genoa, to north of Trieste, at the head of the Adriatic Sea. The section properly called Alpine is the border district that includes the highest masses, made up of weathered Hercynian rocks, dating from the Carboniferous and Permian periods (approximately 360 million to 250 million years ago). The Alps have rugged, very high peaks, reaching more than 12,800 feet (3,900 metres) in various spectacular formations, characterized as pyramidal, pinnacled, rounded, or needlelike. The valleys were heavily

scoured by glaciers in the Quaternary Period (the past 2.6 million years); there are still more than 1,000 glaciers left, though in a phase of retreat, more than 100 having disappeared in the past half century or so.

The Alpine mountain mass falls into three main groups. First, the Western Alps run north to south in Italy from Aosta to the Cadibona Pass; in this group are Mount Viso (12,602 feet [3,841 metres]) and Gran Paradiso (13,323 feet [4,061 metres]), which is the highest mountain wholly within Italy, both base and peak. Second, the Central Alps run west to east from the Western Alps to the Brenner Pass, leading into Austria and the Trentino–Alto Adige valley, also with high peaks, such as Mont Blanc (with a summit just over the border in France of 15,771 feet [4,807 metres]), the Matterhorn (Italian Monte Cervino; 14,692 feet [4,478 metres]), Monte Rosa (with a summit just over the border in Switzerland of 15,203 feet [4,634 metres]), and Mount Ortles (12,812 feet [3,905 metres]). Lastly, the Eastern Alps run west to east from the Brenner Pass to Trieste and include the Dolomites (Dolomiti) and Mount Marmolada (10,968 feet [3,343 metres]). The Italian foothills of the Alps, which reach no higher than 8,200 feet (2,500 metres), lie between these great ranges and the Po valley. They are composed mainly of limestone and sedimentary rocks. A notable feature is the karst system of underground caves and streams that are especially characteristic of the Carso, the limestone plateau

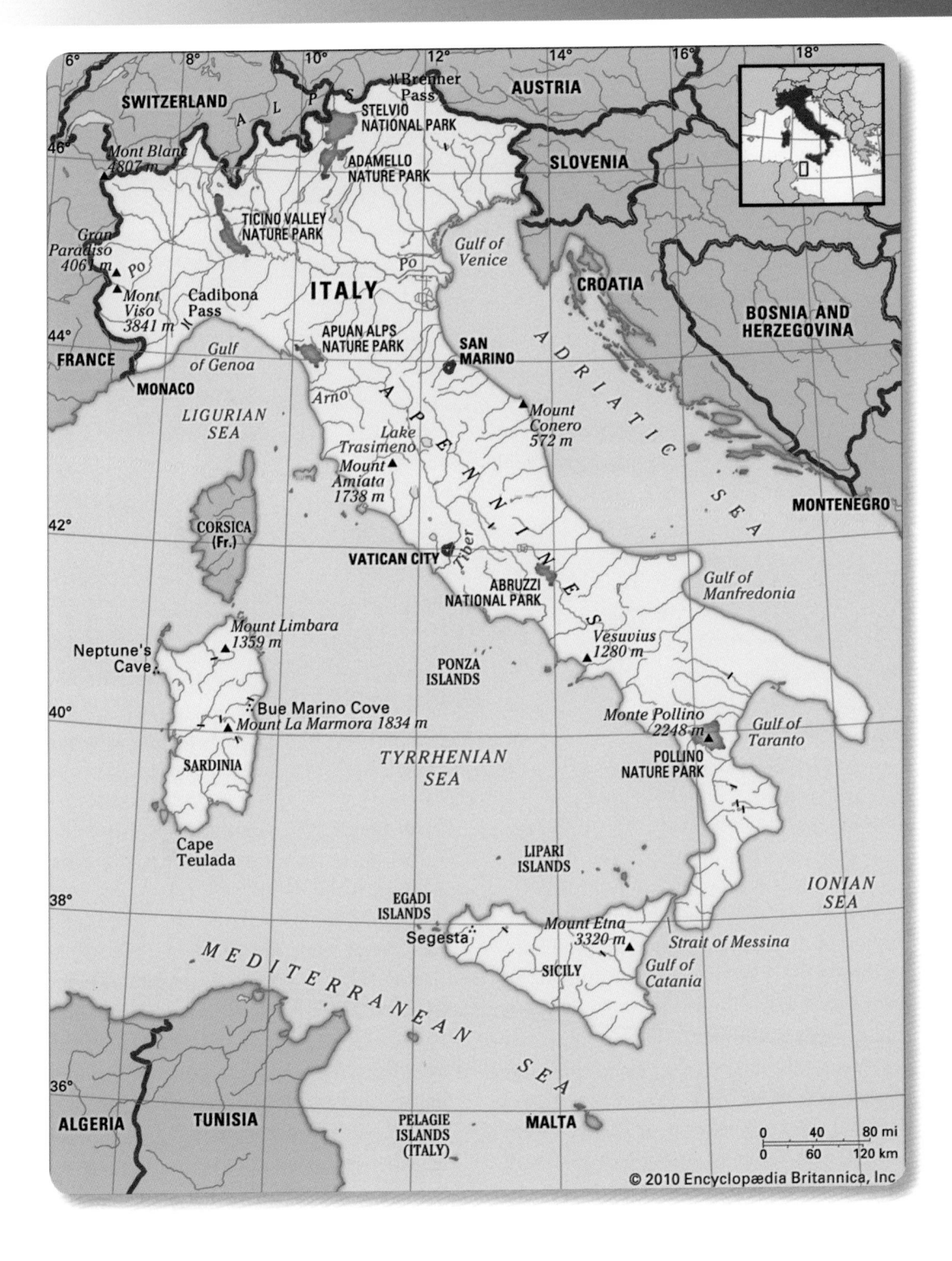

© 2010 Encyclopædia Britannica, Inc

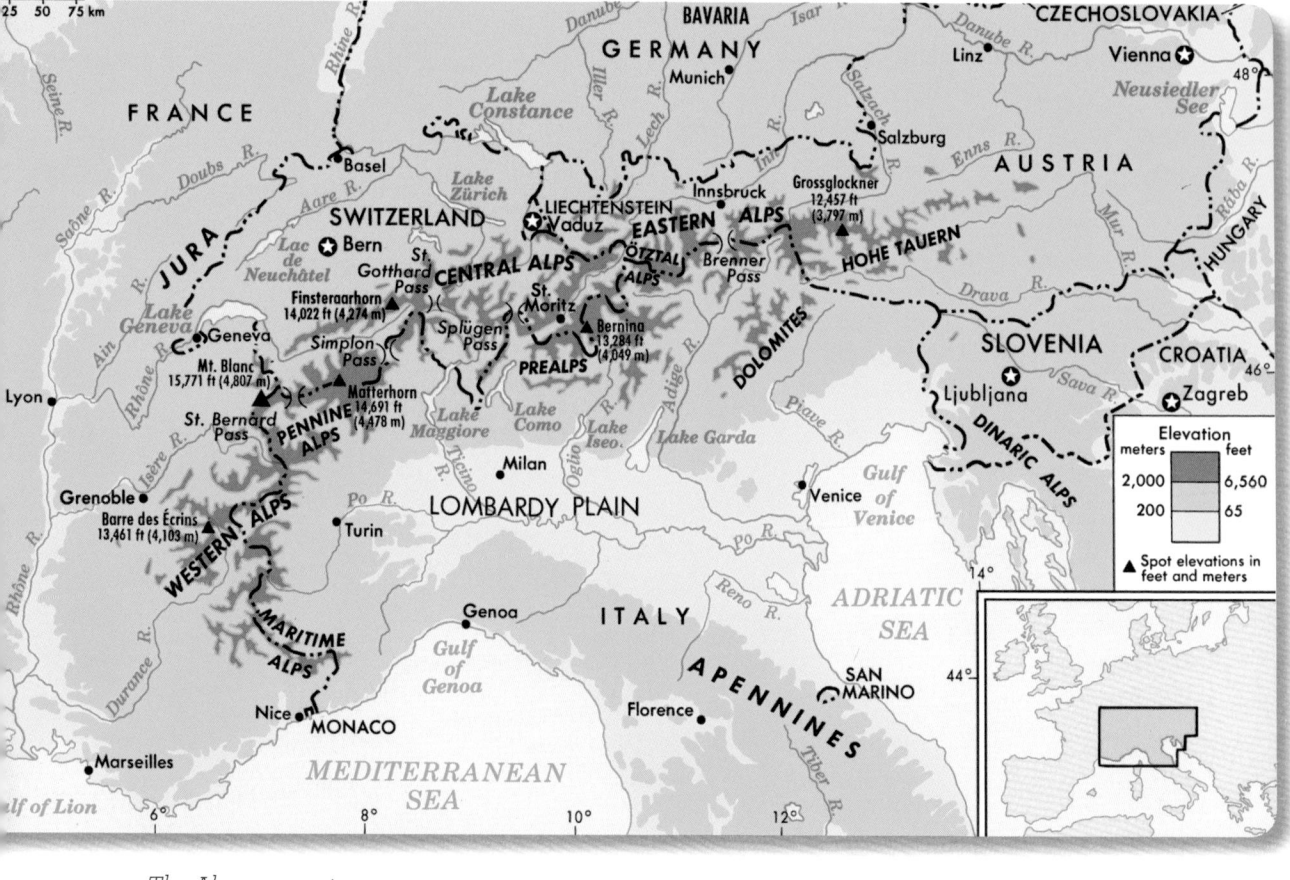

The Alps mountain ranges.

between the Eastern Alps and southwestern Slovenia.

The Apennines are the long system of mountains and hills that run down the Italian peninsula from the Cadibona Pass to the tip of Calabria and continue on the island of Sicily. The range is about 1,245 miles (2,000 km) long; it is only about 20 miles (32 km) wide at either end but about 120 miles (190 km) wide in the Central Apennines, east of Rome, where the "Great Rock of Italy" (Gran Sasso d'Italia) provides the highest Apennine

peak (9,554 feet [2,912 metres]) and the only glacier on the peninsula, Calderone, which is the southernmost in Europe. The Apennines comprise predominantly sandstone and limestone marl (clay) in the north; limestone and dolomite (magnesium limestone) in the centre; and limestone, weathered rock, and Hercynian granite in the south. On either side of the central mass are grouped two considerably lower masses, composed in general of more recent and softer rocks, such as sandstone. These sub-Apennines run in the east from Monferrato to the Gulf of Taranto and in the west from Florence southward through Tuscany and Umbria to Rome. This latter range is separated from the main Apennines by the valleys of the Arno and the Tiber rivers.

At the outer flanks of the sub-Apennines, two allied series of limestone and volcanic rocks extend to the coast. They include, to the west, the Apuane Alps, which are famous for their marbles; farther south, the Metallifere Mountains (more than 3,380 feet [1,030 metres]), abundant in minerals; then various extinct volcanoes occupied by crater lakes, such as that of Bolsena; then cavernous mountains, such as Lepini and Circeo, and the partially or still fully active volcanic group of the Flegrei Plain and Vesuvius; and finally the limestone mountains of the peninsulas of Amalfi and Cilento. The extensions on the Adriatic coast are simpler, comprising only the small promontory of Mount Conero, the higher peninsula of Gargano (3,465 feet [1,056 metres]), and the Salentina Peninsula in Puglia. All these are limestone.

In Sardinia there are two mountain masses, separated by the long plain of Campidano, which runs from the Gulf of Asinara southeastward across the island to the Gulf of Cagliari. The group in the southwest is small and low, formed from sediment, mostly mineralized, perhaps early in the Paleozoic Era (about 540 million to 250 million years ago). The northeastern mass reaches an elevation of more than 6,000 feet (1,830 metres)

The village of Courmayeur in the Pennine Alps, Italy. J. Alex Langley/DPI

at Gennargentu; the underlying foundation is basically metamorphic (heat- and pressure-altered) rock, and it is covered in the northeast by Paleozoic granite and partially covered in the northwest by Mesozoic limestones (those formed about 250 to 65 million years ago) and by sandstone and clays of the Paleogene and Neogene periods (about 65 to 2.6

VESUVIUS

The active volcano Vesuvius rises above the Bay of Naples on the plain of Campania in southern Italy. Its western base rests almost upon the bay. The height of the cone in 1980 was 4,198 feet (1,280 metres), but it varies considerably after each major eruption. At about 1,968 feet a high semicircular ridge, called Mount Somma, begins, girding the cone on the north and rising to 3,714 feet. Between Mount Somma and the cone is the Valle del Gigante (Giant's Valley). At the summit of the cone is a large crater about 1,000 feet deep and 2,000 feet across; it was formed in the eruption of 1944. More than two million people live in the area of Vesuvius and on its lower slopes. There are industrial towns along the coast of the Bay of Naples and small agricultural centres on the northern slopes.

Vesuvius probably originated somewhat less than 200,000 years ago. Although a relatively young volcano, Vesuvius had been dormant for centuries before the great eruption of 79 CE that buried the cities of Pompeii and Stabiae under ashes and lapilli and the city of Herculaneum under a mudflow. Between the years 79 and 1631, several eruptions were reported. The explosions of 512 were so severe that Theodoric the Goth released the people living on the slopes of Vesuvius from payment of taxes.

After some centuries of quiescence, a series of earthquakes, lasting for six months and gradually increasing in violence, preceded a major eruption that took place on December 16, 1631. Many villages on the slopes of the volcano were destroyed; about 3,000 people were killed; the lava flow reached the sea; and the skies were darkened for days.

The slopes of Vesuvius are covered with vineyards and orchards, and the wine grown there is known as Lacrima Christi; in ancient Pompeii the wine jars were frequently marked with the name Vesuvinum. The soil is very fertile, and in the long period of inactivity before the eruption of 1631 there were forests in the crater and three lakes from which pasturing herds drank. In 73 BCE the gladiator Spartacus was besieged by the praetor Publius Claudius Pulcher on the barren summit of Mount Somma, which was then a wide, flat depression walled by rugged rocks festooned with wild vines. He escaped by twisting ropes of vine branches and descending through unguarded fissures in the crater rim.

million years ago). There are caves on the seacoast and inland where limestones predominate.

Present volcanic action had its origins in the Pliocene Epoch (about 5.3 to 2.6 million years ago) and the Quaternary Period (the past 2.6 million years) and is represented by the Flegrei Plain, near Naples, and by the neighbouring islands, such as Ischia; by Vesuvius; by the Eolie, or Lipari, Islands; and by Mount Etna, which is on the island of Sicily. Phenomena that are related to volcanism include thermal springs in the Euganei Hills, *vulcanelli* (mud springs) at Viterbo, and emissions of gas at Pozzuoli. Seismic activity, leading to earthquakes, is rare in the Alps and the Po valley; it is infrequent but occasionally strong in the Alpine foothills; and it may be catastrophic in the central and southern Apennines (as in 1980) and on Sicily.

THE PLAINS

Plains cover less than one-fourth of the area of Italy. Some of these, such as the Po valley and the Apulian Plain, are ancient sea gulfs filled by alluvium. Others, such as the Lecce Plain in Puglia, flank the sea on rocky plateaus about 65 to 100 feet (20 to 30 metres) high, formed of ancient land leveled by the sea and subsequently uplifted. Plains in the interior, such as the long Chiana Valley, are made by alluvial or other filling of ancient basins. The most extensive and important plain in Italy, that of the Po valley, occupies more than 17,000 of the 27,000 square miles (44,000 of the 77,000 square km) of Italian plain land. It ranges in altitude from sea level up to 1,800 feet (550 metres), with the greater part below 330 feet (100 metres). Through it runs the Po River and all its tributaries and the Reno, Adige, Piave, and Tagliamento rivers. The plain falls into several natural divisions. At its highest end, by the Alpine foothills, it is made up of parallel *ferretto* (red loam composed of ferrous clay) ridges, running from north to south, with areas of gravel and permeable sand between them. This section of the plain is terraced

and unproductive, although the rainfall is high. Below this is a section where the rivers rise, their waters eventually providing vital irrigation both for the *marcite* (winter pastures) and for the intensive agriculture of the fertile lower plain. Other notable plains include the *maremme* of Tuscany and Lazio, reclaimed marshland with dunes at the edge of the sea; the Pontine Marshes, a recently reclaimed seaward extension of the Roman countryside (*campagna*); the fertile Campania Plain around Vesuvius; and the rather arid Apulian Plain. In Sicily the Plain of Catania is a good area for growing citrus fruit.

COASTAL AREAS

The seacoasts are quite varied. Along the two Ligurian rivieras, on either side of Genoa, the coast alternates in rapid succession between high, rocky zones and level gravel. From Tuscany to Campania there are long, sandy, crescent beaches and abundant dunes, which are separated by rocky eminences. The coast of Calabria is high and rocky, though sometimes broken by short beaches. The coast of Puglia is level—as is, indeed, most of the Adriatic coast of Italy—although it is dominated by terraced gradients. The majestic delta of the Po River, extending from Rimini to Monfalcone, is riddled with the lagoons that are familiar to visitors to Venice. The Carso, the limestone coastal region between Trieste and Istria, is rocky.

DRAINAGE

Italian rivers are comparatively short; the longest, the Po, is merely 400 miles (645 km) long. While three major rivers flow into the Ionian Sea, in Puglia only two rivers flow to the Adriatic. Along the Adriatic coast a good number run parallel like the teeth of a comb down from the Apennines through Molise, Abruzzo, and Marche regions. The rivers that flow into the Tyrrhenian Sea are longer and more complex and carry greater quantities of water. These include the Volturno, in Campania; the Roman Tiber; and the Arno, which flows through Florence and Pisa. The rivers of the Ligurian rivieras are mainly short and swift-flowing; a few are important simply because cities, such as Genoa, or beach resorts, such as Rapallo, are built on their deltas. But the prince of Italian rivers is the Po. Rising in the Mount Viso area, it runs across the Lombardy Plain, through various important cities such as Turin (Torino) and Cremona, and is steadily enlarged by the numerous tributaries, especially on its left bank. The Po debouches south of Venice, forming a large delta. In Veneto there are also rivers that are not tributaries of the Po. One of these is the Adige, the second longest river in Italy, which flows 254 miles (409 km), passing through Verona and debouching near Adria, south of Venice. The rivers in the south have imposing floods during winter storms, and those that run through zones of impermeable rock may become dangerous; yet during the summer many of these rivers are completely dry. The rivers of the centre and north are dry in the winter because their headwaters are frozen, but they become full in the

Lake Garda, with the town of Malcesine on its eastern shore, northern Italy. ©M. Fritz/SuperStock

spring from melting snow and in the autumn from rainfall.

There are about 1,500 lakes in Italy. The most common type is the small, elevated Alpine lake formed by Quaternary glacial excavation during the last 25,000 years. These are of major importance for hydroelectric schemes. Other lakes, such as Bolsena and Albano, in Lazio, occupy the craters of extinct volcanoes. There are also coastal lagoons, such as Lakes Lesina and Varano, in Puglia, and lakes resulting from prehistoric faulting, such as Lake Alleghe, near Belluno. The best-known, largest, and most important of the Italian lakes, however, are those cut into valleys of the Alpine foothills by Quaternary glaciers. These, listed in order of size, are Lakes Garda, Maggiore, Como, Iseo, and Lugano. They have a semi-Mediterranean climate and are surrounded by groves of olive and citrus trees. Italy also has considerable areas in which, as a result of porous rock, the water systems run underground, forming subterranean streams, sinkholes, and lakes. These are often associated with caves, the most famous of which are those of Castellana, in Puglia.

SOILS

Varying climatic conditions in successive eras and differences in altitude and in types of rock have combined to produce in Italy a wide range of soils. Very common is dark brown podzol, typical in mountains with a lot of flint, where the rainfall is heavy, as in the Alps above about 300 feet (90 metres). In the Apennines, brown podzolic soils predominate, supporting forests and meadows and pastures. Brown Mediterranean soils also are characteristic of the Apennines and are suitable for agriculture. Rendzinas, typically humus-carbonate, are characteristic of limestone and magnesium limestone mountain pastures and of many meadows and beech forests of the Apennines. Red earth—the famous terra rossa, derived from the residue of limestone rocks—is found mainly in the extreme south, especially in Puglia and southeastern Sicily, where it is the usual soil in vineyards, olive groves, and gardens. Sparse rocky earth, clays, dune sands, and gravel are found in the high mountains, in some volcanic zones, and in gullies in the sub-Apennines. There is also a red loam, or *ferretto*, composed of ferrous (iron) clay.

CLIMATE

Geographically, Italy lies in the temperate zone. Because of the considerable length of the peninsula, there is a variation between the climate of the north, attached to the European continent, and that of the south, surrounded by the Mediterranean. The Alps are a partial barrier against westerly and northerly winds, while both the Apennines and the great plain of northern Italy produce special climatic variations. Sardinia is subject to Atlantic winds and Sicily to

African winds. In general, four meteorological situations dominate the Italian climate: the Mediterranean winter cyclone, with a corresponding summer anticyclone; the Alpine summer cyclone, with a consequent winter anticyclone; the Atlantic autumnal cyclone; and the eastern Siberian autumnal anticyclone. The meeting of the two last-mentioned air masses brings heavy and sometimes disastrous rains in the autumn.

Italy can be divided into seven main climatic zones. The most northerly, the Alpine zone, has a continental mountain climate, with temperatures lower and rainfall higher in the east than in the west. At Bardonecchia, in the west, the average temperature is 45.3 °F (7.4 °C), and the average annual rainfall is 26 inches (660 mm); at Cortina d'Ampezzo, in the east, the figures are 43.9 °F (6.6 °C) and 41.5 inches (1,055 mm). In the Valle d'Aosta, in the west, the permanent snow line is at 10,200 feet (3,110 metres), but in the Julian Alps it is as low as 8,350 feet (2,545 metres). In autumn and in late winter the hot, dry wind that is known as the foehn blows from Switzerland or Austria, and in the east the cold, dry bora blows with gusts up to 125 miles (200 km) per hour. Rain falls in the summer in the higher and more remote areas and in the spring and autumn at the periphery. Snow falls only in the winter; the snowfall varies from about 10 to 33 feet (3 to 10 metres) in different years and in relation to altitude or proximity to the sea. More snow falls in the foothills than in the mountains and more in the Eastern than in the Western Alps. Around the lakes the climate is milder, the average temperature in January at Milan being 34 °F (1 °C), while at Salò, on Lake Garda, it is 39 °F (4 °C).

The Po valley has hot summers but severe winters, worse in the interior than toward the eastern coast. At Turin the average winter temperature is 32.5 °F (0.3 °C) and the summer average 74 °F (23 °C). Rain falls mainly in the spring and autumn and increases with elevation. There is scant snow, and that falls only on the high plain. The temperatures along the Adriatic coast rise steadily from north to south, partly because of the descending latitude and partly because the prevailing winds are easterly in the north but southerly in the south. The average annual mean temperature rises from 56.5 °F (13.6 °C) at Venice to 61 °F (16 °C) at Ancona and 63 °F (17 °C) at Bari. There is scant rain: Venice has an average of 29.5 inches (750 mm), Ancona 25.5 inches (650 mm), and Bari 23.6 inches (600 mm).

In the Apennines the winters vary in severity according to the altitude. Except at specific locations, there are but moderate amounts of both rain and snow; in the cyclonic conditions of midwinter there may be sudden snowfalls in the south. The annual mean temperatures are 53.8 °F (12.1 °C) at Urbino, in the east, and 54.5 °F (12.5 °C) at Potenza, in Basilicata; the annual rainfall is, respectively, 35 inches (890 mm) and 39.6 inches (1,000 mm). Along the Tyrrhenian coast and the Ligurian rivieras in the north, both temperature and rainfall are influenced by full exposure to the noonday sun, by the nearness of the sea, with its prevailing southwesterly winds, and by the Apennine range, which protects the area from the cold north winds. The eastern riviera has more rain than the western: rainfall at La Spezia, on the eastern riviera, is 45.2 inches (1,150 mm), while at San Remo, on the western riviera, it is 26.7 inches (680 mm). Farther south, where the coastal areas extend a great distance inland and are flatter, the mean temperature and annual rainfall are 58.6 °F (14.8 °C) and 30.3 inches (770 mm) at Florence and 61.9 °F (16.6 °C) and 31.4 inches (800 mm) at Naples. As a rule, the Tyrrhenian coast is warmer and wetter than the Adriatic coast. Both Calabria and Sicily are mountainous regions that are surrounded by the Mediterranean, and they therefore have higher temperatures than the high regions of the Italian mainland farther north. Winter rains are scarce in the interior and heavier in the west and north of Sicily. At Reggio di Calabria the annual mean temperature is 64.7 °F (18.2 °C) and rainfall is 23.5 inches (595 mm); at Palermo, in Sicily, they are 64.4 °F (18 °C) and 38.2 inches (970 mm). The sirocco, a hot, very humid, and oppressive wind, blows frequently from Africa and the Middle East. In Sardinia conditions are more turbulent on the western side, and the island suffers from the cold mistral blowing from the northwest and also from the sirocco blowing from the southwest. At Sassari, in the northwest, the annual mean temperature is 62.6 °F (17 °C) and the rainfall 22.8 inches (580 mm), while at Orosei, on the east coast, the temperature is 63.5 °F (17.5 °C) and the rainfall 21.2 inches (540 mm).

PLANT LIFE

The native vegetation of Italy reflects the diversity of the prevailing physical environments in the country. There are at least three zones of differing vegetation: the Alps, the Po valley, and the Mediterranean-Apennine area.

From the foot of the Alps to their highest peaks, three bands of vegetation can be distinguished. First, around the Lombard lakes, the most common trees are the evergreen cork oak, the European olive, the cypress, and the cherry laurel. Slightly higher, on the mountain plain, the beech is ubiquitous, giving place gradually to the deciduous larch and the Norway spruce. In the high-altitude zone, twisted shrubs, including rhododendron, green alder, and dwarf juniper, give way to pastureland that is covered with grasses and sedges and wildflowers such as gentian, rock jasmine, campion, sea bindweed, primrose, and saxifrage. Farther up there is curved sedge, with the dwarf willow and the lovely anthophytes. On the snow line there are innumerable mosses, lichens, and a few varieties of hardy pollinating plants, such as flags and saxifrage.

Italian cypress (Cupressus sempervirens). W.H. Hodge

In the Po valley almost nothing remains of the original forests; nearly all the vegetation has been planted or disposed by human activity. Poplars predominate where there is abundant water, but in the drier, more gravelly zones there are a few sedges. On the clayey upland plains, heather abounds, and there are forests of Scotch pine. There are the usual grasses beside the streams and in the bogs and water lilies and pondweed on the banks of the marshes. But the heavily predominant plants are the cultivated crops—wheat, corn (maize), potatoes, rice, and sugar beets.

In the Apennine zone along the whole peninsula, a typical tree is the holm oak, while the area closer to the sea is characterized by the olive, oleander, carob, mastic, and Aleppo pine. There is a notable development of pioneer sea grape on the coastal dunes. The Mediterranean foothill area is characterized by the cork oak and the Aleppo pine. Higher up, in southern Italy, there are still traces of the ancient mountain forest, with truffle oak, chestnut, flowering ash, Oriental oak, white poplar, and Oriental plane. There are quite extensive beech woods in Calabria (on La Sila and Aspromonte massifs) and Puglia, and the silver fir and various kinds of pines thrive in Abruzzo and Calabria. Where the forests have been destroyed in the strictly Mediterranean section of the Apennines, a scrub that is called maquis has grown up. On the island of Sardinia the destruction of the carob forests and on the Apulian Plain the decay of olive trees and shore vegetation have produced steppes of tough plants such as the various sorts of feather grass. Mountain meadowlands are found in Calabria and Basilicata, usually with vetch, bent grass, and white asphodel. The Apennine pasturelands are very much like those of the Alps. The papyrus is quite common in Sicily as a freshwater plant.

ANIMAL LIFE

The extent of animal life in Italy has been much reduced by the long presence of human beings. In the Alps there are many animals, such as marmots, that hibernate and others that change their protective colouring according to the season, such as the ermine, the mountain partridge, and the Alpine rabbit. Larger mammals include the ibex, which is protected in Gran Paradiso National Park, the chamois in the Central Alps, and the roe deer in the eastern Alps. The lynx, the stoat, and the brown bear (protected in Adamello and Brenta) are now rare. Alpine birds include the black grouse, the golden eagle, and, more rarely, the capercaillie, or wood grouse. Among the reptiles are vipers, and among the amphibians are the Alpine salamander and Alpine newt. Species that are found in the Alps also exist in other high mountain regions, where there are, however, more foxes and wolves. In Abruzzo the brown bear may be found, and on the island of Sardinia the fallow deer, the mouflon, and the wild boar are present. Among the freshwater fishes are the brown trout, the sturgeon, and the eel. Among sea fishes, besides common species such as the red mullet and the dentex, there are, especially in southern waters, the white shark, the bluefin tuna, and the swordfish. Among invertebrates there is an abundance of red coral and commercial sponge on the rocks of the warm southern seas. In caves the greater horseshoe bat is found.

ETHNIC GROUPS

Italians cannot be typified by any one physical characteristic, a fact that may be explained by the past domination of parts of the peninsula by different peoples. The Etruscans in Tuscany and Umbria and the Greeks in the south preceded the Romans, who "Latinized" the whole country and maintained unity until the 5th century. Jews arrived in Italy during the Roman Republic, remaining until the present day. With the collapse of the Roman Empire in the West, Italy suffered invasions and colonization, which inevitably affected its ethnic composition. With some exceptions, the north was penetrated by Germanic tribes crossing the Alps, while the south was colonized by Mediterranean peoples arriving by sea. The Byzantines were dominant in the south for five centuries, coinciding with the supremacy of the Lombards (a Germanic tribe) in Benevento and other parts of the mainland. In the 9th century Sicily was invaded by the Saracens, who remained until the Norman invasion in the early 11th century. The Normans were succeeded by the Aragonese in 1282; in 1720 Sicily came under Austrian rule. This mixed ethnic heritage explains the smattering of light-eyed, blond Sicilians in a predominantly dark-eyed, dark-haired people. Except for the Saracen domination, the Kingdom of Naples, which formed the lower part of the peninsula, had a similar experience, whereas the northern part of Italy, separated from the south by the Papal States, was much more influenced by the dominant force of the Austrians. The Austrian admixture, combined with the earlier barbarian invasions, may account for the greater frequency of light-eyed, blond Italians originating in the north. The ethnic mixing continues to the present day. Since the 1970s, Italy has been receiving immigrants from a number of less-developed countries. A predominantly female migration from the Philippines and other Asian countries compares with a predominantly male influx from North Africa. With the accession of numerous former Soviet-bloc countries to the European Union in 2004 and 2007, immigration from eastern Europe soared. In the early 21st century about five million foreigners—roughly half of them from eastern Europe—resided on Italian territory.

LANGUAGES

Standard Italian, as a written administrative and literary language, was in existence well before the unification of Italy in the 1860s. However, in terms of spoken language, Italians were slow to adopt the parlance of the new nation-state, identifying much more strongly with their regional dialects. Emigration in the late 19th and early 20th century played an important role in spreading the standard language; many local dialects had no written form, obliging Italians to learn Italian in order to write to their relatives. The eventual supremacy of the standard language also owes much to the advent of television, which introduced it into almost every home in the country. The extremely rich and, hitherto, resilient tapestry of dialects and foreign languages upon which standard Italian has gradually been superimposed reveals much about Italy's cultural history. Not surprisingly,

the greatest divergence from standard Italian is found in border areas, in the mountains, and on the islands of Sicily and Sardinia.

Only a few languages spoken in limited geographic areas enjoy any legal protection or recognition. These are French, in Valle d'Aosta; German and the Rhaetian dialect Ladino in some parts of the Trentino–Alto Adige; Slovene in the province of Trieste; Friulian (another Rhaetian dialect) and Sardinian, spoken by the two largest linguistic minorities in Italy, received official recognition in 1992. Linguistic minorities persisting in the Alps are, broadly speaking, the result of migratory movements from neighbouring countries or changes in the borderline. The French and Franco-Provençal spoken in Valle d'Aosta date from union with Savoy, but the German spoken in the same area dates from the 12th-century emigration of German sheepherders from the upper valleys of the Rhône. The German spoken in the Trentino–Alto Adige dates back to Bavarian occupation in the 5th century, whereas that spoken in the provinces of Verona and Vicenza dates from a more recent colonization in the 12th century.

Some of the Alpine areas have such a complex linguistic makeup that precise measurement of linguistic communities is impossible. In Friuli–Venezia Giulia, for example, many communes are bi-, tri-, and even quadrilingual, as in the case of Canale, where Slovene, Italian, German,

ITALIAN LANGUAGE

Italian is a Romance language spoken by some 66 million persons in Italy (including Sicily and Sardinia), France (including Corsica), Switzerland, and other countries. It is spoken by large numbers of emigrants and their descendants in the Americas, especially in the United States, Argentina, and Canada. Written materials in Italian date from the 10th century (a set of court records with the testimony of the witnesses in the Italian vernacular), and the first literary work of length is the *Ritmo Laurenziano* ("Laurentian Rhythm") of the late 12th century.

Although Italian has a standard literary form, based on the dialect of Florence, the common speech is dialectal or a local variant of Standard Italian. The less formal the occasion and the less educated the speaker, the greater the deviation from standard speech. The following dialect groups are distinguished: Northern Italian, or Gallo-Italian; Venetan, spoken in northeastern Italy; Tuscan (including Corsican); and three related groups from southern and eastern Italy—the dialects of the Marche, Umbria, and Rome; those of Abruzzi, Puglia (Apulia), Naples, Campania, and Lucania; and those of Calabria, Otranto, and Sicily.

The sound system of Italian is quite similar to that of Latin or Spanish. Its grammar is also similar to that of the other modern Romance languages, showing agreement of adjectives and nouns, the use of definite and indefinite articles, loss of noun declension for case, two genders (masculine and feminine), and an elaborate system of perfect and progressive tenses for the verb. The most notable difference between Italian and French or Spanish is that it does not use -*s* or -*es* to form the plural of nouns but instead uses -*e* for most feminine words and -*i* for masculine words (and some feminine words).

and Friulian coexist. In certain Occitan-speaking parts of Piedmont, Italian is the official language, Occitan is spoken at home, and the Piedmontese dialect is used in trading relations with people from lowland areas.

Farther south, in Abruzzo, Basilicata, Calabria, Puglia, and Sicily, isolated linguistic communities persist against the odds. A dialect of Albanian known as Arbëresh is spoken by the descendants of 15th-century Albanian mercenaries; Croatian, the smallest minority language, spoken by some 2,000 people, has survived in splendid isolation in Campobasso province in Molise; and Greek, or "Grico" (of uncertain origin), may be heard in two areas in Calabria and Puglia. Catalan, too, has survived in the town of Alghero in the northwest of Sardinia, dating from the island's capture by the crown of Aragon in 1354.

RELIGION

Roman Catholicism has played a historic and fundamental role in Italy. It was the official religion of the Italian state from 1929, with the signing of the Lateran Treaty, until a concordat was ratified in

1985 that ended the church's position as the state religion, abolished compulsory religious teaching in public schools, and reduced state financial contributions to the church. More than four-fifths of the population declare themselves Roman Catholics, although the number of practicing Catholics is declining. An estimated 450,000 people worship in the Protestant church, including Lutherans, Methodists, Baptists, and Waldensians. They are all members of the Federation of Evangelical Churches in Italy (Federazione delle Chiese Evangeliche in Italia) founded in 1967. Albanian communities in two dioceses and one abbey in the Mezzogiorno practice the Eastern Orthodox rite. Migration that began in the latter third of the 20th century brought with it many people of non-Christian religious beliefs, significantly Muslims, who number more than one million. The Jewish community fluctuated between 30,000 and 47,000 throughout the 20th century. In 1987 Jews obtained special rights from the Italian state allowing them to abstain from work on the Sabbath and to observe Jewish holidays.

TRADITIONAL REGIONS

Italy is divided into 20 administrative regions, which correspond generally with historical traditional regions, though not always with exactly the same boundaries. A better-known and more general way of dividing Italy is into four parts: the north, the centre, the south, and the islands.

The north includes such traditional regions as Piedmont, which is characterized by some French influence and was the seat of united Italy's former royal dynasty; Liguria, extending southward around the Gulf of Genoa; Lombardy, which has long been noted for its productive agriculture and vigorously independent city communes and now for its industrial output; and Veneto, once the territory of the far-flung Venetian empire, reaching from Brescia to Trieste at its greatest extent.

The centre includes Emilia-Romagna, with its prosperous farms; the Marche, on the Adriatic side; Tuscany and Umbria, celebrated for their vestiges of Etruscan civilization and Renaissance traditions of art and culture; Lazio, which contains the Campagna, whose beautiful hills encircle the "Eternal City" of Rome; and the Abruzzo and Molise, regions of the highest central Apennines, which used to support a wild and remote people.

The south, or Mezzogiorno, includes Naples and its surrounding fertile Campania; the region of Puglia, with its great plain crossed by oleander-bordered roads leading to the low Murge Salentine hills and the heel of Italy. This portion of the country also includes the poorer regions of Basilicata and Calabria.

On the islands of Sicily and Sardinia are people who take pride in holding themselves apart from the inhabitants of mainland Italy. However, the south and the islands have changed a great deal since about 1960 and have become more

TUSCANY

The Italian region of Tuscany (Italian: Toscana) covers 8,877 sq mi (22,992 sq km), and its capital is Florence. Originally settled by Etruscans c. 1000 BCE, Tuscany came under Roman rule in the 3rd century BCE. It was a Lombard duchy in the 6th century CE. It comprised several independent city-states in the 12th–13th centuries, which were subsequently united under the Medici family of Florence. Tuscany passed to the house of Lorraine in 1737 and to Sardinia and the Kingdom of Italy in the 1860s. The region suffered severe damage in World War II and extensive floods in 1966. Its mineral resources include the world-famous Carrara marble. Its agricultural products include olives, olive oil, wines, and livestock. Tourism is important at its historical centres, including Florence and Pisa.

modernized. Within these four main divisions, the variety of the much smaller traditional districts is very great and depends on history as well as on topography and economic conditions.

SETTLEMENT PATTERNS

In general, rural life is in decline. The majority of the population of Italy live in cities and villages; only a fraction live in hamlets or in isolated houses. In the long Alpine valleys the economy was always both agricultural and commercial, with towns such as Aosta and Bolzano at the outlets of the lateral valleys and agricultural settlements higher up or on the slopes of hills. The perpetual subdivision of landholdings makes a purely agricultural economy precarious in this region except in the upper Adige, where the Germanic system of primogeniture survived, producing the *masi*, family holdings that are passed on to the eldest son intact. These rural areas now also include an increasing number of skiing and tourist centres, such as Courmayeur and Cortina d'Ampezzo. In the band of Alpine and Apennine foothills, the villages, often situated on the knolls and flanks of the hills, are linked by roads that hold to the heights, away from the humid valley floors. Each village is usually grouped around a church, a castle, or a nobleman's palace, with its fields on the slopes around it and woodlands lower down. There are innumerable plum and cherry orchards and, above all, vineyards; their wines (Conegliano and Monferrato) are famous. Lombardy is the only area in which the ancient rural way of life has been comprehensively displaced by the development of heavy industry. The Padano-Venetian-Emilian plain is the most important agricultural and stock-breeding region of Italy. The upland plain hosts the great industrial centres such as Turin, Milan, and Busto Arsizio, while the lowland plain remains socially as well as economically rural.

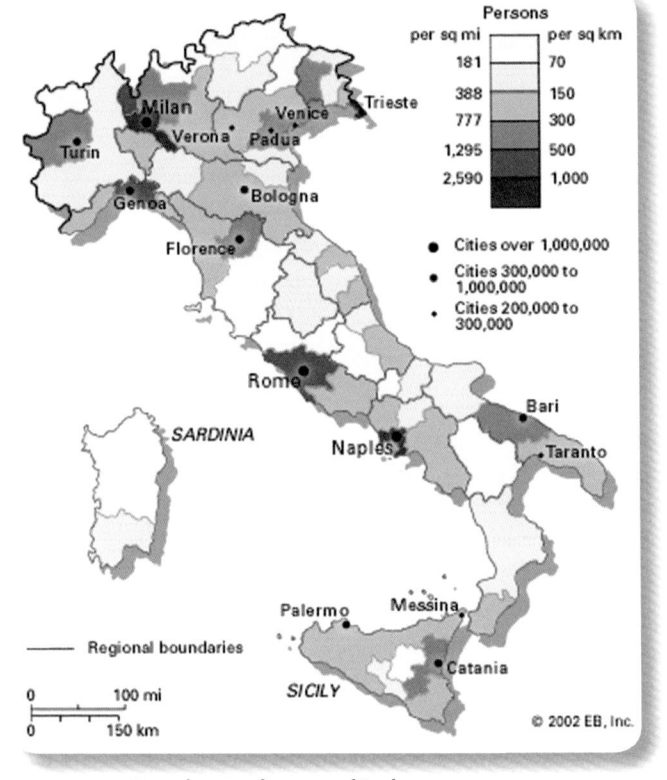

Population density of Italy.

Villages high in the Apennines are less prosperous than those of similar elevation in the Alps. They are still isolated, the ground is infertile, and land is rarely owned by those who work it. Tourism and the expansion of cottage craft industries, such as the porcelain making at Gubbio, near Perugia, have helped these towns survive. The lower hills and plains of Italy are covered with agricultural villages in which a wide variety of crops and vegetables are grown, though often in low yield. In Puglia and Basilicata large farms are staffed by labourers who live in urban centres, such as Cerignola and Altamura,

and travel to work in the countryside. Some fertile and well-watered plains, such as the Neapolitan countryside, have a high level of productivity, especially of market vegetables. Here there is direct ownership of land and fairly dense settlement. In Sicily, settlement is clustered in widely spaced, nucleated towns, with extensive pastureland and farming. In Sardinia the settlement is sparse and mainly inland, and most of the local fishing industry is carried on by men from the mainland.

Italian cities vary greatly in terms of population, economic activities, and cultural traditions. Many of them have developed close economic links with surrounding communities, forming major metropolitan areas, such as Rome, Milan, Naples, and Palermo. Slightly less populous are the urban centres of Genoa–Savona, Bologna, Catania, Messina–Reggio di Calabria, Cagliari, and Trieste–Monfalcone. The geographic pattern shows an even distribution of large metropolitan areas across the whole country, while medium-sized cities are more numerous in the north than in the south, where there is a concentration of small towns.

Historically, the location of Italian urban centres played a central role in their economic development. In the Po valley, cities such as Milan, Pavia, and Cremona were well placed for commerce, being situated at the confluence of roads or rivers. Another group of cities were those on the coast, at the mouths of rivers, or on lagoons protected by sandbars; these included Savona, Genoa, Naples, Messina, Palermo, Ancona, and Venice. At present the most economically viable urban centres are those able to engage in global trade, such as Milan, and medium-sized centres such as those in northern Tuscany that engage in light manufacturing.

DEMOGRAPHIC TRENDS

Throughout the centuries, Italy's population curve has undergone many changes, often in parallel development with population trends in other European countries. The mid-14th-century plague reduced the peninsula's population considerably, and a long period of population growth ended at the beginning of the 17th century. From the early 18th century until unification in the 1860s, a slight, steady growth prevailed, although it was interrupted during the Napoleonic Wars. From the latter half of the 19th century to the latter half of the 20th century, the population more than doubled, despite high levels of emigration. Interestingly, the natural population increase was frequently highest during the decades of highest emigration, although there is no obvious causal relationship between the two.

Italy's overall demographic trends are still fairly consistent with those of other

*The Certosa di Pavia, a Carthusian monastery completed in the 17th century, north of Pavia, Italy.*SCALA/Art Resource, New York

advanced western European countries, which experienced declining fertility and mortality rates following World War II. The growth rate of the population is gradually slowing, with most of the increase coming from immigration; birth rates and death rates are virtually identical. However, the national figures conceal contrasting regional trends. In general, the birth rate and average family size are higher in the south of Italy than in the north, although populations in Molise, Basilicata, and Calabria are declining through continued emigration. The mortality rate is slightly lower in the south than in the north as a result of improved medical care and a younger population; in certain northern regions, especially Liguria, populations are decreasing because the birth rate is falling faster than the mortality rate. For the country as a whole, life expectancy rose during the second half of the 20th century, reflecting higher nutritional, sanitary, and medical standards. At the beginning of the 21st century, the majority of the population was between 20 and 49 years old, with the largest group between ages 30 and 44.

INTERNAL MIGRATION PATTERNS

Since the unification of Italy in the mid-19th century, internal movements have followed a regular pattern—south to north and east to west. People have moved from the southern regions and Sicily to the central regions of Lazio and Tuscany and to the northwest—to Lombardy, Liguria, and Piedmont. They moved in the same way from Veneto to the northwest. Movement from Emilia-Romagna, Marche, and Umbria to regions in the northwest has also been significant. Population movement was relatively slight during the Fascist era between the wars, when permits were required for movement inside the country. Exceptionally, substantial numbers of Italians seeking work at the huge Lingotto vehicle factory run by Fiat were granted permits to go to Turin.

After World War II and the demise of Fascism, Italy entered a period of unprecedented economic growth and high population mobility. The prosperity of the urban areas, especially the industrial triangle of Lombardy-Piedmont-Liguria, contrasted with continuing hardship and poverty in the upland and rural areas, especially in the south. Rapid industrialization in the urban centres acted as a strong "pull" factor, encouraging rural workers to abandon the land and head for the cities. The disparity of wealth and of employment between urban and rural areas triggered a period of intense rural depopulation from the uplands in the Alps, the Apennines, Sicily, and Calabria and an influx of migrants to Rome, Milan, Turin, and Genoa. This movement continues today, although the slowing of economic growth has reduced the "pull" exerted by the industrial areas. Unemployment runs high, especially among the young.

EMIGRATION AND IMMIGRATION

In nearly a century between 1876 and 1970, an estimated 25 million Italians left the country in search of work. Of those, 12 million left for destinations outside Europe. In the 1860s, transatlantic migration was most frequent among northern Italians and was often associated with certain trades; for example, farmers, artists, and street traders tended to emigrate to the United States. Two decades later, however, the trend had become a mass phenomenon, with the main migrants increasingly emanating from the south. Their principal destination was the United States, favoured by more than half the emigrants, the others choosing Argentina, Brazil, and Canada. Some also went to Australia. In the 1920s the United States introduced strict immigration laws, and economic conditions in Brazil and Argentina deteriorated so much that transatlantic emigration was stymied. In addition, the Fascist regime opposed emigration, and during World War II emigration halted almost completely. After 1945 destinations were mainly European, the most popular being France initially and then West Germany and Switzerland. During that period the nature of emigration patterns changed, becoming less stable. In many cases the emigrants were mostly male, as some European countries refused entry to workers' relatives because of housing shortages. Often Italian workers would remain abroad for short periods of time, returning every so often to Italy. On the eve of the 1973 oil embargo, more than 850,000 Italians were working in Switzerland and countries of the European Economic Community (EEC; later succeeded by the European Union [EU]), where the ensuing recession and rising unemployment forced many Italians back home.

In 1972 Italy for the first time registered more people entering the country than leaving, in part because of repatriation but also as a result of immigration from Asia, Africa, and Latin America. For several years the scale of the influx of non-European immigrants was difficult to assess, as no policy existed either to measure or to control it until the mid-1980s. The collapse of communist regimes in eastern Europe brought fresh waves of immigrants from Poland, Romania, Albania, and the Yugoslav region. Many arrived via seaports on the Adriatic coast, claiming refugee status. Some were repatriated, but others were relocated to inland destinations. An ongoing difficulty is the flow of illegal immigrants from Albania. In 2010 there were about five million foreigners in Italy, with a plurality originating from eastern Europe. The majority of new arrivals settled in the north and centre of Italy, but the south had a relatively higher proportion of African and North American immigrants than the north.

CHAPTER 2

THE ITALIAN ECONOMY

The Italian economy has progressed from being one of the weakest economies in Europe following World War II to being one of the most powerful. Its strengths are its metallurgical and engineering industries, and its weaknesses are a lack of raw materials and energy sources. More than four-fifths of Italy's energy requirements are imported. Nonetheless, the chemical sector also flourishes, and textiles constitute one of Italy's largest industries. A strong entrepreneurial bias, combined with liberal trade policies following the war, enabled manufacturing exports to expand at a phenomenal rate, but a cumbersome bureaucracy and insufficient planning hindered an even economic development throughout the country. Services, particularly tourism, are also very important. At the end of the 20th century, Italy, seeking balance with other EU nations, brought its high inflation under control and adopted more conservative fiscal policies, including sweeping privatization.

Although the Italian economy was a relative latecomer to the industrialization process, business in the north of the country caught up with and overtook many of its western European neighbours. Southern Italy, however, lagged behind. The percentage of the labour force working in agriculture is often taken as an indication of the rate of industrialization and wealth of a nation, and in Italy's case the figures clearly illustrate the grave imbalances existing between north and south. Against an EU average of 4.7 percent in 2008, 3.6 percent of the Italian population worked on the land, with as many agricultural labourers from the 8 regions in the south as from the 12 regions in the north and centre. Calabria and Basilicata have the largest concentrations of farm labourers.

Although Italy is not self-sufficient agriculturally, certain commodities form an important part of the export market. Notably, the country is a world leader in olive oil production and a major exporter of rice, tomatoes, and wine. Cattle raising, however, is less advanced; meat and dairy products are imported.

PUBLIC AND PRIVATE SECTORS

The Italian economy is mixed, and until the beginning of the 1990s the state owned a substantial number of enterprises. At that time the economy was organized as a pyramid, with a holding company at the top, a middle layer of financial holding companies divided according to sector of activity, and below them a mass of companies operating in diverse sectors, ranging from banking, expressway construction, media, and telecommunications to manufacturing, engineering, and shipbuilding. One example, the Institute for Industrial Reconstruction (Istituto per la Ricostruzione Industriale; IRI), set up in 1933 and closed in 2000, was a holding company that regulated public industries and banking. Many of those companies were partly owned by private shareholders and listed on the stock exchange. By the 1980s moves had already been made to increase private participation in some companies. The most notable

examples were Mediobanca SpA, Italy's foremost merchant bank, with shareholdings in major industrial concerns; Alitalia, the national airline, which filed for bankruptcy protection in 2008 before being sold to a private investment group; and the telecommunications company Telecom Italia SpA, which was created in 1994 through the merger of five state-run telecommunications concerns. Many other banks were also partially privatized under the Banking Act of 1990.

In 1992 a wide privatization program began when four of the main state-controlled holding companies were converted into public limited corporations. The four were the IRI, the National Hydrocarbons Agency (Ente Nazionale Idrocarburi; ENI), the National Electrical Energy Fund (Ente Nazionale per l'Energia Elettrica; ENEL), and the State Insurance Fund (Istituto Nazionale delle Assicurazioni; INA). Other principal agencies include the Azienda Nazionale Autonoma delle Strade Statali (ANAS), responsible for some 190,000 miles (350,000 km) of the road network, and the Ente Ferrovie dello Stato (FS; "State Railways"), which controls the majority of the rail network.

The private sector was once characterized by a multitude of small companies, many of which were family-run and employed few or no workers outside the family. In the early 21st century, businesses with fewer than 50 employees still represented more than half of total firms, reflecting a trend that showed a decline in large production units and an increase of smaller, more-specialized ones. This trend was especially pronounced in the automobile industry, textiles, electrical goods, and agricultural, industrial, and office equipment.

Following World War II, the economy in the south was mainly dominated by the interests of the government and the public sector. The Southern Development Fund (Cassa per il Mezzogiorno), a state-financed fund set up to stimulate economic and industrial development between 1950 and 1984, met with limited success. It supported early land reform—including land reclamation, irrigation work, infrastructure building, and provision of electricity and water to rural areas—but did little to stimulate the economy. Later the fund financed development of heavy industry in selected areas, hoping that major industrial concerns might attract satellite industries and lay the foundation for sustained economic activity. Yet these projects became known as "cathedrals in the desert"; not only did they fail to attract other smaller industries, they also suffered from high absenteeism among workers. The most successful project was undertaken by Finsider, which in 1964 opened what was Europe's most modern steelworks, in Taranto.

POSTWAR ECONOMIC DEVELOPMENT

The development of the Italian economy after World War II was one of the country's major success stories. Economic reconstruction was followed by unprecedented economic growth between 1950 and 1963. Gross domestic product (GDP) rose by an average of 5.9 percent annually during this time, reaching a peak of 8.3 percent in 1961. The years from 1958 to 1963 were known as Italy's economic miracle. The growth in industrial output peaked at over 10 percent per year during this period, a rate surpassed only by Japan and West Germany. The country enjoyed practically full employment, and in 1963 investment reached 27 percent of GDP.

The success was partially due to the decision to foster free market policies and to open up international trade. From the very beginning, Italy was an enthusiastic proponent of European integration, which favoured the Italian manufacturing industry, which expanded enormously during this period. Certain products, such as Olivetti typewriters and Fiat automobiles, dominated European and world markets in just a few years. The economy slowed down after 1963 and took a downturn after the 1973 increase in petroleum prices. By the late 1980s, however, it was again prospering.

LATER ECONOMIC TRENDS

The economy entered the mid-1980s with a healthy growth rate, which it maintained through the end of the century. However, there were serious battles to be waged: against inflation, a trade deficit, currency restrictions, and tax evasion.

Journalists gather around a Fiat 500, being presented to the press at a racetrack in Kent, England, 1957. Edward Miller/Hulton Archive/Getty Images

Inflation reached nearly 22 percent in 1980. This was principally due to union strength in wage bargaining throughout the 1970s and a mechanism called the *scala mobile*, which adjusted wages to inflation on a quarterly basis for all wage and salary earners. The high degree of job security enjoyed by the Italian workforce raised production costs, which in turn contributed to inflation. Beginning with a decree in 1984 that imposed a ceiling on payments, the *scala mobile* was gradually dismantled (and abolished in 1992) under pressure from the employers'

association, the Confederation of Industries (Confindustria). This was reflected in a sharp fall in inflation to 12 percent in 1984 and down to 4.2 percent in 1986. However, a three-year contract signed in 1987 between Confindustria and trade unions representing all civil servants and some private industrial workers awarded pay raises over the rate of inflation, and by 1991 inflation was again up to 7 percent—3 percent higher than in Germany or France. In 2000 inflation in Italy was at 10 percent. Overall, however, the inflation rate was three times smaller throughout the 1990s than in the 1980s.

Italy's public debt grew steadily throughout the 1980s despite a series of emergency measures designed to reduce public borrowing. By 1991 public debt exceeded GDP, and the cost of servicing it was more than $100 billion, accounting for the entire government budget deficit for the year. In 2010 Italy's public debt still exceeded GDP.

Italy underwent currency reform in the 1980s and '90s in an effort to come into line with the fiscal standards set by the EU. At the end of the century, Italy joined the single currency of the EU, adopting the euro in 1999. From the late 20th century the Italian economy has been dogged by the government's inefficient levying of direct taxes. Since the creation of the republic after World War II, the economy has relied on public loans to finance public works and enterprises, and many Italians did not start paying income tax until the 1970s. Italy also has a thriving underground economy that inevitably deprives the state of revenue. While indirect taxes, including VAT (value-added taxes), were raised several times throughout the 1980s, moves to enforce payment of direct taxes met with resistance. In 1985 a bill was introduced to curtail tax evasion among the self-employed, leading to a one-day national strike. The 1990 budget also included measures to reduce tax evasion. The names of the country's top taxpayers are publicized annually in an attempt to encourage compliance with tax laws.

During the 1990s the annual GDP growth rates were very modest. In 2000, in response to a healthy international economy and to steps taken to improve the Italian finance system—including reduced public spending and increased taxation—the GDP grew 3 percent, its biggest increase since 1988, but the recovery would not be sustained indefinitely. In 2009 the global recession that began in 2007–08 arrived in Italy. The economy stagnated, GDP fell, and unemployment topped 10 percent. The chronic instability of the government of Prime Minister Silvio Berlusconi amplified concern over Italy's public debt, and the ratings agencies Standard & Poor's and Moody's downgraded the country's credit rating in 2011. Italy found itself grouped into the acronym "PIIGS" (Portugal, Ireland, Italy, Greece, Spain), which was used to describe the countries that were at greatest risk in the euro-zone debt crisis. As Italy's euro-zone partners constructed ever-larger financial firewalls in an effort to head off contagion, the technocratic government led by Mario Monti, who became prime minister in 2011, implemented a series of austerity measures to reduce Italy's deficit.

AGRICULTURE, FORESTRY, AND FISHING

Like other branches of the Italian economy, agriculture has been characterized historically by a series of inequalities, both regional and social. Until the Land Reform Acts of 1950, much of Italy's cultivable land was owned and idly managed by a few leisured noblemen, while the majority of agricultural workers struggled under harsh conditions as wage labourers or owned derisory plots of land, too small for self-sufficiency. Agricultural workers had few rights, and unemployment ran high, especially in Calabria, where the impetus for land reform was generated. Reform entailed the redistribution of large tracts of land among the landless peasantry, thereby absorbing greater amounts of labour and encouraging more efficient land use.

Although partially successful, the reform created many farms that were still too small to be viable and plots that were scattered in parcels and often located in unfertile uplands. Another negative aspect of the reform was that it had the effect of damaging the social structure of rural communities. Initially, the EEC did little to help Italy's small farmers, located primarily in the south, while wealthier, larger farms in the north benefited from EEC subsidies. However, in 1975 specific aid was directed at upland farmers, and in 1978 another package provided them advisory support and aid for irrigation. Today, most farms are owned and operated by families.

Since World War II, Italy has maintained a negative trade balance in agricultural products, many of which are consumed domestically because of the country's high population density. The majority of foreign agricultural and food-related trade is with other EU countries, in particular with France and Germany.

Italy's plains constitute only one-fourth of the land under cultivation, indicating widespread cultivation of hilly environments where agriculture has been possible only as a result of modifying the natural landscape and resources through terracing, irrigation, and soil management. The most fertile area is the Po valley, where precipitation is fairly evenly distributed throughout the year, but mean rainfall decreases southward. Coastal areas in Puglia, Sicily, and Sardinia may register only about 12–16 inches (300–400 mm) of annual precipitation, compared with about 118 inches (3,000 mm) in Alpine regions. In general, agricultural land use is divided into four types—field crops, tree crops, pasture, and forestry.

FIELD CROPS

While prime minister in 1922–43, Benito Mussolini strove to make Italy self-sufficient in the production of wheat, but since that time the land given over to its cultivation has been reduced from more than 12 million acres to just over 5 million acres (about 50,000 to 20,000 square km). Hard wheat used for making pasta is traditionally grown in the south, whereas soft wheat used for making bread, biscuits, and pizza crust predominates in the northern lowlands. Yields in the north can be up to three times those in the south because of improved mechanization techniques and more suitable terrain.

Italy is a major exporter of rice, which is grown mostly on the Po plain. Corn (maize) also is grown in that area. Of the other field crops, tomatoes are the most important for domestic and export markets. Naples and Emilia-Romagna specialize in that crop. By the early 21st century the area given over to growing tomatoes had increased more than twofold, and production quadrupled as a result of improved production techniques.

TREE CROPS AND VITICULTURE

Olives and grapes are Italy's two most lucrative agricultural exports. Olive production is suited to the arid conditions

A Tuscan villa with vineyards and olive trees in the foreground. Italy is known for its wine and olive products. wjarek/Shutterstock.com

of Puglia, Sicily, and Calabria, the oil content being enhanced by the long, dry summers. The output is erratic, however, as the olives are susceptible to late frosts. Italy is the world's biggest exporter of olive oil, although Spain dominates the more lucrative sector of table olives. While olives are traditionally grown in conjunction with other crops or livestock, nearly half the olive-producing land now excludes other types of cultivation, reflecting the demise of traditional peasant farming methods.

Wine is produced in every region of Italy and, together with olive oil, enjoys a positive trade balance. Competition is stiffening, however, with the burgeoning eastern European market undercutting western prices. Much of the heavier wine from the south is used to produce vermouth or marsala, while the best-known wines—Soave, Valpolicella, Barolo, and Asti—are produced in the north. About three-fifths of Italy's citrus fruit production is Sicilian, with most of the rest growing in sheltered and irrigated lowlands in Calabria and Campania. Deciduous fruits, on the other hand, are widespread. Campania is best known for its cherries, apricots, nectarines, and hazelnuts, while Emilia-Romagna produces mostly peaches, plums, and pears. Sicily and Puglia are noted for almond production.

PASTURE

Pastureland makes up about one-sixth of the land in use. Meat production in Italy is traditionally weak. Cattle production was relatively stagnant in the second half of the 20th century. There is a marked geographic difference in the distribution of farms; while bovine, swine, and aviculturist farms are mainly found in the north, ovine farms are more widespread in the south. Butter production satisfies domestic consumption, and some cheeses, including Gorgonzola and Parmesan, are made for export. Raising buffalo is a popular activity in Tuscany and Campania, where their milk is used for mozzarella cheese. The production of goats' milk is still modest, although it has become more lucrative, being regarded as a luxury item for the urban market instead of peasant fare. The breeding of pigs has increased most dramatically, mostly in the northern regions of Lombardy and Emilia-Romagna. Peasant families traditionally keep pigs for their own consumption. Competition from other EU countries has threatened the Italian meat market, which suffers from high production costs because of the necessity for irrigation.

FORESTRY

Italian forestry has suffered from overexploitation in the past, first in antiquity by the Romans and then again in the 19th century, when much wood was needed for building mine shafts and railway sleepers. Less than one-third of the land is classified as forest and other woodland. Strenuous efforts to reforest certain areas are gradually producing positive results;

for example, at the end of the 20th century, the production of roundwood, after dipping by 40 percent in the mid-1970s, nearly returned to the high levels it had maintained in the 1960s.

Most of Italy's forest area is made up of broad-leaved trees, with conifers making up about one-fifth of the total. Broad-leaved forests are fairly well spread over the country, with the exceptions of Puglia, Sicily, and Sardinia. Conifers are for the most part concentrated in the Alpine foothills, especially in the Trentino–Alto Adige adjacent to the Austrian border. Chestnut forests are widespread in the northern Apennines and the Calabrian Sila. The North Italian Plain, Puglia, and the southern half of Sicily are virtually devoid of woodland.

FISHING

Italian fish production doubled in the last four decades of the 20th century, but consumption is met mainly by imports. About four-fifths of the fish come from the Mediterranean and the Black Sea and about one-tenth from the Atlantic Ocean, the remaining one-tenth coming from inland waters.

RESOURCES AND POWER

The Italian peninsula is a geologically young land formation and therefore contains few mineral resources, especially metalliferous ones. What few exist are poor in quality, scant in quantity, and widely dispersed. The meagreness of its natural resources partially explains Italy's slow transition from an agricultural to an industrial economy, which began only in the late 19th century. The lack of iron ore and coal especially hindered industrial progress, impeding the production of steel necessary for building machines, railways, and other essential elements of an industrial infrastructure.

Half of Italy's iron output comes from the island of Elba, one of the oldest geologic areas. Another important area of production is Cogne in the Alpine region of Valle d'Aosta; that deposit lies at 2,000 feet (610 metres) above sea level. Little iron-bearing ore has been produced in Italy since 1984. Coal is found in small amounts principally in Tuscany, but it is of inferior quality, and its exploitation has been almost negligible. The vast majority of Italy's coal is imported, mostly from Russia, South Africa, the United States, and China.

During the late 20th century, production of almost all of Italy's minerals steadily decreased, with the exception of rock salt, petroleum, and natural gas. In the early 1970s Italy was a major producer of pyrites (from the Tuscan Maremma), asbestos (from the Balangero mines near Turin), fluorite (fluorspar; found in Sicily and northern Italy), and salt. At the same time, it was self-sufficient in aluminum (from Gargano in Puglia), sulfur (from Sicily), lead, and zinc (from Sardinia). By the beginning of the 1990s, however, it had lost all its world-ranking positions and was no longer self-sufficient in those resources.

Fuel deposits, too, were unable to keep pace with the spiraling demands of energy-hungry industries and domestic consumers. Although domestic production figures rose throughout the late 20th century, Italy remains a net energy importer. Small amounts of oil and natural gas used to be produced in the Po valley in the 1930s, and asphalt was produced in Ragusa in Sicily. This exploitation was followed by further oil discoveries in the Abruzzo and richer amounts again in Ragusa and in nearby Gela. Natural gas is the most important natural resource in the peninsula, found mainly on the northern plain but also in Basilicata, Sicily, and Puglia.

Italy is one of the world's leading producers of pumice, pozzolana, and feldspar. Another mineral resource for which Italy is well-known is marble, especially the world-famous white marble from the Carrara and Massa quarries in Tuscany. However, the reputation of these exceptional stones is disproportionately large when compared with the percentage of gross national product (GNP) accounted for by their exploitation.

Italy's lack of energy resources undoubtedly hindered the process of industrialization on the peninsula, but the limited stocks of coal, oil, and natural gas led to innovation in the development of new energy sources. It was the death of coal in the late 19th century that encouraged the pioneering of hydroelectricity, and in 1885 Italy became one of the first countries to transmit hydroelectricity to a large urban centre—from Tivoli to Rome, along a 5,000-volt line. Rapid expansion of the sector developed in the Alps (with water passing efficiently over nonporous rocks) and also in the Apennines (with less efficient transport over porous rocks). Though uneven precipitation on the peninsula marred continuing growth in hydroelectricity, it comprised a healthy slice of the country's energy consumption by 1920. In the aftermath of World War II, more than half of Italy's electric power was accounted for by hydroelectricity, but there was little room left for expansion, and the country was in need of energy to feed its rapid industrialization. By the 21st century, hydroelectric power, its output unable to keep pace with increasing demand, amounted to less than 20 percent of the country's electricity production. This led to the development of thermal electricity generation fired by coal, natural gas, oil, nuclear power, and geothermal energy.

In 1949 oil was discovered off Sicily, but supplies were limited, and Italy began to rely heavily on imported oil, mainly from North Africa and the Middle East. With oil in such short supply, Italy was, not surprisingly, at the vanguard of nuclear research, and by 1965 three nuclear power stations were operating on Italian soil; a fourth opened in 1981. Nonetheless, by 1987, nuclear power accounted for only 0.1 percent of Italy's total electricity production, and a public referendum of the same year led to the decommissioning of all four plants. The issue was revisited in the early 21st century, and a proposal to dramatically increase Italy's nuclear power capacity was presented by the government. In a referendum held in June 2011, just months after the Fukushima nuclear accident in Japan, the proposal was rejected. Italy remained a significant consumer of nuclear-generated power, with much of its imported electricity originating in France and Switzerland.

Natural gas has been the most significant discovery. It was first found in the 1920s, and its most important exploitation was in the Po valley. Later exploration focused on offshore supplies along the Adriatic coast. Increased reliance on imports began in the 1970s, and by the beginning of the 21st century about three-fourths of Italy's natural gas was imported, primarily from Algeria, Russia, and the Netherlands. There are about 19,000 miles (30,000 km) of pipelines. The use of natural gas has risen at the expense of oil, which in the 1990s was the dominant energy source for electricity production in Italy. By the 21st century natural gas provided more than half of Italy's total energy production. Overall, fossil fuels comprised some 90 percent of Italy's total energy consumption.

MANUFACTURING

The most remarkable feature of Italian economic development after World War II was the spectacular increase in manufacturing and, in particular, manufacturing exports. The most significant contributory factors to this growth were the Marshall Plan (1948–51), a U.S.-sponsored program to regenerate the postwar economies of western Europe; the 1952 foundation of the European Coal and Steel Community (ECSC), later under the European Federation of Iron and Steel Industries; the start in 1958 of the EEC, which contributed to the liberalization of trade; and the abundance of manpower that fueled the growth of northern industrial concerns.

The material that transformed the Italian economy with a flourish was steel. Despite the lack of mineral resources, the Italian government opted to join the ECSC at its inception, and skeptics watched as Italian steel developed so quickly that by 1980 it accounted for 21.5 percent of production in the EEC (which by then had nine members) and in western Europe. Moreover, Italy was second to West Germany among western European steel producers. Steel formed the backbone of the metallurgical and engineering industries, known as *metalmeccanica*. These enjoyed their heyday between 1951 and 1975, when mechanical exports rose 20-fold and the workforce employed in the industries doubled. The number of people working in the automobile industry tripled, and metallurgical exports increased 25 times. The steel industry, which declined in the last decades of the century, was privatized in 1992–97.

The main branches of *metalmeccanica* included arms manufacture, textile machinery, machine tools, automobiles and other transport vehicles, and domestic appliances. The automobile industry has been dominated by Fiat since the founding of the company in Turin in 1899. Milan and Brescia became the other main automaking centres until Alfa Romeo opened its plant near Naples, leading to a decentralization of the industry. Automobile production took off in the 1950s and soared until the mid-1970s, when it began to stagnate. In the 1980s imports from Japan and an economic recession further dampened the industry, though new markets were opened in eastern Europe at the end of the Cold War in the early 1990s. In 2011 Fiat acquired a majority stake in the American auto company Chrysler, and Fiat's involvement saw the car maker return to profitability for the first time in years. Today, Italy has one of the highest numbers of cars per capita in the world.

Notable large firms notwithstanding, the manufacturing sector is characterized by the presence of small and medium-size industries, which are found mainly in northeastern and north-central Italy. This area, concentrated in industrial districts within Veneto, Emilia-Romagna, and Tuscany, is referred to as the "third Italy," to distinguish it from the "first Italy," represented by the industrial triangle formed by the cities of Milan, Turin, and Genoa, and from the "second Italy," which includes the Mezzogiorno. Each industrial district in the third Italy generally specializes in a particular area of light manufacturing, such as textiles or paper products, although more traditional manufacturing is also present. For instance, in Prato, Tuscany, the specialty is textile products; Sassuolo and Cento, both in Emilia-Romagna, engage in ceramic tile production and mechanical engineering, respectively; while Nogara, in Veneto, is known for wooden furniture.

Italy dominated the postwar domestic appliance market, which boomed until the first international oil crisis, in 1973, when small businesses were hard-hit by the increase in energy prices. Olivetti and Zanussi were market leaders, and Italian-produced "white goods," such as refrigerators and washing machines, were much in demand. The textile industry has been important in Italy since the Middle Ages, when Lombardy and Tuscany were leading centres for the wool and silk industry. Other important products now include artificial and synthetic fibres, cotton, and jute yarn. Textiles and leather goods were surpassed by the metallurgical sector in the 1960s, but they remain important components of manufacturing.

The chemicals industry is one of the more recent members of the Italian industrial family. It is often categorized into primary chemicals, dominated by giant enterprises, including Edison, Eni SpA, and SNIA; secondary chemicals, made up of thousands of firms; and a third component comprising firms financed by foreign capital. From 1868 until World War I the chemical industry was restricted to products such as fertilizers and fungicides, but the oil discoveries of the 1950s opened up the

FIAT SPA

Fiat, formerly Fabbrica Italiana Automobili Torino, is an international holding company and a major Italian manufacturer of automobiles, trucks, and industrial vehicles and components. It is the largest family-owned corporation in Italy as well as a massive multinational firm with assembly plants and licenses in many European and overseas countries. Among its automotive names are Ferrari, Maserati, and Lancia. The company also has interests in retailing, chemicals, and civil engineering in addition to manufacturing farm equipment, earth-moving machinery, and a vast array of automotive components. Headquarters are in Turin.

Fiat was incorporated in 1906 as the successor to a company formed in 1899 by Giovanni Agnelli. Because of the high level of skilled workers in Turin and the local school of engineering, the company was able to gain an early lead on its competitors.

The success of Fiat was in large part the work of two men. Founder Giovanni Agnelli, whose family still holds a major interest in the company, led the firm from its formative years until his death in 1945. An intellectual socialist, he saw the automotive industry as a means of providing transportation to the masses, as well as producing jobs for workers. This odd combination of socialism and industrialism proved to be a potent combination in the Italian automotive industry. By 1910 the firm was the largest in Italy, a position it has maintained since. The other major figure in the firm's development was Vittorio Valletta, an unusually skilled administrator, who as general manager guided the day-to-day activities of the company. By the early 1920s Fiat manufactured more than 80 percent of the automobiles sold in Italy, and the company maintained this near monopoly of the domestic market in the decades after World War II.

In 1979 the corporation converted to a holding company by spinning off a number of autonomous companies covering various separate operations. In 1986 Fiat acquired Alfa Romeo SpA, an ailing Italian company that manufactured sports cars. Fiat, once the largest auto company in Europe, began to face stiff competition from larger and more global rivals, such as Volkswagen Group (Volkswagen AG), from the late 1980s. In 2000 the American automobile company General Motors Corporation (GM) acquired a 20 percent stake in Fiat in a technology-sharing deal; in 2005 GM paid $2 billion to terminate the partnership. In June 2009 Fiat finalized a deal with Chrysler LLC in which it acquired most of the troubled American automaker's assets as well as a 20 percent stake in the company, with the possibility that its share could increase if certain requirements were met. The deal resulted in the formation of a new company, Chrysler Group LLC. In 2010 Fiat announced that it was spinning off its industrial unit, which produced trucks and tractors as well as marine equipment, in order to focus on automobiles. The following year Fiat became the majority shareholder in Chrysler after acquiring the remaining stakes held by the U.S. and Canadian governments.

vast field of petrochemicals. The discovery, too, of natural gas near Ravenna triggered the production of synthetic rubber, resins, artificial fibre, and more fertilizers. The industry boomed until the 1973 oil crisis launched a protracted slump, which rebounded somewhat in the 1980s as the sector was rationalized. During the 1990s the chemical industry was confronted with limits defined by environmental protection policies and the restructuring of small and medium-size enterprises.

The food and beverage industry is also important, in particular the traditional products olive oil, wine, fruit, and tomatoes. Additionally, the pulp and paper, printing and publishing, and pottery, glass, and ceramics industries are prominent.

The housing sector was affected by three main factors following World War II: the postwar economic boom, massive rural-to-urban migration, and government incentives to the private construction sector. Approximately

An employee inspects spools of yarn in a textile factory near Varese, Italy. Textiles have long been one of the country's leading industries. Bloomberg/Getty Images

500,000 homes were destroyed in the war and another 250,000 severely damaged. A period of frenzied building ensued, reaching a peak during 1961–65, when an average of 380,000 houses were built each year. Much of the building was undertaken by private companies that engaged heavily in speculative construction and paid scant regard to regulations. This led to overcrowding and a severe lack of services in peripheral urban areas. The problem was exacerbated by the migration of hundreds of thousands of southern Italians to the big northern towns in search of work.

Construction slackened during the late 1960s and '70s as a result of economic recession, although many Italians were still living in substandard dwellings and awaiting rehousing. A 1980 earthquake in the Naples area destroyed a quarter of a million homes and resulted in a localized building boom lasting almost a decade. In the late 1990s the construction sector showed signs of recovery mainly related to investments in public works and the availability of financial incentives for residential housing. As the Italian economy declined near the end of the first decade of the 2000s, the construction industry was especially hard-hit. New building of both private homes and public works contracted sharply as financing became more difficult to secure and government funding for infrastructure improvement dried up.

Mining is not an important sector of the Italian economy. Minerals are widely dispersed, and, unlike other industries, mining and quarrying traditionally have been more prevalent in the south than in the north. In the early 21st century, increased demand for construction materials and fertilizers led to the expansion of northern-based quarrying industries specializing in lime and chalk (for the production of fertilizers and cement, an important industry), along with coloured granites and marbles. Conversely, in the north, extraction of metalliferous minerals (such as iron ore, manganese, and zinc) declined. Nonmetalliferous minerals, including graphite, amianthus (a type of asbestos), and coal, shared a similar fate throughout Italy. As a primary fuel, coal satisfied just over one-tenth of the country's energy demands in the early 21st century. Mining has fared badly on the islands, where it once prospered, with a decline in the extraction of sulfur in Sicily and of lead and zinc in Sardinia. Industrial minerals that remain significant are barite, cement, clay, fluorspar, marble, talc, feldspar, and pumice.

FINANCE

Italy's financial and banking system has a number of unique features, although its framework is similar to that of other European countries. The Bank of Italy is the central bank and the sole bank of issue. Since the introduction of the euro in 2002, the Bank of Italy has been responsible for the production and circulation of euro notes in accordance with EU policy. Execution of monetary policy is vested in the Interministerial Committee for Credit and Savings, headed by the minister for the economy and finance. In practice, the Bank of Italy enjoys wide discretionary powers (within the constraints of the Maastricht Treaty and other agreements that govern the euro zone) and plays an important role in euro-zone economic policy making. The bank's primary function also includes the control of credit.

There are three main types of banking and credit institutions. First, there are the commercial banks, which include three national banks, several chartered banks, popular cooperative banks—whose activities do not extend beyond the provincial level—and ordinary private banks. Second, there is a special category of savings banks organized on a provincial or regional basis. Finally, there are the investment institutions, which collect medium- and long-term funds by issuing bonds and supply medium- and long-term credit for industry, public works, and agriculture. The 1990 Banking Act reduced the level of public ownership of banks and facilitated the raising of external capital. All remaining controls on capital movements were also lifted, enabling Italians to bank unlimited amounts of foreign capital in Italy.

There are many institutes of various kinds supplying medium- and long-term credit. These special credit institutions have as their primary aim the increase of the flow and the reduction of the cost of development finance, either to preferential areas or to priority sectors (for example, agriculture or research) or to small and medium-size business. In addition to this network of special credit institutions, there is a subsystem of credit under which the government shoulders part of the interest burden.

The bond market in Italy is well-developed. Mainly as a result of the special structure of government-sponsored institutions for development finance and subsidized interest rates, the growth of the capital market and stock exchanges was far less important than in other Western industrialized countries. The development of the stock exchange in Italy was initially hampered by the archaic structure and rules of the markets and by tax problems connected with the registration of shares. More recently, however, the market was modernized; the Borsa Italiana, which manages the stock exchange, became operational in 1998.

TRADE

Italy has a great trading tradition. Jutting out deeply into the Mediterranean Sea, the country occupies a position of strategic importance, enhancing its trading potential not only with eastern Europe but also with North Africa and the Middle East. Italy has historically maintained active relations with eastern European countries, Libya, and the Palestinian peoples. These links have been preserved even at times of great political tension, such as during the Cold War and the Persian Gulf War of 1991. Membership in the EC from 1957 increased Italy's potential for trade still further, giving rise to rapid economic growth. However, from that time, the economy was subject to an ever-widening trade deficit. Between 1985 and 1989 the only trading partner with which Italy did not run a deficit was the United States. Italy began showing a positive balance again in the mid-1990s. Trade with other EU members accounts for more than half of Italy's transactions. Other major trading partners include the United States, Russia, China, and members of the Organization of the Petroleum Exporting Countries (OPEC).

Italy's trading strength was traditionally built on textiles, food products, and manufactured goods. During the second half of the 20th century, however, products from Italy's burgeoning metal and engineering sector, including automobiles, rose to account for a majority share of the total exports, which it still retains; they are followed by the textiles, clothing, and leather goods sector. The most avid customers of Italian exports are Germany, France, the United States, the United Kingdom, and Spain. Italy's main imports are metal and engineering products, principally from Germany, France, the United States, and the United Kingdom. Chemicals, vehicle, and mineral imports are also important commodities. Italy is a major importer of energy, with much of its oil supply coming from North Africa and the Middle East.

Membership in the EEC was the most beneficial economic factor in Italian trade during the post-World War II period. The later accession of Greece, Spain, and Portugal to the EEC created stiff competition for Mediterranean agricultural products, especially fruit, wine, and cooking oil. At the beginning of the 21st century, however, the expanded EU and the weakness of the new euro currency allowed for export growth in Italy. As the euro reached and ultimately surpassed parity with the U.S. dollar, this advantage was lost, and for the first decade of the 21st century Italy maintained a negative trade balance.

SERVICES AND TOURISM

The service sector is one of the most important in Italy in terms of the number of people employed. If the definition extends to cover tourism, the hotel industry, restaurants, the service trades, transport and communications, domestic workers, financial services, and public administration, well over half of the workforce operates in the sector. A fully accurate measure is impossible, however, because of the existence of a burgeoning black market.

A plentiful supply of labour has nourished the service sector, especially in the large urban areas, since the 1950s. This labour came initially from rural areas of northern Italy such as Veneto; later the Italian peasantry from the Mezzogiorno migrated north; and more recently immigrants from less-developed countries—many of whom work for low wages, without job security, and under substandard work conditions—have filled low-grade urban service jobs. High-level service jobs include those involved with information technologies, which are used by one-third of Italian business. Factors that have contributed to the growth of the service sector include the rise in the standard of living in Italy and Europe in general, leading to an increase in mobility, financial transactions, business, demand for leisure activities, and tourism.

Italy is renowned as a tourist destination; it attracted more than 40 million foreign visitors annually in the early 21st century. Conversely, less than one-fifth of Italians take their holidays abroad. The tourist industry in Italy experienced a decline from 1987 onward, including a slump during the Persian Gulf War and world recession, but it rebounded in the 1990s, posting gains in the number of

VATICAN CITY

Map of Vatican City.

Vatican City (full name: State of the Vatican City) is the seat of the head of the Roman Catholic Church and is an independent papal state with an area of 109 acres (44 hectares) located within the commune of Rome. In 2010, its estimated population was 800.

The Vatican City flag.

Vatican City's medieval and Renaissance walls form its boundaries except onto the southeast at St. Peter's Square. Within the walls is the world's smallest independent nation-state, with its own diplomatic missions, newspaper, post office, radio station, banking system, army of 100 Swiss Guards, and publishing house. Extraterritoriality of the state extends to Castel Gandolfo and to several churches and palaces in Rome proper. Its independent sovereignty was recognized in the Lateran Treaty of 1929. The pope has absolute executive, legislative, and judicial powers within the city. He appoints the members of the Vatican's government organs, which are separate from those of the Holy See, the name given to the government of the Roman Catholic Church.

The many imposing buildings include St. Peter's Basilica, the Vatican Palace, and the Vatican Museums. Frescoes by Michelangelo in the Sistine Chapel, by Pinturicchio in the Borgia Apartment, and by Raphael in the Stanze (rooms in the papal apartments) are also there. The Vatican Library contains a priceless collection of manuscripts from the pre-Christian and Christian eras. The pope and other representatives of the papal state travel widely to maintain international relations.

overseas and domestic tourists. In addition, the Jubilee celebrations promoted by the Roman Catholic Church in 2000 to mark the advent of its third millennium attracted millions of tourists to Rome and its enclave, Vatican City, the seat of the church.

The tourist industry has flourished under both national and international patronage. The most popular locations, apart from the great cultural centres of Rome, Florence, Venice, and Naples, are the coastal resorts and islands or the Alpine hills and lakes of the north; the Ligurian and Amalfi rivieras; the northern Adriatic coast; the small islands in the Tyrrhenian Sea (Elba, Capri, and Ischia); the Emerald Coast of Sardinia; Sicily; Gran Paradiso National Park and the Dolomites; and Abruzzo National Park.

LABOUR AND TAXATION

Women constitute about two-fifths of the labour force, though they are more likely to take on fixed-term and part-time employment than men. The activity rate of male employment is consistent throughout Italy, but females have a much lower rate of participation in the south.

Because of the *scala mobile*, which adjusted wages to inflation, Italian workers benefited from high job security for decades after World War II. Beginning in the 1980s, though, as the government moved to get inflation under control, the *scala mobile* came under attack and was eventually terminated in 1992.

The strength of trade unions was in decline by the end of the 20th century, but large general strikes were not uncommon. The right to strike is guaranteed by the constitution and remains a very potent weapon in the hands of the trade unions. Three major labour federations exist, each closely tied to different political factions: the General Italian Confederation of Labour (Confederazione Generale Italiana del Lavoro), which is tied to the left; the Italian Confederation of Workers' Unions (Confederazione Italiana di Sindicati Liberi), with ties to the Catholic movement; and the Italian Labour Union (Unione Italiana del Lavoro), related to the secular parties. A number of independent unions are also active, especially in the public service sector. They increasingly challenge the monopoly of the three confederations on national contractual negotiations and are quite militant.

The government has undertaken reforms in tax collection. Historically, it has been unsuccessful in gathering income taxes with consistency, in part because of tax evasion and a black market on goods.

TRANSPORTATION AND TELECOMMUNICATIONS

As a centre of trade, culture, and tourism over the centuries, Italy has developed remarkably complete transportation and communication networks that have been key to its economic development. From the early days of regional trading, boats and ferries were at the service of merchants and travelers to Italy's many ports; later, an extensive rail system allowed faster access to points throughout the interior. The period after World War II was a particularly active time in the development of the country's road, rail, and air transportation systems, much of whose growth was accomplished through government planning and funding.

WATER TRANSPORT

Water transport was the first important means of linking Italy with its Mediterranean trading partners, even though its only navigable internal water is the Po River. At the time of unification in the 19th century, the ports of Venice, Palermo, and Naples were of great significance, and the Italian merchant fleet was preeminent in the Mediterranean Sea. The 4,600 miles (7,400 km) of Italian coastline are punctuated by many ports, and a large majority of imports and exports arrive and leave the country by sea. The principal dry-cargo ports are Venice, Cagliari, Civitavecchia, Gioia Tauro, and Piombino, while those handling chiefly petroleum products are Genoa, Augusta, Trieste, Bari, and Savona. Naples and Livorno handle both types of cargo. Half of the commercial port traffic is concentrated on only one-tenth of the coastline. The industries of Piedmont and Lombardy make heavy demands on the maritime outlets, particularly Genoa, which is the most extensive and important Italian port but which has great difficulty expanding because of the mountains surrounding it.

RAIL TRANSPORT

The main period of railway construction was about the time of unification, from 1860 until 1873. The heavy costs involved in laying down the infrastructure caused the government to sell off its stake in 1865. By this time the networks serving Milan, Genoa, and Turin in the north were well-developed. These were followed by links through the Po valley to Venice; to Bari, along the Adriatic coast; down the Tyrrhenian coast, through Naples, to Reggio di Calabria; and from Rome to the Adriatic cities of Ancona and Pescara. The Sicilian and Sardinian networks also were built. A period of rationalization and modernization followed in 1905 when the network was renationalized; building of new rail lines continued throughout the 20th century. An exceptional feature was the early electrification of the lines, many of which ran through long tunnels and were ill-suited to steam power. This modernization was due to Italy's early development of hydroelectricity.

Although the rail network is well distributed throughout the peninsula, there are important qualitative differences between its northern and southern components. The north enjoys more frequent services, faster trains, and more double track lines than the south. Compared with other European networks, the Italian trains carry little freight but many passengers, partly because the railways failed to keep pace with the rapid rate of industrialization after World War II, while the passenger lines were made inexpensive through government subsidies. Eighty percent of the rail network was controlled by the state via Ferrovie dello Stato ("State Railways") before it was privatized in 1992.

The Italian railways are connected with the rest of Europe by a series of mountain routes, linking Turin with

Fréjus in France, Milan with Switzerland via the Simplon Tunnel, Verona to Austria and Germany via the Brenner Pass, and Venice to eastern Europe via Tarvisio. In the late 20th century routes were expanded, extended, and modernized, including the addition of high-speed lines and computerized booking and freight control systems. The railway network extends some 10,000 miles (16,000 km).

ROAD TRANSPORT

The Italian road network is subdivided into four administrative categories—express highways (*autostrade*) and national, provincial, and municipal roads (*strade statali, strade provinciali,* and *strade comunali,* respectively). Road construction in Italy flourished between 1955 and 1975. Between 1951 and 1980, surfaced roads, excluding highways and urban streets, increased by 72 percent to cover more than 183,000 miles (295,000 km). Automobile sales increased faster than in any other western European economy during this period. Much of this was due to mass production of cheap models by Fiat. Road construction in the south particularly benefited from funds released by the Southern Development Fund.

More spectacular than general road construction was the development of the highway system. This project was farmed out to concessionary companies and financed by tolls, releasing it from the slow state bureaucracy and explaining its rapid progress. By the 1980s the network extended over 3,700 miles (6,000 km), making it second in Europe (only West Germany's was bigger). The main axis runs north-south from Chiasso on the Swiss border via Milan, Bologna, Florence, and Rome all the way south to Reggio di Calabria at the very tip of the peninsula. Another major route cuts southward from the Brenner Pass along the Adriatic coast to Bari and Taranto. A dense latticework of highways serves the north, linking Turin to Milan, Venice, and Trieste on an east-west axis and to Bologna and Genoa. Other east-west routes link Rome to Pescara across the Apennines and connect Naples to Bari. Commercial road transport has increased in recent years; Italy has one of the five largest trucking fleets in Europe.

Congestion is one of the main problems facing Italy's urban streets. Many town centres are based on medieval street plans and are unable to cope with levels of traffic and pollution generated by a population with one of the highest rates of automobile ownership in western Europe. Several cities, including Rome and Milan, have introduced measures to reduce the number of cars entering the city centres at peak hours and promoted other modes of transport. In the 21st century some towns took these steps even further, embracing a trend that came to be known as the "Slow City" movement. By completely banning automobiles from historic city centres and promoting the use of local products, the dozens of towns that adhered to the "Slow City" philosophy sought to preserve their traditional character.

AIR TRANSPORT

Of the small proportion of freight passing through Italian airports, a majority of it is processed either at Malpensa Airport near Milan or at Leonardo da Vinci Airport (in Fiumicino) near Rome. These airports, nearly equally, also handle the bulk of passenger traffic, though Linate Airport in Milan and Marco Polo (Tessera) Airport in Venice carry a large number as well. Many of the other regional airports (including those at Turin, Genoa, Verona, Bologna, Rimini, Pisa, Naples, Brindisi, Palermo, Catania, and Cagliari) are used for domestic flights, except during the peak tourist season, when they may absorb some of the vacation traffic from other European destinations.

The most frenetic developments in air transport occurred in the 1960s, with a 10-fold increase in freight traffic and a sevenfold increase in passengers. At that time Alitalia, Italy's national airline, became one of the largest in Europe. It remained viable by surviving the oil crisis of the 1970s, diversifying as a result of airline deregulation in the 1980s, and forming partnerships with foreign airlines in the 1990s and early 21st century. Alitalia filed for bankruptcy in 2008 and was purchased by an Italian investment group. Italy's flagship carrier was merged with Air One, a domestic competitor, and years of restructuring led to a more competitive airline.

TELECOMMUNICATIONS

Italy had put into use some 13 million broadband Internet connections, 22 million personal computers, and 21 million main telephone lines by the early 21st century. Roughly half of all Italians were regular Internet users, and cellular phones had achieved an astonishing level of penetration. Italy was one of the largest wireless markets in Europe, and, with more than 80 million active mobile phones in 2010, the number of cellular phones in Italy outstripped its population by nearly one-third.

CHAPTER 3

ITALIAN GOVERNMENT AND SOCIETY

The Italian state grew out of the kingdom of Sardinia-Piedmont, where in 1848 King Charles Albert introduced a constitution that remained the basic law, of his kingdom and later of Italy, for nearly 100 years. It provided for a bicameral parliament with a cabinet appointed by the king. With time, the power of the crown diminished, and ministers became responsible to parliament rather than to the king. Although the constitution remained formally in force after the Fascists seized power in 1922, it was devoid of substantial value. After World War II, on June 2, 1946, the Italians voted in a referendum to replace the monarchy with a republic. A Constituent Assembly worked out a new constitution, which came into force on January 1, 1948.

The constitution of Italy has built-in guarantees against easy amendment, in order to make it virtually impossible to replace it with a dictatorial regime. It is upheld and watched over by the Constitutional Court, and the republican form of government cannot be changed. The constitution contains some preceptive principles, applicable from the moment it came into force, and some programmatic principles, which can be realized only by further enabling legislation.

The constitution is preceded by the statement of certain basic principles, including the definition of Italy as a democratic republic, in which sovereignty belongs to the people (Article 1). Other principles concern the inviolable rights of man, the equality of all citizens before the law, and the obligation of the state to abolish social and economic obstacles that limit the freedom and equality of citizens and hinder the

CONSTITUTIONAL COURT

Similar to those of some other European countries, Italy's Constitutional Court is a court of constitutional review. It is composed of 15 judges, of whom 5 are nominated by the president of the republic, 5 are elected by parliament, and 5 are elected by judges from other courts. Members must have certain legal qualifications and experience. The term of office is nine years, and Constitutional Court judges are not eligible for reappointment.

The court performs four major functions. First, it judges the constitutionality of state and regional laws and of acts having the force of law. Second, the court resolves jurisdictional conflicts between ministries or administrative offices of the central government or between the state and a particular region or between two regions. Third, it judges indictments instituted by parliament. When acting as a court of indictment, the 15 Constitutional Court judges are joined by 16 additional lay judges chosen by parliament. Fourth, the court determines whether or not it is permissible to hold referenda on particular topics. The constitution specifically excludes from the field of referenda financial decisions, the granting of amnesties and pardons, and the ratification of treaties.

full development of individuals (Articles 2 and 3).

Many forms of personal freedom are guaranteed by the constitution: the privacy of correspondence (Article 15); the right to travel at home and abroad (Article 16); the right of association for all purposes that are legal, except in secret or paramilitary societies (Article 18); and the right to hold public meetings, if these are consistent with security and public safety (Article 17). There is no press censorship, and freedom of speech and writing is limited only by standards of public morality (Article 21). The constitution stresses the equality of spouses in marriage and the equality of their children to each other (Articles 29 and 30). Family law has seen many reforms, including the abolition of the husband's status as head of the household and the legalization of divorce and abortion. One special article in the constitution concerns the protection of linguistic minorities (Article 6).

The constitution establishes the liberty of all religions before the law (Article 8) but also recognizes the special status granted the Roman Catholic Church by the Lateran Treaty in 1929 (Article 7). That special status was modified and reduced in importance by a new agreement between church and state in 1985. Because of these changes and the liberal tendencies manifested by the church after the Second Vatican Council in the 1960s, religion is much less a cause of political and social friction in contemporary Italy than it was in the past.

THE LEGISLATURE

Parliament is bicameral and comprises the Chamber of Deputies and the Senate. All members of the Chamber of Deputies (the lower house) are popularly elected via a system of proportional representation, which serves to benefit minor parties. Most members of the Senate (the higher chamber) are elected in the same manner, but the Senate also includes several members appointed by the president and former presidents appearing ex officio, all of whom serve life terms.

In theory, the Senate should represent the regions and in this way differ from the lower chamber, but in practice the only real difference between them lies in the minimum age required for the electorate and the candidates: 18 and 25 years, respectively, for deputies and 25 and 40 for senators. Deputies and senators alike are elected for a term of five years, which can be extended only in case of war. Parliamentarians cannot be penalized for opinions expressed or votes cast, and deputies or senators are not obligated to vote according to the wishes of their constituents. Unless removed by parliamentary action, deputies and senators enjoy immunity from arrest, criminal trial, and search. Their salary is established by law, and they qualify for a pension.

Both houses are officially organized into parliamentary parties. Each house also is organized into standing committees, which reflect the proportions of the parliamentary groups. However, the chairmanship of parliamentary committees is not the exclusive monopoly of the majority. Besides studying bills, these committees act as legislative bodies. The parliamentary rules have followed the United States' pattern and have given the standing committees extensive powers of control over the government and administration. All these features explain why the government has a limited ability to control the legislative agenda and why parliamentarians are often able to vote contrary to party instructions and to avoid electoral accountability. The abolition of secret voting on most parliamentary matters at the end of the 1980s did not significantly change this situation.

Special majorities are required for constitutional legislation and for the election of the president of the republic, Constitutional Court judges, and members of the Superior Council of the Magistrature. The two houses meet jointly to elect and swear in the president of the republic and to elect one-third of the members of the Superior Council of the Magistrature and one-third of the judges of the Constitutional Court. They may also convene to impeach the president of the republic, the president of the Council of Ministers, or individual ministers.

Each year, the annual budget and the account of expenditure for the past financial year are presented to parliament for approval. The budget, however, does not cover all public expenditure, nor does it include details of the budgets of many public bodies, over which, therefore, parliament has no adequate control. International treaties are ratified by means of special laws.

The most important function of parliament is ordinary legislation. Bills may

*A view of the Chamber of Deputies, the lower house of Italy's national legislature, during the 2006 opening session.*Franco Origlia/Getty Images

be presented in parliament by the government, by individual members, or by bodies such as the National Council for Economy and Labour, various regional councils, or communes, as well as by petition of 50,000 citizens of the electorate or through a referendum. Bills are passed either by the standing committees or by parliament as a whole. In either case, the basic procedure is the same. First, there is a general debate followed by a vote; then, each of the bill's separate articles is discussed and voted on; finally, a last vote is taken on the entire bill. All bills must be approved by both houses before they become law; thus, whenever one house introduces an amendment to the draft approved by the other house, the latter must approve the amended draft.

The law is then promulgated by the president of the republic. If the president considers it unconstitutional or inappropriate, it is remanded to parliament for reconsideration. If the bill is, nevertheless, passed a second time, the president is obliged to promulgate it. The law comes into force when published in the *Gazzetta Ufficiale*.

THE PRESIDENTIAL OFFICE

The president of the republic is the head of state and serves a term of seven years. The prosecutorial immunity that applies to members of the legislature does not extend to the chief executive, and the president can be impeached for high treason or offenses against the constitution, even while in office. The president is elected by a college comprising both chambers of parliament, together with three representatives from every region. The two-thirds majority required guarantees that the president is acceptable to a sufficient proportion of the populace and the political partners. The minimum age for presidential candidates is 50 years. If the president is temporarily unable to carry out his functions, the president of the Senate acts as the deputy. If the impediment is permanent or if it is a case of death or resignation, a presidential election must be held within 15 days.

Special powers and responsibilities are vested in the president of the republic, who promulgates laws and decrees having the force of law, calls special sessions of parliament, delays legislation, authorizes the presentation of government bills in parliament, and, with parliamentary authorization, ratifies treaties and declares war. However, some of these acts are duties that must be performed by the president, whereas others have no validity unless countersigned by the government. The president commands the armed forces and presides over the Supreme Council of Defense and the Superior Council of the Magistrature.

Presidents may dissolve parliament either on their own initiative (except during the last six months of their term of office), having consulted the presidents of both chambers, or at the request of the government. They may appoint 5 lifetime members of the Senate, and they appoint 5 of the 15 Constitutional Court judges. They also appoint the president of the

Council of Ministers, the equivalent of a prime minister. Whenever a government is defeated or resigns, it is the duty of the president of the republic, after consulting eminent politicians and party leaders, to appoint the person most likely to win the confidence of parliament; this person is usually designated by the majority parties, and the president has limited choice.

THE COUNCIL OF MINISTERS

The government comprises the president of the Council of Ministers and the various other ministers responsible for particular departments. Ministerial appointments are negotiated by the parties constituting the government majority. Each new government must receive a vote of confidence in both houses of parliament within 10 days of its appointment. If at any time the government fails to maintain the confidence of either house, it must resign. Splits in the coalition of two or more parties that had united to form a government have caused most of the resignations of governments.

According to the constitution, the president of the Council of Ministers is solely responsible for directing government policies and coordinating administrative policy and activity. In reality, the president tends to function as a negotiator between government parties and factions. The government can issue emergency decree laws signed by the president of the republic, provided such laws are presented to parliament for authorization the day they are issued and receive its approval within 60 days. Without such approval, they automatically lapse. The government and, in certain cases, individual ministers issue administrative regulations and provisions, which are then promulgated by presidential decree.

REGIONAL AND LOCAL GOVERNMENT

The republic is divided into regions (*regioni*), provinces (*province*), and communes (*comuni*). There are 15 ordinary regions and an additional 5 to which special autonomy has been granted. The regions with ordinary powers are Piedmont, Lombardy, Veneto, Liguria, Emilia-Romagna, Tuscany, Umbria, Marche, Lazio, Abruzzo, Molise, Campania, Puglia, Basilicata, and Calabria. Italy can thus be considered a regional state. The modern regions correspond to the traditional territorial divisions. The powers of the five special regions—which are Sicily, Sardinia, Trentino–Alto Adige, Friuli–Venezia Giulia, and Valle d'Aosta—derive from special statutes adopted through constitutional laws.

The organs of regional government are the regional council, a popularly elected deliberative body with power to pass laws and issue administrative regulations; the regional committee, an executive body elected by the council from among its own members; and the president of the regional committee. The regional committee and its president are

Map of Italy detailing the country's political regions. Encyclopædia Britannica, Inc.

required to resign if they fail to retain the confidence of the council. Voting in the regional councils is rarely by secret ballot.

Participation in national government is a principal function of the regions: regional councils may initiate parliamentary legislation, propose referenda, and appoint three delegates to assist in presidential elections, except for the Valle d'Aosta region, which has only one delegate. With regard to regional legislation, the five special regions have exclusive competence in certain fields—such as agriculture, forestry, and town planning—while the ordinary regions have competence over them within the limits of fundamental principles established by state laws.

The legislative powers of both special and ordinary regions are subject to certain constitutional limitations, the most important of which is that regional acts may not conflict with national interests. The regions can also enact legislation necessary for the enforcement of state laws when the latter contain the necessary provisions. The regions have administrative competence in all fields in which they have legislative competence. Additional administrative functions can be delegated by state laws. The regions have the right to acquire property and the right to collect certain revenues and taxes.

The state has powers of control over the regions. The validity of regional laws that are claimed to be illegal can be tested in the Constitutional Court, while those considered inexpedient can be challenged in parliament. State supervisory committees presided over by government-appointed commissioners exercise control over administrative acts. The government has power to dissolve regional councils that have acted contrary to the constitution or have violated the law. In such an event, elections must be held within three months.

The organs of the commune, the smallest local government unit, are the popularly elected communal council, the communal committee, or executive body, and the mayor. The communes have the power to levy and collect limited local taxes, and they have their own police, although their powers are much inferior to those exercised by the national police. The communes issue ordinances and run certain public health services, and they are responsible for such services as public transportation, garbage collection, and street lighting. Regions have some control over the activity of the communes. Communal councils may be dissolved for reasons of public order or for continued neglect of their duties.

The organization of the provinces, units midway in size between regions and communes, is analogous to that of the communes; they each have councils, committees, and presidents. Since 1990 several laws that modify the organization of these local autonomies have been introduced in a trend toward greater decentralization.

There are certain central government officials whose duties lie in the sphere of local government. These include the government commissioner of each region, who supervises the administrative functions performed by the state and coordinates them with those performed by the region; the prefect, resident in each province, who is responsible for enforcing the orders of the central government and has powers of control over the organs of the province and communes; and the *questore*, who is the provincial chief of the state-run police.

Particular local government officials also have central government duties: among them are the president of the regional committee who, in directing the administrative functions that the state delegates to the region, performs a specific state duty; and the mayor of a commune who, in his capacity as an agent of the central government, registers births, deaths, marriages, and migrations, maintains public order (though in practice this is dealt with by the national police), and can, in cases of emergency, issue ordinances concerning public health, town planning, and the local police.

JUSTICE

The Italian judicial system consists of a series of courts and a body of judges who are civil servants. Judges and prosecutors belong to the same civil service sector, and their positions are interchangeable. The judicial system is unified, with every court being part of the national network. The highest court in the central hierarchy is the Supreme Court of Cassation; it has appellate jurisdiction and gives judgments only on points of law. The 1948 constitution prohibits special courts with the exception of administrative courts and courts-martial, although a vast network of tax courts has survived from an earlier period. The administrative courts have two functions: the protection of *interessi legittimi*—that is, the protection of individual interests directly connected with public interests and protected only for that reason—and the supervision and control of public funds.

Administrative courts are also provided by the judicial sections of the Council of State, the oldest juridical-administrative advisory organ of government. The Court of Accounts has both an administrative and a judicial function; the latter involves primarily fiscal affairs. The Superior Council of the Magistrature, provided for by the constitution and intended to guarantee the independence and integrity of the judiciary, was formed only in 1958. It attends to the careers, assignments, and disciplining of judges. Two-thirds of its members are elected by the judges and one-third by parliament. The president and the public prosecutor of the Court of Cassation also belong to it. Elections tend to politicize the council, which has become an influential force in Italian politics.

Italian law is codified and based on Roman law, in particular as regards civil law. The codes of the kingdom of Sardinia in civil and penal affairs, derived from the Napoleonic Code, were extended to the whole of Italy when unification was achieved in the mid-19th century. In the period between World War I and II, these codes were revised. The Constitutional Court has declared a number of articles unconstitutional. The revised 1990 penal code replaced the old inquisitory system with an accusatory system akin to that of common-law countries. Besides the codes, there are innumerable statute laws that integrate the codes and regulate areas of law, such as public law, for which no codes exist.

The constitution stresses the principle that the judiciary should be independent of the legislature and the executive. For this reason, jurisdictional functions can be performed only by ordinary magistrates, and extraordinary tribunals may not be set up. Judges cannot be dismissed, they are not subject to hierarchical superiors, and their careers rest on seniority.

The organized crime group known collectively as the Mafia (though regionally recognized as the Camorra in Naples, the 'Ndrangheta in Calabria, and the Sacra Corona Unita in Puglia)

Police surveying the damage from a 1992 Mafia bomb attack in Palermo, Sicily, that killed an Italian judge. Scorcelletti/Sestini/Gamma-Rapho/Getty Images

has a long history in Italy, particularly in Sicily, and it has followed the Italian diaspora to foreign countries, notably the United States. Nearly eliminated by Benito Mussolini during the interwar period and revived after World War II, the Mafia resurged in the mid-20th century with the rise of international drug trafficking but faced increased homeland opposition from the Italian justice system in the later years of the century. As government prosecution of its activities increased in the 1970s, '80s, and early '90s, the Mafia struck back by assassinating magistrates and judges who had aggressively targeted organized crime.

Popular resistance to the Mafia increased in the early 21st century as business owners increasingly refused to pay the *pizzo*, a "protection" fee demanded by local crime organizations. The *pizzo*, which extracted an estimated €200 million per day from Italian businesses, represented a vital revenue stream for the Mafia. The Addiopizzo ("Goodbye, *pizzo*") movement coalesced around consumers and businesses who rejected the Mafia's presence in everyday life, and Italy's most powerful business association threatened to expel any of its members who paid the *pizzo*.

POLITICAL PROCESS

For almost half a century after World War II, Italy's electoral system was based on proportional representation, a system in which seats in an elected body are awarded to political parties according to the proportion of the total vote that they receive. Between 1993 and 1995, several changes were made by national legislation and popular referenda. Following these changes, on the national level the Chamber of Deputies and the Senate were elected by a combination of proportionality and plurality. Seventy-five percent of the seats in these two chambers were filled from single-member districts by individual candidates who won the largest number of votes in each district. The other 25 percent of the seats were awarded to candidates from party lists on a proportional basis. The number of votes obtained by the winner in single-member districts was fully (for senators) or partially (for deputies) subtracted before allocating proportional seats, thus introducing a further element of proportionality. A new electoral law passed in late 2005 overturned this system by restoring full proportional representation. However, the law also allocated a number of bonus seats in the Chamber of Deputies to the winning coalition—thus guaranteeing a majority for the victors.

In regional elections, voters cast two ballots. The first is cast in a contest for 80 percent of the seats in the regional council, which are awarded on a proportional basis. The second ballot is employed in a plurality vote; the regional coalition that wins a plurality is awarded all the remaining seats as well as the presidency of the regional government. Split voting is allowed.

In provincial elections, only one vote is cast. If a single provincial list wins more than 50 percent of the votes, seats are divided among all the lists according to their proportion of the vote, and the presidency goes to the head of the winning list. Otherwise, a runoff election must take place between the two most successful lists, with the winner taking 60 percent of the seats.

A similar system is employed in municipal elections in cities with more than 15,000 inhabitants. In this case, however, two ballots are cast, one for mayor and one for the council. Split voting is permitted. In smaller cities only one ballot is cast; the winning list is awarded two-thirds of the seats as well as the mayoralty.

All citizens 18 years and older may vote. The turnout for elections in Italy is high, often reaching well over 80 percent of the electorate for parliamentary elections. Citizens may also subscribe to national referenda or petitions designed to abrogate a law or an executive order; such a petition must be signed by 500,000 members of the electorate or sponsored by five regional councils. Abrogative referenda have been used extensively since the 1970s to make possible a wide range of institutional and civic reforms. Abrogative referenda are provided for with regard to all regional legislation, and some regions have a provision for holding ordinary referenda. The constitution also provides that 50,000 members of the electorate may jointly present a draft bill to parliament.

From the end of World War II until the 1990s, Italy had a multiparty system with two dominant parties, the Christian Democratic Party (Partito della Democrazia Cristiana; DC) and the Italian Communist Party (Partito Comunista Italiano; PCI), and a number of small yet influential parties. The smaller parties ranged from the neofascist Italian Social Movement (Movimento Sociale Italiano; MSI) on the right to the Italian Socialist Party (Partito Socialista Italiano; PSI) on the left; a number of small secular parties occupied the centre. The DC, in various alliances with smaller parties of the centre and left, was the dominant governing party, and the principal opposition parties were the PCI and the MSI.

The postwar party system was radically altered by the fall of communism in the Soviet bloc in 1991, a wave of judicial prosecutions of corrupt officials that involved most Italian political parties, and, finally, the electoral reforms of the 1990s. The DC, riven by scandal, was replaced by a much smaller organization, the Italian Popular Party (Partito Popolare Italiano; PPI), which played a diminished role after elections in 1994. By that time three new parties had arisen to dominate the political right and centre-right: Forza Italia (FI; loosely translatable as "Go Italy"), an alliance created in 1994 by the media tycoon Silvio Berlusconi and dedicated to the principles of the market economy; the Northern League (Lega Nord; LN), formed in 1991, a federalist and fiscal-reform movement with large support in the northern regions; and the National Alliance (Alleanza Nazionale; AN), which succeeded the MSI in 1994 but whose political platform renounced its neofascist past. Meanwhile, the PCI remained an important electoral force under a new name, the Democratic Party of the Left (Partito Democratico della Sinistra; PDS), later shortened to the Democrats of the Left (Democratici di Sinistra; DS). Thus, the Italian political spectrum, which had previously been dominated by parties of the centre, became polarized between parties of the right and left. The political centre was left to be divided by various short-lived multiparty alliances—for example, at the turn of the 21st century, the centre-right House of Freedoms and the centre-left Olive Tree. In 2007 a new centre-left party, known simply as the Democratic Party (Partito Democratico), emerged when the DS merged with the centrist Daisy (Margherita) party. Soon afterward the FI joined with the AN to create the new centre-right People of Freedom (Popolo della Libertà; PdL) party. AN leader Gianfranco Fini withdrew from the alliance in 2010 to form the rival centre-right Future and Freedom for Italy (Futuro e libertà per l'Italia; FLI) party.

SECURITY

The armed forces are commanded by the president of the republic, who also presides over the Supreme Council of Defense, comprising the president of the Council of Ministers; the ministers of defense, the interior, foreign affairs, industry, and the treasury; and the chief of defense general staff. Military service for men was obligatory until 2005, when conscription was abolished. Women may serve in any branch of the armed forces. Although the constitution specifies that the armed forces must embody the democratic spirit of the republic, their activity is free from any political control. Italy's membership in the North Atlantic Treaty Organization (NATO) since 1949 has given the allied command a certain degree of control over the Italian forces.

There are two police forces in Italy with general duties: the Polizia di Stato ("State Police"), which is under the authority of the minister of the interior, and the Carabinieri, a corps of the armed forces that reports to both the minister of the interior and the minister of defense. The functions of the police are the prevention, suppression, and investigation of crimes. All functions are performed by both police forces. When engaged in criminal investigation, the police are placed by the constitution under the authority of the courts; however, the actual subordination of the two forces to two different government ministries is a source of conflict with regard to their technical subordination to the judiciary. In addition to these two police forces, there are special police for customs and for excise and revenue, prison guards, and a forestry corps.

CARABINIERI

The Arma dei Carabinieri (Italian: "Army of Carabinieri"), also called Arma Benemerita ("Meritorious Army"), is one of the national police forces of Italy. Its members are known as carabinieri (singular, carabiniere), a term that comes from the name of a type of military firearm. Originally an elite military organization in the Savoyard states, the corps became part of the Italian armed forces at the time of national unification (1861). For almost 140 years the Carabinieri were considered part of the army, but in 2000 the corps became an independent branch of the Italian armed forces.

Members of the corps wear a variety of uniforms, from military-style fatigues to an ensemble that resembles that of the civilian police force to full Napoleonic regalia. Virtually all of these uniforms include a white bandolier, the presence of which indicates that an officer is on duty. Carabinieri are housed in barracks, and the corps has a variety of military duties: it polices the armed forces, guards military installations, enforces recruiting laws, and has specific military responsibilities in the event of war. In these capacities it is responsible to the minister of defense.

The corps also acts as a civil police force, with responsibility for protecting public order and detecting crime. In those areas its function overlaps that of the Polizia di Stato, which, like the guards, is responsible to the minister of the interior.

Members of the Carabinieri, sporting their white bandoliers across their chests, stand guard in St. Peter's Square in Vatican City. Franco Origlia/Getty Images

HEALTH AND WELFARE

Italy possesses an extensive social security and welfare system that provides coverage for the great majority of the population. The system is run by a sprawling number of state agencies that supervise all social services, make available benefits in the case of accident, illness, disability, or unemployment, and provide assistance for the elderly. The largest of these agencies, which administers a wide range of benefits, is the National Social Insurance Institute (Istituto Nazionale della Previdenza Sociale).

A comprehensive national health service and national medical insurance were created in 1978 and based on Local Medical Units (Unità Sanitarie Locali, later renamed Aziende Sanitarie Locali). In 1992–99 a radical reorganization of the national health system was carried out. Key features of the new system were the rationalization of public expenditures and the improvement of patient care services.

HOUSING

The second half of the 20th century began with a massive housing boom that slowed in the mid-1970s and then resurged again at century's end. Overcrowding continues to be a problem, particularly in the cities of Rome, Milan, and Naples; Portici, a suburb of Naples near Mount Vesuvius, is one of the most congested towns in Italy. Although high demand continued into the 21st century, Italy's real estate market managed to avoid the bubble effect that devastated the economies of the United States, Ireland, and Spain in 2008–09. On average, housing comprises about one-third of a household's monthly expenditure.

EDUCATION

The constitution guarantees the freedom of art, science, and teaching. It also provides for state schools and guarantees the independence of the universities. Private schools (mainly run by religious bodies) are permitted. The constitution further states that the public schools are open to all and makes provision for scholarships and grants.

Education is compulsory only for those age 6 to 16 years. The school system begins with kindergarten for the 3- to 6-year-olds. Primary schools are attended by children between the ages of 6 and 11, at which stage most go on to secondary schools for 11- to 14-year-olds, but those wishing to study music go directly to the conservatories.

Postsecondary schooling is not compulsory and includes a wide range of technical and trade schools, art schools, teacher-training schools, and scientific and humanistic preparatory schools. Pupils from these schools can then continue their education attending either non-university- or university-level courses. University education is composed of three levels.

UNIVERSITY OF BOLOGNA

The University of Bologna (Italian: Università degli Studi di Bologna) is one of the oldest and most famous universities in Europe. It was founded in the city of Bologna in the 11th century; in the 12th and 13th centuries it became the principal centre for studies in civil and canon law and attracted students from all over Europe. Since it then had no fixed site or student housing, scholars of like nationality formed free associations, or guilds, to secure protections that they could not claim as citizens. The organizations formed at Bologna became models for modern universities. In 1158 Emperor Frederick I Barbarossa granted privileges to scholars of Bologna that were eventually extended to all Italian universities.

The students at Bologna were mostly mature men; as the civil law and canon law were at first the only branches of study, they attracted men already filling office in some department of the church or state—archdeacons, heads of schools, canons of cathedrals, and like functionaries. About the year 1200 the faculties of medicine and philosophy (or liberal arts) were formed. The medical faculty became famous in the 13th century for reviving the practice of human dissection, which had not been used in Europe since Roman times. The faculty of science was developed in the 17th century, and in the 18th century women were admitted as students and teachers.

After a period of decline, Bologna was reorganized in 1860 and resumed its place among Italy's foremost universities. The contemporary university includes faculties of jurisprudence, political science, letters and philosophy, medicine, and engineering.

At the first level, it takes between two and three years to gain a diploma. At the second level, between four and six years are spent to gain a university degree. At the third level, specialized courses of two to five years' duration or doctorate courses lasting three to four years are offered.

At the beginning of the 21st century, more than one-third of the population had a high school diploma, about one-third had a junior high school diploma, and more than one-tenth had obtained a college degree. But educational attainment is higher in the younger generations. About two-thirds of people of university age attend university, and almost nine-tenths of people of high school age attend high school. Most schools and universities are run by the state, with programs that are uniform across the country. Less than one-tenth of students attend private schools. University fees are low, and enrollment is unrestricted for most students with a postsecondary school diploma.

CHAPTER 4

CULTURAL LIFE IN ITALY

The 20th century saw the transformation of Italy from a highly traditional, agricultural society to a progressive, industrialized state. Although the country was politically unified in 1861, regional identity remains strong, and the nation has developed unevenly as a cultural entity. Many regional differences are lessening with the increasing influence of television and other mass media as well as a nationally shared school curriculum. Though Italians have long tended to consider themselves citizens of their town or city first, followed by their region or province and so on, this is changing as Italy becomes more closely integrated into the European Union (EU) and as Italians come to think of themselves as part of a supranational community made up of many peoples.

Since World War II, Italian society has profoundly changed, with a significant impact on daily life. One of the main elements of change is the more visible role women play in society outside the home, such as increased participation in higher education and the professions. One aspect of this changed role is that Italy records one of the lowest average numbers of children per woman in the world, as well as some of the lowest birth and fertility rates. The declining number of births was a subject of much concern in the first years of the 21st century, and some towns and villages, particularly in the depopulated rural south, were offering cash premiums and tax incentives for newborns. Of equal concern was the concomitant graying of Italy; in 2010 about one-fifth of the population was over age 65.

For Italian families, among the most popular daily leisure activities are watching television, listening to the radio, reading newspapers, and going to the cinema; reading books and engaging in sports are less common among the majority of people. According to surveys, Italians are very satisfied with their family relations, friendships, and health status, while their economic status and their working positions are less satisfactory. This is especially the case in southern Italy, where there are fewer job opportunities and where unemployment is high.

Though the popularity of home and wireless entertainment has grown, the use of public spaces remains important. Young Italians meet friends on a daily basis, often in the cities' piazzas in the evenings, making frequent trips to bars, cinemas, pizzerias, and discos. Social media Web sites and mobile phones allowed Italians—especially those of younger generations—to maintain ties with friends, but online communication

A crowd dining at a restaurant near the Piazza delle Erbe in Verona. Italy's piazzas, which are akin to town squares, are popular gathering spots. Lonely Planet/Getty Images

was generally seen as a method to facilitate, rather than replace, face-to-face interaction. Coastal areas are popular destinations in the summer. The automobile retains a strong hold on daily life as well. Ownership levels are high, and many cities and towns suffer severe congestion and pollution as a result.

Food is traditionally a primary element of Italian life. Work patterns in Italy revolve around the midday meal, though the leisurely two-hour-long lunch break is disappearing. Bars and trattorie cater cheaply and quickly to the casual diner. The culinary traditions of Italy proudly bear several ancestries, chiefly Etruscan, Greek, and Saracen: to the Etruscans is owed the heavy use of grain, to the Greeks the widespread presence of herb-cooked fish, and to the Saracens the country's love of pastries, rice, and citrus fruits. Although there is no one style of Italian cooking, there being a wide variety of regional differences, Italians everywhere share a love of noodles, and pastas bear such euphonious names as spaghetti ("little strings"), penne ("feathers"), macaroni ("little dear things"), and orecchiette ("little ears"). In the south, noodles are often dressed with sauces made of olive oil, tomatoes, and spices. In the north, especially in Piedmont, they are coated in cream, butter, and cheese. Many foreigners have grown accustomed to these regional variations, as Italian cuisine has become a popular cultural export.

International dishes such as pasta and pizza and ingredients such as olive oil are popular back home in Italy, of course, but Italian cuisine remains characterized by strong regional traditions, local geography, way of life, and history. Northern Italian gastronomy is well known for its use of butter, rice, polenta, and cheeses. Seafood and shellfish are prevalent on the coasts. Meat dishes are popular in central Italy; for instance, wild boar is cooked in Tuscany and Umbria. The south is renowned for citrus fruits, olive groves, and vineyards.

PIAZZA

The squares and marketplaces of Italian towns and cities are known as piazzas, a word that is cognate with the French and English "place" and Spanish "plaza" (all of which are ultimately derived from the Greek *plateia*, "broad street"). The most celebrated Italian piazza is that designed by Gian Lorenzo Bernini in front of St. Peter's Basilica, Rome. It is 650 feet (198 metres) wide and is bounded on the sides by fourfold Tuscan colonnades.

The name became more widely used from the 16th to the 18th century, denoting any large open space with buildings around it. In 17th- and 18th-century England, long covered walks or galleries with roofs supported by columns were called piazzas, and, in the United States during the 19th century, piazza was another name for a veranda formed by projecting eaves.

Italy is also one of the world's largest wine producers, and every region in Italy is known for wine—to name just a few, Barbera and Barolo in Piedmont, Valpolicella and Soave in Veneto, Chianti in Tuscany, Primitivo in Puglia, Cirò in Calabria, and Marsala in Sicily.

For most Italians in the 21st century, religious activity plays a much smaller role in daily life than it did in the prior century and is usually concentrated on Sundays or on special celebrations such as Christmas and Easter. However, older generations, especially in rural settlements, tend to be more involved and may attend mass every day.

Regional life in Italy is typified by a diversity of customs and a great variety of festivals, even if it is their appeal to the tourist industry and to television that helps keep them alive. The majority of religious festivals are Roman Catholic, dedicated to the Madonna or to different saints. The feast of the Epiphany on January 6 exemplifies religious diversification as well as the pagan elements

Costumed Venetians gliding down the Grand Canal during a historical regatta parade in 2010. AFP/Getty Images

present in some of these celebrations. Traditionally, a witch called the Befana brings gifts to children on this day. However, in the villages of Mezzojuso and Piana degli Albanesi, both near Palermo, the Epiphany is celebrated according to the Byzantine and Albanian rites, respectively. The most notable Carnival celebrations are held at Viareggio and Venice, where in 1992 they were financed for the first time by major sponsors.

Italy's strong agricultural tradition gives rise to a multitude of festivals celebrating the harvest, food, country, and seafaring pursuits. These festivals reflect the traditional activities of the area in which they are held. For example, the olive and bruschetta festival at Spello (near Perugia) marks the end of the olive harvest, the fish festival at Termoli reflects the fishing tradition in the port, and the hazelnut festival in Canelli (near Asti) gives testimony to the importance of that local crop. At Senale (near Bolzano) the traditional migration of sheep across the Giorgio glaciers is celebrated, while fishermen in the port of Aci Trezza (near Catania) stage a farcical swordfish hunt every June.

Some festivals are more sporting in nature, such as the historic horse race the Corsa del Palio in Siena, Florence's "football match" in 16th-century costume, and the regattas of Venice, while others commemorate historical events, such as the Lily Festival at Nola (near Naples), recalling the return of St. Paulinus of Nola in 394 after a long imprisonment in Africa, and the festival of Piedigrotta in Naples, commemorating the battle of Velletri in 1744. The Venice Biennale, established in 1895, convenes every other year to celebrate the visual and performing arts.

THE ARTS

Italy was at the forefront of the artistic and intellectual developments of the Renaissance, which drew their impetus from a reappraisal of the Classical Greek and Roman world. Artists and scholars in Italy were especially well placed to take the lead in such a revival, since they were surrounded by the material remains of antiquity. Earlier Romanesque and Gothic forms in both art and architecture were supplanted by the Renaissance, which escalated with a flourish into the Baroque styles of the 16th century.

VISUAL ARTS

The great names in Italian art through the centuries make a long list that includes, among many others, Giotto, Donatello, Brunelleschi, Michelangelo, Leonardo da Vinci, Titian, Bernini, and Tiepolo. Broadly characterized by a warmth of colour and light, Italian painting enjoyed preeminence in Europe for hundreds of years. Continuous subjection to foreign powers, however, eventually enfeebled Italy's artistic contribution, which sank into provincialism. Ties with European art were renewed about 1910 by the work of the Futurists, led by the poet Filippo Marinetti and the painters Umberto

A model striking a pose during a 2012 fashion show in Milan, the city that is considered the centre of Italy's fashion industry. Pier Marco Tacca/Getty Images

Boccioni and Giacomo Balla. Amedeo Modigliani spent time in Paris in the first decades of the 20th century and produced penetrating portraits that were little known in his lifetime. Also of note were the Metaphysical paintings of Giorgio de Chirico, who influenced the Surrealists until the 1920s, when he began to produce more traditional canvases. The subtle, quietist paintings of Giorgio Morandi placed him in increasingly high regard since his death in 1964. Argentinian-born Lucio Fontana's work exemplifies the modern artist's quest for form, expressed, for example, by a blank canvas slashed open by a knife. Modern additions to the Italian tradition of sculpture include the works of Giacomo Manzù, Gio Pomodoro, Marino Marini, Luciano Minguzzi, Alberto Viani, Harry Bertoia, Mirko Basaldella, and Emilio Greco.

Italy is a world leader in high fashion, an industry centred in Milan, a haven for models, designers, and photographers who come to work in the houses of Versace, Gucci, Krizia, Ferragamo, Valentino, Dolce & Gabbana, Prada, and Armani, among many others. Italian design houses such as Modigliani and Alessi have also been strongly influential.

ARCHITECTURE

The traditional image of old Italian towns situated around piazzas adorned with fountains remains valid in a country where ruins from Classical antiquity may stand alongside modern construction marvels. The Rationalist architecture movement of 1926 produced one of the outstanding Italian architect-engineers of the 20th century, Pier Luigi Nervi, architect of the Turin exhibition complex and the UNESCO headquarters in Paris. Marcello Piacentini was responsible for much of the imposing architecture of the Fascist period, such as the Esposizione Universale di Roma (EUR) area in Rome. Innovative architecture is represented in Milan's Marchiondi Spagliardi Institute, by Vittoriano Viganò. Other architects of note include Renzo Piano, known for his international museums; Aldo Rossi, whose critical writings rivaled his built works; and Paolo Portoghesi, who created public buildings from curvilinear forms.

LITERATURE

Italian literature, and indeed standard Italian, have their origins in the 14th-century Tuscan dialect—the language of its three founding fathers, Dante, Petrarch, and Boccaccio. The thread of literature bound these pioneers together with later practitioners, such as the scientist and philosopher Galileo, dramatist Carlo Goldoni, lyric poet Giacomo Leopardi, Romantic novelist Alessandro Manzoni, and poet Giosuè Carducci. Women writers of the Renaissance such as Veronica Gàmbara, Vittoria Colonna, and Gaspara Stampa were also influential in their time. Rediscovered and reissued in critical editions in the 1990s, their work prompted an interest in women writers of all eras within Italy.

After the unification of Italy, writers began to explore subjects theretofore considered too lowly for literary consideration, such as poverty and living conditions in the Mezzogiorno. Writers such as Giovanni Verga invented a new vocabulary to give expression to them. Among women writers was a Sardinian, Grazia Deledda, who won the 1926 Nobel Prize for Literature. However, the most prominent Italian woman writer of the 20th century was Elsa Morante.

The themes of writers in the 20th century ranged widely. The flamboyant patriotism of Gabriele d'Annunzio in the early decades of the century gave way to the existentialist concerns of Deledda and Ugo Ojetti, who focused on local aspects of Italian life. The Fascist period forced many writers underground but at the same time provided inspiration for their work, as in the case of Ignazio Silone and Carlo Levi. Italo Svevo and Luigi Pirandello pioneered the psychoanalytic literary genre, prior to the revival of realism by writers such as Elio Vittorini. Alberto Moravia wrote of the corruption of the upper-middle classes and gained notoriety for the eroticism of his narrative.

By the 1960s the literary world joined the protest movement against the corruption of the state, and poetry eclipsed the novel as the primary literary genre. Pier Paolo Pasolini, a poet, critic, and filmmaker, was the dominant creative figure of the period. Eugenio Montale and Salvatore Quasimodo won Nobel Prizes for their poetry, and Giuseppe Ungaretti founded Hermeticism. A onetime disciple of that movement, the spiritual poet Mario Luzi was frequently nominated for the Nobel Prize.

Of literature in the late 20th century, the work of Italo Calvino, Umberto Eco, and Primo Levi met with much success abroad; within Italy the work of Cesare Pavese, Carlo Emilio Gadda, Natalia Ginzburg, and Leonardo Sciascia was also well received. The last decades of the century saw the revival of the narrative and the historical novel, together with new forms of experimental and innovative language. In 1997 Dario Fo, a playwright known for his improvisational style, won the Nobel Prize for Literature. Writers active in the first years of the 21st century, working in a variety of genres, included Niccolò Ammaniti, Andrea Camilleri, Antonio Tabuchi, and Carlo Lucarelli.

MUSIC

Italian music has been one of the supreme expressions of that art in Europe: the Gregorian chant, the innovation of modern musical notation in the 11th century, the troubadour song, the madrigal, and the work of Palestrina and Monteverdi all form part of Italy's proud musical heritage, as do such composers as Vivaldi, Alessandro and Domenico Scarlatti, Rossini, Donizetti, Verdi, Puccini, and Bellini.

Music in contemporary Italy, though less illustrious than in the past, continues to be important. Italy hosts many music festivals of all types—classical, jazz, and pop—throughout the year. In particular, Italian pop music is represented annually at the Festival of San Remo. The annual Festival of Two Worlds in Spoleto has achieved world fame. The state broadcasting company, Radiotelevisione Italiana (RAI), has four orchestras, and others are attached to opera houses; one of the best is at La Scala in Milan. The violinists Uto Ughi and Salvatore Accardo and the pianist Maurizio Pollini have gained international acclaim, as have the composers Luciano Berio, Luigi Dallapiccola, and Luigi Nono.

Contemporary productions maintain Italy's eminence in opera, notably at La Scala in Milan, as well as at other opera houses such as the San Carlo in Naples and La Fenice Theatre in Venice, and the annual summer opera productions in the Roman arena in Verona. Tenors Luciano Pavarotti and Andrea Bocelli were among Italy's most acclaimed performers at the turn of the 21st century.

THEATRE

There are a large number of theatres in Italy, many of which are privately run. A number of publicly operated permanent theatres (*teatri stabili*) are funded by the state and supervised by the Ministry for Tourism. Three public organizations to promote theatrical activity in Italy are the Italian Theatre Board (Ente Teatrale Italiano), the Institute for Italian Drama (Istituto Dramma ItalianoI), concerned with promoting Italian repertory, and the National Institute for Ancient Drama (Istituto Nazionale del Dramma Antico). In 1990 the government tightened its legislation on eligibility for funding, which severely affected fringe and experimental theatres. Financial constraints in subsequent years led to an increasing number of international coproductions.

Italian theatre has been active in producing outstanding contemporary European work and in staging important revivals, although no native playwright has produced works that can rival those of Luigi Pirandello from the early 20th century. In the late 20th century, Dario Fo received international acclaim for his highly improvisational style.

FILM

The heyday of the Italian film was in the 1950s. Neorealism, best represented in the work of Roberto Rossellini and Vittorio De Sica, diverged from the escapism favoured during the interwar

Fascist dictator Benito Mussolini (left, with hands on hips) *posing during a visit to a movie studio in 1940.* Time & Life Pictures/Getty Images

years to take a candid look at prevailing conditions in postwar Italy. This new style attracted world attention. Cinecittà, the complex of film studios built by Mussolini near Rome, became known as the Hollywood of Europe. Rome became the centre for the international jet set, who frequented the grand hotels and smart cafés of the Via Veneto, attracting a new breed of celebrity-hungry photographers known as paparazzi.

Federico Fellini propagated this image of the capital in films such as *Roma* (1972) and *La dolce vita* (1960; "The Sweet Life"). Pier Paolo Pasolini, on the other hand, took a grittier look at the Italian underworld in films such as *Accattone* (1961; *The Beggar*). Other directors who made a lasting contribution to the cinema of the day were Luchino Visconti, with masterpieces such as *Morte a Venezia* (1971; *Death in Venice*); brothers Paolo and Vittorio Taviani (*La notte di San Lorenzo*

[1982; *Night of the Shooting Stars*]); and the screenwriter Cesare Zavattini. Some directors, such as Michelangelo Antonioni, Franco Zeffirelli, Sergio Leone, and Fellini, enjoyed more success abroad than at home.

In the late 20th century, Italian cinema fell into recession. Nevertheless, Italy can still claim some major international successes, including Bernardo Bertolucci's *The Last Emperor* (1987), Giuseppe Tornatore's *Cinema Paradiso* (1990), Gabriele Salvatores's *Mediterraneo* (1991), and Michael Radford's *Il Postino* (1994; *The Postman*). Silvio Soldini's *Pane e tulipani* (2000; *Bread and Tulips*), Marco Tullio Giordana's *I cento passi* (2000; *The Hundred Steps*) and *La meglio gioventù* (2003, *The Best of Youth*), as well as Matteo Garrone's *Gomorra* (2008, *Gomorrah*) were well received critically. Other directors of note are Gianni Amelio and Roberto Benigni, who won

NEOREALISM

Neorealism (Italian: *neorealismo*) was an aesthetic movement that flourished in Italy especially after World War II. It sought to deal realistically with the events leading up to the war and with their resulting social problems. Rooted in the 1920s, it was similar to the *verismo* ("realism") movement, from which it originated, but differed in that its upsurge resulted from the intense feelings inspired by Fascist repression, the Resistance, and the war. Neorealist writers include Italo Calvino, Alberto Moravia, and Cesare Pavese. During the Fascist years many Neorealist writers went into hiding, were imprisoned or exiled, or joined the Resistance. The movement reemerged in full strength after the war. Neorealism in film embraced a documentary-like objectivity; actors were often amatuers, and the action centred on commonplace situations. Often crudely and hastily made, Neorealist productions stood in stark contrast to traditional escapist feature films. Two notable examples of Neorealist films are Roberto Rossellini's *Open City* (1945) and Vittorio De Sica's *The Bicycle Thief* (1948).

the Academy Award for best actor for a film he directed, *La vita è bella* (1997; *Life Is Beautiful*), which also won for best foreign movie. Italian films are increasingly coproductions of cinema and television companies. The Radiotelevisione Italiana (RAI) and Fininvest are presently Italy's largest film producers, accounting for more than half of the film output, which numbers several hundred films and television productions each year. Rome's Cinecittà also sees many non-Italian productions each year, particularly of films treating historical themes; examples include *Gangs of New York* (directed by Martin Scorsese, 2002), *The Passion of the Christ* (directed by Mel Gibson, 2003), and *The Life Aquatic with Steve Zissou* (directed by Wes Anderson, 2004).

CULTURAL INSTITUTIONS

Italy's cultural heritage is an inescapable presence. The south and centre abound in vestiges of Greek and Etruscan civilization, and substantial Roman remains are visible throughout the peninsula. The most notable examples are the ancient Roman towns of Pompeii and Herculaneum near Naples and the remains in Rome itself. A wealth of monuments, churches, and palaces testify to Italy's cultural past, and the contents of its museums and galleries number more than 35 million pieces. Italy also has more than 700 cultural institutes, over 300 theatres, and about 6,000 libraries, housing well over 100 million books.

The Temple of Hera, Agrigento, Sicily. .V.Dia—Scala/Art Resource, New York

Italy contains dozens of historic places designated by the United Nations Educational, Scientific and Cultural Organization (UNESCO) as World Heritage sites. Among the places officially noted are the old city centres in Ferrara, Pienza, San Gimignano, Siena, and Urbino; archaeological sites in Agrigento, Aquileia, and Valcamonica; and the whole of the Amalfi coast and the Eolie Islands. Later additions to the World Heritage List include the Dolomites, the historic centre of Genoa, and the Rhaetian Railway.

Italy's museums contain some of the most important collections of artifacts from ancient civilizations. The permanent collection in the National Museum in Taranto provides one of the most important insights into the history of Magna Graecia, while the archaeological collections in the Roman National Museum in Rome and in the National Archaeological Museum in Naples are considered among the best in the world. The same may be said of the Etruscan collection in the National Archaeological

SISTINE CHAPEL

One of the world's leading cultural attractions is the Sistine Chapel, in the Vatican Palace. It was erected in 1473–81 by the architect Giovanni dei Dolci for Pope Sixtus IV (hence its name) and is famous for its Renaissance frescoes by Michelangelo. The Sistine Chapel is a rectangular brick building with six arched windows on each of the two main (or side) walls and a barrel-vaulted ceiling. The chapel's exterior is drab and unadorned, but its interior walls and ceiling are decorated with frescoes by many Florentine Renaissance masters. The frescoes on the side walls of the chapel were painted from 1481 to 1483. On the north wall are six frescoes depicting events from the life of Christ as painted by Perugino, Pinturicchio, Sandro Botticelli, Domenico Ghirlandaio, and Cosimo Rosselli. On the south wall are six other frescoes depicting events from the life of Moses by Perugino, Pinturicchio, Botticelli, Domenico and Benedetto Ghirlandaio, Rosselli, Luca Signorelli, and Bartolomeo della Gatta. Above these works, smaller frescoes between the windows depict various popes. For great ceremonial occasions the lowest portions of the side walls were covered with a series of tapestries depicting events from the Gospels and the Acts of the Apostles. These were designed by Raphael and woven in 1515–19 at Brussels.

The most important artworks in the chapel are the frescoes by Michelangelo on the ceiling and on the west wall behind the altar. The frescoes on the ceiling, collectively known as the Sistine Ceiling, were commissioned by Pope Julius II in 1508 and were painted by Michelangelo in the years from 1508 to 1512. They depict incidents and personages from the Old Testament. The *Last Judgment* fresco on the west wall was painted by Michelangelo for Pope Paul III in the period from 1534 to 1541. These two gigantic frescoes are among the greatest achievements of Western painting. A 10-year-long cleaning and restoration of the Sistine Ceiling completed in 1989 removed several centuries' accumulation of dirt, smoke, and varnish. Cleaning and restoration of the *Last Judgment* was completed in 1994.

As the pope's own chapel, the Sistine Chapel is the site of the principal papal ceremonies and is used by the Sacred College of Cardinals for their election of a new pope when there is a vacancy.

Museum of Umbria in Perugia, the Classical sculptures in the Capitoline Museums in Rome, and the Egyptian collection in the Egyptian Museum in Turin.

Italy's towering artistic achievement during the Renaissance is reflected in the magnificent collections in the Uffizi Gallery, the National Museum of the Bargello, and other galleries in Florence. In addition to the Old Masters, the Uffizi,

a public gallery since 1765, contains masterpieces by Michelangelo, Leonardo da Vinci, Botticelli, Piero della Francesca, Giovanni Bellini, and Titian. The Bargello holds a superb collection of Florentine sculpture, with works by Michelangelo, Cellini, Donatello, and the Della Robbia family. The Pitti Palace houses an impressive collection of paintings by Raphael, together with about 500 important works of the 16th and 17th centuries collected by the Medici and Lorraine families.

Many of Italy's major galleries are concerned primarily with their own regional heritage. For example, the Brera Art Gallery in Milan is rich in work from the northern Italian Lombard school, and the Galleries of the Academy of Venice are the major exponent of Venetian painting, as the National Art Gallery in Siena is of the Sienese school. The Vatican Museums, in the enclave of Vatican City, are noted above all for the frescoes by Michelangelo in the Sistine Chapel, which were restored in the 1980s and '90s in one of the most ambitious conservation projects undertaken in Europe.

A quarter of Italy's museums belong to the Italian state, just under half to local authorities, and a small proportion to public bodies, religious organizations, and private owners. The numbers of museum visitors are dependent on overall tourism trends, but individual museums routinely count their annual attendance totals in the millions. In the early 21st century more than 5 million people a year passed through the Vatican Museums, and more than 1.5 million visited the Uffizi Gallery.

Italy's national library system is controlled by the Central Office for Books, Manuscripts, and Cultural Institutes. This body oversees the work of cataloging and conserving the nation's books and directly controls the State Record Library and some 50 state libraries. The two principal national libraries are based in Rome and Florence. Their work is supported by the main national libraries of Bari, Naples, Venice, Palermo, and Milan and their provincial branches. Each of these concentrates to a significant extent on the literary heritage of its own region. The university libraries are primarily concerned with the promotion of academic research.

Academies and societies, representing a multitude of interests, have proliferated in Italy. Indeed, academies of the fine arts had their origins in Italy. For example, the Academy of Fine Arts of Florence was founded as the Academy of Arts of Design in 1563, and the academy of Perugia dates to 1573. Rome's Academy of San Luca was a guild of painters, founded in 1577. Italy's most famous learned society is the National Academy of Lincei, of which Galileo was once a member. The most-distinguished literary society is the Academy of Crusca, founded in Florence in 1582. There are also many historical and scientific societies, including the Cimento Academy, which opened in Florence in 1657. Foreign schools that were established for the study of Italian art and culture contribute significantly to Italian academic life.

SPORTS AND RECREATION

For a country in which only a small percentage of the population is actively involved in sports, Italy has produced an impressive number of champions in cycling, skiing, basketball, water polo, volleyball, and football (soccer). Especially popular is football, which some Italian scholars claim was invented in 16th-century Italy as *calcio* and introduced at the Palio festivals of Florence and Siena. Italian football teams excelled in international play in the 1930s and from the late 1960s onward. The national team has won the World Cup four times, most recently in 2006.

Automobile racing also is widely popular in Italy, and Italian engineers and drivers have contributed much to the sport. Ferrari racing cars, first manufactured in 1946, have won more than 5,000 major races and set many world records.

Italian athletes have participated in every modern Olympiad. The Alpine town of Cortina d'Ampezzo hosted the 1956 Winter Olympics; the 1960 Summer Games were held in Rome; and Turin was host of the 2006 Winter Games. Italy's notable Olympians include fencer Edoardo Mangiarotti, diver Klaus Dibiasi, Alpine skier Alberto Tomba, and Nordic skier Stefania Belmondo. In the first decade of the 21st century, Italy typically finished among the top 10 medal winners at the Summer and Winter Games.

ROBERTO BAGGIO

The Italian professional football (soccer) player Roberto Baggio (born February 18, 1967, Caldogno, Italy), also called "the Divine Ponytail," is widely considered one of the greatest forwards in his country's storied football history. He won the Fédération Internationale de Football Association (FIFA) World Player of the Year award in 1993. He is also famous among football fans for missing the penalty kick that sealed the victory for Brazil in the 1994 World Cup final.

Baggio first played professional football in 1982, with the lower-division team Vicenza. In 1985 he joined Fiorentina, in Florence, a member of Italy's top division, Serie A. Baggio blossomed into stardom with Fiorentina, his distinctive ponytail becoming famous throughout the country. When he transferred to Juventus for a then

Soccer player Roberto Baggio, sporting his "divine" ponytail, in action during a match in 2002. Getty Images

MEDIA AND PUBLISHING

The legalization of local, independent broadcasting stations in 1976 radically changed the media landscape. Since then the number of newspapers and magazines published has declined, while commercial television and radio channels have mushroomed. The broadcasting sector is dominated by the three state channels of RAI and by three major commercial channels—Canale 5, Italia 1, and Rete 4. The latter three are owned by Fininvest, a multimedia company controlled by Silvio Berlusconi, who built up a virtual monopoly in the private television, advertising, and publishing sectors before becoming prime minister (1994; 2001–06; 2008–11). The French channel France 2 competes for viewers in northern and central Italy. About a dozen additional private stations struggle to secure the remaining one-tenth of the national viewership. Italian television has one of the highest numbers of television broadcasts in the EU and produces

record fee in 1990, there were riots in Florence. In his first match against Fiorentina as a member of Juventus, Baggio refused to take a penalty kick, an act that endeared him to his fans in Florence but alienated supporters of his new team. His rocky relationship with Juventus fans was smoothed over in the following years as Baggio led the team to a Union of European Football Associations (UEFA) Cup title in 1993 and a Serie A championship in 1995.

Soon after that championship, he was transferred to AC Milan, where he played a supporting role as his new team won the Serie A title in his first year there. The rest of Baggio's tenure with Milan was not particularly successful, however, and he signed with Bologna in 1997 in an attempt to revive his career. He scored a career-high 22 goals during the 1997–98 season and then signed a lucrative deal with Inter Milan. Baggio spent two seasons with Inter before closing out his domestic career with four years playing for Brescia.

Baggio had made his international debut for Italy in 1988. He played primarily as a substitute in the 1990 World Cup, but four years later he starred for Italy as it advanced to the final against Brazil. A scoreless tie after regulation play and two overtimes, the match went into a penalty kick shoot-out. With Italy trailing in the shoot-out 3–2, Baggio sent his side's final shot over the crossbar, and Brazil won the World Cup. His playing time was limited during the 1998 World Cup, but he scored twice in the tournament and became the first Italian with goals in three World Cups.

After he retired from the game in 2004, Baggio was much celebrated for his charitable endeavours. His autobiography, *Una porta nel cielo* ("A Goal in the Sky"), was published in 2002.

the largest number of films. Well-funded game shows and cabarets proliferate on the major channels, while small local channels provide a fare dominated by films and locally produced advertising.

The commercial television sector developed in a legislative vacuum for its first decade after 1976. This had adverse effects for other sectors of the media. Because of its high viewing figures, television drew the major share of advertising revenue away from its habitual market in films and print media. The effects were especially disastrous for the cinema, but newspapers and magazines also suffered from lack of advertising revenue. As it became increasingly difficult for publishers to operate their newspapers and magazines at a profit, these were gradually taken over by larger industrial and business concerns, often with some compromising of their editorial freedom. In the 1990s legislation to reorganize the broadcasting industry—to prevent the creation of monopolies and to regulate restrictions on the press—proved highly contentious.

The major national newspapers are *Corriere della Sera*, *La Repubblica*, *La Stampa*, and *Il Giorno*. Local and regional papers are particularly vital in Italy, underlining once again the strength of regional identity in Italian culture. Among the newspapers with the largest circulation are the sports titles *La Gazzetta dello Sport* and *Corriere dello Sport*.

CHAPTER 5

ITALIAN HISTORY: EARLY MIDDLE AGES THROUGH THE 13TH CENTURY

Italy was only a part, though an important part, of the international political system of the Roman Empire. When the empire fell, a series of barbarian kingdoms initially ruled the peninsula, but, after the Lombard invasion of 568–569, a network of smaller political entities arose throughout Italy. How each of these developed—in parallel with the others, out of the ruins of the Roman world—is one principal theme of this section. The survival and development of the Roman city is another. The urban focus of politics and economic life inherited from the Romans continued and expanded in the early Middle Ages and was the unifying element in the development of Italy's regions.

THE LATE ROMAN EMPIRE AND THE OSTROGOTHS

The military emperors of the late 3rd century, most notably Diocletian (284–305), reformed the political structures of the Roman Empire. They restructured the army after the disasters of the previous 50 years, extensively developed the civil bureaucracy and the ceremonial rituals of imperial rule, and, above all, reorganized and enlarged the tax system. The fiscal weight of the late Roman Empire was heavy, given the resources of the period: its major support, the land tax, collected by local city governments, took at least one-fifth, and probably one-third, of the agricultural produce. On the other hand, the administration and the army that the tax system

*Roman monochrome floor mosaic, 3rd century AD; in the Portico delle Corporazioni, Ostia, Italy.*SCALA/Art Resource, New York

paid for reestablished a measure of stability for the empire in the 4th century.

Central government was not always stable; there were several periods of civil war in the 4th century, notably in the decade after Diocletian's retirement and in the years around 390. But succession disputes had been a normal part of imperial politics since the Julio-Claudians in the 1st century CE; in general, self-confidence in the 4th-century empire was fairly high. Aggressive emperors such as Valentinian I (364–375) could not have imagined that within a century nearly all of the Western Empire was to be under barbarian rule. Nor was this lack of a sense of doom a simple delusion; after all, in the richer Eastern provinces the imperial system held firm for many centuries, in the form of the Byzantine Empire.

FIFTH-CENTURY POLITICAL TRENDS

The Germanic invasions of the years after 400 did not, then, strike at an enfeebled political system. But in facing them, ultimately unsuccessfully, Roman emperors and generals found themselves in a steadily weaker position, and much of the coherence of the late Roman state dissolved in the environment of the continuous emergencies of the 5th century. One of the tasks of the historian must be to assess the extent of the survival of Roman institutions in each of the regions of the West conquered by the Germans, for this varied greatly. It was considerable in the North Africa of the Vandals, for example, as Africa was a rich and stable province and was conquered relatively quickly (429–442); it was more limited in northern Gaul, a less Romanized area to begin with, which experienced 80 years of war and confusion (406–486) before it finally came under the control of the Franks. In Italy the 4th-century system remained relatively unchanged for a long time. The government of the Western Empire, which was permanently based at Ravenna after 402, became progressively weaker but remained substantially intact. While the Germanic king Odoacer ruled Italy after 476, the peninsula was not conquered by a Germanic tribe until the Ostrogothic invasion in 489–493. Although the peninsula had faced invasions, such as those of Alaric the Visigoth in 401–410, Italian politics continued

ODOACER

Odoacer (born *c.* 433—died March 15, 493, Ravenna, Italy) was the first barbarian king of Italy. His assumption of power in 476 is traditionally considered the end of the Western Roman Empire. Odoacer (who was also called Odovacar or Odovakar) was a German warrior, the son of Idico (Edeco) and probably a member of the Sciri tribe. About 470 he entered Italy with the Sciri; he joined the Roman army and rose to a position of command. After the overthrow of the Western emperor Julius Nepos by the Roman general Orestes (475), Odoacer led his tribesmen in a revolt against Orestes, who had reneged on his promise to give the tribal leaders land in Italy. On August 23, 476, Odoacer was proclaimed king by his troops, and five days later Orestes was captured and executed in Placentia (now Piacenza), Italy. Odoacer then deposed and exiled Orestes's young son, the emperor Romulus Augustulus.

Odoacer's aim was to keep the administration of Italy in his own hands while recognizing the overlordship of the Eastern emperor, Zeno, who granted him the rank of *patricius*—local ruler for the Eastern Empire. Odoacer, however, styled himself *rex*—king of his Germanic army of Sciri, Rugians, and Heruls—and refused to acknowledge Julius Nepos, Zeno's candidate, as Western emperor.

Odoacer introduced few important changes into the administrative system of Italy. He had the support of the Senate at Rome and, apparently without serious opposition from the Romans, was able to distribute land to his followers. Unrest among the German tribesmen led to violence in 477–478, but evidently no such disturbances occurred during the later period of his reign. Although Odoacer was an Arian Christian, he rarely intervened in the affairs of the Roman Catholic Church.

In 480 Odoacer invaded Dalmatia (in present Croatia) and within two years conquered the region. When Illus, master of soldiers of the Eastern Empire, begged Odoacer's help (484) in his struggle to depose Zeno, Odoacer attacked Zeno's westernmost provinces. The emperor responded by inciting the Rugi (of present Austria) to attack Italy. During the winter of 487–488 Odoacer crossed the Danube and defeated the Rugi in their own territory. Although he lost some land to the Visigothic king Euric, who overran northwest Italy, Odoacer recovered Sicily (apart from Lilybaeum) from the Vandals. Nevertheless, he proved to be no match for the Ostrogothic king Theodoric, who was appointed king of Italy by Zeno in 488 in order to prevent the Ostrogoths from raiding in the Eastern Empire. Theodoric invaded Italy in 489 and by August 490 had captured almost the entire peninsula, forcing Odoacer to take refuge in Ravenna. The city surrendered on March 5, 493; Theodoric invited Odoacer to a banquet and there killed him.

during the 5th century to be those of the Roman Empire. This meant, in the context of the military crisis of the period, a continual struggle between civil and military leaders, with the emperors themselves more or less pawns in the middle.

The careers of three of these leaders serve as examples of 5th-century political trends. Aetius controlled the armies of the West between 429 and his murder in 454; he was the last man to be active in both Italy and Gaul, as a Roman senatorial leader of a barbarian army that was Germanic, Hunnic, or both. His career was typical of those in the military tradition of Roman politics, and, had his life not been cut short, he might well have become emperor. The makeup of his army was, however, already significantly different from that of Diocletian or Valentinian, and its growing number of non-Roman military detachments tended increasingly to have their own ethnic leaders and to be organized according to their own rules. Ricimer (in power 456–472, by this time only in Italy) was a Germanic tribesman, not a Roman. He was culturally highly Romanized and, as such, was himself part of a tradition of Romano-Germanic military leadership that went back to the 370s, but he could not, as a "barbarian," be emperor, and he made and unmade several emperors in a search for a stable ruler who would not undermine his own power. Significantly, in 456–457 and 465–467 he ruled alone, subordinate only to the Eastern emperor in Constantinople. Odoacer was militarily supreme from 476 to 493. In a coup in 476 he replaced the last ethnic-Roman military commander, Orestes, and deposed Orestes' son, Romulus Augustulus, the child emperor and the last of the Western emperors. Odoacer pushed Ricimer's politics to its logical conclusion and ruled without an emperor except for the nominal recognition of Constantinople as supreme authority. To what extent he was a military commander of a Roman army as opposed to being a German "tribal" leader was by now impossible to tell. Nonetheless, he, like Ricimer, was an effective defender of Italy against invaders for a long time.

THE OSTROGOTHIC KINGDOM

After his conquest of Italy and assassination of Odoacer in 493, Theodoric, king of the Ostrogoths, began decades of Ostrogothic rule in Italy (493–552). This can be seen as the first true period of Germanic rule in the peninsula, for an entire tribe of 100,000 to 200,000 people came with Theodoric. Still, the Ostrogothic kingdom continued to operate inside a largely Roman political system. Like Odoacer, Theodoric courted the Roman aristocracy, both the civil administrators at Ravenna and the great landowners who made up the Senate at Rome. He needed them to run a still largely functioning tax system, which continued, in part, to pay for the army, though the latter was now entirely Ostrogothic. Roman law remained the basis of political and civil life except for the Ostrogoths, who continued to observe their own customary laws and practices. Theodoric, who did not want the Ostrogoths to become Romanized, encouraged them to keep their distance from the Romans. Yet such apartheid did not last. Some Romans joined the army; many more Goths became landowners, legally or illegally, and adopted civilian Roman cultural traditions.

Theodoric's rule was probably the most peaceful and prosperous period of Italian history since Valentinian, but a decade after his death Italy was already in ruins. Theodoric himself had fallen out with an important, traditionalist senatorial faction and had executed several senators, including the philosopher-politician Boethius in 524; the Roman elites looked increasingly to Constantinople as a result. The Goths began to split between factions representing more-Roman or more-Germanic cultural traditions; when the latter faction murdered Theodoric's daughter and successor, Amalasuntha (regent 526–534; queen 534–535), a crisis began that was to end the kingdom.

THE END OF THE ROMAN WORLD

The Eastern emperors in Constantinople regarded themselves as the legitimate rulers of the West, including Italy, after 476; both Odoacer and, for a time, Theodoric had recognized them, and they had strong links with the Roman Senate. In 533–534 Belisarius, general for the Eastern emperor Justinian I (527–565), conquered Vandal Africa; Amalasuntha's death was the necessary excuse to invade Italy. Belisarius arrived in Sicily in 535, and by 540 he had fought his way north to Ravenna. The Ostrogothic king

Witigis (536–540) surrendered to him. The Gothic armies of the north, however, elected new kings, and Totila (541–552), the most successful of them, kept the war going throughout the peninsula until his death in battle.

The Gothic wars were a disaster for Italy; almost no region was untouched by them. Together with the subsequent wars of the Lombard conquest (568–605), they mark the end of the Roman world there. In the 550s and the early 560s, however, the Eastern (thenceforth, Byzantine) Empire succeeded in reestablishing its political order in Italy, and in 554 Justinian issued the Pragmatic Sanction setting forth its terms: Italy was made a province of the Byzantine Empire, with its capital still at Ravenna (Sicily, Sardinia, and Corsica, however, were to remain administratively separate), and the Ostrogothic political system was to be dissolved. Indeed, the Ostrogoths virtually vanished as a people from then on; it is assumed they were absorbed into the Roman population or into that of the Lombards.

LOMBARDS AND BYZANTINES

In 568–569 a different Germanic tribe, the Lombards, invaded Italy under their king, Alboin (c. 565–572). They came from Pannonia (modern western Hungary), which had itself been a Roman province. Exactly how Romanized they were is a matter of dispute, but they certainly did not have the political coherence of the Ostrogoths, and they never conquered

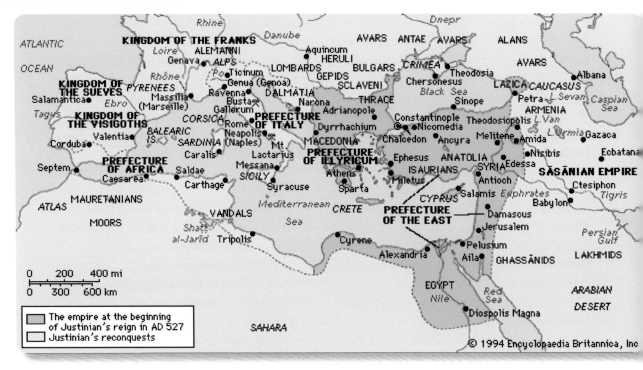

The Byzantine Empire at the death of Justinian I in AD 565.

the whole of Italy. Alboin took the north but was soon murdered, probably with Byzantine connivance. His successor, Cleph (572–574), was murdered as well, and for a decade (574–584) the Lombards broke up into local duchies with no king at all. The Byzantines seem to have been partially responsible for this, too; at that time they did not have the military capacity to drive the invaders back, and it was easier for them to divide the Lombard leadership and buy some of them into the Byzantine camp. For the rest of the century, even after the reestablishment of Lombard kingship under Authari (584–590) and then Agilulf (590–616), nearly as many Lombard leaders seem to

have been fighting with the Byzantines as against them. In 584, in the face of Frankish invasions from beyond the Alps, the Lombard dukes met and elected Authari king, ceding him considerable lands; in the process, Agilulf managed to unify the duchies of the north into a single kingdom. But the confusion of the first decades of the Lombard kingdom did not favour the development of a coherent political system, and, when the wars stopped in 605, Italy was divided into several pieces with boundaries that were in some cases to survive for centuries.

The largest of these pieces was the Lombard kingdom of northern Italy and Tuscany. By the 620s its capital was at

Pavia, which remained the capital of the north until the 11th century; other major centres were Verona, Milan, Turin (Torino), Lucca, and Cividale, the capital of the duchy of Friuli. Friuli played an important role as the Italian frontier against the Avars, a powerful military confederation of Central Asian origin that had taken over Pannonia. The two great southern duchies of the Lombards, Spoleto in the central Apennines and Benevento in the mountains and plains of the south, are best considered independent states; they were not connected to the Lombard kingdom geographically and seem to have developed separately, as territories conquered in the 6th century by Lombard detachments originally in some sense under Byzantine control. They were part of the same political structure as the north only for brief periods, most notably the 660s and the 730s–760s.

Byzantine Italy was nominally a single unit, but it, too, in reality fell into several separate pieces. Its political centre was Ravenna, which was ruled by a military leader appointed from Constantinople and called exarch from about 590. Exarchs were changed quite frequently, probably because military figures far from the centre of the empire who developed a local following might revolt (as happened in 619 and 651) or else turn themselves into autonomous rulers. But the impermanence of the exarchs made it easier for their local subordinates to gain some measure of autonomy. The duke of Naples, the largest city of the south, was effectively independent by the 8th century, as was the duke of the newly formed lagoon city of Venice. The most important of these local rulers, however, was the pope, the bishop of Rome, for Rome remained the largest city of Italy and its bishop, in theory the spiritual head of the whole of Latin Christendom, had considerable status. Rome had dukes, too, but they did not have the local support the popes had, and they remain shadowy figures. The popes, on the other hand, had a political position that in practice equaled that of the exarchs and lasted a great deal longer. In the far south, Sicily remained administratively separate from Ravenna, as did Sardinia, which followed its own path under increasingly independent "judges" in almost total obscurity until the Pisan and Genoese invasions of the 11th and 12th centuries. The Lombards of Benevento took Apulia (now Puglia) from the Byzantines, except for Otranto at its southern tip, in the late 7th century; southern Calabria remained under Byzantine control and was Greek-speaking by the 10th century.

THE LOMBARD KINGDOM

King Authari ensured the survival of the Lombards, threatened as they were by both the Byzantines and the Franks. The last Frankish invasion, in 590, probably resulted in some sort of Frankish supremacy; the Lombards payed tribute, at least for a time, and sent detachments to fight in the Frankish army as late as the 620s. King Agilulf reorganized the kingdom and suppressed several dukes with pretensions to autonomy. He also concluded a treaty with the Byzantines in 605 that established permanent borders with the exarchate, which scarcely changed over the next century (the only major exception being the Lombard conquest of the Ligurian coast in the early 640s). Agilulf also seems to have reorganized the central government with the help of Roman administrators, and indeed he imitated or reestablished some late Roman and Byzantine court rituals; he did not, however, exact the land tax and must have lived mostly off his substantial royal estates.

Agilulf seems to have been a pagan in his personal religion, though he may have been an Arian Christian; there were certainly many Arians among the Lombards, including most of the kings between 568 and 652. His wife and son were, however, Catholic, and Catholics were common among the Lombards as a whole from at least the 590s as well. Germanic peoples had often been Arians in the 5th and 6th centuries (the Ostrogoths were, for example), but the Lombards seem to have been less committed to Arianism than were the Goths or the Vandals, and they abandoned it without documented struggle in the mid-7th century. Although the Lombards do not in any case seem to have been religious fanatics, it may well have been Agilulf who laid the basis for a peaceful conversion of his people to Catholicism, owing to his careful cultivation of links to Catholic figures such as Pope Gregory I (despite his wars with Rome) or to the Irish missionary Columban, who founded the monastery of Bobbio, near Pavia, about 612.

For the political history of the Lombards, scholars rely primarily on one source, Paul the Deacon's *History of the Lombards*, written in the 790s. For the reigns of Agilulf and his predecessors, Paul's information is in part contemporary, for it is based on a lost historical work by Secundus of Non, one of the Romans at Agilulf's court. Secundus's work, however, seems to have ended after 616, and Paul's knowledge—and thus posterity's—becomes much more fragmentary. Paul says little, for example, about Rothari (636–652) except that he was militarily successful (it was he who conquered Liguria) and, most importantly, that he was the first king to set out Lombard custom, in his Edict of 643, a substantial law code that survives independently. It is evident, however, that the basic institutions of the kingdom were by then fairly stable. Between 616 and 712 the Bavarian dynasty—the family of Agilulf's wife, Theodelinda—dominated the succession; kings who were not members of this family, such as Rothari and Grimoald of Benevento (662–671), married into it. Grimoald was the only southern duke to claim the throne of Pavia; like Rothari, he fought the Byzantines and made laws. Male-line Bavarian kings such as Perctarit (661–662, 672–688) and his son Cunipert (680–700) preferred peace and seem to have developed the ceremonial role of the royal court. This contrast may

Italy, AD 700.

have represented a real political difference, but, if so, it was only a difference of emphasis. Every king accepted the cornerstones of the Lombard political tradition: Agilulf's Romanized court and Rothari's Lombard law.

Coups dominated the Lombard political succession, like that of the Visigoths in Spain, and between 700 and 712 these became particularly savage, resulting in the end of the Bavarian dynasty. Liutprand (712–744) reestablished peace; he is generally regarded as the most successful Lombard king. He issued a series of laws, as a conscious and well-organized updating of Rothari's Edict, which introduced a fair amount of Roman law into the Lombard system. He also waged war on the Byzantine exarchate and the southern duchies alike. The duchies of Spoleto and Benevento had, as noted, maintained their independence and their separate political traditions. Liutprand conquered the southern duchies in the 730s, setting up his own dukes in both; by his death, Spoleto (though not Benevento) was stably in Pavia's orbit. He also took about half the land controlled by the exarch and occupied Ravenna itself, temporarily, in 743. His attitude toward Rome is less clear; he took some papal territory but never threatened the city itself. During Liutprand's reign the Lombard king, for the first time since 568, was militarily dominant in the peninsula. He seems, however, to have still accepted the right of the exarch and the pope to an independent existence.

Aistulf (749–756) followed Liutprand's policies to their logical conclusion: he conquered Ravenna in 751, ending the exarchate; he ruled in Spoleto without a duke from 751 to 756; and in 752 he began to move on Rome, demanding tribute from the pope. But times had changed for the Lombards. In the 740s the popes had become close to the rising Carolingian dynasty in Francia, and in 751 its head, Pippin III, was recognized as king of the Franks by Pope Zacharias (741–752). Faced with Aistulf's attacks, Zacharias's successor, Stephen II (752–757), went to the Franks and sought their military support. In 754 and again in 756, Pippin invaded Italy and defeated Aistulf; he took Ravenna from the Lombard king and gave it directly to the pope, notwithstanding protests both from Byzantium and from the inhabitants of Ravenna itself. This pattern was to persist. Aistulf's successor, Desiderius (757–774), allied himself by marriage with the Franks and kept control of the southern duchies. But when he, too, threatened Rome in 772–773, the Frankish king, Charlemagne, invaded and this time conquered the Lombard kingdom outright (773–774). Italy became absorbed into the Carolingian lands right down to the border of Benevento, which remained independent.

POPES AND EXARCHS

The Byzantine lands in Italy were, in theory, only provinces of the empire of Constantinople and to that extent do not have much of an independent political history. Although Ravenna often found itself politically opposed to Constantinople, few exarchs made a permanent impression. The most consistent local political tradition was probably that of the archbishops of Ravenna, who were rich and powerful and, like their counterparts in Rome, had a considerable role in the civil administration.

It was in this context that the popes gradually increased their secular authority. The exarchs did relatively little to defend Rome, which was largely cut off from Ravenna by the Lombard states; the papal city thus had to develop its own political institutions. In the late 6th century, responsibility for feeding the population of Rome and, by the 590s, for defending it from the Lombards (both of Pavia and Spoleto) slowly shifted from the fast-disintegrating Roman Senate to the popes, who themselves still tended to come from senatorial families. Gregory I (the Great; 590–604) was the most important of these, and, thanks to his own extensive theological writings and collection of letters, his papacy is by far the best-documented of this period. In the course of the 7th century, his successors slowly detached themselves from the power of the exarchs, and by about 700 they could successfully defy any attempt from Ravenna to remove them. This also meant that they had gained autonomy from the more distant authority of the Byzantine emperor, with whom they were also often in religious disagreement. Pope Martin I could in 653 still be arrested for such disagreement (he died in exile in the East in 655), but not his successors. This autonomy became particularly important in the 730s because Emperor Leo III (717–741) was an iconoclast (i.e., opposed to religious images, or icons) and the popes were firmly opposed to iconoclasm. The emperor confiscated papal rights in southern Italy and Sicily from Rome for the popes' defiance, but he could not remove a pope. From then on, however, the Byzantine army no longer helped the popes, who were increasingly reliant on their lands in the Campagna (now part of Lazio) around Rome for food and military support. It was in this context that the popes began to look to the Franks for help against the Lombards. But the popes were also, in the face of nothing but hostility from Byzantium, beginning to think for the first time in terms of their own practical independence.

This came to fruition when the popes gained control over Ravenna itself after 756. By 774, when Charlemagne conquered northern and central Italy, Pope Adrian I (772–795) had extensive territorial designs in the peninsula. Yet these came to nothing, and indeed Adrian and Pope Leo III (795–816) found Charlemagne a far more intrusive patron than the Byzantines had ever been. But the popes kept control of the Campagna, and the belt of papal lands between Rome and Ravenna remained intact as well; the Papal States, as reconstituted by the late-medieval popes, reproduced almost exactly the boundaries of the former exarchate.

ETHNIC IDENTITY AND GOVERNMENT

The Ostrogothic kingdom used so many Roman governmental institutions that it can best be understood as a virtual continuation of the late Roman imperial system. Lombard rule marked much more of a break, without doubt. But exactly how much the Lombard states owed to the Roman past and how much to Germanic traditions is an ongoing debate. The basic notion of the kingdom as a political system was a Germanic concept in large part, for the legitimacy of the king rested on his direct relationship with the free Lombard people in arms—the *exercitales*, or *arimanni*, who formed the basis of the Lombard army. This concept did not leave much room for Romans, who indeed largely disappear from the evidence, even when documents increase again in the 8th century; it is likely that any Romans who wished to remain politically important in the Lombard kingdom had to become "Lombardized." It is even in dispute, for that matter, how many such Romans there were. Paul the Deacon, for instance, claimed that the Roman aristocracy were largely killed in the first generation of the Lombard invasion. But this was certainly an exaggeration, because the Lombards adopted too many customs from the Romans for the latter to have been reduced entirely to subjection. Some Roman aristocratic families must have survived among the Lombards, as is suggested, for example, by the name of a

Iron Crown of Lombardy, 9th century; in the collection of the Cathedral of Monza, Italy. SCALA/Art Resource, New York

royal protégé and founder of a monastery in Pavia in 714: Senator, son of Albinus.

The Lombards seem to have settled largely in the region to the north of the Po River, the area with the majority of Lombard place-names and Germanic-style archaeological finds (mostly from cemetery sites). But even there Lombards must have been a minority, and they must have been even more so farther south. There were probably few concentrations of Germanic settlers entirely immune to Roman cultural influence. The Lombard language seems to have disappeared by the 8th century, leaving few loanwords in the Italian language. The impression conveyed is of a gradual Romanization of the society and culture of the Lombards within the framework of their continuing political dominance. When the Franks invaded, Lombards and Romans moved together still more as a conquered, by now "Italian," people: the *regnum Langobardorum* ("kingdom of the Lombards") of the Lombard period was called the *regnum Italiae* ("kingdom of Italy") from the 9th century onward.

The evidence of Lombard law reinforces this pattern. Rothari's Edict and Liutprand's laws look much like the legislation of the Franks and of other Germanic peoples; they deal, for example, with the carefully calculated compensations for various crimes of violence that aimed to replace violent feuds or at least to make easier the resolution of feuding. These ideas were certainly foreign to traditional Roman law. When Liutprand in 731 restricted the scope of the judicial duel, for he suspected that it was unjust, he explicitly recognized that it could not be abandoned altogether, as it was part of Lombard custom. Within this Lombard frame, however, the content of law was often in practice heavily Roman. Lombard land law, for example, was almost entirely late Roman, except for the rules for inheritance.

The administrative system of the Lombard state was even more Roman than its laws. This is not very surprising, for Roman models offered far more power to rulers than did any Germanic tradition of government. The Lombards, like other Germanic invaders, took what they could from their new subjects and used Roman administrators where they could find them. Their system, as it is visible in documents from the 8th century, seems to have been more coherent than that of most other Romano-Germanic kingdoms. It was based on a central government in Pavia with numerous permanent administrators (such as the *referendarii*, who organized the writing of royal charters) and legal experts; there is evidence of legal appeals to judges in Pavia, and some of them were settled by the king himself.

Locally, cities provided the basis of government, which was another Roman tradition. In the kingdom, either a duke or a *gastald* governed each city and its territory; the difference seems to have been principally one of status. In the southern duchies, local rulers were all *gastald*s. These officials were in charge of the local law courts, led the city army, and administered the royal lands in the city's territory. (These three duties more or less exhausted the functions of government in the early Middle Ages.) Such responsibilities were typical everywhere in the post-Roman world; in Lombard Italy, however, the local power of dukes and *gastalds* seems to have maintained a more official character than in, say, Francia, with less development of private, or family, power and more royal intervention in local political processes. The Lombard kingdom also differed from Francia in the relatively limited political importance of its bishops and other churchmen; the kings of Pavia used church institutions as an element to bolster their power less than did any other rulers in the West (including the Byzantines in Italy). This may well show that secular institutions were strong enough for kings to rule through them without ecclesiastical help; if so, the reason must have been the survival of a relatively complex social and political life in the cities themselves. Eighth-century documents, particularly for Lucca, show a network of medium-level aristocratic families based in cities, who tended to furnish both counts and bishops for their localities and whose genealogies can sometimes be traced for centuries to come. The stability of city-based regional governments was probably the essential foundation for the political coherence of the Lombard kingdom itself.

Byzantine Italy was different from the Lombard lands in obvious and crucial respects. It was not independent; it was not ruled by an incoming, ethnically distinct group; and it gave more political space to the church. Perhaps above all, it still exacted the land tax and thus could afford a salaried army and a far more complex administrative system than the Lombards ever had. But in some respects it had a very similar development. The local power of the army and the constant need for defense led to the formation of a militarized landed aristocracy and indeed to a military identity for free landowners at all levels and thus to social patterns that were not at all unlike those in the Lombard states. For that matter, the foreign origin (Greek or Armenian) of many newly landed army leaders made the ethnic mix in the Byzantine lands almost as visible as in the lands of their Germanic neighbours. The civilian aristocracy of the Roman Empire vanished; Roman landowners who wished to maintain political influence had to become militarized and "Byzantinized," at least

if they did not attach themselves to the bureaucratic network around the popes and the archbishops of Ravenna.

Even the church became increasingly militarized; by the 9th century the bishop and the duke of Naples were sometimes the same person. The dominance of local military aristocracies in ecclesiastical politics appeared most clearly in the civil wars in Rome in the late 760s, the first period of effective papal independence and one in which rival families fought it out for the papal office. Roman politics was to take on this internecine character again when popes became politically independent; the next sequences of violence occurred in the years around 900 and in the early 11th century.

The Lombard states and the Byzantine provinces in Italy thus resembled each other more than either did the Roman Empire of the 5th century. The Lombard kings had a far less complex administrative system than had existed before 550, based as it was on royal landowning rather than the complex tax-raising mechanisms of the Roman world. One example of this is that they usually minted only a high-value gold currency rather than the gold, silver, and bronze coins normal under the empire; their state did not need as complex a financial system as the Romans had had. But the complexity of public life could more easily survive in Lombard Italy than farther north in Germanic Europe, owing above all to the vitality of Italian city society: in this sense, the Lombards looked far more Roman than did the Franks or, still less, the Anglo-Saxons. This city society must have been fairly similar on both sides of the Lombard-Byzantine frontier, in Ravenna as in Pavia, in Rimini or Naples as in Lucca or Verona. And, as the Byzantines developed local military aristocracies resembling those of the Lombards, so the cultural traditions of the two parts of the peninsula tended to move in the same direction. They were never identical, however; major Byzantine cities seem to have been larger than Lombard ones, and the Byzantine political system remained the more complex and articulated of the two to the end.

CAROLINGIAN AND POST-CAROLINGIAN ITALY

The Carolingian kingdom of Italy occupied the northern and central peninsula down to Rome, with the sole exception of the nominally Byzantine duchy of Venice. The former exarchate and all the Lombard lands except Benevento (to be dealt with separately) were part of it.

THE KINGDOM OF ITALY

Charlemagne called himself "king of the Franks and the Lombards," thus recognizing the separate identity of Italy inside the Carolingian empire. He left the Lombard dukes and *gastalds* in place unless they openly rebelled against him. Indeed, Italy was so much more tightly governed than Francia that to some extent it served as a model for Charlemagne's governmental reforms. However, these reforms were

intended for the entire empire, and, in general, the reign of Charlemagne in Italy (774–814) effected the slow integration of the latter into the political world of the Franks. Frankish names for institutions and offices replaced Italian ones; for example, dukes and *gastalds* became counts, *gasindi* (private military dependents) became *vassi* ("vassals"), and minor judicial officials were henceforth called *scabini*, as their counterparts were called north of the Alps. As in Francia, the church acquired greater political importance, for the Carolingians in Italy used bishops in their central and local administrations almost as much as they used counts. And, as long as the Carolingian empire remained united, its legislation, with some modifications, was as valid south of the Alps as it was to the north. The Frankish conquest began, then, a period of slow change rather than rupture; certainly, there was less rupture than with the Lombard conquest in 568. Few Franks, in fact, settled in Italy. These were mostly aristocrats, and indeed they made up almost the entire body of Italian counts appointed after about 800. The Lombard aristocracy, however, remained in the cities and supplied most of the bishops, and bishops were steadily gaining in political importance.

Carolingian government, which is better-documented than that of the Lombards, seems to have slowly increased in sophistication. Carolingian rule in northern and central Italy (774–887) brought a century of uninterrupted peace, and kings had time to perfect the already systematic ties between Pavia and the increasingly literate city-based administrations. The king's messengers regularly brought royal commands to the cities, and appeals came back to a complex judicial network in Pavia. Locally, legal procedures became standardized and reliable, as surviving documents of court cases show. This does not mean that government or laws were equitable or just, and there is plenty of evidence to indicate they were not, but they were at least systematic. This administrative network remained, even after the crisis of royal power in the early 10th century.

For most of the 70 years after 774, the kings of Italy were either children or living in the north of Europe. Charlemagne rarely came to Italy; his son Louis the Pious (814–840) never did. Charlemagne was at least involved with Roman politics, and Pope Leo III crowned him emperor in 800; but this title held little practical significance until the German emperors reestablished it in 962, and Louis was anyway crowned emperor in Aachen (now in Germany), not in Rome, in 813. Louis's brother Pippin was subking of Italy until his death in 810, and he was succeeded by his son Bernard (812–817). Louis, however, replaced Bernard with his own son Lothar I (817–855); Bernard revolted, but he was captured and blinded, and he died in 818. Lothar, like his father and grandfather, was more interested in Frankish politics, particularly during the Frankish civil wars of the 830s.

After the Treaty of Verdun in 843, the Carolingian empire began to be divided between the male heirs of the dynasty. Lothar's portion included Italy and the rest of Francia Media, which he later divided among his own heirs. His son Louis II (844–875) was king-emperor only in Italy. Louis II, whose reign was in many ways the high point of the Carolingian kingdom in the peninsula, was an active interventionist king. He used both the Pavia administration and new legislation to restore royal authority, which had slipped a little during the civil wars in Francia. His laws of 850, in particular, directed against robbery and the abuse of power by the rich, attest to the seriousness of his intent. Louis, and an entourage of powerful bishops and lay aristocrats (notably the Supponids, relatives of his wife Engelberga), reestablished firm royal hegemony in northern Italy in the 850s.

Rome was in practice part of Carolingian Italy, but the popes had a great deal of autonomy and also religious status. Nicholas I (858–867), for example, was particularly influential in Francia. The 9th-century popes controlled a complex local administrative apparatus and, like their predecessors, played an important role in military defense, particularly against Arab sea raids from North Africa and Sicily (which was conquered by the Arabs in the years 827–902). Leo IV (847–855) in particular refortified Rome; John VIII (872–882) tried hard to develop military alliances against the Arabs; John X

TREATY OF VERDUN

The Treaty of Verdun (August 843) partitioned the Carolingian empire among the three surviving sons of the emperor Louis I (the Pious). The treaty was the first stage in the dissolution of the empire of Charlemagne and foreshadowed the formation of the modern countries of western Europe. Louis I had carefully planned his three elder sons' inheritances, but from 829 onward his attempts to allocate substantial territory to the future Charles II (the Bald), his young son by a second wife, led to revolts by Charles's half brothers. After Louis's death (840) open warfare broke out; Louis's third son, Louis the German, allied with Charles in attacking the eldest son, the emperor Lothar I. Defeated at Fontenoy, in present Belgium (June 841), and driven from Aix-la-Chapelle (Aachen, Germany, 842), Lothar sued for peace. At Verdun (in present northeastern France) the following year, Lothar was confirmed in possession of the imperial title and received Francia Media, a long central strip of territory including parts of modern Belgium, the Netherlands, western Germany, eastern France, Switzerland, and much of Italy. Louis the German received Francia Orientalis (East Francia), the land east of the Rhine River. Charles received Francia Occidentalis (West Francia), the remainder of modern France.

(914–928) eventually succeeded in this, and a coalition of cities uprooted the Arabs from their stronghold on the sea near Gaeta in 915.

The Arabs were a threat to southern Italy, too, particularly after they occupied Bari in 847 during the Beneventan civil war (839–849). Louis II helped to negotiate an end to that war and was interested in rebuilding Liutprand's southern hegemony. In 866–867 he called up a large army, probably the largest seen in Italy in the entire century, and marched on Bari, which fell to a Frankish, Beneventan, and Byzantine coalition (largely owing to a Byzantine-Slavic naval blockade) in 871. Louis, however, did not leave the south; the Beneventans had to capture him and hold him prisoner for a few days to induce him to return home. This debacle ended

Carolingian attempts at hegemony over the entire peninsula; their Ottonian successors were to have no better luck.

Louis II died in 875 without male heirs. He was succeeded by a series of short-lived uncles and cousins, who came from either France or Germany and stayed in Italy as short a time as possible. But after the fall of the last of these, Charles the Fat (king in Italy 879–887), most of the Carolingian kingdoms turned to non-Carolingian aristocratic families to rule them. In Italy, Berengar I, a female-line Carolingian and also marquess of the still-important border area of Friuli, was well placed to be elected as a king with genuine Italian commitments in 888. However, since Carolingians did not have a monopoly over the succession, anyone could claim the kingship; indeed,

Berengar during his long reign (888–924) faced five such rivals, most of them militarily more successful than he was. Berengar was, in fact, not only long-lived but also unpopular; he spent much of the early part of his reign confined in his power base, Friuli. Even when he did not have internal rivals, as in 898–900, he was unlucky; in 899 the Hungarians invaded Italy, destroying Berengar's army and initiating a series of raids that were to last, off and on, until the 950s.

Berengar I's reign was a key period in Italian history. At its beginning the Italian kingdom was still a powerful and coherent institution, worth fighting civil wars to control. By his death the relevance of kingship itself was in doubt. This development resulted partly from Berengar's personality, which was unadventurous and, militarily, unusually inept—but only partly. As the Carolingian political system had settled in, over four generations, local politics had become more stable and inward-looking. Hereditary families had taken over many counties, particularly the big marches of Friuli, Tuscany, and Spoleto. Sometimes local power was balanced between count and bishop, and the king's capacity to intervene locally increasingly depended on their ability to maintain this balance of power. They usually accomplished this by supporting bishops, conceding more judicial and administrative power to them, particularly after 888. Sometimes, as at Bergamo or Cremona, counts were excluded from inside the city walls altogether. This was occasionally dangerous, for bishops, however loyal, were not royal officials and were more interested in the politics of the city than in those of the kingdom; it also represented a clear move toward both the institutionalization of local power autonomous from kings and the fragmentation of that power. In the face of the Hungarian danger, Berengar took this development one step further and localized military defense; after 900 he issued large numbers of grants to private persons, lay and ecclesiastical, of rights to build and fortify castles. His intention was carefully strategic, and his defense in depth was quite effective, but these castles in turn slowly became local centres of personalized military power, and they gained rights of private justice by the 11th century as well.

Carolingian government had always worked better when strengthened by private relationships of a political and military nature; for example, counts relied on their vassals more than on other subordinates to do their bidding, for vassals had sworn personal oaths of loyalty to them. In the castles of the 10th century, personal military bonds became the basis for effective local action. The office of count, too, was to become more and more the basis for private family power, particularly with the appearance in the counties during the early 10th century of newer ruling families with primarily local roots and fewer national pretensions. Cities remained important administrative centres, but they increasingly became points of reference for the family politics of the military aristocracy rather than bases for royal intervention. These processes had begun well before 888 and were not to be complete until the 11th century, but it is arguable that Berengar's reign marked the turning point. They were crucial for the development of later urban autonomies, culminating in the city communes, but they were disastrous for kings.

Berengar gained 15 years of unopposed rule (905–921) by his cessions of rights and lands after 900. But power was slipping away. Tuscany and Spoleto were semiautonomous under their marquesses; so was the Rome of John X (pope 1914–18) and of the powerful senator Marozia and her son, the princeps (prince) Alberic, who were able and effective rulers between 924 and 954. Hugh of Arles (king 926–947) found the situation irreversible. He could no longer use Carolingian-style procedures, such as new legislation or local administrative intervention, to assert his power. His most typical solution was to overthrow all obvious rivals and replace them with his own relatives, who would in theory be more loyal to him. As a result, he seemed simply violent and high-handed. But the fact is that royal power by now seemed to consist of outside intervention; kings, though still influential and rich, were outsiders to most of Italy. When Hugh faced a coup in 945, his support melted away, and he fell. When Otto I of Germany conquered the Italian kingdom, almost bloodlessly, in 962, his entirely non-Italian power base may simply have seemed to the Italians the logical conclusion of the kingship's increasing marginality. The Italian kingdom was to survive as a coherent administrative structure at least until the 1080s, and Frederick Barbarossa even in the 1150s could seek to revive it with some success, but it was by now external to the immediate interests of most of its subjects. After Hugh, no king could establish stable power in the peninsula without a foreign power base and a foreign army.

AUTONOMY IN THE SOUTH

When Charlemagne conquered central and northern Italy, Duke Arichis II of Benevento (758–787) responded by titling himself prince and claiming the legitimist tradition of the Lombards. Lombard princes then ruled in the south for 300 years, until the Norman conquest. Arichis and his son Grimoald III (787–806) were powerful rulers who held off the Franks, even if Grimoald temporarily had to pay tribute to Charlemagne after an invasion in 787. They controlled the entire southern mainland except for the Bay of Naples and the end of the "heel" and "toe" of the peninsula, using a governmental system similar to that in the north. But this area is largely barren mountain land and difficult to rule completely; many of the remoter gastalds were independent-minded and resentful of Beneventan power. Two of the early 9th-century princes were murdered in aristocratic plots—Grimoald IV in 817 and Sicard in 839. The second of these plots sparked a 10-year civil war that resulted, in 849, in the creation of two rival principalities, based at Benevento and Salerno. The *gastald* of Capua, Landulf I (815–843), also was interested in independence, and by the end of the century Capua was in effect a third state in the old Beneventan principality.

Even Naples, though much smaller, was affected by this move toward local autonomy, for the mid-9th century saw the effective secession of nearby Amalfi from Neapolitan control, and the consuls of Gaeta, on the coast toward Rome, were autonomous from the 860s onward. These three cities, like Venice in the Adriatic, were becoming important maritime powers in this century; Salerno was to join them later. The disintegration of the political system of the 8th century was pushed further by the Arabs, who conquered Sicily from the Byzantines after 827 and established bases such as Bari on the coasts of the Italian mainland from the 840s. Gaeta and Amalfi probably owed much of their naval activity and early commercial development to alliances with the Arabs; but others found the Arabs a rather serious danger, notably Bari's neighbours in Puglia and the great monasteries inland from Capua—Montecassino and San Vincenzo al Volturno, which were sacked in 883 and 881, respectively.

It was this confused world that Louis II wished to dominate in his great expedition of 867–871, but he failed. More successful was the Byzantine emperor Basil I (867–886), who followed up his blockade of Bari with a set of campaigns that aimed at taking the whole southern mainland from the Lombard princes. Shortly after his death, the latter were pushed out of the plains of Puglia, and by 900 only parts of the Capua-Salerno plain and of the south-central Apennines remained Lombard. In that year the count of Capua, Atenulf I, conquered Benevento, and the Lombard-Byzantine border stabilized. Capua-Benevento maintained a certain cohesion under a single dynasty until the 980s, its most notable prince being Pandulf I (Ironhead; 961–981).

After the departure of the Arabs (except from Sicily) and the straightening out of the political boundaries, the south was much more peaceful in the 10th century than it had been in the 9th. The Byzantines dominated the south through a local ruler, or *catepan*, who headed an administrative and fiscal system that was apparently more complex and stable than that of the exarchs had been. Culturally, the Byzantines were by now entirely Greek, and southern Calabria was, as already noted, Greek-speaking; in Puglia, however, the Italian-speaking Lombards dominated, and the Byzantines had to rule through them. They managed this effectively until a series of urban uprisings in 1009–18 brought more autonomy for the Puglian cities—as well as the first Norman mercenaries.

The Lombard states and the independent coastal cities were much weaker. They recognized some sort of Byzantine hegemony, except for the brief periods when the Ottonian emperors sent armies from the north. Their internal structures were less coherent than those of the territories under direct Byzantine rule. During the 10th century castles were built everywhere in southern Italy, just as in the Po plain; in the south (including the papal territories and the march of Spoleto), however, their social effect was in many areas more considerable than in the north because the scattered population living in the territory of a castle tended to move, or be moved, inside its walls. This process, called in Italian *incastellamento*, created a network of fortified hilltop settlements, some of which still survive. The state could direct and control this process, as in the Byzantine lands, but in Lombard areas private landowners undertook it, which greatly extended their local control. The Lombard princes could not control this steady political localization, particularly in the mountains. They instead concentrated on the richer plains between Gaeta and Salerno. Unfortunately, in this small area there were by now six independent states—Gaeta, Capua, Benevento (when it regained independence in the 980s), Naples, Amalfi, and Salerno. They spent a great deal of time fighting each other after Pandulf I's death in 981, and the Normans in the next century had little difficulty conquering them. The only local success story was international trade, which benefited all the coastal cities (Amalfi being the best known); their fleets had good relationships with Arabs, Byzantines, and Latin Christians and conveyed goods among all three. They dominated long-distance commerce in the western Mediterranean until the rise of the more militarily aggressive cities in the north—Genoa and Pisa—in the 11th century.

ITALIAN LITERATURE AND ART IN THE EARLY MIDDLE AGES

The early Middle Ages produced relatively few complex literary works; the elaborate educational system of the Roman Empire depended on a level of aristocratic wealth and a style of civilian culture that did not outlast the Gothic wars, and the ecclesiastical educational traditions that succeeded it were not well rooted in Italy outside Rome until the 9th century. Italy's—and antiquity's—last great philosopher, Boethius (died 524), had no successors, nor did Pope Gregory the Great (died 604) in the field of theology. Hagiography, an important early medieval genre in Francia, became almost unknown in Latin Italy after Gregory the Great's *Dialogues*. The writing of history, too, was only rarely practiced in this period: Paul the Deacon's *History of the Lombards*, dating from the 790s, is far shorter than Gregory of Tours's history of the Franks or Bede's of the English, and it had few parallels except for episcopal histories in Rome, Ravenna, and Naples. Nor did the Rule of St. Benedict, written by Benedict of Nursia (died *c.* 547) for his monastery, Montecassino, have immediate successors, and as yet it indeed had relatively little effect on Italian culture: 8th-century monasteries did follow it, but the Rule owes its international importance to the Anglo-Saxons and to the patronage of the court of Louis the Pious in Francia.

Italy did not lose all of its cultural traditions, and it developed new ones around the emerging centres of political power of the early Middle Ages. Rome maintained a level of intellectual life owing largely to its links with the Greek culture of the East; it experienced a flowering of new writing in the 9th century around international figures such as Anastasius the Librarian (died *c.* 878), who had contacts with both Constantinople and the courts of the Frankish kings. Pavia, for its part, developed a largely secular court culture; Paul the Deacon, who was a poet and an orator as well as a historian, was partially trained there, and later so was Liutprand of Cremona (died *c.* 972), whose *Antapodosis* is a florid but highly literate satire of the kings of the first half of the 10th century. Charlemagne's court drew Italian intellectuals to it and away from the peninsula, but Carolingian patronage returned to the cities of northern Italy in the mid-9th century, and systematic literary education began to develop in several of them. Tenth-century writers included not only Liutprand but also Atto of Vercelli (died 961), who wrote his denunciations of contemporary society in a Latin so difficult that few have ever understood it. The major intellectual activity in early medieval Italy was, however, law. The lawyers at Pavia were already a big group in the 9th century; in the 10th century they undertook a large-scale compilation of Lombard law and its Carolingian updatings, usually called the Liber Papiensis. This text was the source for 11th-century glosses and expositions and juristic arguments over legal theory that led directly to the 12th-century revival of Roman law at Bologna. The study of law in the Lombard and Carolingian capital may have been early medieval Italy's major contribution to the development of intellectual life in Europe.

The visual arts showed a more obvious continuity. The architects of Ravenna's monumental mosaic churches and secular buildings from the Ostrogothic kingdom and the years following the Byzantine reconquest developed new styles, but they did so as an expansion of late Roman ideologies of public buildings along Byzantine lines. In Ravenna the great period had ended by 700; in Rome, however, the same tradition continued, if at a reduced level, throughout the early Middle Ages. Sixth-century popes were builders, and their 7th-century counterparts, though less ambitious, were at least rebuilders; from Adrian I onward there was an intense revival reaching its height with large, richly decorated constructions such as the church of Santa Prassede built by Paschal I (817–824). Rome's surviving early medieval buildings are mostly churches, which is not surprising given its rulers; here as elsewhere, however, one must reckon with secular buildings that have not survived and, of course, with a continuous occupation and reuse of the huge array of Classical monuments.

In Lombard Italy, building on a monumental scale continued as well, notably in the royal palaces at Pavia and at Monza outside Milan (these do not survive, but Paul the Deacon described parts of the latter). This type of monumental architecture may have incorporated a fairly strong tradition of decorative figured stonework, with central European analogues, that survives best at Cividale del Friuli. What has been excavated or otherwise studied in the north, however, is strikingly small in scale, such as the urban monastery of San Salvatore (shortly thereafter renamed Santa Giulia) at Brescia, set up by King Desiderius about 760; the late 8th-century chapel at Cividale del Friuli; and the tiny frescoed church of Santa Maria at Castelseprio, which may date from the early 9th century. It may be that the Lombards, including their kings, had lost the rhetoric of size that the Romans had had (and that the early medieval Romans kept). The late Roman tradition that survived best was an emphasis on internal decoration, and Italy had many separate schools of fresco painters (as well as, more rarely, mosaicists) by the 9th century. However, 9th-century buildings could be large, as was the case with the monastic buildings of San Vincenzo al Volturno on the Benevento-Spoleto border, which were excavated in the late 20th century. They were sumptuously frescoed in both northern and southern Italian artistic styles during the first half of the 9th century. Building techniques declined in sophistication in the early

Outside the medieval town walls of Montagnana, Italy. Dal Pra/M. Grimoldi

medieval period, and older materials were frequently reused. However, artisans apparently continued to cut and make good-quality stone and brick in a Roman tradition. It is likely that there were far fewer builders than during the empire but that they continued ancient traditions in major cities. A price book for northern Italian builders from the early 8th century shows that they could make sophisticated private housing. Urban excavations now reveal, however, that more buildings were constructed of wood than would have been the case under the empire.

SOCIOECONOMIC DEVELOPMENTS IN THE COUNTRYSIDE

Early medieval Italy was an overwhelmingly agrarian society, as it had been before and as it was to be for centuries. Wealth thus derived above all from the ownership of landed estates. Estates were exploited by subsistence tenants on a standard medieval pattern. The slave plantations of 1st-century central Italy had long disappeared, and the word *servus* now usually just meant a tenant without public rights as a freeman; the remaining slaves on the land were mostly skilled specialists. Free and servile tenants essentially paid rent, in money or kind, to their landlords. For the late 8th and 9th centuries, at least in northern Italy and Tuscany, there is evidence of more organized estates, which were the equivalent of the manors of England and the *villae* of 9th-century northern France. Here tenants also had to work without pay on the lord's demesne, an area whose produce went entirely to the lord. These estates, mostly royal or ecclesiastical, could be huge, as were, for example, those of Bobbio and Santa Giulia at Brescia, whose estate records survive. They produced a sizable agricultural surplus, which the estates' owners often sold in the cities (Santa Giulia, at least, had its own merchants). Not all estates, however, were organized this tightly; elsewhere demesnes, though common, tended to be smaller and less economically important; and in the south they were always rare.

In the 10th century, Italian landowners increasingly took money rents rather than crops from at least their free tenants, as is known from their surviving written contracts (*libelli*). Money rents were more flexible and could better survive the fragmentation of property between coheirs or its alienation in bits to others, both practices being very common in Italy. It should be stressed that tenants' ability to pay in coin demonstrates that by this point a fair amount of small-scale commercial exchange was taking place in the countryside; indeed, the new castles of the 10th century, which themselves commanded estates, typically had markets. In the 10th century, too, more and more servile tenants gained their freedom, whether legally (by formal manumission) or illegally; a law of Otto III in the 990s that intended to restrict the rights of "slaves gasping for freedom" had little effect. On the other hand, by 1000, with landlords' acquisition of private judicial powers over tenants, there were new methods of rural coercion that did not depend on tenants' servile status, since landlords could also apply these methods to free peasants.

Italian agriculture was organized for subsistence first; growing crops exclusively for sale was rare in the early Middle Ages. Thus, rents in kind tended to reflect what peasants grew for themselves. One finds standard Mediterranean crops such as grain (rye in northern Italy, wheat elsewhere) and wine on 9th-century rent lists; olive oil was common in central and southern Italy but rare in the north (as it is today), except in specialist farms on the Italian lakes. Early medieval Italy was far more forested than it is today, and peasants seem to have depended substantially on woodland gathering to supplement their diet. Italian peasants probably ate a fair amount of meat, too, more than they were to eat in later centuries. Meat was, however, becoming a sign of an aristocratic lifestyle by the end of the early Middle Ages; Liutprand of Cremona looked down on the Byzantine emperor Nicephorus II Phocas (963–969) for eating vegetables. Specialist stock raising was still rare; sheep, cows, and pigs were raised by subsistence cultivators. As a result, specialists probably did not yet make cloth and leather either, except for luxury goods made by urban craftsmen with an aristocratic clientele. Large-scale urban cloth working, a central part of high medieval Italian life, still lay in the future. The clearest exception to this was perhaps the linen produced in 10th-century Naples.

Not all subsistence cultivators were tenants; there were many free peasant owners in early medieval Italy. How many of them were descended from small Roman proprietors, how many from Roman tenants who had seized their chance in the confusions of the 6th century, and how many from the rank and file of the Lombard army is unclear. Ethnic Lombards must have been a small minority, but by the 8th century nearly all landowners in the Italian kingdom professed Lombard law. Most landowning in the 8th and 9th centuries was highly fragmented, with even great landlords owning hundreds or thousands of small parcels of land that were scattered among those of other owners, whether aristocratic, peasant, or ecclesiastical. Such a pattern gave a certain independence to village life, where small local owners may often have been quite influential. (Great lords more often lived in cities, farther away from direct participation in local society.) Village communities were, however, usually still informal bodies with little of the coherence they were to gain from the 12th century onward.

The existence of this stratum of free smallholders gave a certain reality to the Lombard, and indeed Frankish, constitutional tradition that based royal power on the nation of free warriors at arms. The rise of the aristocracy, however, gravely challenged this tradition. Already in the Lombard period the aristocracy was in practice politically dominant, and probably always had been, in patterns unbroken from the Gothic and Roman period. Yet the 8th-century aristocracy does not seem to have been as wealthy as either its Roman predecessors or its Carolingian and post-Carolingian successors, and this may imply a relative independence for the free peasantry. Under Charlemagne and his descendants this slowly changed. Incoming Frankish nobles acquired large lands, and churches dramatically increased their holdings. That these developments were often at the expense of the poor is shown by a number of 9th-century court cases in which peasants claimed their land, or sometimes their freedom, usually without success; in some of these cases, peasants were clearly in the right. Kings themselves confirmed this, for in the 9th century they worried greatly that the oppressions of the poor would lessen the latter's participation in the public obligations of all freemen—army service, attendance at court, and road and bridge building—and they made laws against such exploitations. The laws were futile, however, and aristocratic landowning and political dominance continued to grow.

In the 10th century, with the breakdown in royal power, these tendencies developed further. In the countryside, castles became the centres of de facto political power that great landowners exercised over their free neighbours. A new, highly militarized small nobility began to emerge, based on these castles. Their ancestors had been of mixed origins—vassals of counts, local diocesan landowners, and even rising free peasants—but they now held, as a group, a virtual monopoly over armed force; indeed, in the sources they are frequently called *milites* ("soldiers"). Counts, where they kept their own power, did so only as leaders of private armies of these *milites*, who, though still their vassals, were now much more autonomous. Churches, to keep control over their extensive lands, had to give much of it out in lease or fief to such military families, and only the strongest churchmen, such as the archbishop of Milan, managed to keep any real power over their new military

dependents. This new castle-holding stratum was to become the basic aristocratic class of the 11th to 13th centuries, with only a few of them aspiring to the official titles of count or viscount. Such a tendency was, in fact, common throughout Europe; in Italy the chief difference was that *milites* were never quite as dominant as elsewhere, for cities remained powerful political and military centres, and peasant owners continued to exist in the countryside. The major exception to this was probably the south, where the new pattern of fortified settlements kept the peasantry within a more rigid political framework than existed in the more scattered villages of the north. Even within such a framework of political control, however, some of these fortified villages achieved a new sort of prosperity, for artisans could work in them, and merchants would come there, too.

SOCIOECONOMIC DEVELOPMENTS IN THE CITY

Most Roman cities survived into the early Middle Ages as political and economic centres. (The majority of those that failed were in the Apennines and, to a lesser extent, on the coast.) Their function as political centres has already been discussed; there is more dispute about their economic role, however. They must certainly have looked dilapidated, with their Roman monumental structures serving as quarries for rebuilding elsewhere; early medieval public buildings were, as noted, smaller and also probably fewer in number—the cathedral and the local royal palace being the most important ones by far. Archaeologists in cities such as Brescia or Verona have found a much less dense settlement network inside the walls of the early medieval cities than in the preceding or later ones, with lower buildings, more courtyards, many more open spaces used for agriculture, and, often, a trend toward building in wood. But both of these cities and several others still followed Roman street plans. It is likely that many cities maintained an urban economic identity, with some commercial and artisanal specialization (at least in luxury goods). Lucca's documents in the 8th century show, among others, gold workers, cauldron makers, physicians, and builders, and such figures also appear in texts for Milan and other cities in the 9th century. Essentially, this kind of artisanal activity relied on the city's role as the residence not only of bishops, dukes, counts, and administrative officials but also of a high proportion of the local aristocracy. The local political interests of the latter can be seen in a wave of competitive church building in the 8th and early 9th centuries; dozens of (probably very small) churches existed in each major centre by 900.

Commerce was undoubtedly far weaker in the early Middle Ages than under the Roman Empire. Archaeology shows it very clearly: the large number of African amphorae and fine ceramics found on every late Roman site in peninsular Italy decreases sharply in the 5th century, and these artifacts vanish in the 6th century. Only from the 8th century onward is there evidence again of pottery-exchange networks, but exclusively on the level of the city territory and, as far as is yet known, only around some cities—notably Rome, which remained the largest city in Italy, though it was only a fraction of its former size. City-country exchange networks were probably relatively weak in the 7th and 8th centuries, although they never altogether disappeared. From the 9th century onward, however, consistent documentary evidence of urban markets shows that these networks were developing again.

Most Classical cities had not been major centres of international commerce, or, at least, such commerce was less important as a reason for their existence than the fact that major landowners lived in them. The sharp decline of this commerce in the early Middle Ages was thus not in itself a threat to city life. But its slow revival from about 750 onward did help these cities, for they were still at the nodes of surviving Roman river and road networks that, with few changes, were to become the commercial routes of the High Middle Ages.

In the early 8th century King Liutprand issued a text that regulated the salt trade from the Venetian lagoon up the Po River. In the following century this trade developed and increasingly came into the hands of local rather than Venetian merchants. Cremona, among other cities, had become a major mercantile centre by the late 10th century, and not, by then, only for salt;

CREMONA

The city of Cremona, in the Lombardy region, is located on the north bank of the Po River southeast of Milan. It was founded by the Romans in 218 BCE on the site of an earlier Gallic village of the Cenomani. Virgil, the Roman poet, went to school there. With the decline of the Roman Empire, Cremona was repeatedly sacked by the Goths and the Huns before being rebuilt by the Lombards in the 7th century. A bishopric since the 9th century and an independent commune after 1098, it initially supported Emperor Frederick I Barbarossa in his conflict with the Lombards out of hostility to Milan, but it finally joined the Lombard League (an alliance of northern Italian towns) in 1167. The city was controlled by the Visconti family and, later, by the Sforzas, of Milan, from 1334 to 1535, except for a period of Venetian rule (1499–1509). It was Spanish from 1535 and Austrian after 1707; its later history followed that of Lombardy.

Cremona centres on the cathedral square, with the finely proportioned Romanesque cathedral (consecrated 1190); the adjoining Torrazzo (c. 1250), reputedly the highest bell tower in Italy (nearly 400 feet [120 metres]); the octagonal baptistery (1167); the city hall (1206–45); and the Loggia dei Militi (1292). Many of Cremona's numerous churches and palaces are notable for frescoes by painters of the 15th–16th-century Cremona school. Important buildings include the churches of Sant'Agostino (1339) and San Pietro al Po (1563) and the Renaissance Fodri, Raimondi, and Stanga palaces. Claudio Monteverdi, one of the founders of opera as an art form, was born there in 1567.

Cremona is famous for the violins and violas made there in the 16th–18th centuries by the Amati family and their pupils, the Guarneri and Antonio Stradivari. The School of Violin and Viola Makers has a museum of antique stringed instruments in the Palazzo dell'Arte. The university school of musical paleography is unique in Italy. An important centre for agricultural and dairy produce, Cremona manufactures agricultural machinery, silk textiles, bricks, and pianos.

the Venetians, on their way to Pavia, brought—among other wares—spices, ivory, and Byzantine cloth. Venice itself was the focus of this international trade by the 9th century; the will of its duke Giustiniano Parteciaco (also spelled Partecipazio), dating from 829, includes the first reference in medieval history to capital investment, in ships and their goods. By the end of the 10th century the Venetians dominated the trade of

the Adriatic Sea and controlled much of its eastern coast.

Inland, however, the spread of both international and local commerce was bringing a new and visible prosperity by the 10th century to many cities, including Cremona, Pavia—the old political capital still automatically visited by many traders from Venice—the southern cities, and, above all, Milan, which was fast becoming the major economic centre of the

Italian kingdom. The northern Italian trade routes, along the Adriatic coast, up the Po River, and across the Alps, were coming to rival the older routes around the western coast of Italy, via Amalfi and Gaeta (or, later, Pisa and Genoa) and up the Rhône River. Both routes were to develop dramatically in the following centuries. But they did not in themselves create urban life in Italy; that was done by the local aristocracy. The continuing domination of Italian cities by landed aristocrats was to condition much of their future history.

ITALY UNDER THE SAXON EMPERORS

In the second half of the 10th century, Italy began a slow recovery from the turmoils of late Carolingian Europe. During the previous century the Po River valley had been exposed to Magyar raiders. Sardinia, Corsica, and Sicily had fallen to the Muslims; even Rome had felt their threat. In the north the Lombard kingdom was little more than a collection of great lordships vying with one another for the Carolingian inheritance. In the south the peninsula was shared by the remnants of the Byzantine and Lombard states and by local powers. The 10th-century papacy had fallen into the hands of various Roman aristocratic factions. But already there were signs of revival. Genoa, Pisa, and Venice were joining other cities in developing local and international trade. In Germany the last of the East Frankish

Carolingians had died, and in 911 Conrad I of Franconia became king, to be succeeded in 919 by the energetic Henry the Fowler, duke of Saxony and founder of the Saxon dynasty of German emperors. In France the Carolingians yielded to the Capetians before the century was out. In the monasteries of Burgundy and Lorraine a new spirit of religious reform arose, which reached outward to the whole of Latin Europe and soon influenced the rich monastic traditions of Italy.

THE OTTONIAN SYSTEM

In the midst of these favourable signs, the Italian political landscape offered little ground for optimism. The only hope for stability and eventual unity lay with the contenders for the former Carolingian kingdom of Italy. Hugh of Provence, nominally king of Italy, cast ambitious eyes across the mountains to the Po valley; he aimed to pull together the fragments of the original Lotharingia, including Italy. But at his death in 947 his son Lothar and later his son's widow, Adelaide of Burgundy, faced strong opposition from Berengario, marchese d'Ivrea e di Gisla, who assumed the crown of Italy as Berengar II. Adelaide summoned the German king, Otto I (936–973), son of Henry the Fowler, to her aid. Although much involved in affairs in Germany, he came to Italy in 951 and married Adelaide, but he returned quickly to Germany to deal with a rebellion by Liudolf, duke of Swabia, his son from an earlier marriage.

SAINT ADELAIDE

One of the most influential women of 10th-century Europe was Adelaide (born c. 931—died December 16, 999, Seltz, Alsace [now in France]), the consort of the Holy Roman emperor Otto I and, later, regent for her grandson Otto III. She helped strengthen the German church while subordinating it to imperial power. The daughter of Rudolf II (died 937), king of Burgundy, and Bertha of Swabia, Adelaide was married (947) to Lothar, who succeeded his father, Hugh of Arles, as king of Italy in the same year. After Lothar died (950), Berengario, marchese d'Ivrea e di Gisla, his old rival, seized the Italian throne and imprisoned Adelaide (April 951) at Garda. After her escape four months later, she asked the German king Otto I (the Great) to help her regain the throne. Otto marched into Lombardy (September 951), declared himself king, and married her (October/November 951). They were crowned emperor and empress by Pope John XII in Rome in 962. She promoted Cluniac monasticism and strengthened the allegiance of the German church to the emperor, playing an important role in Otto I's distribution of ecclesiastical privileges and participating in his Italian expeditions.

After Otto's death (May 7, 973), Adelaide exercised influence over her son Otto II until their estrangement in 978, when she left the court and lived in Burgundy with her brother King Conrad. At Conrad's urging she became reconciled with her son, and, before his death in 983, Otto appointed her his regent in Italy. With her daughter-in-law, Empress Theophano, she upheld the right of her three-year-old grandson, Otto III, to the German throne. She lived in Lombardy from 985 to 991, when she returned to Germany to serve as sole regent after Theophano's death (991). She governed until Otto III came of age (994), and, when he became Holy Roman emperor in 996, she retired from court life, devoting herself to founding churches, monasteries, and convents. Her feast day is December 16.

Moreover, events in Germany forced him to fight the Magyars in 955 at the Battle of Lechfeld, where his decisive victory ended their attacks on German lands.

At the request of Pope John XII (955–964), Otto returned to Italy, where in 962 he realized his dream of securing the imperial crown. The coronation of Otto as emperor was, like that of Charlemagne, a recognition of a political reality. Otto was the leading figure among all European rulers of his day. He was a great military victor and a champion of order. He also had built a close alliance with the German bishops. The imperial title, which had dwindled into a virtually worthless symbol, once again legitimated effective political power.

After his coronation, Otto proceeded to consolidate his power by moving against Berengar II, the enemy of his wife's family. Pope John XII, recognizing the emperor's intention of exerting imperial supremacy over the papacy, began to fear for his own future. His activities provoked Otto to move against him. At a Roman synod in December 963 the assembled bishops, mostly loyal supporters of Otto from northern Italy, deposed John and replaced him with Leo VIII (963–965). Otto's decisive action paved the way for his mastery of the kingdom of Italy.

Within two years Berengar was captured. The papacy entered a turbulent decade that ended with the election of Benedict VII (974–983). Otto built his rule on the foundation provided by bishops loyal to the empire; these bishops, many of German origin, owed their promotion to Otto himself. He also relied upon the support of such powerful figures as the marquess of Tuscany and the duke of Spoleto. He pressed his imperial claims with the Byzantines even as he aggressively supported the Latinization of the southern Italian hierarchy (i.e., subjection to the jurisdiction of Rome rather than Constantinople). The chief fruit of his policy in southern Italy was the marriage of his son, Otto II, to the Byzantine princess Theophano. Otto I had laid the foundation for strong imperial rule in Italy, but he lacked the means to bring it to fruition. Nonetheless, fragile as his foundation in Italy was, it represented a move away from the anarchy of the previous age toward a new era of prosperity and hope for the future.

The focus of imperial policy on Italy under Otto II (973–983) was an inevitable result of the achievements of his father. One should not, however, view Otto II's efforts as a desertion of Germany in quest of the glories of ancient Rome. Rather, the policy of the German monarchy, while grounded partly in the idealization of the ancient Roman Empire, aimed to achieve a vision of Europe that derived from the pragmatic realities of the Carolingian age. The transfer of power on the death of Otto II in 983 to his son, Otto III (983–1002), a mere child, demonstrates the widespread acceptance of this policy. While the succession did arouse a conflict over the regency in Germany, the succession itself faced no serious challenge. The brilliant Gerbert of Aurillac, former abbot of Bobbio and later Pope Sylvester II (999–1003), served as principal adviser and tutor of the young king, whose mother, Theophano, controlled the regency until her death in 991. Otto's grandmother, Adelaide, still an indomitable figure, then served as regent until he assumed power in 994. Despite his youth, Otto was both able and vigorous. He continued the Italian policy of his father and grandfather but expressed it more explicitly.

Many scholars have argued that Otto III's Byzantine connections shaped his conception of imperial rule. Some have suggested that his ideas were anachronistic; others that he failed to follow the path dictated by the national interests of Germany and Italy. But Otto, who had been schooled in a hard and practical court, aimed in his Italian policies at creating an enduring transnational unity in imperial administration under the imperial chancellor. When his seal employed the style "Renovatio imperii Romanorum" ("Renewal of the empire of the Romans"), this invoked an image not so much of Roman antiquity as of the empire of Charlemagne. The "renewal" referred to a new commitment to the Carolingian design for Europe, viewed from the vantage point of the 10th century. Otto's imperial coronation in 996 by Pope Gregory V (996–999), his own nominee, was reminiscent of that of his grandfather in that he did not hesitate to intervene in Roman affairs. When influential Romans drove out Gregory and thought to placate Otto by the election of his former Greek tutor Johannes Philagathus as pope (John XVI; antipope 997–998), the emperor returned and in 998 exacted a terrible price from all. He also secured the election of Gerbert of Aurillac as Sylvester II. He did not, however, subscribe to the view of the papal position found in the Donation of Constantine. He rejected this forgery, which purported to list the rights and properties conferred on Pope Sylvester I. Otto supported the claims of the Italian bishops against the lesser aristocracy, who were attempting to make their lands, which they leased from the church, virtually hereditary. For him as for his predecessors, support of the bishops helped establish royal control over the cities of central and northern Italy.

Otto III died on January 23, 1002. His body was quickly taken to Aachen (now in Germany) and laid to rest beside Charlemagne. The German princes elected the duke of Bavaria, who became Henry II (1002–24), the last emperor of the Saxon dynasty. Notwithstanding reassurances to his German supporters of his commitment to effective rule in Germany, Henry's view of his imperial role differed little from that of his Ottonian predecessors. In Italy he supported the bishops and opposed Arduin of Ivrea, who had seized power after the death of Otto III. It was not, however, until 1013 that Henry was free to come to Italy. After his coronation by Pope Benedict VIII (1012–24) in 1014, he returned to Germany, leaving the bishops the task of disposing of Arduin. In 1021 Henry returned to Italy once more but was unable to extend imperial rule in the south beyond the Lombard principalities of Benevento and Capua.

SOCIAL AND ECONOMIC DEVELOPMENTS

The 10th and early 11th centuries witnessed significant changes in the social and economic life of all parts of Italy. As noted earlier, the upheavals of the early 10th century had vastly increased the need for security, leading in the countryside to the fortification of villages. While this process provided security for the peasants, it also strengthened the control over them by both lay and ecclesiastical lords. The reliance of the Ottonian emperors on the lay and ecclesiastical aristocracy tended to consolidate this arrangement. The number of great noble families grew rapidly as a direct result of imperial action. These families, often from north of the Alps, were part of the effort to subject Italy more directly to imperial authority. At the same time, however, increases in population, the growth of the cities, and the development of a landed class of knights and lesser nobles (vavasours), began to undermine the Ottonian system based on the support of the bishops and the great marquesses. The entry of these new social groups into the quest for land created competition not merely between clergy and laity but also within these groups; indeed, the interests of clergy and laity were often interconnected.

THE REFORM MOVEMENT AND THE SALIAN EMPERORS

Profound dissatisfaction with the pervasive violence, rapacity, and greed of the age, combined with concerns particularly among the monks about their own vulnerability and that of the poor and weak, fueled a movement for monastic reform. Some early monastic reformers identified their cause with that of the Ottonians. St. Romuald of Ravenna, for example, actively supported the missionary program of Otto III. The empire represented order and stability, ideals that appealed to many monks. But some were also beginning to perceive that the imperial order helped foster the competition for rights and domains. The reign of Conrad II (1024–39), the first emperor of the Salian dynasty, permitted and even encouraged such competition. Conrad took the side of the vavasours, who wanted their lands to be hereditary, against the bishops, and he generally supported the interests of the lay aristocracy. Although there is no indication that he intended any permanent change in imperial relations with the bishops—his ties to the papacy were close enough—his actions certainly alarmed Italian ecclesiastical circles. Ultimately, Conrad's policy did not cause any major adjustment in relations between the bishops and the empire.

Conrad's son and successor, Henry III (1039–56), was energetic, strong-willed, and devout. He was no innovator, but his attachment to the church served to reduce the tensions that his father's rule had created. Indeed, he resumed the close relations between the crown and the monastic reformers that had characterized the reign of Otto III and Henry II. His Italian policy bears striking resemblance to that of Charlemagne and Otto I. But he lived in different times. His efforts to settle differences among the factions disputing the archbishopric of Milan and his intervention in papal affairs in Rome placed him in the Ottonian tradition.

Henry supported reform, and reform in turn supported the empire. Some historians have portrayed his actions, particularly his interventions in papal elections, as inimical to the interests of the empire, but they, too, often overlook this point. By emphasizing Henry's piety and his attachment to reform, these historians have de-emphasized the political aspects of his policy. Actually, there was a concurrence between his goals and the desires of the reformers. When Henry arrived in Rome in 1046, he found the papacy in disarray. In the continuing competition among leading Roman families for control of the papacy, the Tusculan faction had elected the corrupt Benedict IX (1032–44), but the Romans drove him from the city and replaced him with the candidate of the Crescentians, Sylvester III (1045). Benedict regained the papacy in 1045, but he sold the office to a supporter of reform, John Gratian, who was then elected as Gregory VI (1045–46). Henry therefore faced an uncertain situation just when he was seeking imperial coronation. The synods of Sutri and Rome resolved the difficulty by deposing the three previous claimants. At the behest of Henry, the bishop of Bamberg was elected as Clement II (1046–47). The new pope immediately proceeded to Henry's coronation on Christmas Day, 1046. The Carolingian precedent—Charlemagne's coronation also took place on Christmas Day—could hardly have been lost on his audience.

Henry III took Gregory VI back to Germany with him, aiming in this way to prevent a resurgence of internal conflict in Rome. But death soon overtook Clement, and Benedict IX again reclaimed the papacy. Henry ordered Boniface of Tuscany to drive Benedict from Rome once again and had the German Damasus II (1048) installed as pope, but Damasus died within a month. Again Henry intervened, securing the election of Bruno of Toul, who took the name Leo IX (1049–54). Leo combined strong attachment to the imperial cause with dedication to the cause of reform.

Profoundly influenced by the monastic centres of reform in Germany and Burgundy, he turned especially to them for collaborators in the work of rebuilding the battered prestige of the Roman church. He brought to Rome men like the theologian Frederick of Lorraine, Hugo Candidus, and Humbert of Moyenmoutier, who became cardinal-bishop of Silva Candida, a Roman suburban diocese. The deacon Hildebrand, who had accompanied Gregory VI to Germany as his secretary, also returned to Rome and joined the papal entourage. Under Leo's leadership the ancient body of cardinals was transformed into an effective instrument for administration of the church and promotion of reform. Leo held synods in northern Europe and Italy aimed at stirring local commitment for the program of the reformers. That program was chiefly directed at freeing churches from lay control, especially by the appointment of unworthy candidates to ecclesiastical office through simony (i.e., the practice of buying church offices), and at forbidding the pervasive practice of clerical marriage and concubinage, which threatened the substance of the church. Leo's efforts drew their inspiration from the monastic reform movement, which had already succeeded in regaining control of many monastic properties and preventing their further alienation not only at the hands of the laity but also at those of other ecclesiastics. Although couched in moral terms, the program of the reformers served eminently practical ends.

THE PAPACY AND THE NORMANS

Having arrived in southern Italy in small groups just prior to 1020, perhaps in part as petitioners at the court of Pope Benedict VIII and in part as pilgrims returning from the Holy Land, Normans joined Lombard rebels in their effort to throw off Byzantine rule in Bari. Although this proved a failure, Norman mercenaries continued to enlist in the armies of various southern Italian rulers. In 1030 Sergius, duke of Naples, granted the county of Aversa to the Norman Rainulf in return for his support against Pandulf of Capua. Rainulf was able to add Gaeta to his holdings, and his nephew, Count Richard, who had succeeded to Aversa in 1047, added the principality of Capua. The next wave of Normans, led by the sons of a lesser Norman landholder, Tancred of Hauteville, undertook a full-scale effort to conquer the south. Robert Guiscard, Tancred's fourth son, assumed a commanding role in southern Italian affairs.

Leo, who remained committed to the imperial ideal, opposed the Normans because he felt that they threatened not only Rome and the papacy but also the interests of the German emperor and relations between East and West. The continued expansion of the Normans in southern Italy and their aggressive assertion of titles—William de Hauteville (William Iron Arm), for example, assumed the title of count of Puglia—influenced Leo to forge an alliance of papal, imperial, and Byzantine forces.

With himself in the company of imperial troops but without awaiting the arrival of promised help from the Byzantines, he met the Normans at Civitate on June 16, 1053. The ensuing defeat was a deep humiliation for Leo, though the Normans treated him with respect. The forced peace profoundly disturbed the balance that he had sought in Italy.

His policy also received a serious setback from the conflict that arose in Constantinople between his legates (Humbert of Silva Candida, Frederick of Lorraine, and Peter, archbishop of Amalfi) and the Eastern patriarch, Michael Cerularius. Scholars differ on the reasons for this conflict, but it arose at least in part from the clash between the papal policies of Latinization of the churches in southern Italy and the claims of Constantinople to jurisdiction in that region. Scholars have often viewed the mutual excommunications launched by the legates and the patriarch in 1054, after the death of Leo, as the beginning of the schism between the Eastern and Western churches; however, that view probably overstates the significance of these events. More particularly, the breach with Constantinople closed the door on the approach taken by Leo IX and led to a major shift in papal policy in favour of the Normans.

Leo's successor, Pope Victor II (1055–57), formerly the bishop of Eichstätt (Bavaria), the fourth pope chosen under the aegis of Henry III, tried to follow in the footsteps of his predecessor. But the death of Henry in 1056 and the failure of Leo's policies in southern Italy limited his role. The Normans continued to strengthen their position in southern Italy. Victor II thus was constrained not only by the failed mission to Byzantium but also by the threat from the south. Moreover, on Henry III's death, the empire came to his six-year-old son, Henry IV (1056–1106), with his mother, Agnes of Poitou, as the regent. Although the succession to the throne was not in doubt, the inevitable intrigues surrounding the regency deprived the papacy of imperial support. When Victor died in 1057, a party of the reformers moved to take advantage of this vacuum. They acted quickly to elect Frederick of Lorraine as pope, under the name Stephen IX (or X; 1057–58), without any effort to consult the regency.

Stephen, who had succeeded to the papacy while abbot of Montecassino, summoned Peter Damian from the monastery of Fonte Avellana to become cardinal-bishop of Ostia. The election of a pope whose brother had been a rebel against the regency suggests that the strong ties that had bound the reform movement to the empire had been somewhat weakened. At the same time, the position of the reformers in Rome was also weakened. When Stephen died in 1058, the Roman nobles supported the election of Bishop John of Velletri as Benedict X (antipope 1058–59), thereby attempting a return to the pro-aristocratic and pro-Roman policies of Benedict VIII and Benedict IX. These circumstances forced the reformers to seek support from the empress Agnes. Their candidate, the Burgundian bishop of Florence, Gerard, was installed on the papal throne as Pope Nicholas II (1059–61).

The reign of Nicholas was pivotal. Not only did Nicholas preside over a major shift in the papacy's relations with the Normans but he also issued a decree in 1059 regulating future papal elections that began the process of concentrating electoral powers in the hands of the cardinals. The consequences of the papal defeat at Civitate in 1053 had already laid the foundation for a change in papal relations with the Normans. Leo IX had earlier appointed Humbert of Silva Candida as archbishop in Sicily and now entrusted the conquest of Calabria and Arab-dominated Sicily to the Normans with the provision that they should remain a hereditary fief of the papacy. This assertion of papal overlordship, often read solely in political terms, represented an effort on the part of the papacy to ensure its claims to jurisdiction over the churches of the still-unconquered lands against the claims by Constantinople. Nicholas's Norman alliance was less a dramatic diplomatic revolution than a response to the changes that confronted the papacy from Civitate onward. The alliance safeguarded papal interests in the south, ensured a measure of stability in Rome during a period of imperial impotence, and promised the independence that the reformers had sought in their notion of *libertas ecclesiae* (i.e., church immunity from secular control and jurisdiction). But the weakness of the empire also led the papacy to seek support in northern Italy.

THE INVESTITURE CONTROVERSY

The kingdom of Italy, a creation of the Lombards, had all but ceased to exist as a separate entity in the early 11th century. Pavia no longer functioned as an administrative centre after 1024, when the royal palace was destroyed. The great beneficiary of the new situation was Milan, whose archbishop Heribert (Ariberto) of Antimiano had played the role of king-maker in the selection of Conrad II as Italian king in 1026. But the archbishop faced considerable opposition from his lesser vassals, the vavasours, who revolted on his return to Milan after supporting Conrad in Burgundy. The roots of this revolt lay in a dispute between two ranks of Milan's warrior elite, the *capitanei* and the vavasours, over the inheritance of fiefs. Conrad was able to restore peace between these factions in 1037 by the Constitutio de feudis, which made the fiefs of the vavasours hereditary. The settlement, however, did not create a lasting peace. A group of vavasours and lower clergy led by Arialdo and Erlembaldo opposed the archbishop, who was supported by the *capitanei*. The dissidents, known as *pataria* (most probably meaning "rag pickers"), also had ties to the reform movement. There were also disorders in a number of other cities. Nearby Brescia, for example, forced its bishop to flee the city. In Florence, John Gualbert, one of the leaders of the monastic reform movement, opposed the city's bishop, an admitted simoniac (i.e., a person guilty of using money to obtain clerical office). Yet the unrests were too varied to fit a simple explanation. The experience of Lucca, for example, differed substantially from that of Florence. Bishop Anselm of Lucca, one of the strongest leaders of the reform movement among the Italian bishops, was chosen by the cardinals as the successor of Nicholas II in 1061 and became Pope Alexander II (1061–73). His position at Lucca was due in large measure to the support of Countess Matilda of Canossa, a principal figure in Italian politics throughout the period. She provided the necessary weight to support papal reform policies in northern Italy and provided the papacy with a counterbalance to the risky alliance with the Normans.

The threat posed to the imperial order in northern Italy by the cities and the crucial role of the reform papacy and its ally, Countess Matilda, evoked a strong response from the imperial party at the death of Pope Nicholas. The Lombard bishops and their allies called upon the youthful Henry to provide a successor. Even though the reformers had already selected Anselm of Lucca as Alexander II in accordance with the election decree of 1059, Henry proceeded to appoint Cadalo, bishop of Parma, who took the name Honorius II as antipope in 1061. The Cadalan schism brought together segments of the Roman nobility and the Lombard bishops, who were opposed to reform. The empire, which had been a partner in reform, was emerging as the enemy of reform. Under the legitimate pope, Alexander II, Hildebrand, former secretary of Pope Gregory VI and now archdeacon of the Roman church, succeeded Humbert of Silva Candida as the leading architect of reform. The papacy increasingly reached out beyond Italy in its effort to extend the influence of the reform movement. Alexander II lent his support, most probably with the advice of Hildebrand, to the conquest of England by William, duke of Normandy, in 1066. Likewise, the papacy became more fully involved in the efforts of the kings of Spain to reconquer lands from the Muslims. The internationalization of the Roman Curia, begun by Leo IX, continued to attract important leaders of the reform to Rome. Under Alexander II the papacy succeeded in escaping the shadows of Roman aristocratic domination and imperial control and in moving onto the European stage.

Against this background, King Henry IV reached his majority and began to assert his rights in both Germany and Italy. Alexander and Hildebrand continued papal support for the *pataria* in Milan; as noted, the reformers demanded an end to marriage of the clergy, to the buying of church offices, and to lay control of appointments to church offices. The issue of lay investiture (the practice whereby secular rulers formally presented to clerics the symbols of their various offices) gained paramount importance in Alexander II's reform program. The reformers' opposition to lay investiture

was a major challenge to the Ottonian system, which rested in part on the emperor's long-standing rights to appoint and control church officials. The issue drove a deep wedge between the advocates of reform and the supporters of the empire, even dividing the reformers themselves.

From the imperial point of view, it was impossible to separate the issue of lay investiture from the changes occurring in the political life of the northern Italian cities. Indeed, the struggle over lay investiture lent legitimacy to movements directed against imperial bishops. Milan was one among a number of northern Italian cities in which a reform movement struggled to secure greater independence from imperial control. Similar movements developed in southern Italy as well. The religious confraternity dedicated to St. Nicholas, whose body had been brought to Bari from Anatolia, served to rally local sentiment. The 11th-century reform movement grew partly out of the emergence of communes, the political organizations of the towns, particularly in central and northern Italy.

The climax of the Investiture Controversy came under Alexander II's successor, Hildebrand, who took the name Gregory VII (1073–85). With Gregory the reform movement achieved its most revolutionary form, although Gregory hardly thought of himself and his contemporary reformers in such terms. Their ideal was a restoration of the church to its primitive freedom, summed up in the Donation of Constantine, a document forged in the 8th century but generally regarded as genuine throughout the Middle Ages. According to this document, the emperor Constantine in the 4th century had granted to Pope Sylvester I and his successors spiritual supremacy and temporal dominion over Rome and the entire Western Empire. Gregory and the reformers, for whom the freedom of the church meant freedom from imperial intervention and the ability of the pope to act without restraint for the good of Christendom, used the Donation of Constantine to bolster their program of reform. That the Donation cast a long shadow over the program of Gregory VII is especially evident in the *Dictatus Papae* ("Treatise of the Pope"), a list of brief statements inserted in Gregory's register asserting papal claims. For example, the eighth title states that the pope alone can use the imperial insignia (the symbols of temporal power). Fruit of an assiduous combing of various sources, the *Dictatus* (which dates to 1075) seems to anticipate the controversies of the coming years. Certainly, it suggests the direction in which the thought of the Roman Curia was moving. The notion of a revival of a golden age also found its expression in the artistic and architectural works of the period—for example, in the mosaics of the basilica constructed at Montecassino by Abbot Desiderius and in the newly built cathedral of Salerno.

The conflict between Gregory VII and Henry IV (1056–1106) over lay investiture was a culmination of developments in Italy that had their origins in the last years of the pontificate of Leo IX. At the Roman synod of 1075, Gregory signaled his determination to bring an end to the practice of lay investiture. There could be no doubt that this policy would have its most drastic impact on Germany and northern Italy, where the remains of the Ottonian system constituted important vestiges of imperial control. Henry IV and his counselors realized these implications and replied at the synod of Worms in 1076. Henry employed a frontal attack on Gregory, challenging the legitimacy of his election. Gregory's response was equally provocative: he excommunicated Henry, which released his subjects from their allegiance. This calculated political response aimed at undermining Henry's position with the German aristocracy. Faced with rebellion, Henry made his celebrated trek across the Alps to meet the pope before he could come to Germany. Pope and emperor met at Matilda's castle in Canossa. There, amid the snows of winter, Henry stood for three days as a penitent until the pope received and absolved him. Henry's action at Canossa saved him temporarily, but he remained in jeopardy. When the conflict resumed in 1080, Gregory again excommunicated Henry, who proceeded to gather his supporters. A synod at Brixen under Henry's control elected Guibert of Ravenna as pope under the name Clement III (elected antipope in 1080; enthroned antipope in 1084–1100). Henry led his army into Italy and laid siege to Rome. Gregory turned for assistance to Robert Guiscard and the Normans, who drove

Clement and Henry from Rome but also sacked the city (1084). Gregory went south with Guiscard and the Normans, where he died in Salerno in 1085.

Gregory's defeat did nothing to strengthen the position of the empire in northern Italy, while it drove the papacy closer to the Normans. The election of Abbot Desiderius of Montecassino as Pope Victor III (1086–87) illustrates this change, since Desiderius had long functioned as an intermediary between the papacy and the Normans. The election of Urban II (1088–99), formerly a monk of Cluny in Burgundy and a strong supporter of Gregory's policy, showed the continued strength of the Roman Curia's resolve and at the same time initiated closer ties to the Capetian kings of France as a counterweight to the empire and an alternative to the Normans. Urban was also effective in gaining support for reform among the cities of northern Italy. Yet his most dramatic endeavour was his summons of the First Crusade at Clermont in 1095, presaged by his earlier meeting with Byzantine envoys in Italy. Urban's commitment to the Crusade proceeded from his desire to heal the schism between the Eastern and Western churches, to extend the papal reform program to the Eastern churches, and to forge a new alliance within Christendom against Islam, its foremost external enemy. The Crusade offered new opportunities for the maritime cities of northern Italy, which for some time had been opposing Muslim power in Sardinia, Corsica, and Sicily. Urban also worked closely with Roger I, count of Sicily, to reestablish the Latin church on the island, but he came into conflict with him over the degree of direct papal control to be exercised there. The apostolic legation that he granted to Roger and his son limited direct papal intervention in the ecclesiastical affairs of the island and thereby joined the reconstruction of the church to the interests of the Norman monarchy. At his death in 1099, Urban had greatly enhanced the prestige of the papacy, yet the conflict with the empire remained unresolved.

The settlement of the investiture struggle that finally emerged under Popes Paschal II (1099–1118) and Calixtus II (1119–24) had a far-reaching impact on the church and on civil society. The settlement represented a compromise between the reformist church and the empire. The agreement reached between Paschal II and King Henry I of England, which limited the role of the king in the appointment of bishops, marked the direction for the eventual solution reached by Calixtus II and Henry V (1106–25) in the Concordat of Worms in 1122. Thenceforward, the emperor was denied the right to invest prelates with the spiritual symbols of their offices; however, as their temporal overlord he retained certain rights (the ones for Germany differing substantially from those for Burgundy and Italy). An earlier attempt at settlement had proposed a near-total severance of the ties between the bishops and the monarchy and thus an end to the Ottonian system. While such an arrangement would have satisfied every aim of the reformers, it would have plunged the empire into chaos. The bishops, well aware of their role as linchpins, objected strongly to such a radical solution, and the plan foundered. But the compromise at Worms was also fraught with danger for the empire. The reformers gained much more than the actual agreement granted. The chief beneficiary was the papacy, which succeeded in freeing itself from imperial restraints. In the temporal sphere, however, and largely by accident, northern and central Italy also faced a new situation as a result of this settlement.

THE RISE OF COMMUNES

During the 12th century, communes, or city-states, developed throughout central and northern Italy. After early beginnings in cities such as Pisa and Genoa, virtually every episcopal city in the north formed a communal government prior to 1140. The origins and developments of communes are complex, and attempts to explain them in simple terms are doomed to failure. The emphasis of 19th-century liberal historians on communal revolts against ecclesiastical repression as well as the later Marxist focus on class conflict in the development of the communes have proved too narrow. They have failed to recognize both the many different causes of violence in the communes and the diversities within the communal movement. Violence resulted from such diverse factors as the conflicting interests of ecclesiastical institutions, the complex ties of loyalty that bound men to one another and to the institutions of their society, and shifts in the distribution of power.

The Investiture Controversy focused the efforts of the higher clergy on consolidating their rights against infringement not merely by the lay aristocracy but also by ecclesiastical competitors. Examples of conflict from various places and periods show how relationships changed dramatically, often within a short period. At Brescia, for example, the bishops, who contested the abbots of Leno for control of the church of Gambara, drew support from a faction of the *milites*, the landed aristocracy, as well as from the *popolo*, which was composed of professional people, craftsmen, and merchants. Elsewhere, local circumstances dictated other alliances. During the period in which the cities were expanding their power into the *contado* (the region surrounding the city), elements drawn from town and countryside continually struggled for control of the commune. Alliances shifted depending on the success or failure of these efforts. At Lucca the bishop and the commune were jointly concerned about the claims of the Abbey of Fucecchio because of its ties to neighbouring Pisa. But the efforts of bishops to establish their rights in the *contado* could also provoke conflict with the commune. Much depended on the makeup of the commune, which varied widely not only from city to city but also from period to period. The relative influence of urban merchants or rural landholders depended on the size of each group within a particular community. Where one group was small, it allied itself with others. The quest for power led to shifting and, at times, strange alliances; for example, at Brescia in the early 13th century, one faction of local magnates drew support from heretics. Even when the commune brought together various factions in sworn associations, it still faced not only the problem of its enemies in the city and countryside but also that of the fragile nature of the coalition on which it rested. Communes created elaborate systems of checks on power that aimed to prevent dominance by any single faction. Term limits were imposed to force changes in the ruling councils. The consuls, so named from Roman precedent, similarly faced limits on their power.

From its inception it was clear that communal government aspired not merely to political independence but also to control of the *contado*. As a result, a complex relationship developed in which the *contado* found markets for its products, offered opportunities for investment for city dwellers, and suffered oppression from urban interests. The city, in turn, offered opportunities to the people of the countryside and helped to ensure a measure of security. There is probably no way for scholars to establish the balance of benefits and disadvantages, but one may be certain that it shifted continuously, depending on region, local conditions, and the general economic climate at a given time.

It is evident, however, that the communes of northern and central Italy benefited from the Investiture Controversy. The ineffectiveness of imperial power in Italy during the first half of the 12th century, which favoured the development of the communes, stemmed largely from the struggle over investitures and the attendant political instability in Germany. These external factors, however, do not in themselves account for the rise of the communes. For that, one must turn to internal factors, particularly the dynamics among various factions and the social dislocations during and following the Investiture Controversy that accompanied rising populations and increased prosperity. The reformers' success in weakening the bonds between church and empire remained a decisive force throughout the 12th century and well into the 13th century. The partisan perspectives of contemporaries oversimplified the Investiture Controversy, showing it either as a struggle for the freedom of the church from lay power or as an effort to preserve the traditional—that is, imperial—order within society. Actually, however, given the complex network of local loyalties within both church and secular society, the controversy fragmented loyalties of both the clergy and the laity. If the old order was weakened, it was not merely a secular order that lost but an ecclesiastical order as well. Nor was it merely the unreformed monasteries and imperial bishoprics that lost; at times, communal authority emerged stronger than any ecclesiastical power in the region. Certainly, by the early 13th century this was true in Genoa, and it was soon to be the case in Milan, Florence, Bologna, and elsewhere.

THE AGE OF THE HOHENSTAUFEN

During the 12th century a new political order developed in Italy. It was not a tidy process, however. In the south the ascendancy established by the Normans of Capua and by the Hautevilles gained strength with the conquest of Sicily from the Muslims in the late 11th century. Following the death of Robert Guiscard, his brother, Roger I, count of Sicily, went to the mainland to consolidate his position. His son, Roger II, succeeded in establishing a Norman kingdom. Recognition for it, however, was slow in coming. Roger first obtained it from the antipope Anacletus II (1130–38) and then, under conditions that revealed the weakness of the papacy before Norman power, from Pope Innocent II (1130–43) in 1139. The papacy continued to seek support from the French monarchy

in order to offset growing Norman influence.

On the other hand, victory in the Investiture Controversy, even though compromised, created a situation that enabled the 12th-century papacy to assume leadership of the reform movement throughout Europe. The Lateran Councils of 1123, 1139, and 1179 marked important stages in the development of the reform papacy. From Urban II on, the central administration of the church expanded. By the mid-12th century— about the time that the monk Gratian was compiling his *Decretum*, the most important collection of ecclesiastical law up to that time—Rome's position as a court of appeals was growing faster than its judicial machinery could possibly accommodate.

The process of definition and extension of papal control over ecclesiastical matters inevitably led to conflict with secular rulers. The determination of the papacy to protect its independence and, after the death of Matilda of Canossa in 1115, to hold onto the vast inheritance she had bequeathed to the Roman church in central Italy, as well as the ties that united the papacy to the reform bishops and to many of the laity who had supported the reform in their cities, signaled changes that had taken place since the Concordat of Worms in 1122. Finally, the keystone of the new order lay in the strength, as yet untested, of the communes. Vestiges of imperial support certainly remained both in the cities and in the countryside, but

Italy in the late 12th century.

the old cause had given way before the real interests that were taking shape during this period.

The emperors of the Hohenstaufen dynasty that succeeded the Salian dynasty attempted to revive the imperial position in Italy. The first efforts of both pope and emperor in the period following the Concordat of Worms were, however, based upon the assumption that something of the old relationship remained. In part, this attitude may have been encouraged by the slight attention that Lothar II (or III; 1125–37) and Conrad III (1138–52) paid to Italian affairs. Lothar's efforts against the Normans were ineffectual,

and he focused primarily on civil war in Germany. His rival and successor, Conrad III, the first Hohenstaufen king, devoted considerable energy to the Second Crusade, which had been promoted by the Cistercian monk and monastic reformer Bernard of Clairvaux. The dominant role of Bernard of Clairvaux certainly influenced the selection of his former disciple, Eugenius III (1145–53), as pope. Forced to seek refuge in France by the political situation in Rome, where the radical reformer Arnold of Brescia stirred both feelings of independence and a demand for more-extreme reforms within the church, Eugenius cooperated with Bernard in the preaching of the Second Crusade. Although the Crusade was conceived originally as an enterprise to be led by the Capetian monarch Louis VII (1137–80), Conrad III was included when it became clear that there would be large-scale German participation. The Crusade fell well short of expectations, and Conrad returned to Germany in 1149 to resume his imperial program. Eugenius, who faced Arnold and the rebellious Romans and who was heavily dependent on Roger II of Sicily during Conrad's absence on Crusade, hoped that Conrad's return would provide the means to reestablish papal control in Rome, but turmoil in Germany prevented the realization of his desire. Conrad died without being able to journey to Italy to receive imperial coronation. Eugenius died the following year.

The reign of Conrad's successor and nephew, the duke of Swabia,

ARNOLD OF BRESCIA

The radical religious reformer Arnold of Brescia (born c. 1100, Brescia, Republic of Venice—died c. June 1155, Civita Castellana or Monterotondo, Papal States) was noted for his outspoken criticism of clerical wealth and corruption and for his strenuous opposition to the temporal power of the popes. He was prior of the monastery at Brescia, where in 1137 he participated in a popular revolt against the government of Bishop Manfred. His proposals for reforming the clergy and for ending the church's temporal powers caused him to be condemned as a schismatic by Pope Innocent II in 1139.

Banished from Italy, Arnold went to France, where he became a supporter of the renowned theologian and philosopher Peter Abelard. Both were condemned as heretics at the Council of Sens, France, in 1141, through the influence of St. Bernard of Clairvaux. Though Abelard submitted, Arnold defiantly continued teaching in Paris until, through the insistence of Bernard, he was exiled by King Louis VII the Young of France in 1141. Arnold fled first to Zürich, then to Passau, Germany, where he was protected by Cardinal Guido, through whose mediation he was reconciled with Pope Eugenius III at Viterbo, Papal States, in September 1145.

Two years earlier the *renovatio senatus* ("renewal of the Senate"), seeking independence from ecclesiastical control, had expelled Innocent and the cardinals, revived the ancient senate, and proclaimed Rome a republic. Eugenius sent Arnold to Rome on a penitential pilgrimage. He soon allied himself with the insurgents and resumed his preaching against the pope and cardinals. He was excommunicated in July 1148. Arnold's agitation for ecclesiastical reform vitalized the revolt against the pope as temporal ruler, and he soon controlled the Romans. He also worked to consolidate the citizens' newly won independence.

Pope Adrian IV placed Rome under interdict in 1155 and asked the citizens to surrender Arnold. The Senate submitted, the republic collapsed, and the papal government was restored. Arnold, who had fled, was captured by the forces of the Holy Roman emperor Frederick I Barbarossa, then visiting Rome for his imperial coronation. Arnold was tried by an ecclesiastical tribunal, condemned for heresy, and transferred to the Emperor for execution. He was hanged, his body burned, and his ashes cast into the Tiber River.

Arnold's character was austere and his mode of life ascetic. His followers, known as Arnoldists, postulated an incompatibility between spiritual power and material possessions and rejected any temporal powers of the church. They were condemned in 1184 at the Synod of Verona, Republic of Venice. Arnold's personality has been distorted through modern poets and dramatists and Italian politicians. He was foremost a religious reformer, constrained by circumstances to become a political revolutionary.

Frederick I (1152–90), brought a major reassertion of imperial rule in Italy. Frederick saw himself not as the heir to a compromise but as a restorer of the Romano-Carolingian heritage of the German monarchy.

PAPAL-IMPERIAL RELATIONS

During the 19th and early 20th centuries, nationalistic and liberal historians popularized a view of Frederick I, whom the Italians called Barbarossa ("Redbeard"), that was surrounded by legend and embroidered by myth. Since World War II, however, scholars have moved away from nationalistic interpretations to reevaluate the imperial-papal relationship within its actual historical context. For example, the Treaty of Constance of March 23, 1153, by which both pope and emperor dedicated themselves almost to a return to the former status quo in both northern and southern Italy, demonstrated their effort to retain essential elements of the traditional order. But events soon showed how illusory this effort was. There was in fact little trust between the papal and imperial sides. Frederick made his descent into Italy in 1154 in order to secure his coronation as emperor. His troops were few, chiefly a band of knights under Henry III (the Lion), duke of Saxony. He put Milan under the ban of the empire for refusing to answer charges laid against it by Lodi, Pavia, and Cremona. But he could do little else. He moved quickly to Rome, where a new pope, Adrian IV (1154–59), the only Englishman ever to hold the papal see, had succeeded Pope Anastasius IV (1153–54). Adrian had little choice but to continue the arrangements made at Constance, although he and his chief adviser, Cardinal Roland Bandinelli (who later succeeded Adrian as Pope Alexander III), opposed Frederick's reassertion of imperial claims to participate in papal elections. Still, they needed his support to quell the continuing unrest created by Arnold of Brescia. The forces of the emperor captured Arnold and turned him over to the prefect of the city, who executed him. Frederick, however, did not move against the Normans, although King Roger II of Sicily had died, and Adrian concluded a treaty with King William I (1154–66) of Sicily in 1156. Frederick's first Italian trip thus served chiefly to demonstrate the impossibility of the kind of restoration that Frederick had envisaged in the Treaty of Constance, but that did not mean that he was prepared to surrender the rights of the empire. Quite the contrary, it helped to move the issues into a new arena.

Perhaps no more dramatic expression of the nature of this change could be imagined than the event that took place at Besançon, where the cardinals Bernard of San Clemente and Roland met with Frederick in October 1157 and delivered a letter from Pope Adrian. The pope reminded Frederick of his imperial coronation and informed him that he wished to confer great *beneficia* on him. The term, which could mean either favours or, in a more specific sense, offices, was translated into German by Frederick's imperial chancellor Rainald of Dassel as "fiefs," which implied that the emperor held the empire from the pope as a vassal. This caused an uproar among those present, particularly since Cardinal Roland went on to ask: "From whom then does he receive the empire...?" Although Pope Adrian denied the interpretation made by Rainald, the damage was done. More importantly, however, this incident shows that contemporaries were quite aware that they were treading on new ground. Frederick firmly rejected any implications of papal overlordship and asserted that he held the empire "from God alone by the election of the princes." That his policies were grounded in political realities is confirmed by his actions in 1158, when again he set forth to Italy. This time he sought neither a rapprochement with the papacy nor a return to the old order. He came as a ruler intent on restoring order in his domains. Having humiliated Milan, which had attempted to oppose him, he met with the cities on the plain at Roncaglia to define the royal regalia (rights) on the basis of customary law. Four Bolognese lawyers joined 28 urban representatives in this task. The text of the three laws issued at Roncaglia, however, shows the increasing influence of Roman law at Frederick's court.

INSTITUTIONAL REFORMS

Already in the second half of the 11th century, studies of Roman law underwent a revival at the University of Bologna under the influence of the jurist Irnerius and his school. Earlier emperors had, in fact, employed Roman law in their judgments and legislation. But Frederick was more conscious of its importance as a source justifying imperial actions. He issued a special privilege for scholars studying law, the so-called *Authentica Habita* (c. 1155), and played a leading role in the gradual evolution of the law schools at Bologna. Roman law, however, was merely one source that contributed to the development of more clearly defined social and political institutions in the 12th century. The profound changes occurring in Italy in this period made innovation inevitable. Communes everywhere were experimenting with new political forms, often concealing their novelty behind traditional names. In the Norman kingdom the effort to fashion royal institutions for disparate regions and populations led not only to a layering of administrative institutions within the royal court but to a great diversity from one region to another. Everywhere, attempts at reconciling widely divergent legal and customary arrangements demonstrated a desire for legal uniformity; the view that each group should live by its own law no longer served the needs of society. More and more, Roman and canon law provided sources useful for reconciling differences. Frederick Barbarossa saw himself as an agent of unification. Although he represented the traditional order and was so viewed by his numerous enemies in Italy, he identified himself with the changing order that was emerging in the mid-12th century. Roncaglia was a new constitutional statement despite its conservative reliance on regalian right.

NORTHERN ITALY

Roncaglia laid the foundation for a new regime in northern Italy. The regalia produced an enormous income from such sources as minting coinage and collecting tolls, making Frederick the wealthiest of all European monarchs. This led him to reconceive the position of Italy within the empire. His aggressive policies could not help but alarm Milan and its allies, and they also caused profound concerns for the papacy. The death of Adrian IV in 1159 revealed a division among the cardinals. A pro-imperial group supported Octavian of Monticello, while the opposition chose Cardinal Roland of Siena. Amid angry recriminations, the two claimants assumed the papal title, Octavian as Victor IV (antipope 1159–64) and Roland as Alexander III (1159–81). At a poorly attended council in Pavia, Frederick abandoned his neutrality and supported Victor IV. But Victor found little support beyond the boundaries of the empire. Even Bishop Eberhard of Bamberg, one of Frederick's closest advisers, made his acceptance of Victor conditional on Victor gaining recognition from the whole church. Nevertheless, Frederick's support was sufficient to give life to the schism. Alexander III relied chiefly on France, England, the Lombard cities allied with Milan, and the Normans in southern Italy and Sicily. On the whole, Frederick's position was the weaker one, but he refused to make concessions. Failing to win over Louis VII of France, he journeyed once again to Italy, only to face strong opposition from the patriarch of Grado, who organized the anti-imperial League of Verona. When Victor IV died in 1164, Rainald of Dassel arranged for the election of the strongly imperial Paschal III (antipope 1164–68) as a rival to Alexander III. But Alexander also faced difficulties. The controversy between King Henry II of England and Archbishop Thomas Becket threatened to deprive Alexander of English support. Moreover, feeling increased uncertainty about his position in France, where he had fled to in 1162, Alexander returned to Rome in 1165 and sought support from the Normans. The death of William I of Sicily in 1166 prevented the realization of this goal, and he once again had to look to France as his mainstay.

Frederick sought a decisive solution in Italy in 1166. He marched with a large force to Rome, but a devastating outbreak of malaria among his troops while in the city put an end to the emperor's plans. In 1167 the Lombard cities formed a league to defend against Frederick's expedition that included Milan, Venice, Padua, Mantua, Brescia, and Lodi.

Despite his setback, Frederick was determined to stay the course. Indeed, by this time, he could hardly turn back without accepting a near-total surrender. Failing to muster support in Germany, Frederick was forced to rely on the limited resources left to him. On May 29, 1176, he met his enemies at Legnano in northern Italy. The army of the Lombard League, under the leadership of Milan, and Frederick's army engaged in a pitched battle, in which the supporters of the empire were thoroughly routed. Accepting the realities created by his defeat, Frederick waged a diplomatic campaign that secured the remarkable treaty concluded with Alexander (whom he now recognized as pope) and the Lombard communes in Venice in July 1177. This agreement settled little definitively, but Frederick obtained a six-year truce with the Lombards and was able to hold onto the Mathildine lands in Tuscany for 15 years. He restored his position in Germany and recovered from the losses endured in Rome. In 1183 Frederick converted the truce of Venice into the Peace of Constance, in which he renounced the regalia claimed at Roncaglia but preserved the administrative rights of the crown. From defeat he thus managed to salvage a considerable portion of his imperial power.

Frederick launched his final expedition to Italy in 1184, where he met with Pope Lucius III (1181–85). He also witnessed a diplomatic turnabout on the part of the Norman ruler, William II (1166–89), who espoused his aunt Constance, the daughter of Roger II of Sicily, to Henry, the second son of Frederick. Although Constance was not expected to inherit the Sicilian throne because William and his queen might still have children, the implications of the agreement were nonetheless momentous. The papacy found itself faced with an intolerable situation. Frederick, now aiming to build a power base in Tuscany instead of Lombardy, attempted to annex the Mathildine lands. Although he failed in this, he secured the *spolia* (spoils) and regalia of vacant bishoprics and abbacies from Clement III (1187–91). Yet Frederick did not live to consolidate this effort. The defeat of the Crusader army at Ḥaṭṭīn in the Holy Land in July 1187 and the subsequent fall of Jerusalem sent a great shock through the West and inspired the Third Crusade. Frederick took the cross; the kings of England and France followed suit. Frederick Barbarossa drowned in the Saleph River in Anatolia on June 10, 1190. The Crusade was able to save ʿAkko (Acre) and assure the continued Crusader presence in the East, but it left Jerusalem in Muslim hands.

ECONOMIC AND CULTURAL DEVELOPMENTS

Frederick was the giant of the 12th-century Italian stage. He lived through a period of dramatic social and economic changes. Genoa, Pisa, and Venice became international powers during this period, with commercial interests stretching from northern Europe to Africa and the Levant. The growth of population in both town and countryside brought about an increase in public works, ranging from town walls to canals. The development of guilds and confraternities reflected the growing complexity of economic organization. Even the smallest cities had their professional elite of judges and notaries alongside the nobles, merchants, and craftsmen. The vigour of the economy found its expression in the construction of new and larger cathedrals, the one at Pisa being among the most notable. Overseas trade and investment increased domestic wealth, leading to the embellishment of cities.

Culture, in turn, produced its own coin. In the Norman south, medical studies developed in Salerno. Although the kingdom of Sicily did not become a major centre for the transmission of Byzantine and Islamic cultures to Europe as did Spain, it nonetheless played a significant subsidiary role. Al-Sharīf al-Idrīsī, the famous Arab geographer, dedicated his three major works on geography to Roger II of Sicily. George of Antioch and, later, Eugenius the Admiral were important translators of Greek works into Latin. Capua, Montecassino, Benevento, and Salerno contributed to the Latin cultural tradition from their own rich patrimonies. Historical writing flourished in the hands of Amatus of Montecassino, Romuald of Salerno, Geoffrey Malaterra, and Falco of Benevento. Already in the 11th century an international clerical culture had emerged in the writings of reformers such as Humbert of Silva Candida and Peter Damian, and it grew under the influence of figures such as Bernard of Clairvaux and John of Salisbury. On the local level, Roman civic culture found its expression in clerical circles around the great basilicas and in secular circles around the prefect and, later, the senators. The north produced an early harvest of the civic spirit in the annals of the Genoese Caffaro di Caschifellone and his successors. Although imperial themes often found a place in these cultural developments, underlying loyalties were local. Only slowly did signs of an international lay culture—largely under French influence—emerge. By the late 12th century the whole of Italy had undergone a major economic and cultural transformation that was to provide a rich basis for the 13th century.

HENRY VI

The death of Frederick Barbarossa's eldest son, Frederick of Swabia, on the Crusade brought to the German throne his second son, Henry VI (1190–97), who had stayed behind in Germany. Thus, strangely, the son who had not expected to become king and who was husband to a princess who also had not expected to inherit a throne found himself in a position to claim both the German and the Sicilian crowns. In Germany the strength of Henry's support and the prestige of his father made succession certain, the more so because he defeated his father's enemy, Henry the Lion, and held his sons hostage. But the Sicilian inheritance of Constance was another matter. The nobility of the kingdom supported the popular Tancred of Lecce (1190–94), as did the English king, Richard I (the Lion-Heart), the old ally of King William II of Sicily. But Henry had secured a promise of imperial coronation from Pope Clement III prior to his death, and his successor, Pope Celestine III (1191–98), who deliberately stalled by engaging in negotiations with Henry, nonetheless proceeded with the coronation on the day following his own consecration. Henry immediately turned his attention to his wife's Sicilian inheritance, but an outbreak of typhus forced him to abandon his plans and return north. Constance herself was captured and held in Salerno. Pope Celestine declared for Tancred and recognized him as king. In Germany much of the Rhineland joined Richard the Lion-Heart and Celestine against Henry. But the capture of Richard on his return from the Crusade strengthened the emperor's hand; Henry demanded an enormous ransom and conspired with King Philip II of France to keep Richard a prisoner. When Henry finally reached an agreement with Henry the Lion in the spring of 1194, the way was open for his return to Italy.

Some scholars have speculated that Henry's Italian policy implies a program of world domination, but such a view is too grandiose. Henry was essentially a practical man. He was also an opportunist. Lacking sources that would provide real insight into his thinking, one can only conclude that he was aware of the policies of his father and that his own aims were extensions, with some modification due to changed circumstance, of those policies. The crown of Sicily was the chief new element. In 1194 he returned to Italy and conquered the Sicilian kingdom; Tancred had died shortly before his campaign began. Aided by the Pisans and Genoese, Henry entered Palermo and was crowned as king on Christmas Day. Constance had remained at Jesi, where she gave birth to a son named Constantine, to be known as Frederick Roger (later Frederick II) in honour of his paternal and maternal grandfathers. Henry aimed to establish German control over the bureaucracy of the Sicilian kingdom and to integrate its administration into that of the empire, employing imperial *ministeriales* for this purpose. These were originally servants of unfree origin who had risen to become important administrators in the imperial government of the Hohenstaufen. Henry gave the trusted ministerial Markward of Anweiler the duchy of Ravenna and the march of Ancona as hereditary fiefs, thereby ensuring that the land route between the kingdom of Italy and the kingdom of Sicily was in safe hands. These measures reveal the centralizing goals that were at the heart of his vision. He tried to ensure that the German (i.e., imperial) crown would be hereditary in his family, a plan that was on its way to realization when, amid his preparations for a Crusade, he succumbed to typhus in Messina and died on September 28, 1197. In Germany the Hohenstaufen future rested with the efforts of Henry's younger brother, Philip of Swabia, to secure the succession for Frederick Roger. In the kingdom of Sicily, Constance succeeded immediately and moved to assert her authority.

OTTO IV

In northern Italy, Henry had endeavoured to preserve the gains that Frederick Barbarossa had made. But Frederick's departure on Crusade and Henry's own concern with the kingdom of Sicily permitted the communes to recover from the reassertion of imperial control after the Peace of Constance in 1183. Henry's death and the ensuing imperial election bought still more time for the communes. The empress Constance withdrew her son, the heir to the kingdom of Sicily, as a candidate for the German throne and entrusted him to the regency of the newly elected pope, Innocent III (1198–1216), before she died in 1198. Philip of Swabia and Otto of Brunswick, son of Henry the Lion of the Welf dynasty, contested the German election. But when on June 9, 1208, Otto of Wittelsbach assassinated Philip in a private quarrel, Otto IV (1208–15) emerged triumphant and began preparations for his coronation, which took place on October 4, 1209. Despite his concessions to the pope, Otto had no intention of dropping imperial claims in Italy; the practical aims that had driven the Hohenstaufen shaped his policy as well. When the new emperor made clear his intention to move on the kingdom of Sicily, Innocent had no choice but to excommunicate him (1210). On the advice of King Philip II of France, the pope transferred his support to the young Frederick, thus paving the way for his accession to the German throne.

FREDERICK II

The youthful king of Sicily knew little peace during the years following the death of his mother. Though Innocent III was nominally his guardian, Markward of Anweiler attempted to control the child-king, basing his claim to the regency on Henry VI's last will. After Markward's death in 1202, Frederick was caught between factions in the kingdom. Only after his marriage to Constance of Aragon in 1209 did his position improve. Then, in 1211, Innocent III turned to him as his candidate for the German throne. This dramatic reversal on the part of the pope and his seeming willingness to jeopardize what most historians have viewed as the papal position in Italy has raised serious questions. True, Innocent exacted a promise from Frederick to maintain the German kingdom separate from the kingdom of Sicily, with his son Henry to be king of Sicily while he became emperor. But acceptance of such a solution raised the question whether the papacy was really committed to any long-term policy, at least one that was consistently dedicated to the separation of the Sicilian kingdom from the German empire. In any case, Frederick spent the next eight years in Germany pursuing and consolidating his position as head of the German kingdom. The kingdom of Sicily was again thrown into turmoil by the competing factions among the nobility, by the efforts of towns and cities to assert greater independence, and by growing tensions between Sicilian Muslims and their Christian neighbours. In northern Italy, imperial authority atrophied; in most places it was little more than a hollow shell. Even in Germany, the new king found that he needed to gain the support of the German church through a broad grant of privileges. In addition, Frederick took the cross at Aachen in 1215, aligning himself with the plan of Innocent III for a new Crusade.

Historians concerned chiefly with papal-imperial conflicts have often missed the positive tone in the relationship between Frederick and the papacy during these early years. The keynote of these years was papal-imperial cooperation, especially on the successful completion of a Crusade. The limited results of the Third Crusade and the bitter fruit of the Fourth Crusade, which had led to the capture of Constantinople and large parts of the Byzantine Empire, had prompted Pope Innocent III to reformulate papal involvement in the Crusades, as outlined in the decree *Ad liberandam* ("To Free the Holy Land") at the fourth Lateran Council in 1215. Innocent's program required a level of commitment never before achieved, especially in financial and logistical terms. Frederick's assumption of the cross demonstrated his support for Innocent's program but raised problems, chiefly because of the uncertain state of affairs in Germany, even after the defeat of Otto IV by Philip Augustus at Bouvines in 1214, and outstanding issues in northern Italy. With the death of Innocent III in 1216, many thought the papal plan for a Fifth Crusade was in jeopardy, but his successor, Honorius III (1216–27), strove to maintain Innocent's

schedule as much as possible. Honorius pressed Frederick and other leaders of the Crusade to hasten their preparations. Although the first contingents from the north were prepared to leave in 1217, Frederick was not among them, partly because he underestimated his capacity to resolve his problems in Germany and Italy and partly because of the speed of preparations for the Crusade. It was not until 1220 that Frederick came to Italy for his imperial coronation and to reenter his Sicilian kingdom. His repeated postponements of his departure for the East, granted by a cooperative Honorius, ultimately prevented him from joining the Crusade. The defeat of the Crusaders in Egypt in 1221 delivered a serious blow to the policy of cooperation initiated by Innocent III and nurtured by Honorius.

Nevertheless, it was a notable period of cooperation. Even the various Italian cities increasingly relied on mediation to settle differences. While Frederick made few concessions, Honorius showed that he was willing to trust in Frederick's promises to reach a final settlement of the Mathildine lands and to keep the administration of the kingdom of Sicily separate from that of the empire. Frederick promulgated imperial laws against heresy, based on the decrees of the fourth Lateran Council. Following his coronation, he began to restore royal authority in the kingdom of Sicily. His Assizes of Capua (1220) set forth a program to regain control of royal rights alienated since the reign of Henry VI.

He also began to establish a more effective central administration. He worked to secure the support of important members of the ecclesiastical hierarchy, including the abbots of Montecassino and La Cava as well as the bishops of the kingdom. He built support among the great nobles, especially the counts of Aquino, but he also encountered considerable resistance from a large segment of the nobility. Faced with this opposition and a revolt among the Muslims of Sicily, he again had to postpone his participation in a new Crusade, although he was careful to send aid and troops. The death of Honorius III in 1227 and Frederick's cancellation of his departure for the East because of illness broke the dam of recriminations and distrust that had been building. The new pope, Gregory IX (1227–41), excommunicated Frederick for his repeated postponements and his alleged abuse of the rights of Sicilian churches during papal vacancies.

An excommunicated Frederick embarked for the East, where he negotiated an agreement with the sultan al-Malik al-Kāmil of Egypt for the return of Jerusalem on terms somewhat less favourable than the sultan had earlier offered the Crusaders in return for Damietta. Frederick, who had married the heiress to the kingdom of Jerusalem in 1225 and had an infant son Conrad from this marriage, laid claim to the kingdom. He set up a regency and embarked on a program to strengthen royal administration. In the meantime, Gregory IX, claiming provocation by the imperial vicar Reginald (or Rainald) of Spoleto, gathered an army and invaded the kingdom of Sicily. Frederick returned from the East, defeated the papal forces, and reached an agreement with the pope at Ceprano in 1230 that did much to restore the basis for cooperation. He could at last devote his efforts to Italy.

The kingdom of Sicily was Frederick's first priority. It had long suffered neglect from his absence and internal strife. The Constitutions of Melfi, or *Liber Augustalis*, promulgated by Frederick in 1231, was a model of the new legislation developing from the study of Roman and canon law. The intent of this legislation was to bring together the disparate elements within the kingdom and to unify them more effectively under royal leadership. It provided for improvements in royal administration, greater efficiency in the courts, and a rationalization of civil and criminal procedures in the interests of justice. Frederick also worked to promote the general welfare of his kingdom. In 1224 he founded the University of Naples. His legislation then dealt with medical education and licensing, public health, and air and water pollution. But he did not lose sight of the place that the kingdom occupied within imperial thinking. Increasingly in the 1230s he was drawn into affairs in northern Italy and Germany that made him conscious of the importance of the Sicilian kingdom as a base for his imperial power. Very possibly, circumstance played a greater role than ideology in forcing this conclusion upon him.

As a part of the settlement reached between him and Honorius III at the time of his coronation in 1220, Frederick had arranged to have his son Henry crowned as king of the Romans (i.e., ruler of Germany) while retaining the imperial, Italian, and Sicilian crowns for himself. Henry, encouraged by some people at his court, embarked on a policy that threatened Frederick's relations with the German aristocracy. As a result, Frederick moved against Henry and placated the German nobles with his Constitution in Favour of the Princes (1232). Yet, whereas Frederick was willing to trade away some of his authority in Germany, he was determined to assert imperial rights in northern Italy. The Lombard cities, as early as 1226, had renewed the Lombard League. While Frederick was dealing with the problems caused by Henry's rebellion between 1233 and 1235, the Lombards grew increasingly restless. Frederick confirmed their fears with his decision to summon a diet to Piacenza in 1236 to impose his imperial authority on them. His action demonstrated his lack of interest in papal efforts to arrange compromises between him and the Lombards. Moreover, the emergence of his chancellor, Pietro della Vigna, as his chief spokesman signaled a shift away from the quiet diplomacy between emperor and papacy that he had carried on with the aid of Hermann von Salza, the grand master of the Teutonic Order, a man respected by the pope and the Roman Curia. Pietro's rhetoric was well fashioned for a propaganda war. On his side, Gregory appointed the strongly anti-imperial Cardinal James of Palestrina as his new legate in northern Italy and blocked Frederick's planned diet. In his propaganda Frederick portrayed himself as the champion of orthodoxy working to prevent the spread of heresy in Lombardy, thus building on the theme of the cooperation between him and Honorius III aimed at stopping the growth of heresy. Gregory's rhetoric appealed to papal claims based on the Donation of Constantine and expressed his earlier concerns about Frederick's abuse of ecclesiastical rights.

The growing rift between Frederick and the papacy was not merely a revival of the papal-imperial conflict of the 12th century, though it certainly had elements in common. It had its immediate roots in the failure of the policy of cooperation employed under Innocent III, Honorius, and even Gregory himself. There is every indication that Frederick valued this relationship, but he increasingly came to see it as an obstacle to securing his imperial rights in northern Italy. The papacy had also worked to preserve good relations. But fear of Frederick's policies in northern Italy evoked memories of Frederick Barbarossa among members of the Curia. Above all, neither the emperor nor the pope could turn back the clock on the development of the communes. In fact, from the very outset Frederick seemed more a pawn of the emerging forces in northern Italy than a restorer of the ideal of empire. The new forces were represented above all by two tyrants, Ezzelino and his brother, Alberigo, from the ancient da Romano family, who were working to expand their lordship from their base in Verona at the expense of towns such as Padua, Vicenza, and Brescia. Frederick relied on them for support, and in doing so he provoked the opposition of earlier supporters, such as Azzo, marchese d'Este, who now sided with the Lombards. Potentates such as the Romanos were the potential beneficiaries of Frederick's military activities, more so than the emperor himself.

Buoyed by early success in northern Italy, Frederick returned to Germany. He even hoped to repair his differences with Gregory, who proved amenable. However, the attempted settlement broke down. On November 27, 1237, Frederick, back in Italy, dealt the Lombards a heavy blow in the Battle of Cortenuova. He followed his military success with a strong propaganda attack, chiefly directed against Gregory IX. But the victory won at Cortenuova proved difficult to convert into permanent gains. Milan continued to hold out. In the following summer Frederick laid siege to Brescia but failed to take the city. Gregory excommunicated the emperor, repeating previous papal criticisms. What was at stake, however, was not some ideological high ground but recognition that Frederick had violated the rights of the church in the kingdom of Sicily. Gregory attempted to use the machinery developed for the Crusade to the East to gather money and manpower to oppose Frederick, who, in turn, warned his fellow rulers of

the danger that these efforts posed. The papacy accused Frederick of failing to support the Crusade mounted by Thibaut of Champagne in 1239 and delaying its departure for the East. Gregory wished to recall him to the program on which the papacy had been insisting since the reign of Innocent III, but Frederick's own concerns were with his European domains. It was not that he opposed the papacy's desire for a Crusade; he wanted to settle matters in Italy first.

THE FACTORS SHAPING POLITICAL FACTIONS

The breach between emperor and pope that marked the remainder of the reign of Gregory IX and that grew more intense under Innocent IV (1243–54) undoubtedly helped shape political factions in northern Italy throughout the 13th century. But it would be an exaggeration to say that the conflict over church and state determined political developments. As already noted, local and regional factors underlay the politics of the northern communes. The conflict of religious and political ideology emerged chiefly in the second half of the 13th century, but later debates often hearkened to the vituperative papal-imperial propaganda of the 1240s. In some respects the lines had already been drawn, at least in part, by the internal political disputes that had begun to dominate Italian urban life from the mid-11th century on. The role that the reform movement played in the emergence of political factions is known only in part, but its importance cannot be denied. However, it would be a mistake to view this influence solely as a clerical-lay dichotomy. The emergence of papalist and imperial parties that later in the century called themselves Guelf and Ghibelline, respectively—based on terms taken from the divisions between the Welf house of Otto IV and the Hohenstaufen (Waiblingen) house of Philip of Swabia and Frederick II—echoed the struggle over rights. The term *pars ecclesiae* ("party of the church"), which became more common in the second half of the 13th century, has generally been viewed as a reference to support for the papacy, but it also referred to support for local churches. Both meanings of the term are correct, and the earliest usages seem to favour a more local interpretation.

The changing character and composition of communes often followed the fortunes of this struggle over rights. Increasingly, divisions between landowning magnates and *popolo* concealed the process of coalition making characteristic of early 13th-century urban politics. The regime of the podesta (which had its origins in imperial appointees), formed in the second half of the 12th century to provide greater stability and protection against violence, was already becoming more professionalized in the age of Frederick II. The preference for professional officials, strongly evidenced by mid-century in the writings of Albertanus of Brescia and others, aimed

to prevent the military aggrandizement of an Ezzelino da Romano or an Azzo d'Este and to defend communal values.

The *pars ecclesiae* very often controlled the commune and stood for communal independence. Although some disputes with bishops were an inevitable feature of the Italian urban scene, alliances between bishops and communes grew more common in the 13th century. Imperial ideology was largely driven from the field. Likewise, class-based economic disputes varied in importance from one place and time to another; these disputes reflected the fundamental concerns over rights, especially over property, on both the local and the imperial-papal level, that shaped Italian urban politics.

THE END OF HOHENSTAUFEN RULE

The final decade of Frederick II's reign marked the end of the imperial system in Italy. Although Frederick seemed at times on the verge of repeating Barbarossa's achievement, he could not marshal the resources needed for the task. His kingdom of Sicily fell more and more victim to his need for money to fight his war in the north, which all but ended the efforts at good government that had motivated his Constitutions of Melfi (1231). Increasingly, Frederick mortgaged his income from the kingdom to Roman bankers and subordinated the interests of the kingdom to the needs of the empire. His relations with the north-ern Italian maritime powers, save for Pisa and to some degree Venice, continued to deteriorate in the 1240s, but he remained dependent on income from taxes on their trade and could not entirely break ties with them. Instead, he tried to compete directly with them and to control their access to the ports of the Sicilian kingdom. The pressures of war largely determined his policies. The death of Pope Gregory IX in 1241 at first promised the possibility of a resolution. But it soon became clear that the cardinals could not proceed to an election because of their internal division. It was only in 1243 that they finally selected the Genoese cardinal Sinibaldo Fieschi, one of the leading legal experts of the period, who took the name Innocent IV. The new pope soon demonstrated his unwillingness to compromise with Frederick, identifying papal interests closely with those of the Lombard cities. Under threat from the Romans, the pope left Italy and summoned a general council of the church to meet in Lyon in 1245. This council sealed the rupture between Frederick and the papacy and ensured that there would be little chance for a reconciliation in future negotiations. Frederick's position remained militarily secure, but threats of conspiracies and growing opposition marked the final years of his reign. He was the last medieval emperor to assert his rule in northern Italy.

The death of Frederick II at Fiorentino in Puglia on December 13, 1250, ended an era and opened the way for a new political order. The papacy determined that it would no longer tolerate the rule of the Hohenstaufen in Italy and opposed Frederick's son and successor, Conrad IV, as well as Frederick's natural son, Manfred, who became de facto ruler in the kingdom of Sicily and, following Conrad's death in 1254, secured the crown for himself. Conrad's son, Conradin (Conrad V), continued, however, to be the official heir. Even before Innocent IV died in 1254, the papacy tried to secure aid from the English king Henry III (1216–72), promising the Sicilian crown to his younger son Edmund. Innocent's successor, Alexander IV (1254–61), soon discovered the folly of this effort and began to search elsewhere. Meanwhile, Manfred consolidated his position in the kingdom and in the march of Ancona. In northern Italy the passing of Frederick enabled tyrants such as Ezzelino da Romano to assert their virtual independence under the guise of supporting Manfred. Even the death of Ezzelino in 1259 did not impede the trend toward military rule. Almost everywhere, the ethos of strong government overwhelmed the rule of the communes.

The death of Frederick and the virtual failure of his line left a power vacuum. The papacy turned for support to Charles of Anjou, brother of King Louis IX (1226–70) of France. While Frederick was alive, Louis had remained aloof from the conflict and had even expressed his disapproval of the papacy's actions against Frederick. However, after the death of

Conrad, he supported his brother's bid for the Sicilian kingdom against Manfred. At the same time, Charles's arrival in Italy set a new direction for politics in the north, where the Guelfs welcomed him. He proceeded to Rome, followed by a Crusader army that had support from the pope, Clement IV (1265–68), himself a Frenchman. Charles fended off Manfred while awaiting his own army, which had traveled overland. On February 26, 1266, he defeated Manfred and his forces on the plain of Grandella, near Benevento. This battle ended Hohenstaufen rule in Italy and began the Angevin dominance that lasted through most of the rest of the 13th century. Charles succeeded to the Sicilian throne (1266–85) and asserted his leadership in Rome and in northern Italy. He quickly defeated a futile challenge by Conradin and had him executed in Naples (1268).

The papal party of the Guelfs was dominant in the north; the papacy ruled in the centre; the Angevins were in control in Sicily and Naples; and the whole was held together by the strong personality and ambitious dreams of Charles of Anjou (Charles II). As matters turned out, many of his dreams differed but slightly from those of the Hohenstaufens. Moreover, despite their aggressive and grandiose character, most of them seem to have had little basis in reality. Charles had designs on the Byzantine Empire and North Africa, as is evident from Louis IX's Crusade to Tunis in 1270, which ended in disaster. The north of Italy was

growing more and more restive under the rule of Charles. Pope Nicholas III (1277–80), sensing the direction of things, removed Charles from his position as senator at Rome and from his vicarship in Tuscany. The papacy also spearheaded efforts at reconciliation between Guelfs and Ghibellines. But Charles resisted and endeavoured to increase his influence over the papacy. Pope Martin IV (1281–85), a strong Angevin supporter, restored him to his former offices. But before Charles could reap the benefits of his reinstatement, he faced an insurrection in Sicily. The so-called Sicilian Vespers—an uprising on Easter Monday of 1282, when citizens of Palermo attacked the French garrison—led to a protracted war known as the War of the Sicilian Vespers. The king of Aragon, Peter III, came to the aid of the rebellious Sicilians, while Charles received indirect support from his nephew, the king of France, as well as the papacy. After 20 years of intermittent warfare, the outcome was the division of the kingdom founded by the Normans. The mainland of southern Italy continued to be held by Charles's successors (the Angevin dynasty), whereas the island of Sicily came under the rule of the Aragonese.

As the 13th century came to an end, Italy had not yet recovered from the disasters of the age of Frederick II. Milan was dominant among the Lombard communes and was soon to make its bid for hegemony in northern Italy. Florence, meanwhile, had increased in size, wealth, and power to become the dominant force in Tuscany and the chief bulwark against the ambitions of the Visconti, a powerful Milanese family. The papacy vacillated under Angevin influence, while the kings of Naples carried on a vain war to retake the island of Sicily from the Aragonese. External influences, especially from France, increasingly dominated the political life of Italy, culminating at the turn of the century in the disastrous conflict between Pope Boniface VIII (1294–1303) and King Philip IV (the Fair) of France (1285–1314). Italy had escaped imperial dominance only to fall under the shadow of the French. Perhaps there is a certain irony in the country's exchange of one heir of Charlemagne for another.

ECONOMIC AND CULTURAL DEVELOPMENTS IN 13TH-CENTURY ITALY

The 13th century witnessed an enormous increase in prosperity not only in the maritime cities but also in the growing centres of the cloth industry, especially the woolen textile industry in Tuscany. Venice came to dominate the rich trade with the Byzantine Empire, especially after the Fourth Crusade (1204). Genoa, which eclipsed Pisa in the latter part of the century, expanded its trade in the western Mediterranean and in Provence. During the second half of the 13th century, Florentine influence, benefiting from close ties with the Angevins and the papacy, prospered in the kingdom of

Sicily. The new wealth left an imprint on Italian cities. By the end of the century, the first mansions of the rich, although small by later standards, began to adorn the cities, alongside new municipal buildings and the churches of the mendicant orders, especially of the Franciscans and Dominicans.

The culture of this period reflects both the new wealth and the tensions it generated in Italian society. The legal culture that had flourished in Bologna in the 12th century came of age in the 13th century and spread to other parts of Italy. Lawyers formed a large educated class with an appreciation of rhetoric and grammar and some taste for poetry, history, and philosophy. In the first half of the century the court of Frederick II was an important centre for these studies, as is evident in the letters of Pietro della Vigna, the emperor's chief spokesman. The chronicle of Riccardo of San Germano proved the best that the century would produce. Frederick's court also attracted figures such as Michael Scot, whose translation of mathematical and scientific treatises from Arabic into Latin made Sicily an important centre for their transmission. Frederick's own study *De arte venandi cum avibus* ("On the Art of Hunting with Birds") drew not only on earlier writings but also on his own and his contemporaries' observations and experience. The incipient Dominican *studium* in Naples produced Thomas Aquinas, arguably the greatest thinker of the age. Frederick, however,

COSMATI WORK

The mosaic technique known as Cosmati work was practiced by Roman decorators and architects in the 12th and 13th centuries. In Cosmati work, tiny triangles and squares of coloured stone (red porphyry, green serpentine, and white and other coloured marbles) and glass paste were arranged in patterns and combined with large stone disks and strips to produce geometric designs. Cosmati work was applied to architectural surfaces and to church furniture.

The word Cosmati comes from the name Cosma, which belonged to a number of members of the several families involved in the art. Cosmati work differs from the several similar mosaic techniques that flourished in Italy at about the same time mainly by its design, which balances areas of busy, intricate pattern with smooth areas of plain stone following the ancient Roman tradition of clarity, simplicity, and monumentality. The production of Cosmati work was interrupted in the 14th century by the temporary transferral of the papal seat to Avignon, France, and subsequently reappeared only in a debased form.

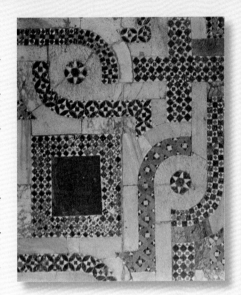

Cosmati mosaic (c. 1085–1132); detail of the floor in the choir of the church of San Nicola, Bari, Italy. SCALA/Art Resource, New York

did not continue the rich Norman tradition of mosaic art and architecture, best represented by the Palatine Chapel in Palermo and the cathedrals of Cefalù and Monreale. Instead, Frederick was more noted for his castles, especially his starkly beautiful Castel del Monte in Puglia.

Thirteenth-century Rome saw a flourishing of the arts in sculpture and in the stonework and mosaics of the Cosmati that adorn the walls of such churches as San Paolo Fuori le Mura and Santa Maria in Trastevere. By the end of the century, Arnolfo di Cambio, whose work in Florence was to gain him greater fame, produced important sculpture in Rome. But Rome was chiefly the centre of the papacy and of an international clerical culture. Although the papal chancery grew apace in this period, producing thousands of polished letters in its distinctive style, other studies found little place there. It was more devoted to practice than to study.

Secular legal studies, grammar, and rhetoric took deep root in the north. Fresh ideas streamed across the Alps from France, influencing the writings of figures such as Albertanus of Brescia, while these same ideas drew numerous Italians northward, including the Florentine scholar Brunetto Latini. In Milan, Bonvesin da la Riva, poet and eulogist of his city, composed his *De magnalibus urbis Mediolani* ("Concerning the Great Works of the City of Milan") in 1288. At Padua, Rolandino reacted against the incursions of Ezzelino da Romano in his *Chronicle*. While in exile from Florence in the early 1300s, Dante Alighieri, the greatest of all Italian poets, completed his towering epic poem, *The Divine Comedy*. Dante's literary art found its visual equivalent in the brilliant frescoes of Giotto di Bondone in Padua (Arena Chapel), Florence (Santa Croce), Assisi (Magdalen Chapel in the lower church of San Francesco), and Naples (destroyed).

CHAPTER 6

ITALY IN THE 14TH AND 15TH CENTURIES

The failure of the Hohenstaufen emperor Frederick II and his successor kings of Sicily to dominate Italy in the course of the 13th century left the peninsula divided among a large number of effectively independent political units. The inability of rulers from beyond the Alps to impose their authority upon it was clearly and finally demonstrated by the expedition (1310–13) of Henry of Luxembourg, crowned as Emperor Henry VII. An idealist who believed that he, as God's secular vicar, had a divine mission to restore peace to "the garden of the Empire," Henry entered Italy in 1310 with the consent of Pope Clement V (1305–14) and seemed at first to prosper. He sought, as an honest broker, to reconcile Guelf (i.e., pro-papal) and Ghibelline (i.e., pro-imperial) factions, but it was soon apparent that any attempt to override those old loyalties entailed a massive assault upon the political status quo, a revolution that would be fiercely resisted. Florence, in particular, opposed not only any concession to its enemies but any restoration of imperial power.

In these circumstances Henry was increasingly driven into exclusive alliance with the opponents of the Guelfs and became himself merely a leader of a faction. As a result, both the papacy and King Robert of Naples, who had originally favoured his coming to the peninsula, returned to their traditional anti-imperial stance. The dream of peace by imperial fiat dissolved, and Henry turned to war, but his death from fever at Buonconvento, near Siena, in August 1313 broke the hopes of the imperialists forever. Later emperors who intervened from the north—Louis IV (the Bavarian; 1327–30) and Charles IV of Bohemia (1354–55, 1368–69)—came with much more limited aims, not as universal monarchs but as short-time players on the Italian scene, seeking there such limited gains as the prestige of imperial coronation at Rome. However much these emperors maintained their formal de jure claims to rule, any imperial central authority in Italy had disappeared. In its place stood a complex, often chaotic grouping of many rival powers whose hostilities and alliances fill, in wearisome detail, the pages of contemporary chroniclers.

This political disunity went along with other divisions in a peninsula that manifested sharp regional differences in climate, land formation, economic development, customs, and language. (A 13th-century chronicler praises a contemporary as a skilled linguist because of his fluency in "French, Lombard, and Tuscan." There was no common literary language before Dante—and then only in verse, not prose.) These very pronounced diversities have led many commentators to rule out any attempt to construct a general unified history of Italy in this period and to insist that a coherent synthesis must be based upon its constituent parts. For these authors, the only true history will consist of separate accounts of the six major powers—Sicily, Naples, the Papal States, Florence, Milan, and Venice—together with those of some 15 to 20 minor powers—such as Mantua, Montferrat, Lucca, and Siena—which were scattered among them. (This ignores the ambiguous case of Genoa, extremely powerful economically but pitifully weak politically.)

There is much in such contentions. It would be unwise to play down the overwhelming spirit of *campanilismo* (local patriotism; the spirit of "our campanile is taller than yours") during the 14th and 15th centuries. Only a minority of people living at that time could ever have heard the word *Italia*, and loyalties were predominantly provincial. It is true that among certain classes, such as merchants who traveled beyond the Alps or scholars who looked back nostalgically to Roman republican or imperial glories, some elements of national consciousness survived. Dante—seeking in his *De vulgari eloquentia* (written 1304–07; "On the Eloquence of the Vernacular") to find, amid what he described as "a thousand different dialects," "the elusive panther" of some basis for a common vernacular literary language—argued that there were some "very simple standards of manners, dress, and speech by which our actions as Italians are weighed and measured." However vague this claim may appear, one can certainly see in the peninsula some elements that, taken together, made a strong contrast to the world beyond the Alps: a common legal culture, high levels of lay education and urban literacy, a close relationship between town and country, and a nobility who frequently engaged in trade.

Yet ultimately one must conclude that the interest or importance of this period springs above all not from any "national" considerations or reflections upon the Italian peninsula as a unity but rather from three particular features that appeared in at least some parts of it. First there was the maturing, often in the face of severe challenges, of the remarkable economic development that had originated in earlier centuries. Though shaken in the course of the 14th century, northern and central Italian trade, manufacture, and mercantile capitalism, together with increasing urbanization, were to continue with extraordinary vigour and to have remarkable influence throughout much of the Mediterranean world and Europe as a whole—a development that served as the necessary preliminary for the expansion of Europe beyond its ancient bounds at the end of the 15th century. Second, in parallel with this, came the extension of de facto independent city-states, which, whether as republics or as powers ruled by one person or family (*signorie*, singular: *signoria*; ruled by *signori*, or lords), created a powerful impression upon contemporaries and posterity. Finally, allied to both these movements was this society that produced the civilization of the Italian Renaissance, the Renaissance that in the 15th and 16th centuries was to spread to the rest of Europe.

THE SOUTHERN KINGDOMS AND THE PAPAL STATES

Not all regions were to undergo favourable economic or constitutional development or to receive anything but reflected rays from the sun of the Renaissance. In the south the Sicilian Vespers of 1282 separated the island of Sicily for more than 150 years from the rest of the kingdom of Sicily, which until then had consisted of both the island and the southern mainland. On the mainland thenceforth, the successors of King Charles of Anjou ruled as vassals of the papacy. Normally described by contemporaries as "kings of Naples" (though resolutely continuing to call themselves "kings of Sicily"), they pursued a 90-year war against the Aragonese kings of (island) Sicily. They financed that war, which was ultimately unsuccessful, through harsh taxation of the only productive element in the kingdom—namely, its impoverished peasantry. This increase in the royal tax burden, already oppressive at the time of the Norman kings, fixed the region in wretched poverty and destroyed all possibility of native capitalist growth. As a result, during the 14th century almost all trade and banking came into the hands of northern Italians, particularly Florentines. At the same time, outside a few restricted areas (Sulmona, coastal Puglia, Campania) that produced considerable surpluses of grain, an arid climate and inferior soil made for poor agricultural development in the Kingdom of Naples.

Against this background, political unrest flourished. Under King Robert (reigned 1309–43; known to his literary flatterers as "Robert the Wise"), who made no less than five attempts to conquer the island of Sicily, the monarchy was able to resist the more extravagant demands of the nobility for rewards for their military and political support. But, with the accession of Robert's granddaughter Joan I (1343–82), royal authority withered away, court factions dominated, and civil war (1347–52) ensued. Quelled for a time, baronial strife revived at the end of Joan's reign in a conflict between two branches of the Angevin family (those of Durazzo versus those of Provence) that claimed recognition as heirs of the queen. The eventual victor, King Ladislas (1386–1414), benefiting from the turbulence provoked by the Great Schism, was able to boast of considerable military success in central Italy and even gained—according to some observers—a brief predominance in the peninsula. But the accession of his sister, Joan II (1414–35), inexperienced and childless (that is to say, without obvious heirs), brought a renewal of anarchy to the Neapolitan kingdom, in which true power rested not with the monarchy but with a few powerful owners of vast estates (latifundia) who were allied to the monarchy through blood or service. Below these barons existed a large number of petty nobles with minuscule fiefs; still lower was the mass of peasants, who eked a bare subsistence from the soil.

Meanwhile, the island kingdom of Sicily—or Trinacria, as it was often called—was ruled from 1296 to 1409 by a cadet branch of the royal house of Aragon. This house, in rebellion against papal claims of suzerainty and engaged in constant war with the Kingdom of Naples, went through a pattern of monarchical weakness and economic decline similar to that shown by the Angevins

of Naples. In Hohenstaufen and early Aragonese Sicily, extensive royal landholdings had given the monarchy effective power throughout the kingdom. With the death of King Frederick III (1337), however, substantial concessions of royal lands to a grasping baronial class increasingly divided the island. Of particular importance in this group were the three great families of the Ventimiglia, the Chiaramonte, and the Passaneto—men so powerful that contemporaries described them as "semi-kings," having below them some 200 lesser, poor, and violent vassals. In these years, with an economy dominated largely by Catalan merchants, Sicily looked to Aragon (which in 1326 had also gained control of the island of Sardinia) and its great port of Barcelona rather than to the peninsula to the north.

If the southern kingdoms limped through the 14th century in internal strife and economic backwardness, so, too, did the Papal States lying to the north of the Kingdom of Naples. In March 1303 Pope Boniface VIII, in conflict with King Philip IV of France over papal jurisdiction, had been seized at the papal residence of Anagni by a small band of French and Roman adventurers. Though released almost immediately, he died a month later of, it was said, deep humiliation. The Papal States had been founded to preserve the independence and spiritual authority of the papacy, yet here, clearly, it seemed to have failed. Partly because of the menacing Roman baronage and partly again through the pressure of the

French king, Pope Clement V decided to abandon the peninsula and seek refuge at Avignon. Here between 1307 and 1377 the papacy was to reside in greater safety. Italy was now "bereft"—as Dante, who witnessed these developments, testified—"of its two suns," both the papacy and the empire.

The effects of that withdrawal were twofold. First, the "lands of the Crucified One," as the church dramatically described its territorial state, were reinforced in their secular anarchy, and everywhere local "tyrants" seized power from papal officials. Yet, at the same time, the traditions of the church inevitably required that the papacy should return to the Rome where St. Peter had, it was said, preached and suffered. Hence, over the years, with fluctuating enthusiasm, the French popes struggled sporadically to establish obedience, peace, and control over their Italian lands. These efforts indeed played an important role in the foreign affairs of the Italian states in the period. Notable were the attempts at reconquest of the Papal States by Cardinal Bertrand du Poujet (1319–34) and Cardinal Gil Albornoz (1353–63). Yet the results were slight. After a heroic expenditure of money and blood, Albornoz attained some measure of order, largely by appointing the more amenable tyrants as "papal vicars" and by securing from them promises of payment of taxes and services in return for acknowledgment of overlordship. But even these muted successes proved unstable. With the outbreak of war between the Avignon papacy and Florence in 1375, most of the vicars cast off their allegiance. Three years later the Papal States fell into even greater disarray with the outbreak of the Great Schism (1378–1417). For almost four decades, until the Council of Constance, unity was shattered by rivalries between popes and antipopes—one French, one Italian, and later a third one, also Italian.

Amid the confused struggles that engulfed the Papal States in this period, one incident in particular stood out for men of the day and excited the imagination of posterity. The city of Rome, deserted by the papacy, presented a sombre picture of shepherds, herdsmen, labourers, and artisans dwelling by ruins that testified to past glory and were now taken over as the residences of powerful aristocratic families. The Colonna, Orsini, and Annibaldi established their fortifications amid the remains of the Mausoleum of Augustus, the Forum, and the Colosseum, and from there they fought out their ancient rivalries. Here in the 1340s rose the remarkable figure of Cola di Rienzo. A notary and the son of an innkeeper, possessing an imagination that easily accepted the most flattering fantasies, he gained esteem from the rumours he circulated that he was the son of Emperor Henry VII. An avid reader of Classical history and an interpreter of ancient inscriptions, intoxicated by the past splendours of Rome, he preached to his fellow citizens the recovery of its former greatness. Inspired by the Lex Regia, the supposed right of the Roman people to confer authority on the emperor, he announced that the citizens of his own day, under his leadership, could assume that right and resolve all disputes between rival claimants to the office. Achieving prominence as the most eloquent member of an embassy dispatched to Avignon to complain of the absence of the papacy, he excited the admiration of many (including the poet Petrarch) at the papal court. On his return in May 1347, with the help of some mercenary soldiers, he seized power in the city, and a parliament summoned at his command awarded him the title of "Nicolai, the Severe and Clement, the Tribune of Freedom, Peace and Justice, and Liberator of the Holy Roman Republic."

The following month Cola invited all the Italian states to appear before him to discuss "the security and peace of Italy." It is a remarkable testimony not so much to his eloquence as to their desperate wish for peace that no less than 25 communes answered his call. During a remarkable round of ceremonies, in the presence of the communes' representatives, Cola announced that the Romans held jurisdiction over the whole world and conferred Roman citizenship upon all citizens of other Italian states. These chimerical pretensions (described by a contemporary as "fantastic stuff which won't last long") very soon came to be unveiled as such. In the following December, faced with an increasingly suspicious pope and a Roman citizenry satiated by novelties, Cola was driven from the city. He returned to Rome and was appointed senator in 1354 (essentially a puppet of Albornoz's

attempt to dominate the Papal States), but within less than three months he faced a popular revolt that ended with his death. Cola's importance lay not so much in anything he had achieved as in the demonstration of how powerful an influence the thought of Classical Rome could exercise on men of the time. He survives in cultural history (as hero, for example, of the German composer Richard Wagner's opera *Rienzi*) and in the myths (certainly no more than myths) that he had planned the unification of Italy and was a prophet of the 19th-century Risorgimento.

THE *POPOLO* AND THE *SIGNORIE* IN CENTRAL AND NORTHERN ITALY

Meanwhile, in the course of a long process extending through the 13th and 14th centuries, within the towns of the Papal States and most towns of northern and central Italy, there arose from the old communes a new form of government, that of the *signoria*. The communes of the 13th century had become increasingly dominated by the conflicts of the nobility who controlled their governments. These divisions, though often moved by the Guelf and Ghibelline parties, in fact largely reflected personal, economic, or quite local political rivalries—all inflamed by ideals of chivalric honour and an everyday acceptance of the traditions of vendetta. In large part as a response to these conflicts, there had arisen within the communes the movement of the *popolo*—i.e., of associations of non-nobles attempting to win a variety of concessions from the nobility.

Within the ranks of the *popolo* were, in the first place, those who had gained wealth through trade, banking, exercise of a profession, or landholding and sought membership in the ruling noble oligarchies. The second group comprised prosperous members of the artisan or shopkeeping classes who, while not normally seeking a direct position in government, sought a more satisfactory administration of the finances of the commune (particularly a more equitable distribution of taxation), a greater voice in matters that most directly concerned them (for example, the licensing of the export of food), and, in particular, the impartial administration of justice between noble and non-noble. Above all, the *popolo* (like many of the nobility themselves) desired a civic order that would end violent party conflicts and lessen the effects of noble vendettas.

In some towns the *popolo* movement succeeded in bringing about constitutional change. In those communes where the nobility did not monopolize all wealth and where the development of trade, industry, and finance had created a complex social structure, the existing oligarchies agreed to come to terms. This came about more easily when the *popolo* succeeded in ending party struggles so violent that they could be described as a form of civil war. Here, often against the background of some disaster, such as defeat in war, it became normal to establish a council of the *popolo*, under a captain of the *popolo*, alongside the old council of the commune under its podesta, as a consultative element in what was now termed the government of "the commune and *popolo*." In Florence, where the movement enjoyed its greatest success, the *popolo*, organized in seven major and five lesser guilds, assumed power in 1282 not simply as the partner of the commune in government but as the dominant element within it. Moreover, in January 1293, by the Ordinances of Justice, it declared that the members of 152 powerful families were "magnates" and, as such, excluded from personal participation in government and subject to particular disadvantages in law vis-à-vis non-magnates.

Nevertheless, in all but a few towns, the *popolo* proved unable to solve the problem of public order, and in these circumstances "the peaceful and tranquil state" of the cities came instead to be established by *signori*, who were powerful party leaders. From the second half of the 13th century, having triumphed over, destroyed, or permanently exiled their opponents, these men began to give institutional form to their power and to pass it on to their sons as a hereditary right. What they offered in return to their subject citizens was the hope of eliminating anarchic civil violence by the exercise of superior force. It was in this way that, in the course of the 14th century, *signoria*, or permanent legal rule by single families, began. From the communes the *signori* obtained their titles, the authority to control the communes "according to their own will," and the right to pass on this grant to their chosen successors. With the passage of time, these usurped legislative trappings lent the appearance of legitimacy to their rule. By the end of the 14th century the *signori* normally sought some legitimization of their power by obtaining authorization from the emperor or pope to act as "vicars" over the territories that their families had come to rule. As such, during the 15th century these hereditary lordships—or, in effect, principalities—seemed to constitute the natural order in large areas of northern Italy.

So, in the Veneto, Verona fell to the della Scala (or Scaligeri) family in the 1260s, as did Vicenza from 1312, while Padua was subject to the Carrara (or Carraresi) family from 1318. In Lombardy the Bonacolsi and then, from 1328, the Gonzaga family came to be sole rulers of Mantua, while the Visconti achieved the *signoria* of Milan from 1311. During the next 35 years the Visconti extended their dominion by gaining power over Cremona (1334), Pavia, Lodi, Bergamo (1332), Como (1335), Piacenza (1337), Tortona, and Parma (1346). In Emilia the Este (Estense) family, already established at Ferrara from 1264, extended their power to Modena (1288) and Reggio (1290). In the northern sector of the Papal States the towns of the Romagna and the Marche fell to signori between 1315 and 1342; when Cardinal Albornoz's attempts at reconquest failed, the papacy granted most of its territories to vicars, including these *signori*. Thus, between about 1250

and 1350, northern and central Italy had undergone a profound transformation in constitutional forms, political life, and attitudes toward authority. The rule of a city-state by one man was no longer seen as a strange and temporary expedient but as a normal aspect of life. Under the new regimes the councils of the communes and *popolo* still remained, but their role was limited to minor administrative tasks or to formal approval of the political decisions of the *signori*. Essentially, all that remained of the old communal system was its administrative service, a core of skilled notaries who kept the machinery of government in operation. Meanwhile, in return for their absolute power, the *signori* restored or created harmony within the upper classes of the towns and reconciled the interests of the *popolo* and the nobility. Nonetheless, the emergence of the *signorie*, however important, was only one element in the constitutional history of the northern and central Italian towns in the 14th century. It was a movement largely confined to the Veneto, Lombardy, Emilia, the Marche, and—subject to the suzerainty of regional princes—Piedmont. In most towns of Umbria and Lazio (Latium) the papacy was able to prevent their establishment. In Tuscany they were largely unsuccessful. Lucca fell to *signori* in the first half of the 14th century, notably with the rule of the remarkable Castruccio Castracani between 1316 and 1328, but the town experienced a strong revival of republican government from 1369 to 1392. Republican Florence underwent only brief interludes of signorial governance. Florence conquered several of its neighbours—Volterra, Prato, Pistoia, San Gimignano—before any signorie arose in them. In Liguria, Genoa was continually unstable because of the violent conflicts of its noble houses. Rather than submit itself to any one family, the town oscillated between communal government and a series of *popolo*-granted life dictatorships—of which the most memorable was that of Simone Boccanegra, future hero of an opera by the Italian composer Giuseppe Verdi. Two communes, Siena (at least in the 14th century) and Venice, rejected signorial government entirely in favour of republican institutions.

During the 14th century then, substantial parts of Italy remained outside the control of *signori*. Alongside the new principates there were some communal governments—including those of Venice and Florence, two of the most powerful cities in the peninsula, which both survived and developed into powerful territorial states with very strong republican traditions. These republics survived partly because it was much more difficult for *signori* to seize control over a patrician oligarchy of bankers and merchants than it was to dominate a society consisting of landowners, artisans, and rural workers. Societies with highly developed economies were much less amenable to princely control. In republics, an economy that would be menaced by internal disunity and a ruling class united at least in its pursuit of commercial advantage helped assure the preservation of public order and the repulsion of any individual or family seeking political domination.

VENICE IN THE 14TH CENTURY

It was, in fact, in the 1290s and the hundred years that followed—broadly speaking, the same period in which the *signorie* were consolidating their position—that the two principal republics established and secured the essentials of their constitutions, which were to last (in the case of Florence) into the 16th and (in the case of Venice) even into the late 18th century. At the beginning of this period the dominion of Venice included the islands of the lagoon and the *dogado*, a thin strip of the mainland around the lagoon, along with an overseas empire consisting of most of the Dalmatian coast, the island of Corfu, various islands in the Aegean, the coasts of the Peloponnese, and Crete. The overseas territories were often valuable in themselves, and they served also as a series of staging areas for Venetian commerce. In the establishment of the city's constitution, the key moment came in February 1297, when the Great Council, in which sovereignty resided, was expanded to take in more than 1,000 members. From that time forward, and in particular from the 1320s, admission to that body became more difficult, and from the 1390s it ceased altogether. What has been traditionally described as "the closing (*serrata*) of the Great Council"—that is, the creation of an oligarchic government dominated by a fixed hereditary caste—did not occur in

Miracle of the True Cross at the Bridge of S. Lorenzo, *oil painting by Gentile Bellini, 1500; in the Gallerie dell'Accademia, Venice.* SCALA/ Art Resource, New York

1297 but actually extended over some 100 years from that date.

From its members the Great Council elected the Senate, the Lesser Council, the Quarantia (judiciary), the Council of Ten, all the committees of government, and, by an extremely elaborate system of lot, the doge. The "Excellent Lord, by the Grace of God, Doge of Venice, Duke of Dalmatia and Croatia, the Most Serene Prince" enjoyed immense prestige and had an important role in the coordination of government. Yet, however powerful his personality, he was increasingly bound by his councils. In reaction against such control, the doge Marin Falier, from one of the greatest families of the city, conspired in April 1355 to overturn the sovereignty of the nobility. He paid for the attempt with his life. A century later

(1457) the patriciate were to show their strength again when the Council of Ten deposed Francesco Foscari. The power of the doge diminished; henceforth, he could promote his own initiatives only by submitting them to the Great Council and the Senate.

The Venetian Senate originally comprised 60 members (the Pregadi), but by 1450 it had grown to 300 members, of whom some 200 had the right to vote. It was particularly concerned with foreign policy, war, and matters of commerce. Its chosen ambassadors constituted the first and finest diplomatic service in Europe. In addition to their regular dispatches, these men were expected on their return from duty to produce a detailed account (*relazione*) of the government and country to which they had been sent. The Senate also organized the fleets and the recruitment and supervision of condottieri; it controlled the markets of grain, salt, wine, and oil; and it built the principal merchant galleys and organized the regular convoys (*mudae*) in which they sailed to "Romania" (Constantinople and the Black Sea), "Flanders" (London and Brugge), and Tunis. The Senate auctioned the lease of ships for each voyage, nominated their master mariners, and laid down elaborate regulations for their crewing and equipment.

Alongside the Great Council and the Senate stood the Council of Ten. In 1310 Baiamonte Tiepolo and other nobles had sought to seize power from the dominant faction in the Great Council. It was after the suppression of this conspiracy that the Great Council created the Council of Ten, armed with exceptional powers. At first it was to exist for a limited time to watch over the security of the state, but, after the attempted coup by Marin Falier in 1355, the Council of Ten became permanently established. Its members controlled the secret police, espionage, and counterespionage, and they exercised in some measure their own judicial system. From that power base they came to exert a strong influence on financial and diplomatic administration.

Below the patrician class, who formed and monopolized all the political offices of the Venetian state, existed a less-privileged class, that of the citizens. Consisting of about 2,500 males of the status of notaries and the like, they controlled the civil service. Their leader, the grand chancellor, though not a patrician, was, as head of the civil service, one of the most important men in the republic. Outside the ranks of the citizens were the disenfranchised majority of the population—labourers, shopkeepers, artisans, and, in great numbers, seamen.

Under this constitution the Serenissima ("Most Serene Republic") produced the most satisfactory form of government and society known in the world at that time. Petrarch's praises of

the most miraculous city of Venice, rich in gold but richer in fame, strong in power but stronger in virtue, built on both solid marble and the harmony of its citizens, secured more by the harmony of its citizens than by its surrounding seas,

echoed a virtually universal praise. Such rhetoric, typical of most discussions of the republic from the 13th to the 16th century, gained its persuasive power from the real social concord that the Venetian government, like no other, indeed provided. This outstanding success at home was matched by victories abroad. In the second (1294–99) and third (1351–55) Genoese-Venetian wars, the Genoese, the Venetians' principal economic rivals, gained numerous victories against the republic, and in the fourth war (1378–81) they temporarily seized Chioggia and Malamocco, on the lagoon at the heart of Venice's power. Yet in the end, with the superiority of its state structure and civic spirit, Venice always won these wars. In the overseas empire a careful administration secured from its peoples, if not passionate loyalty, at least a submission that drew no small strength from the threat of an alternative Turkish dominion.

FLORENCE IN THE 14TH CENTURY

In Florence, the other great republic of northern Italy, the key constitutional moment came in 1293 with the Ordinances of Justice. Though modified somewhat two years later, they preserved a system in which sovereignty explicitly rested with the *popolo*, an elite class drawn from the seven major guilds, or *arti maggiori*—that is, the judges and notaries, the Calimala (bankers and international traders in cloth), the money changers, the silk merchants, the doctors and apothecaries, the wool merchants, and the dealers in furs. Together with dominant figures from five guilds of lesser status (the *arti medie*, or middle guilds, consisting of the butchers, the shoemakers, the smiths, the stonemasons, and the secondhand dealers), the *popolo* gathered every two months to elect six priors who ruled Florence as supreme magistrates.

Behind these forms, the men who effectively ruled were members of the *popolo grasso* ("fat people"), consisting of bankers and businessmen of great wealth, who professed allegiance to the Guelf party. Yet the survival of guild government was, in these years, often precarious. Fierce rivalries often split the dominant faction. In 1302 the "Black" Guelfs, in alliance with Pope Boniface VIII, succeeded in expelling the "Whites." Among the White Guelfs at this time was the poet Dante (1265–1321), who had held public office and who wrote his greatest work during his exile, which lasted for the rest of his life. *The Divine Comedy* still offers eloquent testimony to the extreme bitterness of domestic conflict in these years. Moreover, external pressures forced the city to accept the lordship between 1313 and 1322 of King Robert of Naples and then again, between 1325 and 1328, of Robert's son, Charles of Calabria. It was perhaps fortunate for the continuance of the commune that Robert was too preoccupied with his own kingdom to establish

any full and permanent control and that Charles died prematurely.

Yet, despite such political difficulties, Florence probably reached the apogee of its prosperity during the first three decades of the 14th century. Its population grew to about 95,000 people, and a third circle of walls, constructed between 1284 and 1333, enclosed an area that the city was not to surpass until the middle of the 19th century. In the 1290s, construction began on the new cathedral (Duomo) of Santa Maria del Fiore (the dome was not completed until 1436) and the fortress-residence of the Palazzo Vecchio—both potent symbols of the commune, to which was soon added a third, Giotto's campanile.

Up to the beginning of the 1340s, Florence reigned supreme in long-distance trade and in international banking. From that time, grave shocks struck its economy, and these, combined with failure in war, led to another brief experiment in signorial rule; in 1342 a protégé of King Robert, Walter of Brienne, titular duke of Athens, was appointed *signore* for one year. Almost immediately on his accession, Walter changed this grant to that of a life dictatorship with absolute powers. But his attempt to ally himself with the men of the lower guilds and disenfranchised proletariat, combined with the introduction of a luxuriant cult of personality, soon brought disillusion. An uprising in the following year restored, though in a rather more broadly based form than hitherto, the rule of the *popolo grasso*.

DANTE

The great Italian poet Dante Alighieri (born *c.* May 21–June 20, 1265, Florence, Italy—died September 13/14, 1321, Ravenna, Italy)—often referred to solely by his first name—was of noble ancestry, and his life was shaped by the conflict between papal and imperial partisans (the Guelfs and Ghibellines). When an opposing political faction within the Guelfs (Dante's party) gained ascendancy, he was exiled (1302) from Florence, to which he never returned. His life was given direction by his spiritual love for Beatrice Portinari (died 1290), to whom he dedicated most of his poetry. His great friendship with Guido Cavalcanti shaped his later career as well. *La Vita Nuova* (1293?) celebrates Beatrice in verse. In his difficult years of exile,

Dante wrote the verse collection *The Banquet* (*c.* 1304–07); *De vulgari eloquentia* (1304–07; "Concerning Vernacular Eloquence"), the first theoretical discussion of the Italian literary language; and *On Monarchy* (1313?), a major Latin treatise on medieval political philosophy. He is best known for the monumental epic poem *The Divine Comedy* (written *c.* 1308–21; originally

Dante Reading from the Divine Comedy, *painting by Domenico di Michelino, 1465; in the Cathedral of Santa Maria del Fiore, Florence.* Alinari-Mansell/Art Resource, New York

titled simply *La Commedia*), a profoundly Christian vision of human temporal and eternal destiny. It is an allegory of universal human destiny in the form of a pilgrim's journey through hell and purgatory, guided by the Roman poet Virgil, and then to Paradise, guided by Beatrice. By writing it in Italian rather than Latin, Dante almost singlehandedly made Italian a literary language, and he stands as one of the towering figures of European literature.

Guild rule then continued virtually unchallenged until 1378. In that year the regime was overthrown not by a *signore* but by factions within the ruling class, which in turn provoked the remarkable proletarian Revolt of the Ciompi. In the wool-cloth industry, which dominated the manufacturing economy of Florence, the *lanaioli* (wool entrepreneurs) worked on the putting-out system: they employed large numbers of people (9,000, by some calculations) who worked in their own homes with tools supplied by the *lanaioli* and received wages by the piece. Largely unskilled and semiskilled, these men and women had no rights within the guild and in fact were subjected to harsh controls by the guild. In the Arte della lana (the wool-cloth guild), a "foreign" official was responsible for administering discipline and had the right to beat and even torture or behead workers found guilty of acts of sabotage and theft. The employees, who were often in debt (frequently to their employers), subsisted precariously from day to day, at the mercy of the trade cycle and the varying price of bread. With them, among the ranks of the *popolo minuto* ("little people"), were day labourers in the building trades as well as porters, gardeners, and poor and dependent shopkeepers. On occasion these poor, in Florence as all over Italy, rioted when bread was scarce, but they were normally powerless to organize efficiently against guilds and governments—both of which could impose extreme penalties on anyone who defied their authority.

In effect, the poor rose to revolt only at the prompting of members of the ruling class. So it was in the Revolt of the Ciompi of 1378. In June of that year Salvestro de' Medici, in an attempt to preserve his own power in government, stirred up the lower orders to attack the houses of his enemies among the patriciate. That action, coming at a time when large numbers of ex-soldiers were employed in the cloth industry, many of them as *ciompi* (wool carders), provoked an acute political consciousness among the poor. In their clamour for change, the workers were joined by small masters resentful of their exclusion from the wool guild, by skilled artisans, and by petty shopkeepers. Expectation of change and discontent fed upon each other. In the third week of July, new outbreaks of violence, probably fomented by Salvestro, brought spectacular change: the appointment of a ruling committee (*balìa*) composed of a few patricians, a predominating number of small masters, and 32 representatives of the *ciompi*. Michele di Lando, foreman in a cloth factory, was appointed to the *balia* as "standard-bearer of justice."

In their six-week period of rule, the men of the *balia* sought to meet the demands of the insurgents. The *balia* approved the formation of guilds for the wool carders and other workers to give standing to their members, established more equitable taxation between rich and poor, and declared a moratorium on debt. Yet, angry at the slow pace of change, the poor remained restive. On August 27 a vast crowd assembled and proceeded to the election of the "Eight Saints of God's People." Then they marched on the Palazzo Vecchio with a petition that the Eight Saints should have the right to veto or approve all legislation. But by now all the temporary allies of the poor were alienated from the spirit of revolt. The rich resisted, won over Michele di Lando with a bribe, called out the guild militias, and drove the protesters from the scene.

Normality was reestablished within a few days. The new guilds were abolished, and the poor returned to the impotence that was, throughout Italy, their lot. Malnutrition quenched rebellion, leadership was lacking, and the limited horizons of their lives made any ideal of betterment short-lived. The main effect of the revolt was to introduce at the top of society a regime that was narrower and more oligarchic than that which had ruled for the previous 30 years.

ECONOMIC CHANGE

Meanwhile, changes in the character of the economy in town and country profoundly affected the development of both the republics and the *signorie*. Although scholars today often contend that in this period an "urban economy" drove northern and central Italy, in contrast to the rest of Europe, most Italians still lived on the land, and the prosperity of any town depended greatly on its *contado*, or the rural territory that it governed. Here, despite differences in agriculture due to different climates and types of soil, certain patterns of development occurred within the peninsula. By the end of the 13th century, tenurial serfdom had virtually died away, and other forms of landholding were evolving to take its place. Sometimes peasants worked the land as freeholders (as in fact many peasants had always done, even at the very height of the manorial system). Sometimes (and this was particularly true of large ecclesiastical estates in northern Italy) lands were let out on perpetual hereditary lease for low rents—a procedure that, in effect, often led to the virtual dispossession of church proprietors in favour of secular tenants. But the most common new tenancy from the 13th century was that in which landlords offered short-term leases in return for heavy rents either in money or, more often, in kind. Among such leases the one that came to figure most prominently, especially in well-cultivated land in central and northern Italy, was sharecropping, particularly *mezzadria*. In contracts of *mezzadria*, the landlord provided half the seed sown and in return received half of the tenant's fruits. Frequently the contract was renewable every year—a provision that held considerable insecurity for the lessee, who was obligated to leave the land at term. Often, in order to make sure that the landlord received a full return from his lease, detailed conditions were attached on rotation of crops, plowing, digging, and harrowing. In all, this form of tenure, which was to remain a central feature of northern Italian rural life up to the mid-20th century, can be seen less as an agreement to let land than one to hire labour.

At the same time, a system of more intensive farming was developing. Before the mid-13th century, large homogeneous estates were a rarity, and it was very unusual for one proprietor to own half or more of a parish. From that time on, however, scattered portions were increasingly consolidated into united farms such as the *poderi* of modern Tuscany. Profits from commerce were used to build drainage, plant trees, erect homesteads, and acquire livestock, manure, and agricultural instruments. In these areas the common-field system began to disappear, common pasture declined, and a growing number of individual properties were hedged in. Labourers came to live on the farm, leaving the village to house a reserve of casual workers. Thus, by the end of the 14th century, the old landscape of dispersed strips of land and fortified villages had frequently given way to broad estates dominated by country houses, the leisure seats of urban landowners. Yet these developments were in no way uniform, even in the Emilian plain and in Tuscany, where they were most common. In the south the latifundia, the large estates that only a few major landowners owned, continued to exist, but they were now farmed with hired labour.

Evidence of *bonifiche* (drainage works) and the clearing of wasteland suggests a continual expansion in agricultural production up to the 1340s. So, too, trade, manufacture, and banking also prospered in that period. Within the peninsula, communes had to engage in large-scale marketing of food simply to provision the cities. For a town such as Florence, which at the beginning of the 14th century could gain from its own territories just enough food to feed its population for five months of the year, this commerce was literally a matter of survival. But, at the same time, trade in food and other bulk goods was matched by long-distance commerce in luxuries. With the decline of Pisa in the 13th century, Venice and Genoa remained the principal centres of this traffic. Venetians and Genoese had their own quarters and consulates in Syria and Palestine and at Constantinople and Alexandria. Sailing from their ports or traveling inland to Damascus and Aleppo (heads of the Asian caravan routes), they held a virtual monopoly of East-West trade, exchanging wood, steel, and arms for "spices" (the generic name for all precious goods from the East, including pepper, ginger, cinnamon, nutmeg, silk, dyes such as cochineal and indigo, cotton, drugs, and sugar).

To the northeast, traders from Italy penetrated the Black Sea to draw grain, fish, salt, and slaves from the Crimea. Farther east still, they traveled to Azerbaijan, the Caspian Sea, and China. "The road from Tana [on the Sea of Azov] to Cathay," a Tuscan merchant's handbook told its readers, "is quite safe by day and by night according to the merchants who report having followed it." Indeed, in the first half of the 14th century there were Italian merchant colonies (with husbands taking their wives along) and seven Italian missionary bishops in China.

In the West, too, Italian commerce expanded its empire. The introduction of the compass to the Mediterranean, leading to new marine charts (the *portolani*, the earliest survivors of which date back to the 1290s), gave new wings to maritime daring. From at least 1277 the Genoese and from 1314 the Venetians sent annual galley convoys through the Strait of Gibraltar and thence, on a compass setting, across the Bay of Biscay to English and Flemish ports. Out into the Atlantic, Genoese navigators visited the Canary Islands. At the same time, shipbuilding technology advanced during the 14th century. Trireme galleys expanded from 50 to sometimes 150 tons, and Italian ports began to employ the cog, a square-sailed vessel capable of carrying 150 slaves and ideal for bulk cargoes. Meanwhile in banking, the most prominent of financial houses to extend their operations beyond

the Alps were the Bonsignori company of Siena and the Florentine houses of the Acciaiuoli (with 53 branches throughout Europe), the Peruzzi (83 branches), and the Bardi (even larger than the Peruzzi). Within Tuscany again, beginning in the 14th century, the manufacture of textiles became a major industry.

Growth accompanied changes in the character of commerce. Resident capitalists emerged who held a tight grip on far-flung agents through a network of correspondence, and new mercantile techniques developed in which Italians could boast primacy—account books with Arabic numerals, double-entry bookkeeping, marine insurance, bills of lading, bills of exchange, and a mature law of the sea and law of commerce. The expansion of commerce was uneven; it was rudimentary in the south, and even in central and northern Italy most towns were no more than small market centres for the surrounding countryside. Nevertheless, the major commercial centres in the opening decades of the 14th century sustained an economy that was never again to expand so fast and be, in relation to the rest of Europe, so powerful.

FAMINE, WAR, AND PLAGUE

Italy's thriving economy soon confronted severe challenges. Among these, first, were famines, which affected most of Italy in the years 1339–40, 1346–47, 1352–53, and 1374–75, and a general expansion and intensification of war compounded these catastrophes. The 13th century saw the diffusion of the crossbow, whose bolt far surpassed the arrow of the longbow in its power to penetrate. The crossbow obliged mounted knights to adopt heavier armour for better protection. Hence arose the need for stronger and more-numerous horses. Such technical developments began to make the practice of warfare much more expensive and professional, and in these circumstances mercenary troops came increasingly to supplement and then often to replace the old citizen militias. In the 14th century, Italian states raised these troops in ever larger numbers not by hiring individuals but by drawing up a *condotta* (contract) with a condottiere (contractor), who would engage to bring a band of up to several thousand soldiers in time of war to the aid of a commune or kingdom.

Given the difficulties of securing political control over Italian military leaders (who might, it was feared, take over the state), it became common, beginning in the 1330s, to negotiate with non-Italian condottieri. Their forces rapidly grew to immense size. In the 1350s "The Great Company," founded by Werner of Urslingen, comprised some 10,000 troops and 20,000 camp followers and had its own government, consultative council, bureaucracy, and foreign policy. Throughout the 1360s and '70s these "mobile states"—for example, the companies of the Englishman Sir John Hawkwood and the Germans Albrecht Sterz and Hannekin Baumgarten—dominated war in Italy, and in times of

peace they were all too likely to subject their former employers to a variety of blackmailing threats.

These changes in the practice of war went hand in hand with a considerable expansion in the power of governments. The weak, decentralized communes of the 13th century, with comparatively primitive administration and very light taxation, gave way in the 14th century to republics and *signorie* with much stronger political control and exclusive new means of fiscal exploitation. States raised revenues through property taxes, *gabelle* (e.g., taxes on contracts, sales, transport of goods into and out of town), and forced loans (*prestanze*), while they developed sophisticated measures, including the consolidation of state debts into a form of national debt, to service long-term deficit financing. At Florence, for example, where from 1345 state debtors were issued securities at 5 percent interest, negotiable in the open market, revenues rose from around 130,000 florins in the 1320s to more than 400,000 florins in the 1360s.

Such innovations—fruit of the inter-related needs of food provision, war, and taxation—brought about considerable growth in bureaucratic institutions and in the number of administrative officials. At the same time, however, these innovations allowed war to be waged on a larger scale, and states increasingly diverted productive wealth into war. That is, these innovations helped cause the setbacks that occurred in many sectors

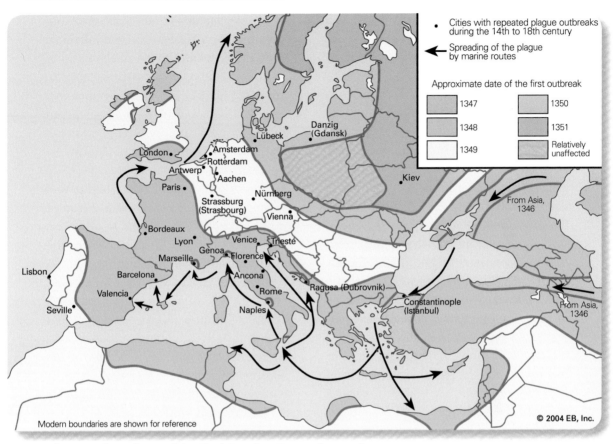

The second pandemic of the Black Death in Europe (1347–51).

of the economy during the 1340s. In that decade, with trade already disrupted by the beginning of the Hundred Years' War in France, the overextension of Italian (particularly Florentine) banks became clear. In 1343 the Peruzzi company collapsed, in 1345 the Acciaiuoli, and in 1346 the Bardi.

Still more disastrous was the arrival from the east of the Black Death. Galleys and cogs brought the plague in its bubonic and pneumonic forms to Messina in early October 1347. By January 1348 it had reached Genoa and Pisa, by February Venice. From these ports it spread throughout the peninsula and on to the rest of Europe. Estimates of the death toll vary between one-third and one-half of the population. Yet the effects were not confined to 1348, as plague was henceforth rooted in Italy. Although slackening in its power and appearing more sporadically, the disease returned to many parts of the peninsula, in both town and countryside, in 1361–62, 1363, 1371, 1373–74, 1382–83, 1398–1400, 1407, and 1410–12. Thereafter it continued as a town disease in individual, sporadic, but continually threatening assaults up to the 18th century.

POLITICAL DEVELOPMENT

From the 1380s to the 1450s Italy was torn by a long series of large-scale wars. The principal aggressor in these conflicts was the Visconti family, who, having seized the *signoria* of Milan, had extended their power to many other cities, from Asti in Piedmont to Reggio in Emilia. From 1385 the ruthless and energetic Gian Galeazzo Visconti (created duke of Milan by Emperor Wenceslas in 1395) embarked on a series of diplomatic and military campaigns that brought him virtual hegemony over northern and central Italy. He extended his power through a series of dynastic marriages—essentially, the bartering of Visconti wealth for noble blood—that gave the family immense prestige. Gian Galeazzo's first wife was Isabella of Valois, daughter of King John II of France; his sister, Violante, was married (albeit briefly) to Lionel, son of Edward III of England; and his nieces were married to the dukes of Bavaria and Austria.

In 1387 Gian Galeazzo seized Verona and Vicenza from their *signori*; in 1388 he took Padua and other territories in the Veneto. These coups provoked the suspicions of Florence, and, after the failure of attempts to delineate their respective spheres of influence, three wars erupted between the two powers (1390–92, 1397–98, 1400–02). Gian Galeazzo

apparently achieved an overwhelming predominance, for he was recognized as *signore* of Pisa and Siena in 1399 and of Perugia, Spoleto, and Assisi in 1400. In June 1402 he took Bologna. Florence was now encircled, and perhaps it was saved from conquest only by Gian Galeazzo's death in September from plague. At his death the state that he had built up collapsed, and his son, the vicious and incompetent Giovanni Maria Visconti (duke 1402–12), was incapable of restoring the dynasty's fortunes. With the accession of Giovanni's brother, Filippo Maria Visconti (duke 1412–47), however, a new era of Visconti expansion dawned. By 1422 Filippo Maria had restored the family's Lombard possessions. Thenceforward, until the middle of the century, there came a series of virtually continuous conflicts against an alliance of Florence and Venice.

Until the 14th century Venice had ruled only the lagoon, the eastern and Adriatic possessions that had served to maintain its commerce, and, on the Italian mainland, a thin strip of land bordering the lagoon. Yet the rise of Visconti power from the 1380s persuaded the Serenissima finally to establish itself as a territorial power on the peninsula. If the old *signori*—the della Scala at Verona and the Carraresi at Padua—had seemed from time to time in the past to threaten the free passage of goods from Venice over the Alpine passes or into Lombardy, the threat of the Visconti dukes with all their power could only reinforce Venetian apprehensions. With Gian Galeazzo's death the republic turned accordingly to extending its control over the mainland. Between 1403 and 1405 it took over Verona, Vicenza, and Padua. Between 1411 and 1420 the city seized the wide territories of the ecclesiastical prince, the patriarch of Aquileia in Friuli. In 1426 it conquered Brescia and in 1428 Bergamo in Lombardy. These acquisitions proved immensely profitable. It was calculated in 1440 that taxes from the new possessions yielded 306,000 ducats, as against 180,000 from the colonial possessions (which were at the same time much more expensive to defend). The "Veneto," as it came to be known, was rich, populous, and fertile—and a good market for the city's trade. In the newly subjected towns the old civic oligarchies continued to hold a measure of local power, though now under the supervision of Venetian podestas and captains. Below them, peasants and urban workers acquiesced in a system that imposed some external check upon exploitation by the town patriciates.

Venetian expansion had taken place through an alliance with its fellow republic, Florence, against Milan. Yet this entente, in part through the Venetians' very success, was shortly to disappear. On the death of Filippo Maria Visconti without male heirs (August 1447), some prominent citizens proclaimed Milan a republic. But they proved incapable of maintaining order in the state, which in 1450 surrendered to Filippo Maria's son-in-law, the powerful condottiere Francesco Sforza. Francesco was swift to proclaim himself duke. This revolution soon led to a revolution in the diplomatic alignments of the peninsula, with Florence then and for more than 40 years afterward adhering to Milan as its principal ally in its search to maintain the status quo and its own power. Following the collapse of the Revolt of the Ciompi, Florence itself had come under the rule of a narrow oligarchic government under the personal domination of Maso degli Albizzi (1382–1417) and then of his son, Rinaldo (until 1434). The Albizzi regime successfully resisted the Visconti and then a temporary threat from King Ladislas of Naples in the years 1408–14, and it also contributed to Florence's expansion over Tuscany, which since the mid-14th century had transformed the city-state into a territorial state like Milan and Venice. The city had absorbed Volterra in 1361 and Arezzo in 1384; now it went on to conquer Pisa, with its port, in 1408 and to purchase Livorno from Genoa in 1421. Seeking further expansion, however, it failed to conquer Lucca in a war fought between 1429 and 1433.

That failure was largely responsible for the fall of the oligarchy dominated by the Albizzi and its replacement with an oligarchy subordinate to Cosimo de' Medici. Cosimo, who attained an unofficial personal dominance over the state in 1434, was to hold it until his death in 1464 and then pass it on to his descendants. Cosimo was the principal architect of an alliance with the Sforza of Milan that culminated in the Peace of Lodi (1454). By this pact Milan, Florence, Venice, and (in

1455) King Alfonso of Aragon and Naples and Pope Nicholas V bound themselves together in an "Italian League" against any power, Italian or foreign, that should disturb the existing balance of power. At the same time, the treaty established special machinery for the peaceful settlement of any disputes that might arise among the states. Despite some local conflicts, the creation of the Italian League brought about a much more peaceful era in the second half of the century. Peace was assisted, above all, by a general exhaustion among most of the major powers, whose economies and societies could no longer support the strains imposed upon them by wars.

THE SOUTHERN MONARCHIES AND THE PAPAL STATES

In the south, Alfonso V of Aragon (1416–58) used the island kingdom of Sicily mainly as a base for his conquest of Naples. Thereafter Sicily was governed by viceroys who subjected its interests to those of Aragon, which became part of Spain in 1479. Examples of Sicily's incorporation into the Spanish state were the establishment there of the Inquisition (1487) and its expulsion of the Jews (1492). So, too, the Kingdom of Naples, conquered by Alfonso between 1435 and 1442, underwent an unpromising development, its peace continually threatened by the rival claims of the Angevin and Aragonese dynasties. On his death in 1458, Alfonso left Naples to his illegitimate son, Ferdinand I (1458–94).

Ferdinand maintained his rule only with difficulty, suppressing baronial revolt with an extreme severity that served to further alienate his subjects.

Ferdinand at least was able to retain control until the days of the French invasion (1494). The Papal States, on the other hand, had virtually dissolved at the time of the Great Schism. Southern Emilia, the Romagna, the Marche, and Umbria were given up to numerous *signori* acting as "papal vicars," among whom the most celebrated were the Este of Ferrara and the Montefeltro of Urbino. In the cities of Bologna and Perugia, the Bentivoglio and Baglioni families, respectively, retained predominance, though without obtaining the vicariate. The church still ruled some territories directly, notably Ancona and much of southern Umbria, but in Lazio strong baronial families threatened its power—in Rome itself antipapal and republican sentiment still survived. Not until the reign of Pope Alexander VI (1492–1503) did the papacy make a determined attempt to assert authority over the whole state. Until then the popes enjoyed the worst of all worlds, condemned for the deep involvement in secular politics that their position as temporal rulers had thrust upon them while, at the same time, remaining largely powerless to extract obedience from their principal vassals.

VENICE

By contrast, Venice in the 15th century, with a population of perhaps 100,000 in the city and 1,000,000 on the mainland, enjoyed a golden age and could be considered a major European power. Its overseas empire expanded with the inheritance of Cyprus from the French Lusignan family in 1489, and its economy still generated large profits. In 1423 the doge Tommaso Mocenigo calculated that the Venetian marine consisted of 45 state and private galleys employing 11,000 seamen, 300 large cargo vessels with 5,000 seamen, and 3,000 smaller craft employing 17,000 men. Either from the Fondaco dei Tedeschi ("Warehouse of the Germans") by the Rialto Bridge or in state-organized convoys, Venetian merchants continued to distribute the precious goods of the East through Europe. In industry, the state-owned Arsenal provided shipbuilding yards and dry and wet docks for the maintenance of huge numbers of vessels. Manufacture flourished, above all in silks and cottons, tanning, and, on the island of Murano, glassblowing. On the mainland, expansion continued with the acquisition of Ravenna in 1441 and of the agricultural Polesine region of Rovigo (north of Ferrara) in 1482–84. For observers throughout Europe, the "myth" of Venice excited admiration originating in surprise that so many could participate in government without producing anarchy. Venice's social stability continued, assisted by a legal system that strove consciously to preserve equal justice for the powerful as well as the weak and by the particular attention given, through some 120 *scuole*, or charitable organizations, to the needs of the poor.

Yet, amid general prosperity, three developments during the second half of the century foreshadowed grave future problems. First, in July 1499 Vasco da Gama returned to Lisbon from India with a small cargo of spices, threatening an end to the virtual monopolization by the Venetians of Eastern trade. Second, the Ottoman Turks, having taken Constantinople in 1453, continued their advance in Greece, the Balkans, and the Mediterranean. In the course of the first Turkish war (1463–79), Turkish cavalry raided Dalmatia and Friuli; Venice lost the strategically important island of Negroponte (Euboea, or Évvoia) and agreed to pay tribute to the sultan. Meanwhile, Venice's expansion on the mainland troubled the republic's fellow Italian states, which feared that it might, in the words of Pope Pius II, "be seeking the monarchy of Italy." However untrue, many contemporaries shared this sentiment, and they united in praising both the beauty of the city and the menace that they detected in its power. So the French statesman Philippe de Commynes, recalling his visit to Venice in 1495, wrote admiringly of its churches, monasteries, and palaces, its 30,000 gondolas, its Grand Canal ("the fairest and best-built street, I think, in the world"), the Basilica of St. Mark, the Arsenal, and other attractions. Venice was, he thought, "the most triumphant city that I have ever seen." Yet its rulers were "so wise and so bent on enlarging their territories, that, if not prevented in time, all the neighbouring states may lament it too late." The suspicion and opposition of its Italian neighbours were the third source of Venice's future weakness, and they hindered the republic in the second Turkish war (1499–1503), which brought still greater losses.

FLORENCE

Venice in the 15th century remained, despite all, an immensely strong power, able to preserve its republican constitution unimpaired. In both these matters, it contrasted with Florence under the Medici. The foundation of the family's fortune was laid by Giovanni di Bicci (1360–1429), who founded the Medici bank and in 1422 was appointed as banker to the papacy. His son Cosimo, who dominated the *reggimento* (principal patrician families) from 1434, united his vast financial resources with a keen intelligence. His natural simplicity of manner and plethora of folksy sayings were well designed to avoid offending (as far as possible) republicans. In a city proud of its traditions of "freedom," he maintained his claim to be a private citizen, refused all titles of lordship, and held the powerful office of "standard-bearer of justice" for only three two-month periods.

Cosimo gained adherents by giving gifts and loans to all orders in society as well as to churches, confraternities, and religious orders and also by granting patronage to writers and artists. He granted commissions to the sculptor Donatello and the architects Michelozzo (Medici Palace) and Filippo Brunelleschi (the choir and nave of San Lorenzo) and constructed villas in the countryside at Careggi and Cafaggiolo. Founder of a great library, he subsidized the scholarship of the Neoplatonist Marsilio Ficino, the humanist Poggio Bracciolini, and the collector of antiquities Cyriacus of Ancona. In politics he moved with moderation, gradually and sporadically. In no way could his rule be considered an exercise of despotic power. Cosimo always had to secure the support of a majority among the *reggimento*, who saw themselves as his allies in retaining their economic and social predominance in the state. By and large the Medici regime was acceptable to the patrician class because it stabilized the conflicts within it that had broken the unity of Florence before 1434.

Certainly, Cosimo's influence was sufficient to allow his son, Piero, to take over this informal rule at his death in 1464. More remarkably, on the death of Piero in 1469, it passed to his son Lorenzo, then only 20 years old. Lorenzo later earned fame as "the Magnificent" (a title given to anyone of prominence at the time), partly as a tribute to the charm of his personality, partly by a careful projection of his own image, and partly through the perceptions of Florentines of a later generation who, looking back through the dark years that followed his death, tended to think of his era as a golden age. Yet in some respects that appellation is exaggerated. In foreign politics Lorenzo made a disastrous error in the 1470s when he attempted to prevent Pope Sixtus IV from establishing a power base in the Romagna. This led to the Medici bank's loss of the papal account and a conspiracy between members of the pope's family and the Florentine Pazzi family to overthrow Medici rule. In April 1478 the Pazzi assassinated Lorenzo's brother Giuliano but failed to kill Lorenzo, and the insurgents, denied support by the citizens, were captured and executed. Yet the "War of the Pazzi" (1478–80) that followed, with Florence pitted against a papacy allied to Naples, proved dangerous and expensive, and Lorenzo emerged from it only with great difficulty.

Thereafter Lorenzo pursued a more cautious and successful path in foreign affairs. On the death of Sixtus in 1484, he made a friend of the successor, Innocent VIII, and through this intimacy Lorenzo acquired a cardinalship for his son Giovanni. (And it was Giovanni, as Pope Leo X, who was to ensure the triumph of the Medici throughout Tuscany in the 16th century.) But the claims made for Lorenzo as "the peacemaker" of Italy, even as a "constructor of a balance of power," have no substance—except insofar as he, as ruler of a militarily weak state in his last years, inevitably took part in a balance of weak states from which only Venice stood out. In addition, Lorenzo—a man of genuine intellectual and aesthetic interests, who had been educated as a humanist rather than as a merchant— can be criticized as a businessman. Even

acknowledging that the Medici bank had to meet political as well as strictly economic ends, with loans to political allies who might be poor risks financially, it remains true that it was inadequately supervised and, for this reason, close to failure by 1492.

In the subject territories of the *contado*, Lorenzo was able to suppress any rebellion. An attempt by Arezzo to free itself from Florentine commercial exploitation in 1471 led to the sack of the town by mercenary troops in Florentine pay (though whether or not this was at Lorenzo's express will is uncertain). In Florence itself during his predominance, the patriciate pursued a more aristocratic lifestyle, expressed among other ways by a revival of jousting and lavish expenditure on clothes, palaces, and the arts—all of which were at odds with older traditions of republicanism. Yet, in public patronage of the arts, Lorenzo— perhaps because he had less money, perhaps because the family's houses were already filled with works of art—did less than his father. Lorenzo preferred small, private pieces, as found in his collection of antique cameos, medals, and gems and in the pastiche-antique model statuettes produced for him by Bertoldo di Giovanni. He also had a creative interest in architecture. Lorenzo read Leon Battista Alberti's *De re aedificatoria* (promulgated 1452, published 1485; *Ten Books on Architecture*), wrote to the duke of Urbino asking to see the plans of his new palace, and entered his own design in the competition for a new facade of the Florence cathedral. Only his death (in April 1492) at the age of 43 saved the judges from what might have been a particularly difficult decision.

MILAN

Within the duchy of Milan, meanwhile, the Sforza family sought to maintain its newly acquired power. Francesco (duke 1450–66) provided his subjects not only relative peace and patronage of humanism and the arts but also the disadvantages of tyrannical rule. His successor, the cruel and lustful Galeazzo Maria Sforza (1466–76), was assassinated in a conspiracy of three young men who combined personal grievances and republican sentiments. His son and heir, Gian Galeazzo, was a minor. In 1480 the regency government came under the control of Galeazzo's brother, Ludovico Sforza ("il Moro"), who ruled as duke from 1494 to 1499. Ludovico maintained the customary splendour of the Milanese court and employed, among many other artists and engineers, Leonardo da Vinci (who painted for him the *Last Supper* at Santa Maria delle Grazie) and Donato Bramante (architectural work at Sant'Ambrogio and Santa Maria delle Grazie). Yet under his rule, extravagant taxation, imposed largely to meet the cost of a virtually standing army, threatened the prosperity of the duchy, which derived from agricultural wealth, silk, and arms manufacture.

From 1463 to 1499 Milan also ruled Genoa. Bitter factional conflicts had, from the mid-14th century, eliminated Genoa as a political force and driven it to dependence on other powers. Yet, despite the advance of the Ottomans in the eastern Mediterranean, which threatened its colonies (Chios, Samos, and Lesbos in the Aegean; Caffa in the Crimea; and Tana at the head of the Sea of Azov), Genoa's economy still prospered. With the support of the Bank of San Giorgio, which served as a state treasury, the city moved toward its 16th-century eminence as one of the great European financial centres. Genoese émigrés (such as, notably, Christopher and Bartholomew Columbus), discouraged now from business in the East, looked to new fields of enterprise in the Iberian Peninsula. By 1492 the city's bankers were dominant in Spain, particularly in Sevilla (Seville), and had already financed a considerable part of the exploration and colonization of the Canary Islands.

THE FIRST FRENCH INVASION

Because the rulers of both France and Spain had dynastic claims in Italy, it was predictable that after the Hundred Years' War in France in 1453 and the conquest of Granada by Spain in 1492 both powers would make Italy the battlefield of their conflicting ambitions. In the event, it was an Italian who called the foreigners into Italy. Prince (later King) Ferdinand of Naples, angry that his grandson-in-law, Gian Galeazzo, duke of Milan, was excluded from power, threatened the regent, Ludovico. In reply, Ludovico successfully urged King Charles VIII of France to vindicate the claims of the French royal house to Naples. Charles's response was at first stunningly effective. He crossed the Alps in early September 1494 and marched south. At Florence, Lorenzo's successor, his son Piero de' Medici, had declared in favour of Ferdinand. But the rapid advance of the French forces demoralized him, and he sued for peace in November. Discredited by this failure, Piero was forced to flee from the anger of his fellow Florentines. Charles entered Rome on the last day of the year and Naples—which he conquered "with the chalk of his billeting officers"—on February 22, 1495. Yet his triumph was short-lived. Alarmed at this sudden increase in French strength, Ludovico, the emperor Maximilian I, the pope, and King Ferdinand II of Aragon came together in the League of Venice in March 1495 to combat Charles's power. Faced by these forces, Charles, leaving behind some of his troops in garrison, decided to return home. Crossing the Apennines at Cisa Pass, he met the army of the league blocking his passage at Fornovo. After an indecisive battle, the French army broke through into Lombardy and passed back to France.

Three years later, when Charles died, his campaign may have seemed merely a passing incident of no importance.

Yet by making Italy a battleground for foreign powers he had profoundly weakened the peninsular states, which now faced a series of invasions that subjected them to domination by "barbarians" (as the Italians were pleased now to call non-Italians). Florence, humiliated by defeat and weakened by the establishment of a new government, struggled to regain control of towns that had seized the occasion to throw off subjection. Naples, devastated by war, fell largely into the hands of Spanish troops. In Milan Ludovico now feared both domestic unpopularity and the accession to the French throne of Louis XII, who claimed to be heir to the Visconti. Venice, characteristically emerging with spoils from the imbroglio (the Neapolitan ports of Otranto, Brindisi, and Trani), was looking for new triumphs, while Pope Alexander VI was considering means to disrupt the peace of Italy on behalf of his son Cesare Borgia.

SAVONAROLA

The French invasion and defeat and the exile of the Medici gave particular prominence within the new republican regime of Florence to a friar, Girolamo Savonarola. The son of a prominent physician, Savonarola had been born at Ferrara, entered the Dominican order at Bologna at the age of 23, and rapidly acquired fame as a theologian and preacher. In the years 1482–85 he served in the convent of San Marco at Florence; he returned there at the express wish of Lorenzo de' Medici and became prior in 1491. In those years Savonarola preached conventional apocalyptic sermons warning of God's punishments that awaited Florentine sinners, including, notably, those guilty of evil in government.

Following the passage of Charles VIII's army, this message took on new forms. Drawing upon earlier Florentine mystical traditions, Savonarola now preached the doctrine that, in return for moral purification, Florence would soon become "the new Rome," enjoying power, dominion, and success in this world. This flattering teaching, which was especially appealing after Florence's humiliation, brought a wide circle of personal adherents (the Piagnoni, or "Wailers," as their opponents called them), who enthusiastically backed Savonarola's campaigns (not in themselves untypical of revivalist movements of the age) against gambling, blasphemy, and illicit sex. From 1497 Savonarola organized bands of young men to go from house to house to persuade their inhabitants to surrender those worldly possessions to which they were particularly attached, such as dice, books, paintings, and elegant dresses. Savonarola's followers then placed these "vanities" on a bonfire and solemnly dedicated their destruction to the Lord. In the controversy of 1495 as to what form of government should replace that of the Medici, Savonarola supported the party seeking the widest extension of popular participation. It is unlikely that Savonarola had any decisive influence on the political fortunes of the city; nonetheless, he came to be associated with the many failures of the government in those years and to be seen as an enemy by the parties of the Bigi (looking for the return of the Medici), the Arrabbiati (who hoped for a much more exclusive, less broadly based, republican government), and the Compagnacci (those who resented the puritanical way of life now imposed on the city). In particular, he attracted enemies through his unflinching support for an alliance with France, which isolated the commune in Italy but brought no response in loyalty from Charles VIII. His foreign-policy stance and his evangelical denunciation of the wickedness of the papacy aroused the hostility of Pope Alexander VI. In June 1497 the friar was excommunicated and commanded to remain silent. Defying this decree, Savonarola resumed preaching early in 1498 and included in his sermons appeals for a general council to reform the church. Such defiance, combined with a certain revulsion against the unrelenting moral crusade, led the secular government in April 1498 to turn against Savonarola. He was accused of heresy, tortured, and finally hanged and burned in the Piazza della Signoria (May 23).

Yet the contrast between the austerity of Savonarola's life and the licentiousness of the Borgia pope who condemned him, as well as the destiny that the friar had prophesied for the Florentines, lingered in the minds of many, including some of the city's most distinguished citizens, and in the last Florentine republic, of 1527–30, the memory of his exalted prophecies was still to sustain those who resisted the Medici and the emperor Charles V.

THE EARLY ITALIAN RENAISSANCE

Against this political and economic background stands the cultural development of Italy in the 14th and 15th centuries. The term Italian Renaissance has not gone unchallenged; its meaning and boundaries have aroused much controversy. From the 1340s the idea of "rebirth" was a commonplace in critical writing. Authors spoke of how, with Dante and Giotto, both poetry and painting had been "reborn," and in the following two centuries the same notion was often applied to other areas such as architecture, sculpture, and philosophy. In this period, "rebirth" was always used in connection with some intellectual or artistic skill; it was not until the 19th century that historians such as the French Jules Michelet and then, above all, the Swiss Jacob Burckhardt (whose *The Civilisation of the Renaissance in Italy* was first published in German at Basel, Switzerland, in 1860) began to write of the Renaissance as a period of time.

For Burckhardt this period consisted, broadly speaking, of the 15th century in Italy, a time and place in which "medieval" man became "modern" man. For him, the Italian of the 15th century was "the first-born among the sons of modern Europe." No historian today would hold to that definition. Nonetheless, the term, redefined, still enjoys overwhelming assent. For some historians (such as Lauro Martines), the Renaissance coincides with the life of the commune, stretching back to the 11th century; for others (such as Hans Baron), it sprang from the ideological battles that accompanied the wars of Florence and Milan at the beginning of the 15th century. A majority consensus, however, still conceives of the Italian Renaissance as a period of cultural history having no very sharp chronological boundaries but stretching over the years from about 1340 to about 1550.

HUMANISM

The early Renaissance had two principal characteristics. Of these the first is humanism, a term that did not carry the present-day ethical or antireligious sense but instead referred to the intensive study of a revived Classical antiquity. Humanism comprised an intense concern with the *studia humanitatis* ("studies of humanity")—that is, grammar, rhetoric, history, poetry, and moral philosophy as read in Classical Latin and, sometimes, Greek texts. As such, it represented not a philosophical system but rather an educational program that largely excluded those subjects taught in the universities: logic, natural philosophy, metaphysics, astronomy, medicine, law, and theology.

The origins of humanism date back to the Italy of the 1290s, in which one finds, in many cities, friends coming together informally to study the ancient world and attempting to reproduce something of the spirit of the Latin classics in their own writings. That the movement should have originated in Italy is not surprising. It was natural that Italians should look back to Rome, particularly since the ruins of Roman civilization still stood about them. In addition, the study of the great corpus of Roman law in the universities of Padua and Bologna led easily to a wish to understand the society that had produced it. Yet even beyond that, in the secular world of the city-states, where lay literates rather than clerics dominated intellectual life, the secular civilization of the Classical world had an irresistible appeal. It was not that the humanists were un-Christian, rather that their Christianity was a lay and, in some sense, secularized Christianity.

The movement advanced in the middle of the 14th century through the work of two men, eminent both as humanists and for their roles in Italian and European literature: Francesco Petrarca (Petrarch; 1304–74) and Giovanni Boccaccio (1313–75). It was consolidated at the end of the century, above all in Florence. Here in the 1390s the inspired teaching of the Byzantine Manuel Chrysoloras made the city the leading centre for the study of Classical Greek in Europe, while Coluccio Salutati (1331–1406) and Leonardo Bruni (1370–1444), both of whom served for some time as chancellors of the republic, claimed that the disciplines of humanism were particularly suitable for the service of the state as studies appropriate to the "active life" of a republican citizen.

Thenceforth humanism dominated intellectual life in the peninsula (and later in much of Europe), influencing vernacular literature, the writing of history, art, education, and style of life. During the 15th century, for the first time, Florentine Greek studies turned scholars from moral back to metaphysical philosophy. Marsilio Ficino (1433–99) translated all of Plato's writings, together with important Neoplatonic texts and the Greek mystical *Corpus Hermeticum*. From these sources he went on to develop his own philosophy of Christian Hermeticism, or Neoplatonism. Subsequently modified and developed by Giovanni Pico della Mirandola (1463–94), whose best-known essay bears the significant title *Oratio de hominis dignitate* (1486; *Oration on the Dignity of Man*), this philosophy, which argued that human beings could independently determine their own salvation by following the natural impulses of love and beauty, presented an immensely optimistic view of humanity and its place in the universe. It was to exercise a strong fascination, particularly over artists and poets, in the following hundred years.

THE ARTS AND INTELLECTUAL LIFE

Humanism does not by itself comprise the whole of the early Italian Renaissance, which should also be understood as a general intense efflorescence of all the arts and intellectual life. From the time of Dante and Giotto through that of the great trio of Donatello, Brunelleschi, and Masaccio at the beginning of the 15th century and on to the age of the High Renaissance, these years present a picture of extraordinary cultural power. In examining its social origins, it has been traditional to point to the economic wealth and early capitalist development of central and northern Italy. Certainly, that development allowed the financing of patronage, advanced literacy, and in many ways offered a new way of looking at the world. Yet high culture developed unevenly throughout the peninsula; for instance, in this period it was insignificant in the great port and thriving economic centre of Genoa. Therefore, wealth did not simply equate with cultural vitality.

It was, in fact, strong states (unlike Genoa) and the peculiar state system of Italy that lay behind most of the intense secular patronage and intellectual life in this period. In painting, sculpture, and architecture the leading patrons were governments, and the patrons' motives were a mixture of aesthetic response, civic pride, and propaganda. The communes took responsibility not only for

Lantern on top of the Cathedral of Santa Maria del Fiore (the Duomo) of Florence, designed by Filippo Brunelleschi, 1436; completed c. 1436–71. Robert Harding Picture Library

the *palazzi comunali*, or city halls, and other communal buildings but also for the building, interior furbishing, and maintenance of their cathedrals and other principal churches (in these, sometimes specifically excluding any ecclesiastical participation in the work). In the same spirit, republics and *signorie* engaged in town planning—in the destruction and reconstruction of town sites, in regulating building and use, and, through appointed conciliar committees, in the siting of new roads, squares, and fountains. At the same time, government involvement in the arts gave them an

The Palazzo Ducale, 1450–1510; in Pesaro, Italy. Shostal/Superstock

increasingly secular character. Political allegories and demands for identifiable portraits of lords or statesmen made new demands upon the artist and stimulated interest in the art of Classical Rome, whose heir the communes claimed to be.

Whether in the republics or the *signorie*, art had a major role as propaganda. Because Italy was divided into many states, political art was not centred at one court—as in England, Scotland, or France—but flourished in city-states throughout the peninsula. Because the states were in intense rivalry, art itself was enlisted in that rivalry. Thus, the fragmentation of Italy, which made it so vulnerable to foreigners in the last years of the 15th century, also contributed to its cultural supremacy. At the same time, the papacy played its own part in this development— particularly from the mid-15th century, when Pope Nicholas V made the first full-scale alliance between the papacy and humanism, planning "majestic buildings, combining taste and beauty" for Rome, to exalt the majesty of the Holy See.

CHAPTER 7

EARLY MODERN ITALY THROUGH UNIFICATION

The calamitous wars that convulsed the Italian peninsula for some four decades after the French invasion of 1494 were not, according to modern historians, the tragic aftermath of a lost world. Rather, they were a further elaboration and intensification of a violent age whose self-definition was transition. War reflected the wider European rivalries that made Italy a prize for plunder and a defensive bulwark against the Ottoman Turks, that led to the explorations and conquests of the New World and to new contacts with Asia, and that erupted into open divisions over religious belief. Above all, war propelled all of Europe into a new economic and demographic expansion that was to shift the centre of power from the garden of Italy in the Mediterranean to north-western Europe and its Atlantic world.

FRENCH AND SPANISH RIVALRIES AFTER 1494

The new political landscape after the 1494 invasion still reflected the contradictions and conflicts of the medieval political past. Rivalries of status, class, family, and neighbourhood continued unabated in the cities of both republics and principalities. Territorial states grew, and their urban capitals dominated neighbouring rural hinterlands even more than in previous decades. And, although independent action by the Italian states now had to yield to powerful initiatives from the newly unified monarchies of France and Spain,

A 19th-century painting depicting French King Charles VIII entering the city of Naples in 1495.
Universal Images Group/Getty Images

such foreign intervention echoed the policies of their medieval Angevin and Aragonese forebears.

The French were not expelled from Naples. Charles VIII left Naples as freely in May 1495 as he had entered it a few months earlier. But an anti-French league led by Venetian and Spanish troops was needed to recover the kingdom for Ferdinand II of Naples (ruled 1495–96). When Spanish naval action cut the supply lines of the embattled French garrisons that had been left behind, a preliminary armistice in 1497 ended the fighting.

The Italian states took advantage of the disequilibrium caused by the invasions for their own territorial aggrandizement. Venice, already more powerful than any of the other Italian states, gained the most. It occupied several important ports in Puglia with the intent of appropriating them, backed Pisa in its long though ultimately unsuccessful revolt against Florence (ending in 1509), and supported the conquest of Milan in 1499 by Louis XII (ruled 1498–1515), the new king of France, in exchange for Cremona and its hinterland.

Louis XII had not given up French pretensions to the Kingdom of Naples, and the acquisition of Milan strengthened his supply position. Powerful aristocrats within the kingdom, led by the pro-French princes of Sanseverino in Calabria, fomented dissension and weakened the already tenuous rule of King Frederick (1496–1501) to the point that both the French and Spanish saw an opportunity to satisfy their ambitions. In the Treaty of Granada (1500) they agreed to invade and partition the kingdom between them into a northern French sphere of the Abruzzi and Campania (including the city of Naples) and a southern Spanish sphere of Calabria and Puglia. Yet the most wily diplomat of the age, Ferdinand II (the Catholic) of Aragon, the king of Spain, hoped not only to forestall French ascendancy and outsmart Louis XII in Italy but also to assert his own claims as the legitimate heir to the Aragonese empire founded by Alfonso V (the Magnanimous) in 1442. In addition, he hoped to resist Ottoman advances that were threatening his possession of Sicily.

In 1501 a French and Spanish invasion divided the Kingdom of Naples according to plan, and Frederick of Naples lived out his life in French exile together with his faithful servant, the great Neapolitan poet Jacopo Sannazzaro. When hostilities broke out in Puglia in 1503 over the large revenues of the sheep customhouse at Foggia, Spanish forces under Gonzalo Fernández de Córdoba (the "Great Captain") outfought the French and occupied the entire Kingdom of Naples by the end of that year. France abandoned its claim to Naples in 1505. During the next 30 years Naples spearheaded Spanish policy in Italy.

During the first decade after the French invasions, Tuscany, the Romagna, and the Marche also underwent political upheavals. The Medici were expelled from Florence in 1494, and Savonarola's powerful sermons inspired a theocratic state. Tuscan cities that the French had liberated from Florentine rule continued their revolt. After Savonarola's execution in 1498, an oligarchic republic was created under the authority of Piero di Tommaso Soderini (ruled 1498–1512; elected gonfaloniere for life in 1502).

Meanwhile, Cesare Borgia, the natural son of Pope Alexander VI, attempted to carve out a dynastic state for himself in the Romagna and the Marche. As the model for political theorist Niccolò Machiavelli's prince, Cesare Borgia had prepared assiduously to seize power upon his father's death. But his plans were thwarted by bad fortune: at the very moment when decisive action was required, he himself was deathly ill. A college of cardinals caught between Spanish and French interests hastily elected a new pope, Pius III, who, however, died only 26 days later. His successor, Julius II (reigned 1503–13), had to win back by force of arms the territories in east-central Italy up to Bologna that Cesare Borgia had taken from the Papal States.

In order to reconquer the lost papal lands, Julius II organized an anti-Venetian alliance, the League of Cambrai (1508). All the great powers of Italy, along with those across the Alps—the Holy Roman Empire, France, and Spain—joined forces to defeat the Venetians at Agnadello (May 14, 1509). But dissension among the victorious allies, who were manipulated by skillful Venetian diplomacy, turned the alliance against France because that kingdom now seemed to be the greatest power in Italy. A Holy League, organized in 1511 to curtail French power in Lombardy, restored the Medici in Florence in 1512 with the help of Spanish arms and allowed Venice to keep its old *terra ferma* (mainland) empire (without its recent acquisitions in Lombardy, the Romagna, and Puglia). Nonetheless, Agnadello profoundly shook Venetian self-confidence and remained the turning point in the republic's imperial ambitions in mainland Italy.

At the same time, Louis XII enjoyed his greatest triumphs, including the defeat of Julius II's Holy League at Ravenna (April 11, 1512). But, with the death of his brilliant general Gaston de Foix in that battle, the French suffered an irreparable loss. Further, in May 1512, 20,000 Swiss troops entered Italy on the papal side, and the French army was recalled to repel invasions of Navarre (Navarra) by the Spanish and of Normandy and Guyenne by the English. Francis I (ruled 1515–47), who succeeded his cousin and father-in-law, Louis XII, reopened hostilities in Italy. His army of 40,000 men defeated the Swiss at Marignano (September 13–14, 1515), which allowed him to retake Milan. The new pope, Leo X (reigned 1513–21), who was a Medici and a dependent of Spain, hurried to secure peace. Within the year, the new king of Spain, Charles I (ruled 1516–56), who had succeeded his maternal grandfather, Ferdinand II, as coruler because of his mother's insanity, signed the Peace of Noyon (August 13, 1516), which gave Milan to France and confirmed Naples for Spain. The peace would not endure, however, as local Italian affairs became subordinated to the dynastic struggle between the young heirs to Habsburg and Valois (the ruling French dynasty) fortunes and to the Reformation movement that intertwined religion and politics into the 17th century.

THE AGE OF CHARLES V

Charles I, who was elected Holy Roman Emperor Charles V in 1519 upon the death of his paternal grandfather, Maximilian, aspired to universal monarchy over the far-flung territories he had inherited, from Germany, the Low Countries, Italy, and Spain to the New World. The Piedmontese humanist Mercurino de

Gattinara, Charles's chancellor from 1518 to 1530, fueled his ambitions, but the providential design for Charles to be a new Charlemagne collided with political realities. The revolt of the *comuneros* (1520–21), an uprising of a group of Spanish cities, was successfully quelled, securing Castile as the bedrock of his empire, but the opposition of Francis I of France, of Süleyman I (the Magnificent; ruled 1520–66) of the Ottoman Empire, and of the Lutheran princes in Germany proved more intractable.

Early success in Italy, nevertheless, provided Charles with the most important base outside Spain for exercising his

A 16th-century tapestry depicting the Battle of Pavia in 1525, considered to be the decisive battle of the war in Italy between Francis I of France and Charles V. DEA/A. Dagli Orti/De Agostini/Getty Images

power. Imperial troops forced the French to retreat from Milan and restored the Sforza in 1522. When a refitted French army of 30,000 men retook Milan in 1524, the new Medici pope, Clement VII (reigned 1523–34), changed sides to become a French ally. But at the most important battle of the Italian wars, fought at Pavia on February 24, 1525, the French were defeated and Francis I was captured. Soon after his release, he abrogated the Treaty of Madrid (January 1526), in which he had been forced, among other concessions, to abandon his Italian claims. He headed a new anti-Spanish alliance, the Holy League of Cognac (May 1526), which united France with the papacy, Milan, Florence, and Venice. With no French forces in the field, some 12,000 of Charles's imperial troops, largely unpaid Lutheran infantry, marched south to Rome. On May 6, 1527, they attacked and sacked the city, forcing the pope to take refuge in the Castel Sant'Angelo. The repercussions of this chastisement of the corrupt church were heard throughout Europe, and some scholars still date the end of the Renaissance in Italy to this event.

New military technologies in siegecraft (cannon and bastion) and new techniques in open-field engagements (mixing pike and harquebus) not only transformed the nature of warfare but also threatened the order of a society still dominated by an aristocratic military caste. In the course of the Italian wars, the non-noble infantry adopted tactical innovations that unseated the cavalry of heavily armoured nobility, which had dominated medieval warfare. Charles VIII's invading army employed the Swiss pike phalanx, whose moving squares of 6,000 men had already developed the ability to engage in offensive as well as defensive maneuvers. In the fighting against France for the Kingdom of Naples, Fernández de Córdoba first developed the Spanish *tercios*, more-flexible units of 3,000 infantrymen using both pikes and harquebuses. Spanish military superiority eventually owed its success to the introduction in 1521 of the musket (an improved harquebus) and to the refinement of pike and musket tactics in the years preceding the Battle of Pavia. Such tactics dominated land warfare until the Battle of Rocroi in 1643.

The new social composition of the enlarged infantry, as well as the need for large quantities of metal and the financial requirements for equipping and launching an army, pushed military affairs further into royal hands, strengthening the growing power of the central monarchy at the expense of the aristocracy. Commoners could forge a new relationship directly with royal authority. They could also, as in the case of the republics, create new images of citizenly power. In 1503 the Florentine republic, for example, planned two monumental mural paintings for the Great Council Hall of the Palazzo Vecchio (town hall) to be executed by two of the giants of High Renaissance art, Leonardo da Vinci and Michelangelo.

The former's *Battle of Anghiari* and the latter's *Battle of Cascina*, if completed, would have emphasized the strength and righteous rage of republican virtue and the necessity for citizens to be vigilant, challenging them to retake Pisa and subdue Tuscany during the republic's ongoing wars. Ludovico Ariosto, singing his epic poetry at the chivalric pro-French court of Ferrara, lamented the loss of glory, honour, valour, and courage to the "wretched and foul invention" of firearms. Even 20 years after the fact, when the diplomat and writer Baldassare Castiglione nostalgically portrayed the graceful court of Urbino of 1508 in *The Courtier* (1528), he did so in order to instruct courtiers and court ladies on how to adapt their roles to the changing times.

In the immediate wake of the sack of Rome and the consequent disgrace of the Medici papacy, the Florentines expelled their Medici overlords. A French army under General Odet de Foix Lautrec finally arrived in 1528, but Andrea Doria, a Genoese admiral and aristocrat whose galleys had formerly been in the service of the French, unexpectedly switched sides and became a staunch supporter of Charles V. Plague took Lautrec's life and decimated the French army, and in 1529 the pope was forced to make peace with Charles in the Treaty of Barcelona—as did Francis I in the Treaty of Cambrai. After almost 40 years of war, Italy submitted to Spanish pacification. Francis I renounced his claims in Italy, as well as in Artois and Flanders. The last Sforza was restored in Milan with the provision that the duchy would pass to Spain upon his death. Venice lost its recent mainland conquests. The Papal States were restored, and in 1530 the pope crowned Charles V emperor and king of Italy and made vague promises to call a council to address the Protestant schism and reform the church. In exchange, Spanish forces reinstated the Medici in Florence.

Italy remained subject to sporadic French incursions into Savoy in 1536–38 and 1542–44 during a third and fourth Habsburg-Valois war, and Spain's Italian possessions were increasingly taxed to support Charles's continual campaigns; however, for the remainder of his reign, Charles's armies fought the French, the Ottomans, and the Protestant princes outside Italy. Notable for Italy was Charles V's capture of Tunis in 1535 and his glorious march up the Italian peninsula in 1536 to confirm his personal rule. But the Ottomans formally allied themselves with France against the Habsburgs thereafter, defeated an allied fleet at Prevesa, retook Tunis in 1538, and stepped up their assault on the Venetian empire in the Mediterranean. With the eventual failure of Charles's attempts to secure Germany, his great continental empire was divided. Italy became a part of the Spanish Habsburg inheritance of his son, Philip II (ruled 1556–98), and, after the Spanish victory over the French at St. Quentin (1557), the Peace of Cateau-Cambrésis (1559) officially confirmed the era of Spanish domination that had existed in Italy since 1530.

SPANISH ITALY

Spain thus established complete hegemony over all the Italian states except Venice, which alone maintained its independence. Several Italian states were ruled directly, while others remained Spanish dependents. Naples, Sicily, and Sardinia (which had all been dependencies of Aragon), as well as Milan, came under direct Spanish rule and owed their allegiance to the sovereign according to their own laws and traditions. Their foreign policy interests were subordinated to the imperial designs of Spain, which also appointed their chief officers (viceroys in Naples, Palermo, and Cagliari; a governor in Milan) and administered their internal affairs through local councils. From the beginning of Philip II's reign, Italian affairs, which had originally been administered by the Council of Aragon, were coordinated by a Council of Italy in Madrid. At this council, the three major states—Naples, Sicily, and Milan—were each represented by two regents, one Castilian and one native. Sardinia remained a dependency of Aragon. The king, however, continued to receive and be responsive to embassies sent by various groups outside official channels until the Spanish Habsburg line died out in 1700.

A vitriolic anti-Spanish polemic has long dominated the historiography of early modern Italy. It accuses Spanish rule of an authoritarianism closed to new ideas and innovation, of presiding over an empty formalism in literary expression, and of promoting *spagnolismo*, an exaggerated and ostentatious pomp—all perceived as the fruits of a decadent, backward-looking colonial domination. Faulting Spain for trying to integrate Italy within its absolutist and imperial program or blaming Italy's 17th-century decline on Spanish social and economic policies has served nationalistic fervour since the 16th century, but it has missed both the benefits of Spanish rule to Italian peace and security and the main causes of crisis in 17th-century Italy. To understand the latter, one must examine the internal conflicts and economic impediments that existed within the Italian states themselves rather than look to an absentee Spanish scapegoat. And, above all, early modern Italy must be understood in a wider European context and in relation to the economic shifts wrought by the new Asian and American trade. The touchstone for modern scholarship is Fernand Braudel's *The Mediterranean and the Mediterranean World in the Age of Philip II* (1949), which continues to inspire and challenge research into Philip II's empire and beyond.

THE KINGDOM OF NAPLES

Pedro de Toledo (viceroy 1532–53) reorganized the Kingdom of Naples and placed it firmly within the Spanish monarchical orbit dominated by Castile. Within the kingdom, he oversaw the eradication of the pro-French barons and attempted to install centralized, absolutist policies. Within the city, he developed new residential quarters and strengthened Spanish defenses against outside attack. He enjoyed unparalleled personal prestige; his daughter Eleonora was married to Cosimo I (the Great), the Medici duke of Tuscany, in 1539. But his power had limits, as was shown by the successful Neapolitan opposition to the introduction of the Inquisition in 1547. Pedro's policy was governed by the principle of "divide and conquer," which played upon rampant inequalities between the barons and the people and between the capital and the countryside.

The most important ruling body in the kingdom was the Collateral Council, comprising five regents presided over by the viceroy, with a judicial council and a financial council exercising their respective competencies at its side. A new elite of lawyers, a "nobility of the robe," began to emerge, sustaining the Spanish regime with its indispensable bureaucratic services. The Neapolitan parliament, which consisted of representatives of the city districts (*seggi*), of the feudal nobility, and of royally owned towns, had only two functions—to authorize taxes and to request rights and privileges from the king in exchange—but this body was suspended in 1642.

In the capital the town council, which seated representatives of the city's five noble *seggi* and of a citywide commoners' *seggio*, emerged as the most important institution of municipal government. The most pressing problem facing the city administration was the provision of food. Naples had grown to 250,000 inhabitants by 1600, which ranked it first in population among the cities of western Europe.

In the countryside, where some 90 percent of the population still lived, the aristocracy retained strong social and economic control. The Spanish government's bureaucracy did attempt to break the barons' political stronghold and to limit the worst abuses, but success depended upon a healthy economy and an emerging middle class, both of which began to falter after 1585. The 12 provinces of the kingdom remained atomized, and their unarticulated markets were often attached to the trading networks of foreign states such as Venice or Genoa rather than integrated to form a national market within the kingdom itself.

THE KINGDOM OF SICILY

Sicily's administration had existed apart from that of the mainland since 1282, when the island had revolted against Angevin rule and come under the Aragonese crown. In the 16th century Sicily remained the cornerstone of the Spanish Mediterranean policy against the Ottomans, and its agricultural products continued to be the staple of long-distance trade.

As in Naples, Spanish policy in Sicily attempted to modify traditional baronial abuses. Spain allowed the barons considerable autonomy over their large agrarian estates, including the exploitation of their tenant farmers, but it prevented open feuds between barons and eroded their political power by excluding them from offices in the central government. Two local councils, one in judicial affairs and the other in public finance and administration, centralized Spanish government from the reign of Charles V. Parliament and the Inquisition competed for power with the viceroy. Parliament, which comprised three branches—clergy, nobility, and royal towns and districts—voted ordinary and special taxes, but its short and infrequent sessions prevented sustained opposition to Spanish policies. The Inquisition, on the other hand, was completely independent of the viceroy and often challenged his jurisdiction, but it received royal backing only in purely religious disputes. Above all, Spain played internal rivalries and sectional interests against one another for its own advantage. Constant struggles weakened all parties, and the numerous autonomous authorities held civil government in such check that it became immobilized and unable to make important decisions.

SARDINIA

Sardinia's links to the kingdom of Aragon dated from the 14th century. Longstanding assimilation to Spanish culture had reinforced the patriarchal structure of the local nobility, whose chief source of wealth was sheep raising. As in Naples and Sicily, the Spanish introduced little change into government, preferring instead to support an aristocratic-monarchist regime. The viceroy was often a Sardinian, the native parliament had three branches, and international politics separated Sardinia from Italian affairs.

THE DUCHY OF MILAN

When Francesco II Sforza died childless in 1535, Milan devolved to Charles V and was administered by a Spanish governor, who maintained traditional institutions. The duchy consisted of nine provinces, each dominated by a small group of families resident in their provincial capitals. Central administration from Milan rested primarily with the Senate, a judicial and legislative body that maintained its authority under Spanish rule despite inevitable confrontations with the governor. Official Spanish policy aimed at maintaining an equilibrium between centralization and home rule.

Two institutional changes, nevertheless, had significant effects upon the society of Milanese Lombardy. First, by 1584 the membership of the Senate was reduced from 28 to 15 as well as altered in its composition; whereas half of its members had been aristocratic landowners and high-ranking clerics, they now were all professional lawyers. As in Naples, the nobility of the robe, who in Milan were lawyers drawn from the urban patriciate, grew at the expense of the old landed nobility and formed an essential alliance with the Spanish crown.

Second, tax reforms aimed at marshaling Milanese resources for the Spanish wars affected the society of the duchy, not only in equalizing the tax burden but also in redistributing power between city and countryside. Merchants, who had previously been tax-exempt, found their wealth (based on annual gross sales) taxed after 1594, and landowners not residing in cities, who had previously been taxed far above city dwellers, benefited from a new assessment system set by elected bodies of rural residents after 1561. These policies had unexpected long-term effects in the 17th century when economic interests were able to regroup and find a foothold in the countryside.

Milan's strategic importance as the gateway to Italy remained a keystone of Spain's imperial design, and, with war and revolt north of the Alps, Milan served as a critical staging area for men and supplies on the "Spanish road" from Genoa to Lombardy and from there through the Alpine passes to the Rhineland. During the Revolt of the Netherlands (1567), the Netherlands' Eighty Years' War (1568–1648) for independence, and the Thirty Years' War (1618–48), Milan was a focal point of Spanish military preparation.

The Roman Catholic Church had unusual influence and autonomy in Milan. Charles Cardinal Borromeo, member of a rich noble family of Milan and nephew of Pope Pius IV (reigned 1559–65), resided in his diocese after 1565 as the model bishop of the Catholic Reformation. He instituted seminaries, diocesan synods, and provincial councils, personally visited some 800 parishes, watched over the spiritual needs of monasteries, convents, and lay confraternities, fought heresy, and supported relief of the poor. Moreover, under his rule the Milanese church enjoyed unusual freedom of action and special privileges in furthering Catholic reform.

PRINCIPATES AND OLIGARCHIC REPUBLICS

Spanish hegemony in Italy extended beyond the states under its direct control. The rulers of Savoy and Tuscany owed their titles to Spain, Genoa acted as Spain's chief banker, the papacy depended heavily on the Spanish monarchy in the age of the Counter-Reformation, and even independent Venice needed Spanish aid in protecting its Mediterranean empire from further erosion by the Turks. Several minor states were so small that they had little political influence; these included the republic of Lucca as well as several duchies that remained under the control of local noble families—the duchies of Modena, Reggio, and Ferrara under the Este family; the duchy of Mantua and Montferrat under the Gonzagas, and the duchy of Parma and Piacenza under the Farnese. These states, too, enjoyed the enforced Spanish peace within Italy and benefited from the security against foreign invasion. Their nobility intermarried with the Spanish aristocracy and absorbed Spanish culture.

SAVOY AND TUSCANY

During the Italian wars, France and Spain had occupied Savoy, a duchy that incorporated most of the present-day Piedmont, between France and the duchy of Milan. Allied with the victorious Spanish at the battle of St. Quentin (1557), its legitimate heir, Duke Emmanuel Philibert (ruled 1559–80), recovered his state with the Peace of Cateau-Cambrésis (1559) and began to rebuild and strengthen it. He transfered the capital across the Alps from Chambéry to Turin, which grew as a fortified and planned city. He limited the power of numerous localities and centralized state finances. Increased taxes and economic recovery allowed him to maintain a small but disciplined standing army, which became the basis of Piedmontese military power. His son Charles Emmanuel I (ruled 1580–1630) followed an expansionist policy with varying success. In 1589 he failed to take Geneva, and in 1601 he ceded some territory to France in exchange for the marquessate of Saluzzo. He also engaged in debilitating wars in an unsuccessful quest to take Montferrat.

When Spanish arms restored the Medici to Florence in 1530, they bestowed on them the title "dukes of Tuscany." After the assassination of the first duke, Alessandro, in 1537, Cosimo I (ruled 1537–74) succeeded him and developed a strong absolutist state. As a Spanish ally, Cosimo fought Siena (1552–55) and annexed it in 1557. The Spanish, however, retained five strategically important seaports, the Stato dei Presidi ("State of the Garrisons"), which were administered by Spanish Naples.

In 1569 Cosimo received the title grand duke of Tuscany. His sons Francis I (ruled 1574–87) and Ferdinand I (ruled 1587–1609) succeeded him, and the latter enlarged the free port of Livorno. In the early modern period the city of Florence had only about one-half of its medieval population, and it receded from the international scene, becoming the capital of a provincial court.

THE REPUBLIC OF GENOA

In 1528 Andrea Doria initiated a constitutional reform by which nobles loyal to him gained power. Factionalism continued, however, especially between the "old" and "new" nobility. When serious disorders erupted in 1575, the old nobility abandoned the city, and a popular faction took their place beside the new nobility. A compromise mediated by Spain and the papacy averted civil war by reconstituting the ruling class. Wealth replaced status as the basis of social stratification and political alliance.

Andrea Doria's support of Charles V bolstered Spain's naval profile in the western Mediterranean. Genoa continued its control over Corsica through its central bank, the Bank of San Giorgio. Genoese bankers, who had extended their family businesses from Naples to Sevilla, replaced the German Fuggers as the primary financiers of the Spanish empire. At home, nobles invested in landed property and city residences, while silk manufacturing employed a large percentage of the Genoese working class.

THE REPUBLIC OF VENICE

Defeat at Agnadello in 1509, followed by pressure from the Spanish Habsburgs in Lombardy and the Austrian Habsburgs to the north of the republic, limited Venice's Italian mainland empire. In addition, Ottoman expansion in the eastern Mediterranean disrupted Venice's trade in the Levant and chipped away at its overseas empire: lost were important ports of call in Albania and Greece in 1503, the Aegean islands north of Crete in 1540, Cyprus in 1571, and Crete itself in 1669. At the same time, Portuguese trade with Asia after 1498 and the rise of the Dutch city of Antwerp as an entrepôt for the distribution of goods to northern Europe seriously challenged Venice's trading monopoly. No longer the most powerful state in Italy, Venice still enjoyed internal cohesion, an extremely effective diplomatic corps, and a strong fleet to navigate an independent policy between Spain and the papacy.

Before the plague of 1576, Venice's population had risen to 180,000, with a patriciate of under 5 percent. A strong oligarchic tendency during the 16th century reinforced the power of the Council of Ten over the Senate, and the cleavage between rich and poor nobles widened. After 1583, however, the old nobility lost its bid to monopolize politics, and the Senate recovered power, which it applied to a more independent foreign policy. Textile manufacturing remained the most important trade until the precipitous decline of the woolen industry in the early 17th century. Venice's population stabilized at about 150,000.

In 1606 a papal interdict condemned Venice for refusing to repeal several laws limiting the church's traditional rights and for trying two priests in civil rather than ecclesiastical courts. Paolo Sarpi, the republic's state theologian, mounted an effective defense by arguing for state sovereignty in temporal affairs. The dispute ended in a compromise, mediated by France and Spain. Sarpi's *The History of the Council of Trent* (1619) later indicted the pope for usurping ecclesiastical authority and for manipulating the reform council to reinforce his power.

THE PAPAL STATES

The papacy engaged in often flamboyant political maneuvers, especially during the reign of Julius II (1503–13), and in the architectural and intellectual renewal of Rome. Save for the brief reign of the last non-Italian pope before the 20th century, Adrian VI (reigned 1522–23), the papacy failed to respond to the spiritual crisis of the day. However, a predisposition for a religious revival, or Catholic Reformation, was fostered

Painting by Titian depicting Pope Paul III (seated), who encouraged reform efforts within the Roman Catholic Church in the 16th century. The Bridgeman Art Library/Getty Images

by the Christian humanist Erasmus of Rotterdam's biblical philosophy of Christ, by prophetic and apocalyptic interpretations of the Italian wars, and by an awareness of long-standing clerical abuses. Yet serious attempts at reform from above did not begin until the reign of Pope Paul III (1534–49). In 1536 he appointed a reform commission, which produced the important blueprint *Consilium de emendanda ecclesia* ("Project for the Reform of the Church"), and in 1537 he made the first attempt at convoking a reform council. By the 1540s, however, hopes for reunification of Catholics and Protestants had foundered. A true Counter-Reformation—that is, the Roman Catholic Church's conscious fight against Protestantism—began to take shape with papal approval of the Jesuit order in 1540 and with the creation of the Holy Office of the Inquisition in 1542. New religious orders such as the Theatines (1524), the Capuchins (1528), and the Jesuits (1534) provided the backbone of the new class of religious leaders, although the apostasy to Calvinism in 1542 of Bernardino Ochino, vicar-general of the Capuchins, was a serious setback. The Jesuits' educational program, above all, began to prepare laymen of high social status for leadership roles. The Council of Trent (1545–63) uncompromisingly defined Catholic dogma and outlined a program for disciplinary reform and administrative centralization. The *Index librorum prohibitorum* (1559; "Index of Forbidden Books"), a list of books condemned by the Roman Catholic Church as pernicious to faith and morals, was compiled by a censorship board that limited orthodox expression to a narrowly controlled range.

In politics, the papacy was dependent on Spain yet eager to find an alternative to Spanish domination in Italy. Although ecclesiastical reform occupied most of the church's energies, Pope Pius V (reigned 1566–72) promoted the Holy League, which checked Ottoman expansion into the western Mediterranean by defeating the Ottoman fleet at Lepanto (1571). Under Pope Gregory XIII (reigned 1572–85) the Julian calendar was reformed into the modern Gregorian calendar. Pope Sixtus V (reigned 1585–90) launched a Catholic missionary counteroffensive in central Europe and reorganized the Roman Curia. He, along with Clement VIII (reigned 1592–1605), also patronized the urban development and new artistic flowering in Rome that culminated in the Baroque creations of Gian Lorenzo Bernini and the architect Francesco Borromini. These two popes also fought rural banditry and brought Ferrara, Urbino, and Castro back under direct papal rule.

CULTURE AND SOCIETY

Cities and courts spawned the high culture of late Renaissance Italy. Ranging from Pietro Aretino's merciless lampoons of the scandalous lives of the princes of the church in Renaissance Rome to the mysticism and Christocentric piety embraced by the intellectual circle surrounding the Spanish humanist Juan de Valdés in Naples, Italian culture in the 16th century defined itself for or against the church. Niccolò Machiavelli, in a famous chapter of *Discorsi sopra la prima deca di tito Livio* (1513–19; "Discourses on the First Ten Books of Livy"), argued that the church was the cause of Italian ills because it had lost its religious moorings and had kept the Italians politically divided. A rigid Counter-Reformation orthodoxy, however, condemned some of Italy's most brilliant intellectuals—philosophers and scientists such as Giordano Bruno, who was burned as a heretic in 1600, Tommaso Campanella, who was imprisoned in 1599 for 27 years, and Galileo Galilei, who was forced to recant his Copernican beliefs and was placed under permanent house arrest in 1633.

At the same time, however, Italy was at the forefront of a movement that fostered scientific exchange by establishing scientific academies—the Roman Accademia dei Lincei (founded in 1603), the Florentine Accademia del Cimento (1657), and the Neapolitan Accademia degli Investiganti (1665). In fields such as drama (both tragedy and comedy), music (both religious and secular), art history, rhetoric, and political theory, Italians of the late Renaissance played formative roles—the poets Torquato Tasso and Giambattista Marino, the composers Giovanni Pierluigi da Palestrina and

NICCOLÒ MACHIAVELLI

Italian statesman, historian, and political theorist Niccolò Machiavelli (born May 3, 1469, Florence, Italy—died June 21, 1527, Florence) rose to power after the overthrow of Girolamo Savonarola in 1498. Working as a diplomat for 14 years, Machiavelli came in contact with the most powerful figures in Europe. He was dismissed when the Medici family returned to power in 1512, and during the next year he was arrested and tortured for conspiracy. Though soon released, he was not permitted to return to public office. His famous treatise *The Prince* (1513, published 1532) is a handbook for rulers; though dedicated to Lorenzo de' Medici, ruler of Florence from 1513, it failed to win Machiavelli his favour. Machiavelli viewed *The Prince* as an objective description of political reality. Because he viewed human nature as venal, grasping, and thoroughly self-serving, he suggested that ruthless cunning is appropriate to the conduct of government. Though admired for its incisive brilliance, the book also has been widely condemned as cynical and amoral, and "Machiavellian" has come to mean deceitful, unscrupulous, and manipulative. His other works include a set of discourses on Livy (completed *c.* 1518), the comedy *The Mandrake* (completed *c.* 1518), *The Art of War* (published 1521), and the *Florentine Histories* (completed *c.* 1525).

Claudio Monteverdi, the artist and art historian Giorgio Vasari, and the political theorist and statesman Giovanni Botero, to name just a few. These examples demonstrate the continuity of Italy's cultural achievement in the period that followed the High Renaissance.

SOCIETY AND ECONOMY

The expanding demographic and economic base of Italy provided the wherewithal for the political and cultural programs of the 16th century. From the mid-15th-century demographic low point after the 1347–48 plague, Italy, along with the rest of western Europe, recovered dramatically. Between 1400 and 1600 the Italian population nearly doubled, increasing from about 7 million to about 13 million, and prices rose sharply, with cereal prices tripling and quadrupling. Increased demand, the increased supply of money from the silver of the New World, and profligate military expenditures fueled high inflation. Italy's most distinctive feature was its highly urbanized life. In 1550, 30 cities—more than in any other region in the West—had populations of more than 10,000.

Rural areas nevertheless still accounted for almost 88 percent of the total population, and, given the relative parity in birth and death rates, cities grew primarily as a result of rural emigration. Wheat and wool were the chief agricultural products, and the spread of capitalist agriculture in the 16th century was an important ingredient in the transition from feudalism to capitalism. Textile production of both woolens and silks continued to be the major industry in the cities, but the precocious economic development of Italy in manufacturing, trade, and finance came to a crashing halt during the dislocations of the 17th century.

The economic recovery of the second half of the 16th century challenged the traditional hierarchical ordering of society. Nobility and clergy, the two most identifiable groups, did not lose their status but slowly changed character. With the demise of old families and the rise of a new nobility based on wealth and public service, social mobility in the cities put the old aristocracy on the defensive until it was able to forge new alliances with the ruling princes and the bourgeois bankers and merchants. At the same time, demographic growth and a yawning gap between wages and prices threatened to create an even larger disparity between rich and poor. In good times, the lower classes could provide a new labour market, fueling industrial production; in economically bad times, however, sickness, unemployment, and the rising price of bread could drive them down into the vortex of poverty and even push them to the point of rebellion.

THE 17TH-CENTURY CRISIS

The economic boom of the late 16th century began to stall throughout Europe.

Engraved illustration showing a doctor dressed in protective gear, complete with birdlike mask, meant to protect the wearer against the plague. Hulton Archive/Getty Images

The first signs of hardship appeared in Italy after 1585, and famine persisted through the 1590s. New waves of plague struck northern Italy and Tuscany in 1630–31 and southern Italy, Lazio, and Genoa in 1656–57, with population losses between one-fourth and one-fifth, respectively. The large cities of Milan, Naples, and Genoa lost as much as half of their population. In addition, war in northern Europe after 1618 and in the Middle East between the Ottomans and the Iranians from 1623–39 disrupted Italy's important export markets; war between Spanish, German, French, and Piedmontese forces moved to Italy between 1628 and 1659; and social conflicts within the Spanish states contributed to the decline of Italy relative to northwestern Europe.

Both agricultural production and urban industries entered into crisis in the decade 1611–20, reaching their low point about 1650. In the south, extensive wheat monoculture exhausted the soil and led to deforestation and soil erosion. Further, noble owners drained off profits for expenditures on urban luxuries, and indebtedness placed commercial grain farmers at greater risk as grain prices fell in the 17th century. In the north, intensive agriculture supported the numerous large cities, but overexpansion onto unproductive land, soil depletion, and the loss of credit pushed the region to the limits of what the population could support. In the cities, wool manufacturing fell by 50 percent in the 1620s and all but disappeared thereafter, although silk production held its own. Commercial

and banking activities, once the fastest-growing industries, now constricted, and foreign imports braked further development at home. Italy's early industrial lead lost to increased competition from northwestern Europe as new products at lower prices replaced the traditional ones in the Italian markets. The Italian guilds' opposition to technological and organizational change, higher taxes, and higher labour costs prevented the adaptability required to surmount the short-term crisis, which instead turned into a long-term structural realignment. Only in Lombardy was there a successful shift to the putting-out system, which transfered urban industries to the countryside.

The economic involution reinforced the social hierarchy, favoured investment in landed property and rents over commerce and industry, and reinvigorated noble pretensions. With capital shifted from the manufacturing and service sectors to agricultural production of cash crops such as olive oil, wine, and raw silk, the number of skilled urban craftsmen and merchants decreased while that of illiterate peasants increased, and landed-noble power intensified. The church reasserted itself in every aspect of social life, from land ownership to ecclesiastical organization, from the defense of orthodoxy and the culture of the Council of Trent to the education of the ruling class. As the economic crisis deepened, middling ranks lost out, and social stratification between rich and poor rigidified.

In the political sphere, Spain's involvement in the Thirty Years' War

(1618–48) and subsequent wars with other European powers—financed in part by taxes on its Italian possessions—drained Italy. As Spain declined, it dragged its Italian realms down with it. Revolts broke out in Palermo and Naples in 1647. In Naples a revolt of July 7 was mistakenly identified as a plebeian rebellion bearing the name of a young fishmonger, Masaniello, although he was murdered within 10 days and had actually been a tool of bourgeois elements seeking greater political power in the city. The uprising spread to the countryside, established a republic that sought French protection, and assumed the character of an open rebellion against Spain and native feudal lords. Internal dissension and the arrival of the Spanish fleet brought an end to the revolt by April 1648. The social and economic crisis deepened in Naples after the failure of the revolt and a recurrence of the plague in 1656. Lost was any hope of an alliance between the middle classes and the urban proletariat or rural masses against the landed aristocracy. Paradoxically, renewed Spanish reliance on the nobility of the robe fostered the very class that was to lead the cultural renewal that made Naples one of the intellectual centres of 18th-century Italy.

REFORM AND ENLIGHTENMENT IN THE 18TH CENTURY

After the death of the last Spanish Habsburg, Charles II (ruled 1665–1700), fighting over the remnants of Spain's European empire consumed the continent's powers in the War of the Spanish Succession (1701–14). The Treaties of Utrecht (1713) and Rastatt (1714) inaugurated a new pattern of state relations in Italy between Austrian Habsburgs, Spanish Bourbons (with Bourbon France always in the background), and the independent states. After complicated military and diplomatic maneuvers, this pattern eventually stabilized into a long-term equilibrium. In the initial treaties, Naples, Sardinia, and Milan (which had incorporated Mantua after the last Gonzaga had sold it to Louis XIV in 1701) passed to the Austrian Habsburgs; and Sicily went to Victor Amadeus II, duke of Savoy, who assumed the title of king of Sicily. Renewed Spanish hostilities, however, forced Victor Amadeus to cede Sicily to Austria in exchange for Sardinia in the Treaty of The Hague (1720). Spain acquired the duchy of Parma and Piacenza in 1731. In 1734, during the War of the Polish Succession, Charles, son of the Bourbon Philip V of Spain, conquered the kingdoms of Naples and Sicily from Austria. Spain had thus regained its two largest Italian possessions. After the Medici dynasty in Tuscany died out in 1737, Francis Stephen (Francis I)—duke of Lorraine, husband of Maria Theresa of Austria, and Holy Roman emperor after 1745—ruled as grand duke of Tuscany from Vienna. And in 1748, after the War of the Austrian Succession (1740–48), Austria regained Milan, which it had lost more than once in the preceding years.

SOCIETY AND ECONOMY

A slow economic recovery began in Italy in the mid-1680s, but it remained weak into the early 18th century. A slump in the 1730s gave way to strong mid-century economic growth, until the famines of 1763–67 highlighted the weakness and inefficiency of government policies. Regional differences in Italy's agricultural structure led to even greater divergences between north and south. Whereas some northern urban industries found refuge in smaller centres and rural settings, the south came to rely economically almost exclusively on agriculture. Overall, Italy's foreign trade decreased and its exports shifted from high-value manufactured goods to relatively inexpensive raw materials (including agricultural products) and semifinished goods, while it became a net importer of finished industrial products. At the same time, the Italian domestic market also contracted, and increasing social and institutional constraints further limited productive and mercantile opportunities. While Italy's population between 1700 and 1800 rose by about one-third, to 18 million, that of the rest of Europe grew at twice that rate. Italy's relative demographic and economic stagnation were to prevent an agrarian or industrial revolution during the 18th century.

The aristocracy retained hegemonic control of politics and economics, dominating land ownership and manipulating legal and political institutions in the towns to maintain their position.

Tensions and conflicts arose from time to time between the central authority of the absolutist states and the nobility, between the rich bourgeoisie or professional classes and the nobility, and among the nobles themselves, but the nobility blocked, worked out compromises with, and co-opted these rival groups to preserve aristocratic predominance. In the north, especially in the republican states, city oligarchies resisted erosion of their power and privileges. In sharp contrast, the social and economic position of the urban masses and the growing rural population deteriorated, while the difficulties of daily life increased.

POLITICAL THOUGHT AND EARLY ATTEMPTS AT REFORM

By the beginning of the 18th century, a new cultural climate opened Italy to a wide range of European ideas—especially the philosophical thought of René Descartes, Pierre Gassendi, Benedict de Spinoza, Pierre Bayle, Thomas Hobbes, John Locke, Sir Isaac Newton, and Hugo Grotius. With it new cultural institutions came to the fore. The Academy of Arcadia, founded in Rome in 1690, exemplified the channeling of energies for rationalism and innovation. Among its more famous members, Gian Vincenzo Gravina, Ludovico Antonio Muratori, and Giambattista Vico gained renown by launching juridical, historical, aesthetic, and "scientific" critiques of society. Vico's *Scienza nuova* (1725; *The New Science*), the most enduring work produced by this group, found tepid reception in its own day, and the author's ideas on a universal philosophy of history won wide acceptance among Enlightenment thinkers only in the 1770s. Paolo Mattia Doria (1662?–1746) and the Medinaceli Academy in Naples also employed historical inquiry to seek remedies for society's ills. Doria revived the idea of a Platonic republicanism of philosophic magistrates, in which an anti-Enlightenment Catholicism would become a kind of civil religion. In Naples he led his group of self-styled "ancients" against the scientific "moderns" led by the Neapolitan diplomat Celestino Galiani and Bartolomeo Intieri, a Florentine factor in Naples who provided a link to Tuscan intellectual circles. The ministerial class that developed in Spanish Italy from the early 16th century helped foster such networks of intellectual exchange between the cities of Italy and between Italy and the broader cosmopolitan centres of 18th-century Europe.

The political and cultural roles of the church—in particular, the supranational character of the papacy, the immunity of clerics from the state's legal and fiscal apparatus, the church's intolerance and intransigence in theological and institutional matters, as well as its wealth and property—constituted the central problems in the reform schemes of Italy's nascent intellectual movement. The most incisive breakthrough came from Pietro Giannone (1676–1748), a Neapolitan jurist, who employed a jurisdictional, historical method to oppose church abuse of power and to break the church's stranglehold on the state. Probably the strongest arguments for church reform came from Enlightenment thinkers Francesco Scipione, marchese di Maffei (1675–1755), and Muratori (1672–1750), who sought to reconcile politics with morality and religion. Muratori's *Della pubblica felicità* (1749; "On Public Happiness") reached Bourbon audiences in French and Spanish translations and was probably read in the Austrian Habsburg realms by Maria Theresa herself.

THE ERA OF ENLIGHTENMENT REFORM

By the mid-18th century, economic recovery, Muratori's program of Enlightenment Catholicism, and a renewed interest in natural science, political economy, and agronomy produced the first stirrings of reform. The dynasties installed after the wars of succession—the Habsburg-Lorraine in Milan and Tuscany and the Bourbon in Naples—led the way.

MILAN

A first wave of reforms under Maria Theresa came to Milan in the early 1740s. The Genoese patrician Gian Luca Pallavicini prepared them as a minister after 1743 and then implemented them as governor after 1750. The reforms reorganized government administration, ended the sale of offices, reordered state finances, founded a public bank, and, most important, in 1749 placed a new cadastral survey—begun in 1718 but interrupted in 1733—under the direction of the Florentine jurist Pompeo Neri. The Theresian cadastral survey took effect in 1760. Applying objective principles of fiscal justice and administrative rationalization, the new method of registering the ownership and value of property not only revamped Milan's fiscal system but also improved agriculture, increased productivity, and centralized control of revenues in impartial hands.

In Vienna the Department of Italy oversaw Milanese affairs after 1757 and orchestrated a second wave of reforms during the 1760s. Another imperial official, Carlo, conte di Firmian of Trent, arrived in 1759 to implement wide-ranging changes. Firmian completed the earlier reforms in political administration, in the judicial system, in ecclesiastical relations, and in educational policy. But strong opposition from diverse social groups defending traditional rights and privileges weakened the reform movement. In 1761–62, however, an important group of young reformist noblemen formed around Pietro Verri (1728–97) and took the name of his militant journal, *Il caffè* (published 1764–66; "The Coffeehouse"). The circle's best-known work, Cesare Beccaria's *Dei delitti e delle pene* (1764; *An Essay On Crimes and Punishments*), castigated torture and capital punishment as symptoms of the injustice and inequality inherent in the society of the old regime.

Joseph II (ruled 1765–90) promoted a new wave of reforms after 1770 that gained strength when he became the sole ruler after Maria Theresa's death in 1780. The old system of public administration and magistratures came under attack and was abolished by 1786. In the 1770s and '80s the reform policies of "Josephism" succeeded in suppressing all the chief political and judicial bodies of the Milanese aristocracy and in establishing modern ones in their place. Joseph's government appointed provincial intendants and reduced the church's power in the state. Educational reform established popular elementary schools as well as new disciplines at the Palatine School of Milan and the University of Pavia.

Such reforms, however, proved to have few long-term cultural or social consequences. Opposition from nobles, local administrators, aristocratic landlords, magistrates, clergy, and even Enlightenment intellectuals, who feared Joseph's new authoritarianism, undermined the reforms. Leopold II (ruled 1790–92), who had ruled Tuscany as Grand Duke Peter Leopold before succeeding his brother Joseph, could not overcome their resistance, which gained strength from the forces unleashed by the French Revolution. Francis II, who succeeded Leopold II in 1792, faced a war with Revolutionary France, which seized Milan in 1796.

TUSCANY

Emmanuel, comte de Richecourt, who served in Tuscany for 20 years as the chief representative of the regent, Francis I, followed the main lines of Habsburg policy in Milan. Local aristocratic divisions, the privileged position of Florence (the Tuscan capital), and the corruption and private enrichment of public officials came under scrutiny. Reforms aimed to restore revenues, reorganize magistratures, control the old nobility, and moderate the influence of the church. Pompeo Neri, who was recalled from Milan to Florence in 1758, advocated the free trade of cereals to address problems of economic scarcity and provide incentives to agricultural production.

Physiocratic solutions to economic problems—that is, solutions based on laissez-faire economics and on the belief that land is the source of all wealth—characterized Tuscany under the leadership of Peter Leopold (later Leopold II), who ruled from 1765 to 1790. The Accademia dei Georgofili, founded in 1753, exercised a wide influence on a range of issues touching on agrarian reform. Legislation confirmed the free trade in grain in 1767, suppressed artisanal guilds in 1771, and eliminated all internal customs duties in 1781. Peter Leopold planned to redistribute church and state land to a new class of independent small farmers. These, in turn, would form a genuine foundation for a new kind of polity based on a constitutional monarchy with representative assemblies. Although the land reform occurred from 1766 to 1784, the constitutional reform never matured. Peter Leopold's reforms completely transformed the bureaucratic and administrative state machinery, vigorously attacked church property and prerogatives, overhauled the judiciary, and promulgated a new penal code, which was the first in Europe to abolish the death penalty. Tuscany served as a true European model of Enlightenment absolutism for 25 years. But, upon the grand duke's election as emperor at his brother Joseph's death in 1790, Tuscany, left to his son, Ferdinand III, erupted in violence as hostile clerics and civil servants manipulated the European crisis of the 1790s against Leopold's reforms.

NAPLES AND SICILY

Under Austrian Habsburg rule after 1707, Naples witnessed numerous reform plans but little concrete action. When Sicily came under Austrian rule in 1720, similar good intentions foundered in the face of local resistance, a worsening international economy, and the political exigencies and fiscal burdens of imminent wars. With the conquest of Naples and Sicily in 1734 by Charles of Bourbon (who ruled as Charles VII until 1759), the Italian south celebrated its nominal independence under a new foreign dynasty. The new regime introduced significant reforms, including new administrative and judicial systems, fostered economic recovery, and patronized an important Enlightenment community. The discipline of political economy originated during this period with the publication in 1751 of Ferdinando Galiani's treatise *Della moneta* ("On Money") and Antonio Genovesi's appointment in 1754 to the first university chair in political economy.

In 1759 Charles abdicated his Neapolitan throne in order to become King Charles III of Spain, leaving his minister Bernardo Tanucci to head the regency council of his son Ferdinand IV (ruled 1759–1825). The turning point in the Neapolitan reform movement came with a catastrophic famine in 1764, which urgently called into question the effectiveness of old-regime structures. After Ferdinand's marriage to Maria Carolina, the daughter of Maria Theresa, Tanucci began to lose favour with the disengaged, weak monarch. He was forced to resign in 1776, having pushed Bourbon reform to its limits, although with few tangible results. Naples moved away from its Spanish Bourbon ties and into the orbit of Habsburg policies. Fearing that the reforms had run their course, Genovesi's students in and out of government—Giuseppe Maria Galanti, Francesco Longano, Traiano Odazzi, and the Grimaldi brothers, Domenico and Francesco Antonio—pursued his interests in solving economic and agricultural problems. The 1780s were the high point of the Neapolitan Enlightenment, both through their work and through the writings of Genovesi's students Francesco Maria Pagano and Gaetano Filangieri. The latter's *Scienza della legislazione* (1780–85; *The Science of Legislation*), which called for equal justice for all, state intervention in economic affairs, and broad educational reforms, ranks among the most important works of the European Enlightenment. At the same time, Domenico Caracciolo, the viceroy to Sicily from 1781 to 1785, implemented a reform program that abolished the Inquisition and challenged the fabric of the feudal system, but again without concrete results. In the end, political ties to Austria and Britain against Revolutionary France put Naples on the defensive, and, when France invaded in January 1799, the monarchs fled to Palermo for safety, and the French established a republic.

THE OTHER ITALIAN STATES

The Papal States, the states governed by the pope—Venice, Genoa, and Savoy—eschewed political-institutional reform. The theocratic monarchy of Rome, however, was open to moderate forms of Enlightenment thought under Clement XII (1730–40) and Benedict XIV (1740–58). Under Bourbon pressure the papacy even disbanded the Jesuits in 1773, albeit sometime after their expulsion from Portugal (1759) and from Bourbon Spain, Naples, and Parma (1767–68). Venice and Genoa lost ground as international powers and remained subject to a shrinking, conservative patriciate. Venice, however, remained Italy's most important publishing centre and home to a lively literary and artistic culture including figures such as the dramatist Carlo Goldoni and the painters Giovanni Antonio Guardi and Giovanni Battista Tiepolo. In Piedmont and Sardinia the long reign of Charles Emmanuel III (ruled 1730–73) further developed Savoyard militaristic absolutism and administrative centralization without the liberal spirit of Enlightenment reform.

THE CRISIS OF THE OLD REGIME

The French Revolution did not create the continentwide crisis that followed in its wake; rather, the revolutionary repercussions that rocked polities and societies after 1789 arose from the longstanding and unaddressed problems of the old regime. French and Austrian Enlightenment thought circulated freely in Italy, and a wide range of Italian intellectuals and ministers contributed to the growing body of Enlightenment thought and practice that emphasized secularization and science. However, this cosmopolitan movement confronted powerful feudal and ecclesiastical estates that controlled vast land and wealth, combated bad government that had grown habitually resistant to rationalization, struggled with the difficult task of reforming a retrograde economic system unsupportive of trade or industry, and, at the same time, found itself out of touch with the daily concerns of the mass of society facing economic hardship and wedded to traditional religious beliefs. Enlightenment culture ultimately exacerbated the problem of reform, since reform from above highlighted the disparities between high and low, raised unrealizable expectations, and imposed solutions that rarely overhauled the structure of power. The

inequalities in Italian society, the obstacles to its economic development, and the political conservatism of its privileged interest groups would not easily yield to reason alone.

THE FRENCH REVOLUTIONARY PERIOD

When French troops invaded Italy in the spring of 1796, they found fertile ground for the revolutionary ideas and practices of their native country. Since the 1780s, Italian newspapers and pamphlets had given full play to news from France, especially to the political struggle between the king and the Parlement of Paris. As the revolution unfolded in France, news reports became more frequent and more dramatic. After 1791 they were further enhanced by the personal testimonies of political émigrés. Vigilant censorship by the Italian governments could not stop the spread of revolutionary ideas. Yet Italians viewed the French Revolution simplistically as a struggle between monarchists and revolutionaries.

THE EARLY YEARS

As the reformist impulse of the 1780s waned, Italians took a growing interest in the French Revolution. Educated landowners and entrepreneurs who had put their trust in the enlightened rulers of their own states and had looked forward to important administrative and political reforms were disappointed. The French example gave them new hope. During the 1780s Masonic lodges had begun to replace scholarly academies and agrarian societies as loci of political discussion. In the 1790s more-radical secret societies emerged, modeled after the Illuminati ("Enlightened Ones") founded in Bavaria by Adam Weishaupt, a professor of canon law, which promoted free thought and democratic political theories.

The Italian governments opposed French revolutionary ideas, recognizing them as a potential threat to stability. The outbreak of the French revolutionary and Napoleonic wars confirmed their fears. After French armies in 1792 occupied Savoy and Nice, which belonged to the kingdom of Sardinia-Piedmont (ruled by the house of Savoy), the kingdom joined the First Coalition, an alliance formed in 1793 by powers opposed to Revolutionary France. The arrival of the French fleet in the Bay of Naples in December 1792 prevented the king of Naples from following the Piedmontese example, but other governments resorted to stern repression of French-inspired protests. Many Italians, however, viewed the revolutionary French legal and administrative system as the only answer to their own grievances against traditional elites. In Piedmont and Naples, where discontent was especially widespread, proponents of democratic ideas organized actual conspiracies. Arrested conspirators who escaped death or jail found refuge in France, where they became influential and active.

Italian émigrés helped to give a sharper focus to the aims of revolutionary protest and to prepare the ground for French intervention in the peninsula. The best-known émigré, the Tuscan nobleman Filippo Buonarroti, served as national commissioner in the Ligurian town of Oneglia, captured by French armies in 1794. Oneglia became the location for the first revolutionary experiment on Italian soil when Buonarroti introduced a republican constitution and the cult of the Supreme Being and abolished seigneurial rights. The "Oneglia experiment" ended abruptly in 1795 with the fall of Maximilien Robespierre's government in France, but Buonarroti persisted in his radical beliefs, becoming a supporter of the French left-wing agitator François-Noël (Gracchus) Babeuf. The precedent he had set was not forgotten.

FRENCH INVASION OF ITALY

The French campaign in Italy, which assured the political future of Napoleon Bonaparte, began in March 1796. According to the Peace of Paris (May 15, 1796), King Victor Amadeus III of Sardinia-Piedmont was forced to cede Savoy and Nice to France and to grant safe passage to the French armies. On the same day, Napoleon's army drove the Austrians out of Milan, pursuing them into the territory of the Republic of Venice. By April 1797 the French controlled the entire Po valley, including Bologna and the northern reaches of the

Republic of Venice, which the pope had ceded to them in the Peace of Tolentino (February 19, 1797). French armies also occupied the duchy of Modena and most of the grand duchy of Tuscany, including the port of Livorno. After defeating the Austrians on Venetian territory during the winter of 1796–97, Napoleon turned his offensive northward, crossing the Tagliamento River and driving for the Habsburg capital, Vienna. In April 1797, at Leoben, Austrian envoys offered to negotiate. In exchange for an end to the French offensive, Austria agreed to partition Venetia and to recognize French sovereignty over Austria's former possessions in the Low Countries and Lombardy. For the next two years the Italian peninsula enjoyed a period of relative freedom and democracy, which ended with the Austro-Russian campaign against France in April 1799.

ROOTS OF THE RISORGIMENTO

The origins of the Italian Risorgimento—the great national "resurgence" of the 19th century—date to this period, insofar as the period gave rise to political groups that affirmed the right of the Italian people to a government suited to their desires and traditions, as well as to the growth of a sense of nationalism and individual responsibility.

In 1800 the Neapolitan historian Vincenzo Cuoco argued that the Italian revolution of the 1790s had been a "passive revolution" without real roots in Italian soil or a national ruling elite. Later generations of historians repeated and endorsed this view, arguing that Italian Jacobinism had imitated Robespierre's ideology. They tried to distinguish between Jacobin republicanism and more moderate, indigenous political movements. However, in reality, the Italian Jacobins often modified their positions from political necessity. Some who had advocated radical republicanism and democracy in the 1780s and '90s accepted important offices in the Napoleonic governments of the early 1800s. The essential difference between moderate and radical Francophiles lay in the different meanings that each group gave to the concept of democracy. The doctrine of equality, for instance, could be restricted to equality before the law, or it could be expanded to include social and economic equality, which would shake the foundation of private property. Depending on their definition of equality, the two groups could take very different approaches to taxation, economic regulation, and public education.

THE ITALIAN REPUBLICS OF 1796–99

During the revolutionary triennium (1796–99), political initiative in Italy remained in French hands. The moderate heads of the post-Jacobin Directory regarded the conquered Italian territories primarily as bargaining chips. However, Napoleon, as commander of the French armies in Italy, worked actively to establish "sister republics." He hoped for financially stable and politically dependable governments that would recognize French hegemony, adopt French legislation, and hold radical elements at bay. Thus, he supported the establishment of moderate republican governments headed by prominent Italian citizens.

The first of these, the Cispadane Republic, was established at Modena in March 1797; in July it merged with the Cisalpine Republic, which encompassed Lombardy. Although strong enough militarily to deter an Austrian offensive, the republic remained torn internally by strife between moderates and radicals. Democratic clubs and newspapers continued to resist control from Paris. Yet the moderates, under French tutelage, gradually emerged as a new bureaucratic and political class. A third republic, the Ligurian Republic, incorporating the former republic of Genoa, was proclaimed on June 6, 1797. It was ruled by members of the local aristocracy, who worked hand in hand with the Directory in Paris and blocked union with the Cisalpine Republic. In Piedmont the Savoy government suppressed Jacobin uprisings until the French forced the king to leave, annexing his territories in February 1799. When Napoleon ceded Venetia to Austria by the Treaty of Campo Formio (October 17, 1797), Italian revolutionaries felt outraged and betrayed. Ugo Foscolo expressed their disillusionment in his novel *Le ultime lettere di Jacopo Ortis* (1798; "The Last Letters of Jacopo Ortis"). To keep both a hostile Pope Pius VI and the democratic clubs in check, the French occupied

Rome in January 1798 and proclaimed a Roman Republic on March 15. Although the democratic Constitutional Club in Rome remained strong, moderate leaders maintained control. The southern exile Vincenzo Russo described these events in his *Pensieri politici* (1798; "Political Meditations"), one of the most important examples of Italian Jacobin thought.

The situation in Italy changed in November 1797 when Napoleon departed on his ill-fated expedition to Egypt. Under pressure from England, King Ferdinand IV of Naples invaded the Roman Republic and attempted to restore the papal government in Rome. The French armies launched a counteroffensive. King Ferdinand took refuge in Sicily under the protection of the British fleet, and French troops occupied Naples on January 23, 1799, and established the Parthenopean Republic. Although the Parthenopean Republic controlled only some of the provinces of the former Bourbon kingdom—others remained under Bourbon rule or in the throes of anarchy—it became the most democratic of all revolutionary governments of the triennium. This owed largely to the French military commander Jean-Étienne Championnet, as well as to the commissioner Marc-Antoine Jullien. Previously a follower of Babeuf, Jullien defied the wishes of the Directory in Paris for a moderate government. The Parthenopean Republic had the enthusiastic support of a number of southern intellectuals and notables (members of the social or economic elite).

COLLAPSE OF THE REPUBLICS

Early in 1799 the French situation in Italy deteriorated rapidly. After the birth of the Second Coalition against France (March 1799), Austrian and Russian troops were able to occupy the Cisalpine Republic and to reach Turin in less than two months. Thus, the French lost the entire Po valley. In addition, most of the French army was forced to withdraw from Naples. The destruction of the Parthenopean Republic was the work of bands of peasants organized by Fabrizio Cardinal Ruffo, a faithful adherent of the king. Ruffo's bands quickly disposed of the weak democratic militia. Their Armata della Santa Fede ("Army of the Holy Faith") was the most important peasant uprising in the history of modern Italy. Invoking God and king, they devastated the castles of the aristocracy and occupied communal lands that the local barons had usurped; they also killed bourgeois leaders who had set up provisional municipal governments. The reaction against the French and the indigenous Jacobins became a great antiaristocratic movement, which the Bourbon monarchy skillfully manipulated to its advantage. Naples surrendered on June 23, 1799, and soon afterward the king returned from Sicily. At the behest of the British admiral Horatio Nelson and Queen Maria Carolina, wife of Ferdinand and a sister of Marie-Antoinette of France, the king (violating the terms of the surrender) ordered the execution of more than 100 revolutionary leaders. Among them were the best southern administrators, jurists, and intellectuals.

The French, who had occupied Tuscany between March and July 1799, were driven out by a violent peasant uprising, the Viva Maria ("Long Live the Virgin Mary"). This movement developed into a march on urban centres, assaults on Jewish residents, and a hunt for real or alleged local Jacobins; it also reestablished the power of the landowning aristocracy and of the clergy. The Roman Republic fell in September 1799. The French resisted only in Genoa, while a large number of Italian Jacobins took refuge in France. Thus ended the revolutionary triennium.

The pro-French *patrioti* ("patriots") had completely failed to enlist the support of the masses. From the summer of 1796 the rural districts were in ferment but almost always in opposition to the new rulers. There were peasant marches on cities in Lombardy, the Romagna, and Tuscany. Armed bands controlled or recaptured parts of the Marche, Tuscany, and the Kingdom of Naples. In some cities, such as Verona and especially Naples, popular dislike of the French and the local Jacobins was manifest. This antirevolutionary sentiment derived to some extent from the influence of the clergy and the high taxes levied by the republican regimes. However, it stemmed primarily from the populace's ingrained and instinctive conservatism, which only the gradual development of a grassroots opposition movement was later able to overcome.

The Italian Jacobins, defeated in domestic political struggles, also suffered a deep loss of respect for their French ally. Money levies for military purposes degenerated into pure plunder; constitutions were not democratically drafted but dictated by the French; supporters of the democratic opposition were jailed or removed from office. Worst of all, Napoleon showed an autocratic tendency and a lack of commitment to republicanism in his policy of returning the king of Sardinia-Piedmont to the throne in the summer of 1796 and of ceding Venetia to the Habsburgs in 1797. Disillusionment with French policies, however, did not reconcile the Italian Jacobins with their former rulers; instead, it bolstered their nationalism. In Piedmont, for instance, a secret society, I Raggi ("The Beams of Light"), advocated a democratic, unionist, and anti-French program that would lead Italy toward unity and independence.

THE FRENCH CONSULATE

After gaining control of France in his coup d'état of 18–19 Brumaire (November 9–10, 1799), Napoleon renewed his Italian campaign. His armies crossed the Alps again, this time through the difficult Great Saint Bernard Pass, and reoccupied Milan on June 2, 1800. A few days later they scored a definitive victory over the Austrians at Marengo, between the Po and Bormida rivers. Defeated also on German soil, the Second Coalition quickly collapsed. The Treaty of Lunéville (February 9, 1801) reestablished the Ligurian and Cisalpine republics. Piedmont was reannexed to France in September 1802, together with Elba and Piombino. The duchy of Parma was also annexed, although annexation became official only in 1808. Even in Tuscany, Austrian influence ended when Louis, son of Ferdinand of Parma, was declared king of Etruria. In northern Italy, Austria retained only Venetia, while France directly or indirectly controlled the areas from the Alps to the Tuscan coast. In the south the papal and Bourbon governments remained in power, but their positions were weak.

The second Cisalpine Republic, established in June 1800, proved to be a transitional regime, since it lacked the necessary combined support of the moderates and landowners. In Paris Napoleon's most trusted adviser on Italian affairs was the Milanese patrician Francesco Melzi d'Eril, who during the triennium had hoped to see northern Italy united in a constitutional monarchy under a Habsburg or Bourbon prince. Melzi was the most clear-sighted exponent of an older moderate ruling class that still yearned for enlightened autocracy. Napoleon also favoured the formation of a large Italian state, provided he could control it. His preference was for an Italian republic with a constitution on the French model. Central authority was to be vested in a president, with a relatively weak representative body divided among three estates—landowners, merchants and tradesmen, and intellectuals and clerics. Napoleon wanted to assume the presidency himself or to name a

Nicolas-André Monsiau's painting showing the meeting during which Napoleon Bonaparte was made president of the new Italian Republic in 1802. DEA/G. Dagli Orti/De Agostini/Getty Images

a secret society, I Raggi ("The Beams of Light"), advocated a democratic, unionist, and anti-French program that would lead Italy toward unity and independence.

THE FRENCH CONSULATE

After gaining control of France in his coup d'état of 18–19 Brumaire (November 9–10, 1799), Napoleon renewed his Italian campaign. His armies crossed the Alps again, this time through the difficult Great Saint Bernard Pass, and reoccupied Milan on June 2, 1800. A few days later they scored a definitive victory over the Austrians at Marengo, between the Po and Bormida rivers. Defeated also on German soil, the Second Coalition quickly collapsed. The Treaty of Lunéville (February 9, 1801)

leaders, the local nobles and educated bourgeois for the first time felt an obligation to govern and defend their country together.

THE NAPOLEONIC EMPIRE

Soon after Napoleon claimed the title of emperor in 1804, the Italian Republic became a kingdom, proclaimed on March 17, 1805. Napoleon, as king of Italy, appointed his stepson, Eugène de Beauharnais, as viceroy and Antonio Aldini as secretary of state, forcing Melzi to step aside. Although Italian autonomy remained limited, Napoleon's victories, which constantly increased the territory of the kingdom, provided some compensation. Venetia was annexed to it by the Treaty of Pressburg (December 26, 1805), and Dalmatia and Istria were attached to the kingdom with a separate constitution. In a reorganization following the Treaty of Schönbrunn (October 14, 1809), Dalmatia and Istria were joined with Trieste and Ragusa (now Dubrovnik), together with other territories ceded by Austria, to form the seven French *départements* of the Illyrian provinces. The Marche became part of the Italian kingdom in April 1808. Liguria was directly annexed to France on June 4, 1805, as was Tuscany in March 1808. In 1809 Napoleon abolished the temporal power of the papacy and annexed Rome and the remainder of the Papal States to France. Pope Pius VII responded by excommunicating Napoleon, who in response held the pontiff prisoner, first in France and later in the Ligurian town of Savona.

As emperor of France and king of Italy, Napoleon directly controlled all of northern and central Italy. During his rule, far-reaching reforms were instituted. Although the new Italian legal codes were translated almost verbatim from the French with little regard for Italian traditions, they introduced a modern jurisprudence responsive to the rights of the individual citizen. Properties held in mortmain, the old feudal ecclesiastical tenure (specifically those of the regular clergy), were transferred to the state and sold. The remaining feudal rights and jurisdictions were abolished. Roads were improved everywhere, and both primary and higher education were strengthened. In return for higher taxes, Italians thus gained a network of new and improved services that were to hasten Italian social and economic progress and cohesion.

The Continental System, a blockade designed to close the entire European continent to British trade, was proclaimed on November 21, 1806. It was freely violated everywhere, including along the Italian coastline. Although the blockade's real purpose was to promote the growth of French manufacturing, especially the silk industry, by protecting it against imports, the war economy and blockade also stimulated Italian production, prompted the emergence of machine-building and metallurgy sectors, and spurred the completion of important public works.

In the south, after the repression and executions of 1799, the Bourbons experimented with some cautious reforms, mainly fiscal and antifeudal. These were implemented to strengthen the loyalty of the rural population, which had already proved so valuable to the monarchy. But the Neapolitan government was desperately weak, both politically and militarily. Indeed, the French reoccupied the country between February and March 1806, and the Bourbon court once more fled to Sicily. On March 30, 1806, Napoleon's brother, Joseph Bonaparte, was proclaimed king of Naples. When he became king of Spain in 1808, he was replaced by one of the most famous French generals, Joachim Murat. Despite this change, the nine years of French rule in southern Italy were a period of continuity, and, consequently, French reforms had a lasting impact. Joachim Murat was more independent of Paris than Joseph Bonaparte had been. During his reign there were fewer French ministers and advisers in proportion to Neapolitan officials, and he opposed the enforcement of the Continental System. Feudal privileges and immunities were finally abolished, although the landed aristocracy retained extensive power in the countryside. By purchasing the property confiscated from the church and from exiled landowners, southern notables subverted Murat's plan to distribute small landholdings to peasant families. Much common land, originally usurped by large landowners, was recovered, but this worked to the benefit of bourgeois notables known in the south as *galantuomini* ("honourable men"). Fiscal, judicial,

and educational reforms, similar to those introduced in the Kingdom of Italy, were implemented in Naples.

Meanwhile, both Sardinia, where the Savoy court took refuge, and Sicily remained apart from the Napoleonic world. In Sicily the Bourbons were under strict English control, not only militarily but also politically. In 1811–12, when the king clashed with the Sicilian nobles, mostly over taxation, the British naval commander Lord William Bentinck intervened. He introduced a moderate constitution that left much power in the hands of the nobles but markedly limited the absolute powers of the throne. Sicily then experienced a short period of autonomy with intense political ferment, which ended in 1816 when the restored Bourbons abrogated the constitution and reunited the island with the Kingdom of Naples to form the Kingdom of the Two Sicilies.

THE END OF FRENCH RULE AND THE RESTORATION

The Napoleonic regime collapsed in Italy as it did in the rest of Europe. Beauharnais and Murat, with their respective armies, had taken part in Napoleon's disastrous Russian campaign of 1812. At the moment of defeat, Murat deserted the emperor, returned to Naples, and made peace with the English and the Austrians. Joining them in their campaign against Beauharnais, though without a full commitment, he advanced with his Neapolitan troops as far as the

Po River (March 1814). By the terms of the armistice of Schiarino-Rizzino (April 16, 1814), Beauharnais was able to retain control of Lombardy. But an insurrection in Milan on April 20 allowed the Austrians to occupy the entire region.

THE VIENNA SETTLEMENT

The Congress of Vienna (1814–15), held by the victorious allies to restore the prerevolutionary European political status quo, determined that the Bourbons should be returned to Naples. For this reason, taking advantage of Napoleon's escape from Elba to France on March 1, 1815, and his return to power, Joachim Murat opted to change sides yet one more time and declared war on Austria on March 15, 1815. In the Rimini proclamation of March 30 he incited all Italian nationalists to war, but no general insurrection occurred. Quickly defeated, Murat was forced to abdicate in May. From his exile in Corsica he moved to a base in Calabria to attempt the reconquest of his kingdom. Recaptured by Bourbon troops, he was executed in October 1815.

The Congress of Vienna established the political order in Italy that lasted until unification between 1859 and 1870. According to the Final Act of the congress, Francis I of Austria also became king of Lombardy-Venetia, which was incorporated into the Habsburg state. The former episcopal principality of Trento was formally annexed to Austria. King Victor Emmanuel I of Savoy recovered his territories (Nice, Savoy, and Piedmont) and acquired the Ligurian coast, including Genoa. The duchy of Parma was granted to Marie-Louise of Habsburg, the daughter of Francis I and Napoleon's second wife. At her death the duchy was to revert to the Bourbon-Parma family, which was also temporarily placed in charge of the duchy of Lucca. The Habsburg-Este family returned to Modena and inherited the duchy of Massa in 1825. Also in Tuscany, the Habsburg-Lorraine family added the State of the Garrisons to its former domains and was given claim to Lucca, which the Bourbon-Parma family was to relinquish in 1847. The pope recovered his temporal domain in central Italy. Ferdinand IV of Naples reassumed control of his former realm under the new title of Ferdinand I, King of the Two Sicilies.

Thus, the Vienna settlement dismantled the three aristocratic republics of Venice, Genoa, and Lucca; it strengthened Piedmont and restored undisputed Austrian hegemony in the peninsula. Austrian troops garrisoned Ferrara, ready to intervene in case of trouble in the Papal States. Austria gained the right to intervene in the Kingdom of the Two Sicilies, if necessary. Members of the house of Habsburg ruled over Parma, Modena, and Tuscany; and Venetia and Lombardy became, in practice, provinces of the Austrian Empire. Only the Savoy kingdom of Sardinia-Piedmont remained outside the Austrian system designed and imposed on Italy by the Austrian foreign minister Klemens, Fürst (prince) von Metternich. Under Russia's secret protection the Savoy government proved dependably reactionary.

On April 7, 1815, Francis I proclaimed the formation of the kingdom of Lombardy-Venetia. The new state was a fiction, however, because the two regions remained separate, each subject to the central ministries in Vienna. Milan lost its role as a capital, most of the Napoleonic administration was dismantled, and the centralizing authority of Vienna became all-pervasive. Many reforms, especially legal reforms, were abolished. Austria reacted to widespread discontent with increasingly severe police measures and stricter censorship, suppressing, for example, the liberal and Romantic periodical *Il conciliatore* ("The Conciliator") after only one year of publication (1818–19).

Returning to Piedmont from his refuge in Sardinia, Victor Emmanuel I of Savoy abolished all laws promulgated by the French and removed from public office all those who had collaborated with them. He invited the Jesuits back into the kingdom and turned many educational institutions over to them and to other religious orders. This extreme reaction provoked liberal opposition among enlightened members of Piedmont's upper classes.

Francis IV of Modena demonstrated comparable intransigence; but, in Parma, Marie-Louise of Habsburg practiced political moderation and preserved many French reforms. Although Francophiles were expelled from the Tuscan administration and some French reforms were abolished, Tuscany under Ferdinand III of Habsburg-Lorraine and his successor, Leopold II, became known for economic liberalism and lenient censorship. Intellectual life flourished in Tuscany with the arrival from other regions of exiled writers, such as the poets Giacomo Leopardi and Niccolò Tommaseo and the historian Pietro Colletta. These men gathered around the Gabinetto di Lettura ("Literary Club") of Gian Pietro Vieusseux, founder of an important periodical, *L'antologia* (1821–33; "The Anthology").

In the Papal States the restoration, achieved principally by the diplomacy of the cautious secretary of state, Ercole Cardinal Consalvi, brought increasing government centralization. Educated men who had held positions of responsibility under the French and Italian governments resented bitterly the restoration of clerical control over all aspects of public life. Dissatisfaction was especially strong in the Romagna.

In Naples the victorious powers made sure that the Bourbons would not repeat the reprisals of 1799. Thus, the restoration appeared to begin well under the balanced policies of a government led by Luigi de' Medici, who absorbed part of Murat's capable bureaucracy. Many judicial and administrative reforms of the French era survived, but concessions made to the church in a concordat concluded in 1818, as well as financial retrenchment, hampered the progress of the bourgeoisie. Especially among the *galantuomini*, who had profited from

French legislation, strong discontent found an outlet in a widespread secret society, I Carbonari ("The Charcoal Burners"). Already in existence under French rule, apparently with a vaguely nationalist program, the society gained strength and formulated more-definite constitutional aims. The southern bourgeoisie was determined to take part in political life and to promote its interests openly. From the south the lodges of the Carbonari quickly spread to the Marche, the Romagna, Piedmont, and Lombardy.

Spain experienced a revolution in 1820, in which the Liberals gained power and reestablished a constitution promulgated in 1812. This event had notable repercussions in Italy. In the Kingdom of the Two Sicilies, former members of Murat's army, affiliated with the Carbonari, marched on Naples (July 2, 1820) to the cry of "Long live liberty and the constitution." They found support in the army and among the bourgeoisie. King Ferdinand was forced to yield to demands for the introduction of the Spanish constitution, which limited royal powers, decreased centralization, and reduced the influence of the capital. The new regime proved short-lived, however, for it had too many enemies. The king sought to recover his former powers; and Sicilian dissidents attempted to reestablish their island's separate status, though their movement was brutally suppressed by the Neapolitan constitutional government, assisted by Austria. Invoking the Austrian right to intervene if necessary to maintain the restored Bourbon monarchy,

in January 1821 Metternich convened an international congress at Laibach (now Ljubljana) attended by representatives of the European powers and of the Italian states, including King Ferdinand himself. Overcoming weak Anglo-French opposition, Ferdinand obtained approval for military intervention. Accordingly, the Austrian army entered the kingdom and occupied Naples on March 23, 1821, reestablishing the king's absolute government.

In Piedmont the more liberal and educated wing of the nobility resented Victor Emmanuel I's reactionary policies and found allies among bourgeois groups that had adopted the constitutional program of the Carbonari. In the wake of the Neapolitan revolution, a conspiracy began with the support of Liberals in Lombardy and, covertly, of the heir apparent to the throne of Sardinia-Piedmont, Charles Albert, principe di Carignano. Between March 9 and 13, 1821, the revolt, organized by military and bourgeois leaders, spread from Alessandria to Turin. Victor Emmanuel I abdicated in favour of his brother, Charles Felix, and, in the latter's absence from the kingdom, appointed Charles Albert as regent. On March 14, Charles Albert proclaimed the Spanish constitution of 1812, though its implementation was contingent on the new king's approval. From his refuge in Modena, Charles Felix refused to accept it; with Austrian help and loyal Piedmontese troops, he quickly occupied the kingdom and established his authority. Three conspirators were executed and many more imprisoned or exiled. Charles Albert succeeded in reconciling with Charles Felix, but his vacillating conduct marked him for years to come. The Liberals never forgave him his compromises with Charles Felix, who ruled until 1831. Although there was no revolution in Lombardy-Venetia, a complex network of opponents of the regime was discovered and suppressed. In October 1820 the Carbonari in Milan were attacked, and some were deported. In March 1821 the police penetrated another secret organization, I Federati ("The Confederates"), led by the Milanese nobleman Federico Confalonieri. The society favoured constitutional government, but its program was more moderate than that of the Carbonari though no less anti-Austrian. From December 1821 to January 1823 members of the conspiracy were unmasked in the army and the upper bureaucracy and received death sentences, all of which were eventually commuted to long prison terms.

ECONOMIC SLUMP AND REVIVAL

A severe economic recession accompanied this period of political reaction, which continued in the Romagna until as late as 1828. After the famine of 1816–17, Russian grain flooded the Italian market and contributed to a crisis of agricultural overproduction. The desperate poverty of the peasantry led to grain riots, brigandage, and the spread of pellagra, a vitamin-deficiency disease endemic among the northern peasantry, whose diet relied heavily on corn (maize). The slump continued until nearly 1830, when successful mulberry cultivation brought renewed rural prosperity and was sufficient, particularly in Piedmont and Lombardy, to reestablish agricultural credit and provide capital for the growth of textile and engineering industries.

Renewed prosperity supported a revival of cultural activities, and many periodicals addressed the country's economic and social problems. The most notable of these publications was the philosopher Gian Domenico Romagnosi's *Annali universali di statistica* ("World Statistical Almanac"), which published the first essays of his most important pupil, Carlo Cattaneo. Until this period Lombard and Tuscan moderates had dominated political and cultural criticism, but they were now joined by expatriates from other regions and by Roman Catholic and democratic thinkers.

THE REBELLIONS OF 1831 AND THEIR AFTERMATH

The July Revolution of 1830 in Paris set in motion an Italian conspiratorial movement in Modena and in other Emilian towns. Two Carbonari, Enrico Misley and Ciro Menotti, put their trust in the duke of Modena, Francis IV of Habsburg-Este, who was looking for an opportunity to expand his small state. But when Francis discovered that the Austrian police knew of the plot, he had Menotti and others arrested. Nevertheless, the revolt spread to the Romagna and to all parts of the Papal States except Lazio. For various reasons the provisional governments of the insurgent cities failed to organize for a common military defense and did not receive the hoped-for help of the French army. During March 1831 the Austrian army intervened and reestablished the status quo ante. The failure of the uprisings of 1831 suggests that the program of the Carbonari had run its course.

The moderate Liberals, most of them Carbonari, had demonstrated a readiness to compromise with the absolute monarchs. They had distrusted democrats and republicans who sought to achieve Italian unification by political revolution and force of arms. Among these were the Adelfi, a secret society of the followers of Filippo Buonarroti. Ultimately, the task of organizing new cadres of democratic and republican opponents of the restoration governments fell to Giuseppe Mazzini, scion of a bourgeois and Jacobin family of Genoa. Exiled in 1830 at the age of 25, Mazzini turned away from both

YOUNG ITALY

The pro-independence movement known as Young Italy (Giovine Italia) was founded by Giuseppe Mazzini in 1831 to work for a united republican Italian nation. Attracting many Italians to the cause, it played an important role in the Risorgimento (struggle for Italian unification).

Mazzini, in exile at Marseille for his revolutionary activities, was prompted to found a new society because of the repeated failures of revolts led by the Carbonari (liberal secret societies). In contrast to the clandestine methods of the Carbonari and their dependence on foreign support, Young Italy was to be based on the moral and spiritual revival of the Italian people; it was to have a popular character and educate the people in their political role. The new movement was declared to stand for a republican government because, as its official program stated, "all the men of the nation are called by the law of God and Humanity to be free and equal brothers, and only a republic could assure this." It also favoured a unitary state because "without unity there is not truly a nation, since without unity there is no strength." To propagate these ideas, Mazzini published the journal *Giovine Italia* from 1832 to 1834.

According to Mazzini, the movement grew from 40 members at its 1831 beginnings to more than 50,000 by 1833. Young Italy spread rapidly in northern Italy (in Liguria and in Piedmont), where a high literacy rate made possible wide distribution of the society's publication, but it always remained a middle-class movement.

Young Italy plotted conspiracies against the existing governments in Italy during the 1830s and the 1840s, but its revolts met with failure. The lack of popular support for insurrection as the road to independence discredited the society. In 1848 Mazzini himself replaced Young Italy with the Italian National Committee (Associazione Nazionale Italiana). After 1850, with Piedmont leading the struggle for unification, Mazzini's influence declined.

Carboneria and Buonarrotism and established his own organization, Giovine Italia (Young Italy). Republican and unionist, Mazzini's organization emphasized popular participation in the national struggle but eschewed Jacobin and social-revolutionary objectives. In 1833–34 the first abortive Mazzinian uprisings took place in Piedmont and Genoa. The latter was organized by Giuseppe Garibaldi, who then fled to France. In 1834 the Austrian police identified as many as 2,000 adherents of Young Italy in Lombardy. In 1836 Mazzini, who had established relationships with democratic revolutionaries in other countries and cofounded Giovine Europa (Young Europe), left Switzerland and settled in London.

Conservative repression convinced the moderates of the futility of conspiracies with limited membership and of the necessity to educate the public about the need for change. Meanwhile, the peace imposed on Italy from 1831 to 1848 favoured economic development, which came in varying degrees everywhere except in the south. There the Bourbon Kingdom of the Two Sicilies remained backward, and the growth of bourgeois landownership that resulted from the division of great aristocratic holdings did nothing to change the situation. Thus, the imbalance between north and south, to be felt even more strongly after unification, continued to increase. Meanwhile, Genoa, Turin, and Milan began to lay the foundation for becoming important European financial and industrial centres. Piedmontese and Lombard manufacturing and banking expanded rapidly. In Venetia important land-reclamation projects were completed, and in Tuscany banking and commerce flourished, especially via the port of Livorno. Throughout the country the construction of a railroad network beginning in the 1840s increased commerce and gave rise to subsidiary industries.

Economic revival made it more difficult for governments to tighten police control. In Milan, Carlo Cattaneo's journal, *Il politecnico* ("The Polytechnic"), founded in 1839, argued that the progress of science and technology necessary to fuel economic growth depended upon government reforms. In the same year, a congress of Italian scientists held its first annual meeting in Pisa. Through 1847 each subsequent meeting assumed a markedly more nationalistic character. Thus, conditions became more favourable for moderates to realize their programs of increasing public education and abolishing censorship and police surveillance. In the cause of economic unification they endeavoured to standardize tolls and trade practices and to increase cultural exchange among the Italian states. They also sought to achieve representative institutions compatible with Italian traditions and with Roman Catholicism.

Vincenzo Gioberti, the most important exponent of liberal Catholicism, envisioned a new and positive role for the temporal power of the papacy. His *Del primato morale e civile degli Italiani*

(1843; "On the Moral and Civil Primacy of Italians") affirmed the idea of progress as the return of the material to the spiritual, of man to God. Because such progress could be realized only through the mediation of the church, Gioberti advocated an Italian federation free from Austrian hegemony and under the nominal presidency of the pope. His ideas were influential among the clergy and most Catholic intellectuals. Under different formulations, this new papalist movement was advanced by Cesare Balbo, Niccolò Tommaseo, and Antonio Rosmini-Serbati.

In the early 1840s, renewed Mazzinian attempts at armed rebellion were ruthlessly suppressed. Among these was the Calabrian expedition of 1844, organized by the Venetian Bandiera brothers and seven of their companions, who were captured and executed by the Bourbon regime. These violent acts of suppression increased the esteem that governments and the general public felt for the moderate opposition. The election of Giovanni Maria Mastai-Ferretti as Pope Pius IX in 1846 augured well for the Papal States; his nomination derived from anti-Austrian feeling in the Curia. In the beginning of his reign, he showed liberal sympathies and granted amnesty to political prisoners. He gradually removed the most reactionary prelates from important government posts, permitted the publication of political periodicals, and finally, in 1847, established a council of state. Although only advisory, the council gave the laity a voice in the affairs of state. Influenced by the pope's liberalism, rulers elsewhere in Italy introduced reforms. Especially important was the Tuscan press law of 1847, by which Grand Duke Leopold II removed most forms of political censorship. The reforms encouraged extremism, however, and the reactionary powers of Europe became convinced that the stability of Italy was in jeopardy. In July 1847 Austrian troops occupied the papal city of Ferrara. This intervention stimulated cooperation among Italian rulers, including Charles Albert of Savoy, whose relations with Austria had been particularly strained. While the rulers discussed reforms—especially the formation of an all-Italian customs union—and the measures needed to cope with famine in several regions, the populace began to stir.

THE REVOLUTIONS OF 1848

The first of the revolutions of 1848 erupted in Palermo on January 9. Starting as a popular insurrection, it soon took on overtones of Sicilian separatism and spread throughout the island. Piecemeal reforms proved inadequate to satisfy the revolutionaries, both noble and bourgeois, who were determined to have a new and more liberal constitution. Ferdinand II of the Kingdom of the Two Sicilies was the first to grant one (January 29, 1848). Other rulers were compelled to follow his example: Leopold II on February 17, Charles Albert on March 4, and Pope Pius IX on March 14. The Austrian government, on the other hand, did not yield to popular pressure. Instead, it reinforced its garrisons in Lombardy-Venetia, arrested opposition leaders in Venice and Milan, and suppressed student demonstrations in the university cities of Padua and Pavia. By March 22–23, when revolution had also reached Budapest and Vienna, Venetian and Milanese insurgents moved to depose their Austrian overlords. Within a few days the Austrian army lost nearly all of Lombardy-Venetia and retreated into the Quadrilateral (the region between Mantua, Peschiera, Verona, and Legnago).

On March 23 Charles Albert of Sardinia-Piedmont declared war on Austria. It was a risky decision, but prospects for a national war seemed promising, and he wanted to seize the initiative to preclude republican and democratic domination of the insurgency. After annexing Parma and Modena, whose rulers had been driven out by insurgents, the Piedmontese won a few more victories before suffering reverses. Pius IX, Leopold II, and Ferdinand II, all of whom had initially sent troops to northern Italy to support the Piedmontese army, hastily withdrew their forces. The pope's address to the cardinals on April 29 revealed his reluctance to back national movements against Austria and did much to discredit him among patriots. Lombardy and Venetia, though not without internal opposition, accepted merger with Piedmont. Nevertheless, the Piedmontese army was unable to withstand the Austrian counteroffensive. After a series of defeats, Charles Albert's forces withdrew from Milan and on August 6 left the city and its insurgents to the mercy of the returning Austrians. Accusations of royal treachery, formulated by Lombard democrats at that moment, long survived in Italian political debates. By the terms of the Salasco armistice (August 9, 1848), the Piedmontese army abandoned Lombardy. In Piedmont the new constitution, the Statuto Albertino (Albertine Statute), remained in force, and democratic ideas survived.

Throughout Europe the forces of reaction were triumphant. The revolutions of 1848 were suppressed in Vienna, Prague, Budapest, and Paris. In Naples the king regained power in a coup on May 15 and went on to reconquer Sicily. Meanwhile, in Rome the papacy reintroduced a range of obscurantist policies. Venice, however, under the dictatorship of Daniele Manin, refused to accept the Salasco armistice and resisted the Austrian siege. Leopold II of Tuscany took refuge in the Bourbon fortress of Gaeta in February 1849, when the democrats Giuseppe Montanelli and Francesco Domenico Guerrazzi were on the verge of taking control of the government and proclaiming an Italian constituent assembly. In Rome the minister Pellegrino Rossi, a former member of the Carbonari who had promoted conciliatory policies after returning from exile in France, was assassinated on November 15, 1848. This event triggered a democratic insurgency and caused Pius IX to flee to the safety of Gaeta. A constituent assembly elected by universal male suffrage proclaimed the Roman Republic on February 5, 1849.

The Italian revolution seemed to have been reborn. However, Charles Albert, pressed by Piedmontese democrats to resume his war with Austria (March 20, 1849), saw his army routed at Novara three days later. On the same day, March 23, he abdicated and went into exile. His successor, Victor Emmanuel II, was granted an honourable armistice because the Austrians did not want a weakened Savoy monarchy that could be exploited to the advantage of its democratic opponents. The defeat of Piedmont made the position of the democratic and republican opposition untenable in other parts of Italy as well. In Tuscany moderates recalled the grand duke, whose Austrian protectors crushed an insurrection in radical Livorno (May 1849). In Lombardy the Austrian reconquest of Brescia in March, after 10 days of fighting, left Venice isolated, though the city resisted enemy forces until August. The Roman Republic, led by Mazzini and Garibaldi, held out until July 3 against a French army sent by Louis-Napoléon Bonaparte, the new president of the French Republic (later the emperor Napoleon III), whose restoration of the papacy repaid his Roman Catholic supporters. The returning sovereigns rapidly set about abrogating constitutions, disbanding parliaments, and, especially in the south, filling the prisons.

Portrait of Venetian political leader Daniele Manin. Hulton Archive/Getty Images

UNIFICATION

In Piedmont Victor Emmanuel II governed with a parliament whose democratic majority refused to ratify the peace treaty with Austria. This was an exception to the general course of reaction. The skillfully worded Proclamation of Moncalieri (November 20, 1849) favourably contrasted Victor Emmanuel's policies with those of other Italian rulers and permitted elections. The victorious Liberals installed a new cabinet under Massimo d'Azeglio, a moderate who was trusted by the king. D'Azeglio introduced the Siccardi law, which curtailed the power of ecclesiastical courts. In October 1850 another prominent moderate, Camillo Benso di Cavour, entered the cabinet and directed a laissez-faire economic policy. He formulated international commercial treaties and drew on foreign capital to reduce the public debt, stimulate economic growth, and develop a railroad system. Cavour's dynamism alarmed conservatives and even d'Azeglio. In 1852, through an alliance with centre-left deputies that became known as the *connubio* ("marriage"), Cavour displaced d'Azeglio as head of the cabinet. Despite disagreements with the king (who favoured the clerical party and occasionally displayed absolutist tendencies), Cavour introduced various ecclesiastical, judicial, and fiscal reforms.

A number of events promoted Piedmont's prestige in Italy and abroad. In March 1854 France and England intervened in support of the Ottoman Empire against Russia in the Crimean War. To obtain Austrian support, they were prepared to guarantee the status quo in Italy. Only Piedmont was in a position to disrupt it at that time, and Cavour negotiated an alliance with the Western powers. In May he sent to the Crimea an army that performed brilliantly. As a result, Piedmont was able to assume a place among the victors at the Congress of Paris (February 1856). From this platform Cavour, achieving a diplomatic coup for Piedmont and Italy, declared that the only threat to peace in Italy, and the root cause of subversive plots, was the burdensome Austrian overlordship. Cavour's pronouncements at the congress increased the standing of Piedmont among nationalists.

Meanwhile, Mazzini's democratic and republican movement was crumbling. In February 1853 an insurrection against the Austrians failed in Milan. The discovery and execution at Belfiore (1852–53) of the leaders of a conspiracy in Mantua, as well as abortive insurrections in Cadore and Lunigiana, discredited the democratic movement and discouraged its most dedicated adherents. Mazzini faced complete isolation for his support of an expedition to the southern mainland to incite insurrection, known as the Sapri expedition (June–July 1857), in which the Neapolitan republican and socialist Carlo Pisacane and some 300 companions lost their lives. The democrats were divided and unable to carry on the revolutionary struggle; nothing was to be expected from the restored governments. In Lombardy-Venetia, Austria carried out stern repressive measures. Pius IX, now under the influence of the reactionary Giacomo Cardinal Antonelli, refused to grant any reforms in Rome. Liberal Catholicism could not remain viable without reforms in the Papal States. In Naples and the duchies, reaction became pervasive, although the grand duke of Tuscany sought to make his subjects forget that he owed his throne to Austrian military intervention. Only in Piedmont was there any hope left for the reformers.

THE WAR OF 1859

In 1857 Italian nationalists founded the monarchist-unionist Italian National Society, which supported the policies of Cavour. Under the presidency of Manin and the vice presidency of Garibaldi, the society achieved wider appeal than it would have achieved under the exclusive leadership of moderates. Although he did not outlaw conspiratorial movements, Cavour was determined to solve the Italian question by international politics rather than by revolution. At a secret conference held at Plombières, France, in July 1858 he arranged with Emperor Napoleon III for French military intervention in the event of Austrian aggression against Piedmont. Cavour's goal was the complete expulsion of Austrian troops from the peninsula. In return for this help Piedmont had to cede Savoy and the county of Nice to France and outlaw the Mazzinian movement; wrongly, Napoleon III held Mazzini's followers responsible for an attempt on his life made by the anarchist Felice Orsini in Paris on January 14, 1859. Despite that event, a Franco-Piedmontese alliance was sealed in January 1859. With Napoleon's

approval, Victor Emmanuel II made a speech from his throne in which he declared himself ready to hear "il grido di dolore" ("the cry of woe") against Austrian oppression that arose from every part of Italy.

Meanwhile, the Austrian military leadership and its sympathizers at court urged Emperor Francis Joseph to declare war on Piedmont. On April 23 an insulting and unacceptable ultimatum demanded the demobilization of Piedmontese troops. Piedmont rejected the ultimatum, and Austria declared war three days later. As Cavour had hoped and planned, France honoured its alliance with Piedmont. In June 1859 the allies won bloody battles at Magenta, Solferino, and San Martino. But, with the Austrian army in retreat, Napoleon III suddenly signed an armistice with the Austrians at Villafranca. This sudden change of policy responded partly to the outcry of French public opinion against the loss of life in the Italian campaign and partly to events in Italy itself, where political unification seemed imminent. On April 27 insurgents had overthrown Leopold II of Tuscany, and moderate political leaders headed by Baron Bettino Ricasoli had formed a provisional government. In June Parma, Modena, and the Papal Legations (the northern Papal States) had rebelled. Only in the Marche and Umbria were papal troops able to suppress the insurgents. Plebiscites in the liberated states urged unification with Piedmont, but France opposed the creation of a powerful new state on its border.

At Villafranca Napoleon III received Lombardy from Austria, which he passed, in turn, to Piedmont. He also agreed that the deposed rulers of Modena and Tuscany would be restored to power and, along with Austria, permitted to join an Italian confederation. In response to this political defeat, Cavour resigned in July 1859 and was replaced by Urbano Rattazzi. Britain, however, opposed the restoration of conservative governments in Modena and Tuscany, and Napoleon III, with his position at home strengthened by the acquisition of Savoy and Nice, reconsidered his position. As a result, Cavour's policy prevailed, and he returned to office on January 21, 1860. New plebiscites in the duchies and the Papal Legations reconfirmed popular sentiment in favour of union with Piedmont. It was fear of a democratic revolution, a desire to weaken Austria, and Britain's wish for a strong Italian state as a counterweight to French influence that induced the Western powers to assist Piedmont in obtaining this great success.

GARIBALDI AND THE THOUSAND

The democratic movement refused to consider the national revolution in any way complete so long as parts of the peninsula remained under the old sovereigns. Sicily, where autonomist opposition to the Bourbon government was endemic and extreme, was the most obvious place for a democratic revival. In April 1860 a Mazzinian-inspired insurrection broke out in Palermo (the Gancia revolt), and, although it was quickly quelled, it spread throughout the island. After the insurrection, Sicilian democrats demonstrated that they could overcome their deep divisions of ideology and class. In May they had the opportunity to assist Garibaldi's Expedition of the Thousand, a volunteer force that had set sail from Liguria to free the Italian south from Bourbon rule.

Despite scant preparations and a shortage of weapons, Garibaldi's volunteers landed at Marsala on May 11, 1860, and in less than three months conquered the entire island of Sicily. Garibaldi's daring and skill and the indigenous revolutionary ferment accounted for the success of the expedition. Still, the attitude of the Sicilian peasants was ambivalent. They initially welcomed the invading force but then quickly became disillusioned at Garibaldi's reluctance to order the breakup of secular, landed estates. Although Garibaldi declared on May 14 that he ruled "in the name of Victor Emmanuel, king of Italy," he entrusted the Sicilian provisional government to his associate, Francesco Crispi, who came into serious conflict with Cavour's emissaries on the island. Cavour feared the implications of a republican coup d'état. Meanwhile, as the European powers attempted mediation, the new king of the Two Sicilies, Francis II, granted a constitution and promised amnesty to Sicilian rebels. At this point, without the consent of Victor Emmanuel II and perhaps even against his wishes, Garibaldi crossed the Strait of Messina on August 19, 1860, and by September 7 made a triumphant entry

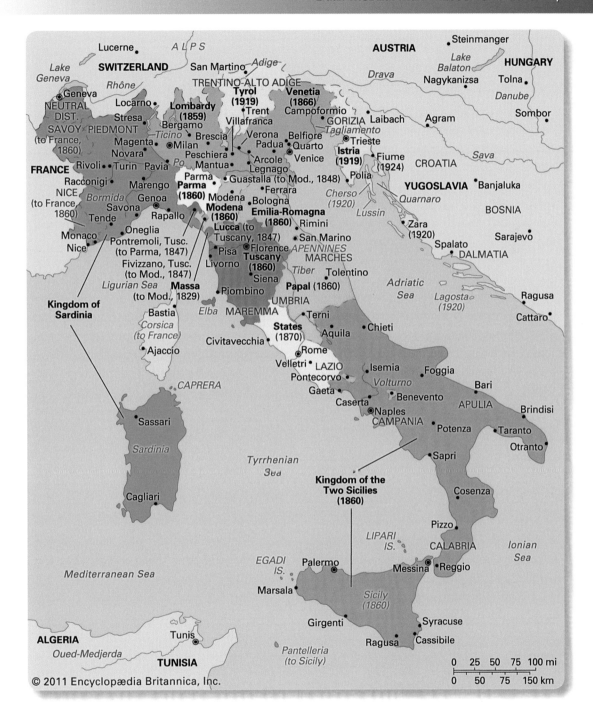

The unification of Italy. The dates are those of annexation, first to Sardinia-Piedmont and after 1861 to the Kingdom of Italy.

into Naples. Francis II fled to Gaeta, and on October 1 the last serious resistance of the Bourbon army collapsed at the Battle of the Volturno, near Caserta.

The prestige of Garibaldi and the democrats had risen so high that Cavour felt compelled to seize the initiative once again. Having persuaded Napoleon III to limit his opposition to lodging a perfunctory protest, Cavour proceeded to occupy the central Papal States (Umbria and the Marche). Rome and its surrounding region (Lazio) remained under papal rule, but the remainder of the Italian peninsula, apart from Austrian Venetia, became one kingdom under a moderate constitution. On October 26, 1860, Victor Emmanuel II met with Garibaldi on Neapolitan soil and was greeted as "king of Italy." During October and November, plebiscites in the former papal and Bourbon provinces overwhelmingly endorsed annexation to the Kingdom of Italy.

The Kingdom of Italy was officially proclaimed on March 17, 1861, by a parliament assembled in Turin. Soon afterward Cavour asserted that Rome must become the capital of the new state within a context of separation between secular and religious authority. However, with Cavour's untimely death on June 6, 1861, the Roman Question remained unresolved.

CONDITION OF THE ITALIAN KINGDOM

In 1861 the kingdom had 26 million inhabitants, 78 percent of whom were illiterate. With some 70 percent of the adult population engaged in agriculture, it seemed unlikely that Italy could achieve the economic progress that other European countries were making in that period. The group winning the majority in parliament in 1861 was from the moderate-conservative right. The coalition principally united a Piedmontese group, which was led by Giovanni Lanza and Quintino Sella and controlled manufacturing and banks, with Ricasoli's Tuscan group, which was interested in commerce and transportation. This elite alliance wanted a centralized government structure that would allow parliament, and hence the executive branch, to control local administration, especially where there was any danger of democratic predominance. By a series of laws enacted in 1865, these moderate notables effected legislative unification and established firm central control over the provinces and the communes through the appointment of handpicked regional prefects. Their democratic opposition, preoccupied with the issue of bringing Rome and Venetia into the new state, offered little resistance to these centralizing and authoritarian tendencies.

The kingdom's centralized government intensified the serious economic imbalance between north and south. The free-trade policy of the moderate governments ruined or badly harmed the weak and unprotected industries of the south, especially woolen-cloth manufacturing in the Salerno area, which the Bourbon government had previously sheltered.

Moreover, railroad construction in southern regions was beset with corruption in the issuance of contracts. Relief for the poor and public education remained miserably inadequate. Naples, the largest city in Italy in 1861, with about 447,000 inhabitants to Turin's 205,000, was plagued with poverty and disease.

Poverty was most acute and widespread in rural areas, where peasant families had gained nothing from the partial division of large feudal estates. Many peasants espoused an especially violent form of brigandage, which, though fomented and often assisted by emissaries of the exiled Francis II, was a form of class warfare against the agrarian bourgeoisie. Men on horseback occupied villages in the south, killed Liberals, and raised the white flag of the Bourbon kingdom. The government sent some 116,000 soldiers—two-fifths of the entire Italian army—to the south to combat this lawlessness. The army's savage action resulted in the execution of at least 5,000 peasants under laws that established special tribunals to deal with the "emergency." Even so, the government did not bring brigandage under control until 1865.

In the country at large, the public remained preoccupied with completing territorial unification. The democrats, who were most interested in solving the Roman Question, saw an opportunity to act in March 1862 when Urbano Rattazzi replaced Bettino Ricasoli as prime minister. Garibaldi assembled a volunteer force in July and August and began a march from the south into Lazio and Rome. Fearful of Austrian reaction and of a military confrontation with the French garrison in Rome, Rattazzi mobilized the regular army. Garibaldi was wounded in the ensuing fighting and was arrested on August 29, 1862, at Aspromonte in Calabria. The subsequent public outrage brought down Rattazzi's government. In 1864 Marco Minghetti, another moderate, negotiated the September Convention, a compromise that required French troops to withdraw from Rome in exchange for an Italian pledge to respect the pope's temporal sovereignty and to remain out of Rome. A secret clause in the agreement also bound Italy to transfer its capital from Turin to Florence, thus implicitly abandoning Cavour's claim to Rome. When this clause became known, severe riots in Turin (September 21–22) left 30 people dead and caused the fall of the Minghetti government.

THE ACQUISITION OF VENETIA AND ROME

Two years later, in June 1866, the outbreak of war between Austria and Prussia diverted attention from Rome to Venetia. The Italian government of Alfonso La Marmora, under the terms of an alliance with Prussia, attacked Austrian-held Venetia when Prussia attacked Austria from the north, but the Italians met defeat both on land at Custoza (June 24) and at sea near Lissa (July 20). In July Garibaldi led a band of volunteers who cooperated with regular army units to achieve some moderate success near Trento, but the government ordered him to withdraw when Austria and Germany concluded an armistice. Through the mediation of Napoleon III, Italy obtained Venetia in the Treaty of Vienna (October 3, 1866). In the spring of 1867, Rattazzi returned to power and permitted Garibaldi to station volunteers along the papal border. However, a renewed attempt to march on Rome merely brought back French troops, who defeated Garibaldi at Mentana on November 3. Arrested once again, he was sentenced to house arrest on the remote island of Caprera, between Sardinia and Corsica, where he owned some property. Italy suffered a marked loss of prestige politically and militarily, and the internal situation was far from favourable. Separatist revolts occurred in Palermo in 1866. In 1869 Parma and other cities rose in rebellion against the *macinato* ("grist tax") and other taxes levied to finance the reorganization of the armed forces.

The Lanza-Sella government, formed in December 1869, was perhaps the most typical among the centre-right cabinets of this period. It repressed Mazzinian opposition, advocated free trade, and was cautious in foreign affairs, although, in its careful subservience to France, it nearly acquiesced to the king's desire to intervene in the Franco-German War. Yet, despite its lack of brilliance, the Lanza-Sella government resolved the Roman Question. Napoleon III's defeat and abdication deprived the pope of French military protection. Therefore, on September 20, 1870, following a token armed resistance by the papal army, Italian troops breached the city's walls at Porta Pia and entered Rome. Refusing to accept Italy's occupation of the city, Pius IX withdrew and declared himself a prisoner in the Vatican palace, a position that his successors maintained until 1929.

CHAPTER 8

ITALY FROM 1870 TO THE PRESENT

Afte the conquest of Rome in 1870, Italian politicians settled down to manage the economy, to build up the country's military power, and—in the telling phrase of the Piedmontese author and statesman Massimo d'Azeglio—to "make Italians." Popular disaffection remained high, especially because of the grist tax that had been introduced in 1869. Governments of the right remained in office, first under Giovanni Lanza (to 1873) and then under Marco Minghetti (1873–76). The right was not an organized party but a group of patriotic, mostly northern landowners committed to a strong currency and free trade. Under both prime ministers the main domestic task was to balance the budget. Minghetti eventually managed this, but raising taxes and squeezing expenditure made the right unpopular, and its candidates did badly in the 1874 elections. In March 1876 the Minghetti government fell when its Tuscan supporters refused to support a state takeover of the railways.

Italy was then ruled for many years by governments of the left, which were usually led by Agostino Depretis (until his death in 1887). The deputies of the left, heirs of the Risorgimento's democratic tradition, were more anticlerical, more frequently members of the middle class (many of them were lawyers), more often from the south, and less concerned about the value of money than the rentier right had been. They were, however, splintered into various groups, and factional disputes became endemic. Left governments abolished the grist tax (1883) and made two years' primary education compulsory (1877).

A main achievement of the left was the widening of suffrage in 1882. The voting age was reduced to 21 (from 25); the requirement to pay 40 lire in direct taxes per annum was halved and was abolished altogether for those with two years' schooling. The electorate thus increased from approximately 500,000 to 2 million men, including now many urban artisans, especially in the north, where schools were more common. Within a few years modern political parties were founded and won seats in northern Italy, but southern constituencies remained dominated by elite groups of lawyers and local notables, often linked to prominent landowners.

Local government was also very significant, and there were often bitter disputes among local factions. The 8,300-odd municipalities (comuni) were in charge of primary schools and most welfare services, raised much of their own revenue, and appointed their own staff. The central government tried to control them by appointing the mayors and also by giving veto powers over municipal decisions to provincial bodies that were strongly influenced by the provincial prefect, a government appointee. The prefect frequently dissolved councils for alleged financial or legal abuses and replaced them with a government "commissioner" until new elections were held, but these dissolutions often occurred when council leaders opposed government candidates at parliamentary elections. However, government attempts to control local government were never really successful. The prefects had to ensure that government candidates would win the next parliamentary elections, and so they had to conciliate, not bully, local elites, including the mayors and municipal councillors. Corruption was therefore often left unchecked. National governments became remarkably dependent on local power holders. Depretis himself won over ("transformed") deputies and kept his governments in office by distributing patronage and favours to local notables.

Trasformismo ("transformism") became the normal way of conducting parliamentary business, for there were few serious disputes among the leading politicians. Virtually all of them accepted the constitutional settlement of 1861, and few disputed foreign and colonial policy, which, in any case, was conducted by foreign ministers and prime ministers without much reference to parliament. In 1881 the French occupation of Tunisia alarmed the government, and the following year, to avoid diplomatic isolation, Italy joined the Triple Alliance with Germany and Austria-Hungary. This was essentially a defensive alliance guaranteeing German and Austrian support against any attack by France, Italy's main rival in the Mediterranean. Meanwhile, Italy embarked on its first real colonial ventures, the takeover of the Red Sea ports of Asseb and Massawa (both now in Eritrea) in 1885. Southern politicians favoured colonial expansion as an outlet for surplus population and agricultural produce; northern ones wanted Italy to be a great power, saw the army as an essential guarantor of public order, and supported high military spending—the army and navy ministries spent more than all other ministries combined between 1862 and 1913.

FORCES OF OPPOSITION

The political elite may have agreed on most issues, but there was plenty of opposition in the country. Most men owned guns, and violent crime was common. There were 3,000 murders a year, many of them a result of vendettas or blood feuds. Brigands were still active in parts of the southern mainland in the 1870s, and banditry was still common in the mountainous zones of Sardinia. In the towns, rioting was frequent; more than 250 people were killed in riots against the grist tax in 1869, and similar riots against local taxes or for land and jobs continued well into the 20th century. The strikes of the 1880s— especially by organized agricultural labourers in Mantua province—much alarmed respectable opinion. Anarchists were active in the Romagna and parts of the south and occasionally attempted to carry out insurrections, as at Matese in 1877, or to kill the king, as Giovanni Passanante attempted to do in 1878.

However, the anarchist leader in the Romagna, Andrea Costa, soon converted to socialist ideas. In 1881 he founded the Revolutionary Socialist Party of Romagna (later the Italian Revolutionary Socialist Party), which preached eventual revolution but also agitated for such causes as universal suffrage and labour and welfare legislation; in 1882, under the new suffrage, Costa became Italy's first socialist deputy. In Lombardy a moderate, labour-oriented Italian Workers' Party, founded in 1885, helped to organize the Po valley peasantry into "leagues" and labour cooperatives. The northern labour movement—unions, mutual aid societies, and cooperatives—adopted either revolutionary or reformist socialist ideas. Reformist local councils began to be elected in central Italy, first in Imola and then in other small agricultural towns.

Republican opposition also survived, particularly in central Italy, long after Mazzini's death in 1872. Republicans ran many of the mutual aid societies and cooperatives. They opposed strikes, nationalizations, and the class struggle but strongly favoured social protective legislation and civil rights. Some of them, including Matteo Renato Imbriani, also advocated an active irredentist foreign policy—that is, a policy that aimed to liberate Italians living in foreign territory; in particular they wanted to wrest Trento and Trieste from Austrian control. They considered the Triple Alliance and colonial expansionism inimical to Italian interests and expressions of Italy's monarchical and conservative political institutions.

Perhaps the most serious opposition force in the country was the Roman Catholic Church. The Risorgimento had deprived the church of the Papal States, including Rome itself, and of much of its

IRREDENTISTS

The Irredentists (Italian: Irredentisti) were a group of Italian patriots prominent in the last quarter of the 19th century and the early 20th century who sought to deliver Italian lands from foreign rule. Their name was derived from the words *Italia irredenta* ("unredeemed Italy"), and their object was to emancipate the lands of Trentino (south Tirol), Gorizia, Istria, Trieste, Ticino, Nice, Corsica, and Malta from Austrian, Swiss, French, and British rule.

The Irredentists aimed especially at gaining several Italian-inhabited areas still controlled by Austria after the process of Italian unification (1860–70). In the last two decades of the 19th century, they opposed Italy's adherence to the Triple Alliance, which included Austria. The Irredentists contributed to the pressure that caused the Italian government to enter World War I on the side of the Allies (May 1915). Italy's acquisition of the Istrian peninsula on the north Adriatic and of south Tirol from Austria after the war fulfilled the hopes of many of the Irredentists.

income. The church had lost its previous virtual monopoly of education and welfare, and compulsory state education was deliberately secular. Many religious orders had been disbanded; monasteries and convents had become public buildings, used by the state. In the south particularly, ecclesiastical organization had relied heavily on monks and friars and could barely continue to function. Bishops needed royal approval, which was often refused, to receive their revenues and take up their posts. The state's Law of Guarantees of 1871 permitted the pope himself to retain only the Vatican and Lateran palaces as well as Castel Gandolfo. Pius IX denounced the new usurping state, forbade Catholics to vote in parliamentary elections or to become candidates, and appointed a new generation of "intransigent" bishops. New laymen's organizations were founded; the Opera dei Congressi, with committees at parish level, became the focus of Catholic resistance to the new state. It organized cooperatives, welfare insurance, credit banks and mutual aid societies, as well as a host of local journals and campaigns against liberal secular proposals (such as a divorce law). Church and state remained mutually suspicious, particularly in the Veneto region, where the Catholic social movement effectively mobilized regionalist opposition to centralizing government and peasant hostility to landlords and free trade.

LAND REFORM

The main issue of political debate in late 19th-century Italy was land ownership. Liberal governments insisted that the municipalities should sell off most of the common land to private owners—at least 740,000 acres (300,000 hectares) were sold by 1880 in southern Italy alone, and more was occupied illegally. Another 1.25 million acres (500,000 hectares) of ecclesiastical estates were similarly sold, often at extremely low prices. Overall, at least 5,000,000 acres (2 million hectares) were transferred. In some regions, including Piedmont, Liguria, and Sardinia, the sales did create a "property-owning democracy"; that is, a large number of rural people became small landowners, albeit with scattered strips that made improvement unprofitable. The sales also introduced people to the market economy because they had to repay their mortgages in cash and find money for high land taxes. Small-scale ownership did not become common in most other regions, despite the land sales. Peasants who did acquire land were often forced to sell it again to meet tax debts or interest payments. However, land transfers did often create a non-noble rural middle class that owned an adequate amount of land or extensive flocks and could dominate local politics. This was particularly true in the former Papal States of central Italy.

Privatization of the commons also had serious environmental and social consequences. Much common land was woodland, bought up and felled by speculators who sold timber to railway companies (for sleepers) or to mines (for roof support). Deforestation became widespread; Sardinia, for example, lost four-fifths of its trees in the 19th century. The results included soil erosion, landslides, stagnant water in valley bottoms, and increased malaria—the greatest scourge of rural Italy, which in turn prevented much fertile low-lying land from being cultivated. Furthermore, the state also abolished traditional rights such as grazing and wood gathering on the remaining unsold common land. Millions of households that had relied on access to this land to obtain fuel for heating and cooking or pasture for their pigs were suddenly forced either to suffer real poverty or to break the law.

PROTECTIONISM

Most agricultural land in Italy produced grain, especially wheat. In the early 1880s world wheat prices fell by one-third, and the incomes of the larger and more prosperous farmers (who grew for the market rather than for their own consumption) collapsed. As landowners were the most powerful pressure group in the country and were strongly represented in parliament, the government could not resist their demands for protectionism.

The most prominent wool and cotton manufacturers of northern Italy also favoured tariff protection, and these industries were second only to the silk industry in importance and numbers employed. Some tariff protection (up to 40 percent) had, in fact, already been given to textiles and other light industries in 1878, but employers naturally wanted more, particularly after the restoration of gold convertibility in 1883 in effect revalued the lira. Moreover, in the 1880s Italy also gained a steel industry (Terni Steelworks, founded 1886), which was designed to build warships and railways but was sold to subsidized industries and was itself unable to survive without protection. All this meant the rise of a strong protectionist lobby, representing large landowners and textile manufacturers and linked to powerful steel and naval interests.

SOCIAL CHANGES

In 1871 there were 26.8 million Italians. Both birth and death rates were high, and almost half the children born alive died before age five. Large-scale transatlantic emigration began in the 1880s; in 1888 alone more than 200,000 Italians went to the Americas in search of jobs, 10 times as many as a decade previously. The most popular destinations were Argentina, Brazil, and the United States.

Most emigrants in this early phase, whether bound for the Americas or for other parts of Europe, were northerners, often seasonal migrants from hill and mountain areas of peasant ownership, where jobs were scarce and where younger sons who stayed behind had little prospect of marriage. But even in 1888 more than a quarter of the emigrants were southerners, and the great exodus of southern emigrants to both North and South America was just about to begin. Most people (nearly 70 percent in 1871) were illiterate and usually spoke only dialect. The compulsory schooling law of 1877 (which was widely ignored in practice) provided for only two years

of schooling, not enough to guarantee the ability to read and count. Conscripts were likely to be taught to read during military service, but only one-fourth of the age group was actually called up into the army. Italian education was more successful at the secondary level in the towns, where the "technical schools" and "technical institutes" taught science, engineering, and accounting and had high prestige among urban parents. As for the universities, they mainly trained lawyers and doctors, both professions in which supply considerably exceeded demand.

THE CRISPI ERA

On the death of Depretis in 1887 the Sicilian and former Mazzinian Francesco Crispi became prime minister and pursued a policy of administrative reforms at home and expansion abroad. His main domestic achievement was to extend suffrage at local elections to all males over age 21 who paid five lire per annum in local taxes—that is, to 3.5 million people. This was a real blow to the local notables who had previously controlled local government. The larger councils (after 1896, all councils) were also permitted to choose their own mayors and were required to meet in public. The Crispi government also brought in a reasonably effective system of administrative law for the first time, through the provincial councils (*giunte*) and the Council of State. The government reformed the

Portrait of Francesco Crispi, Italian prime minister during the late 1800s. DEA/A. Dagli Orti/De Agostini/Getty Images

charities, excluded the clergy from running them, and often diverted the funds to more secular purposes. The minister of justice, Giuseppe Zanardelli, promulgated a new code of criminal law that abolished the death penalty and legalized strikes unless violence or intimidation occurred.

However, the most important act of Crispi's first government was the new tariff of 1887. It was a response to demands from northern steel and textile interests, from farmers (also mainly from the north) who faced imports of cheap American grain or Asian rice, and from social reformers eager to secure legislative measures that employers could afford. A duty of 50 lire per ton was placed on imported wheat by 1888, and later it went higher still; food prices rose sharply, provoking considerable unrest. Similar measures protected steel, shipbuilding, and textiles. Italy's largest trading partner was France, and the French retaliated against Italian goods. A "tariff war" between the two countries lasted until 1898. Franco-Italian trade was more than halved, and entire sectors of Italian agriculture, including wine, silk, cattle, and olive oil, collapsed overnight as their markets were cut off. When excess food supplies drove all agricultural prices down, even grain growers failed to benefit from the new tariff. Moreover, the crisis helped to drag down many of Italy's banks, including one of the largest, the Banca Romana. Resulting inquiries revealed that the bank had made interest-free loans to leading politicians, including Crispi himself and former treasury minister Giovanni Giolitti, who was prime minister from May 1892 to November 1893. Politicians needed the money to finance their election expenses and to run or bribe newspapers. The Banca Romana scandal of 1893 was the first of many famous Italian corruption scandals, and, like the others, it discredited the whole political system.

Crispi's colonial policy brought additional blows. The Italian settlement at Massawa soon provoked conflict with Ethiopia, which claimed Massawa as part of its own territory and whose forces in 1887 killed 500 Italian troops at Dogali. The two countries made peace at Wichale in 1889, and Crispi expanded the Italian possessions along the Red Sea to include most of present-day Eritrea and along the Indian Ocean coast to include eastern and southern Somalia. In 1895 the Italians annexed a large portion of the Ethiopian province of Tigray, and war with Ethiopia began again. In March 1896 the Ethiopians overwhelmed the Italian army at the Battle of Adwa (Adua), killing about 5,000 Italian troops. This disaster forced Crispi to resign and ended Italy's colonial adventures for some years. It was widely seen in Italy as a disgrace to the whole political system and to Italy's aspirations to great-power status; it would have to be avenged in the future.

YEARS OF CRISIS

Economic hardship and political corruption at home, together with military failure abroad, provoked riots and uprisings throughout the country. In the early 1890s the *fasci siciliani* (Sicilian peasant leagues organized by socialists and others) led successful strikes and land occupations until Crispi, in January 1894, used the army to restore order. The *fasci*'s leaders were imprisoned, and the movement soon collapsed. At the same time, the government also suppressed an anarchist insurrection in Lunigiana by martial law. Further riots occurred in 1898, mainly in cities and towns, over civil liberties and the high price of bread. Shortly after troops killed hundreds of rioters in Milan, King Umberto I decorated their commander, General Fiorenzo Bava Beccaris. Governments also exercised repression by attempting to govern without parliament, as Crispi did in 1895; by dissolving opposition associations and unions, as the government of the marchese di Rudinì, Antonio Starabba, did in 1897; and by attempting to restrict civil liberties by royal decree, without parliamentary approval, as the governments of both Rudinì and Luigi Pelloux tried to do in 1898–99. Socialists, anarchists, and syndicalists protested against this authoritarian rule both inside and outside parliament. In 1899 Socialist deputies overturned the parliamentary ballot box to block the passage of a measure.

Repression resulted in a constitutional crisis. Conservative politicians, notably Sidney Sonnino in 1897, argued that the Italian parliament was corrupt and unfit to govern and that the king should provide strong executive rule, according to the letter of the 1848 Statuto (constitution). Most moderate Liberals rejected this argument. The campaign for constitutional government was led by Felice Cavallotti and the Radical group in parliament, who in the 1890s strongly denounced bank scandals, tariff protectionism, colonial wars, and the Triple Alliance. The Radicals were a northern, anticlerical, moralistic group that denounced the corruption of the south (Crispi was the first southern prime minister), of the monarchy, and of the Roman establishment and strongly favoured wider civil liberties and army reform. In 1900, after months of bitter parliamentary dispute and obstructionism, Pelloux called a general election to resolve the constitutional issue, in which the left triumphed; the Radicals won 34 seats, and their allies, the Republicans, won a further 28 out of a total of 557. (The two groups had had 51 seats between them in the previous parliament.)

Furthermore, in 1892 a young Milanese lawyer, Filippo Turati, had helped to found the Italian Workers' Party (Partito dei Lavoratori Italiani), which in 1893 became the Italian Socialist Party (Partito Socialista Italiano; PSI). The PSI united the various socialist and labour groups of northern and central Italy and Sicily and stood in opposition to the anarchist movement. The new party was mainly social democratic and heavily influenced by the German model. It preached class struggle and aspired to parliamentary representation and state socialism. Formally Marxist, it envisaged a long period of evolution before an eventual "revolutionary" transformation of society. Crispi dissolved the party in 1894, but it revived in the late 1890s and won 32 seats in 1900. While its deputies worked closely with the Radicals to secure constitutional liberties and social reforms, ordinary party members were often much more revolutionary in their aims. Other socialist organizations, such as trade unions and cooperatives, also grew in the 1890s and by 1900 were significant in the newly industrializing economy of northern Italy. They campaigned for concrete short-term gains on wages and working conditions and were usually more reformist than the party. However, the more radical syndicalist movement also began to take hold among various groups of workers and peasants at this time, including dockworkers, marble miners in Tuscany, and peasants in Puglia. These organizations preached revolutionary class struggle and opposed the reformist policies of the Socialist Party leadership. Railway workers, who were also influenced by revolutionary syndicalism, formed their own autonomous union, the Italian Railroad Workers Union (Sindacato Ferrovieri Italiani; SFI), in 1907. Moreover, a syndicalist federation, the Italian Syndical Union (Unione Sindacale Italiana; USI), was founded in 1912.

THE GIOLITTI ERA

The elections of June 1900 marked the defeat of the Pelloux government and of attempts to impose illiberal laws. The following month King Umberto I was assassinated by an Italian anarchist, Gaetano Bresci, who had returned from the United States to "avenge" the victims of the 1898 repression. The new king, Victor Emmanuel III, favoured a return to constitutional government, as did the governments led by Pelloux's successors, Giuseppe Saracco, Giuseppe Zanardelli, and Giovanni Giolitti, the last of whom was the most frequent holder of the office of prime minister between 1903 and 1914. Giolitti sought to defuse popular discontent by social reforms, the gradual extension of the right to vote, and public works and to conciliate the major organized opposition groups in the country, the Socialists and the Roman Catholics. In 1912 suffrage was extended to nearly the entire adult male population, from 3.3 to 8.6 million men.

In the south, however, Giolitti's government was less accommodating and often resorted to old-style repression in the face of protest, as in 1903 and 1904. The historian and Socialist Gaetano Salvemini, the fiercest critic of Giolitti's strategy toward the south, accused the government of corruption and of doing nothing to alleviate poverty. Salvemini's pamphlet, first published in 1909 and later collected as *Il ministro della mala vita* (1919; "The Ministry of Evil"), encapsulated this position. Giolitti also embarked on a colonialist war with Turkey in 1911, with the support of the church and the new nationalist movement. Italy conquered Libya and the

King Victor Emmanuel III (far left) and Queen Elena strolling down a city street with Prime Minister Giovanni Giolitti. Alinari Archives/Getty Images

Greek-speaking Dodecanese islands in the Aegean Sea. Both territories became Italian possessions in 1912 and remained so until World War II.

DOMESTIC POLICIES

The social reforms passed in these years included laws that prohibited child labour, established a compulsory maternity fund and compulsory rest days, and limited the working day of women to 11 hours. Central governments also subsidized municipal welfare schemes such as orphanages and senior citizen housing and encouraged municipal transport, housing, and water and sewage schemes—especially in northern Italy, where the municipalities could afford such innovations. Often these schemes were pioneered by Catholic- or Socialist-dominated local councils, which entrusted the management to their own cooperatives; government approval of "municipal socialism" was much resented by local businessmen, shopkeepers, and others. Moreover, Giolitti's governments allowed trade unions to operate in relative freedom and generally avoided interfering in private-sector labour disputes. The government's tolerance of labour organizations was another source of middle-class resentment.

Giolitti enjoyed Radical support, and his governments often included Radical deputies. He also received the tacit support of moderate Socialist deputies and union leaders. Giolitti's accommodation of labour and Socialists was his way of co-opting the socialist movement and, as he put it, placing "Marx in the attic." Trade unionism grew rapidly in the new atmosphere after 1900, not only in industry but among the agricultural labourers of the Po valley and Puglia. A land-workers union, the Federation of Agricultural Labourers (Federterra), was formed in 1901, and the various Socialist-led unions formed a confederation of labour in 1906. Some unions depended heavily on public works schemes subsidized by government. Others, such as Federterra, relied on Giolitti's reform legislation favouring cooperatives and on contracts provided by Socialist councils. All the major Socialist institutions became reliant on government willingness not to repress them. In turn, they abandoned any effort to overthrow the government. However, revolutionary views dominated the Socialist Party membership from 1904 to 1908, which was always more militant than its leaders, especially those in parliament. Moreover, there was also a powerful group of revolutionary syndicalists, who broke away from the Socialist Party in 1907 but retained control of many unions, especially in Liguria and Puglia. This popular militancy ensured that Socialist deputies could not compromise too openly with Giolitti or accept posts in his governments.

Nor could the organized Roman Catholic movement easily make open arrangements with the Giolitti government. The Catholics, too, had founded trade unions and workers' cooperatives, as well as mutual aid societies and rural banks, throughout northern Italy in the 1890s. This development followed Pope Leo XIII's embrace of social concerns in his encyclical *Rerum Novarum* (1891). In opposition both to socialism and the "excesses of capitalism," *Rerum Novarum* called for the organization of Catholics in economic and political life, class conciliation, the creation of small farms, limits on weekend work, and the defense of female workers. Catholic associations were particularly strong among the peasantry of Lombardy, Piedmont, and the Veneto and among the largely female textile workers, and they controlled many local councils. In 1897–98 the Rudinì government dissolved most Catholic associations, but later governments permitted their reestablishment in return for tacit support against socialism. This support even became overt at parliamentary elections; in 1904 and 1909 the papal prohibition on Catholics voting (*non expedit*) was lifted in many constituencies, and Catholics were permitted to vote for Liberal candidates in order to keep Socialists out. In 1913 antisocialists signed a secret electoral agreement known as the Gentiloni pact, named for the president of the Catholic Electoral Union, Vincenzo Ottorino Gentiloni. The old "intransigents" of the Opera dei Congressi, deeply hostile to a united Italy, were replaced early in the century by a new generation of moderate Catholic leaders favoured by Pius X, who even dissolved the Opera dei Congressi in 1904 and brought the Catholic lay movement under the bishops. The Catholic moderates gave Giolitti their support, but they could not enter government or even operate as a lay party independent of the bishops or the Vatican.

ECONOMIC DEVELOPMENTS

Giolitti's political dominance rested on Italy's rapid economic growth after the mid-1890s. Industrial production probably doubled between 1896 and 1913. The tariff dispute with France was settled in 1898. Cotton milling remained the largest industry, but by 1914 Italy had also established—for military reasons—a large, protected steel industry, together with extensive shipbuilding yards in Liguria. Big modern metalworking plants opened or expanded in Piombino, Terni, Brescia, Milan, and Genoa. The railways were nationalized in 1905, and this stimulated demand for rolling stock and engines. Hydroelectricity from the Alps provided cheap, renewable energy for the factories of the northwestern "industrial triangle" (Lombardy, Liguria, and Piedmont). Moreover, a major new industry—automobile production—developed, in which Italy did not have to compete against established interests elsewhere. Fiat, founded in Turin in 1899 by Giovanni Agnelli, soon became one of Europe's largest producers and exporters of automobiles and also made buses, trucks, airplanes, and military vehicles. Lancia was founded in Turin in 1906, and the company that became Alfa Romeo opened in Milan in 1910. Olivetti, founded in 1908 in Ivrea, soon became Europe's leading producer of typewriters and office machines. The state's finances were healthy during this period, and the balance of payments was boosted by remittances from the millions of emigrants elsewhere in Europe and in the Americas.

Agriculture, still the dominant sector of the economy, provided jobs for almost 60 percent of employed adults in 1911. It, too, enjoyed a boom, partly because of state-subsidized land reclamation and irrigation schemes (particularly in the Po valley) and partly because of continued high tariffs on grain imports, which gave ample incentive to produce more food on suitable land. Wheat production rose by about one-third in these years. In central Italy, sugar beet production, another heavily protected sector, stimulated a new refining industry. The Socialists and Catholics founded cooperatives throughout northern and central Italy to help provide seeds and machinery and to market produce, and a network of rural banks provided farmers with much-needed cheap credit.

Economic growth, however, was heavily concentrated in the north. The south languished, and income there was less than half that in the north. The southern economy was arguably linked more closely to northern Europe and South America (to which it exported wine, olive oil, fruit, and labour) than to northern Italy. Southern produce needed markets abroad, and the south was very badly hit by the tariff war with France. Moreover, the positivist school of anthropology, fashionable in the 1890s and later, promoted a widely held view that southerners were more criminal than northerners and even "racially" degenerate—an argument that lent ethnic overtones to the debate on "southern backwardness."

Southern politicians soon began demanding and, when in office, securing tax relief and development schemes, which provided, among other things, roads, schools, and irrigation. In 1897 the first "special law" provided Italy's poorest region, Sardinia, with cheaper credit and funds for irrigation and reforestation. Sardinia's leading politician, Francesco Cocco Ortu, was minister of agriculture. Later laws extended similar or greater benefits to other regions and in 1906 to the entire south. In practice, the legislation had little impact, because World War I interrupted any progress. However, it was the first time that funds derived from taxes paid by the prosperous north were used by central government agencies to stimulate economic activity in the south—or at least to win votes for government supporters.

Continuing southern poverty stimulated mass emigration from Sicily and the southern mainland, which averaged more than 500,000 people per year from about 1901 onward and rose to 900,000 in 1913, mainly to North and South America. About half of the migrants to the New World returned later, bringing new values as well as new money. Others sent back regular payments that contributed to the local economy. Some southerners crossed the Atlantic twice a year, commuting to seasonal agricultural work in Argentina. In the north most emigration to other European countries was seasonal, but many rural dwellers migrated within Italy to jobs in the expanding industrial cities. Migrants were usually young, male, unskilled, and illiterate, but many were also politically aware and militant, as the strong anarchist presence of Italians in the United States testified.

HEALTH AND EDUCATION

The other major social changes in these years, apart from emigration, resulted from the decline in serious illnesses and in illiteracy. Improved water supplies and sewerage meant fewer cholera epidemics—though these still occurred at times, as at Barletta in 1910–12. Malaria, a major scourge of the rural south, declined sharply as quinine became widely available after 1900. Pellagra, a vitamin-deficiency disease endemic among the northern peasantry, rapidly declined as diets improved. By 1901, for the first time, a majority (51.3 percent) of Italians could read and write. Emigrants needed to be able to write home, and so they had an incentive to learn. In 1911 the primary schools were removed from municipal control—poor communes had not been able to build schools or to enforce attendance—and were henceforth run and financed by the central government. Whereas most Italians at the time of national unification had spoken only their regional dialect, millions of people now spoke standard Italian, which they learned in school or in the army or for use as a lingua franca in the cities. A common language, common education, and common experience of military service had begun, by 1914, to "make Italians"—but religion, social class, and local loyalties still sharply divided them.

ITALY DURING WORLD WAR I

On Giolitti's resignation in March 1914, the more conservative Antonio Salandra formed a new government. In June, "Red Week," a period of widespread rioting throughout the Romagna and the Marche, came in response to the killing of three antimilitarist demonstrators at Ancona. When World War I broke out in August, the Salandra government stayed neutral and began to negotiate with both sides—a policy that Foreign Minister Sidney Sonnino described as "sacred egoism." The Austrians eventually agreed to grant Trentino to Italy in exchange for an alliance, but the Triple Entente (France, Britain, and Russia) made a more generous offer, promising Italy not only Trentino but also South Tirol, Trieste, Gorizia, Istria, and northern Dalmatia. The Italians accepted this offer in the secret Treaty of London (April 1915) and joined the war against Austria-Hungary a month later, hoping for major territorial gains.

The negotiations, conducted by the foreign and prime ministers and a handful of diplomats, had been kept secret. The majority of deputies, meanwhile, favoured neutrality, as did former prime minister Giolitti, the major opposition groups (Catholics and Socialists), and most of the population. War therefore was supported only by the conservatives in government, by the Nationalist Association, a group formed in 1910 by Enrico Corradini and others to support

Italian expansionism, by some Liberals who saw it as the culmination of the Risorgimento's fight for national unity, by Republicans and reformist Socialists who knew nothing of the Treaty of London and thought they were fighting for national liberation, and by some syndicalists and extremist Socialists—including Benito Mussolini, then editor of the Socialist Party newspaper—who thought the war would bring about the overthrow of capitalism. Mussolini was soon expelled from the Socialist Party, but with help from the Triple Entente he managed to found his own alternative, pro-war newspaper, *Il Popolo d'Italia* ("The People of Italy"). Futurists and nationalists (including Gabriele D'Annunzio) agitated for intervention.

In April–May 1915 the government, helped by a series of noisy demonstrations by pro-war activists (the so-called "Radiant Days of May"), pushed through its war policy despite the opposition of the majority in parliament and in the country. Neither Giolitti nor any other "neutralist" could form a government without renouncing the Treaty of London, betraying Italy's new allies, and compromising the king. The Salandra government officially declared war against Austria-Hungary on May 23 and entered combat the following day.

Meanwhile, despite a series of defections to the nationalist cause, the Socialist Party expressed its official position in the slogan "Neither adherence, nor sabotage." Unlike its sister parties in the Second International (an international meeting of trade unions and socialist parties), the PSI did not get behind the Italian war effort. The reformist Claudio Treves voiced the pacifist opinions of the movement in parliament in 1917, when he made a plea that the troops should not spend another winter in the trenches. Other Socialists took a more active role against the war and distributed antiwar propaganda or organized desertions. Many Catholics also failed to support Italy's participation in the war, although others took an active part in the conflict. In August 1917 Pope Benedict XV called for an end to what he called a "useless slaughter."

In June 1916, after a series of military failures, the Salandra government resigned. The new prime minister was Paolo Boselli, who, in turn, resigned after the momentous military disaster at Caporetto in October 1917, which enabled the Austrians to occupy much of the Veneto in 1917 and 1918. This single battle left 11,000 Italian soldiers dead, 29,000 injured, and 280,000 taken prisoner. Some 350,000 Italian soldiers deserted or went missing, and 400,000 people became refugees. Only a strong rearguard action in November and December prevented further Austrian advances.

Caporetto signified the end of the war for many Italians and encapsulated the disastrous leadership of General Luigi Cadorna, as well as the terrible conditions under which the war was being fought. In some mountain regions, far

Italian troops retreating after their defeat at the Battle of Caporetto in 1917. Hulton Archive/Getty Images

more soldiers died from cold and starvation than from actual fighting with the Austrians. The generals themselves tended to blame the defeat at Caporetto on poor morale and "defeatism." Cadorna blamed "shirkers" and called Caporetto a "military strike." (Caporetto had coincided with the Russian Revolution of 1917.) Cadorna himself was replaced by General Armando Diaz in November. Nonetheless, the invasion of Italian territory helped consolidate the war effort on the home front, and thousands of support committees, often sustained by middle-class groups, were formed to "defend the nation." Some Socialist deputies and intellectuals, such as Turati, rallied to the war effort as the threat to Italian territory became clearer. After the war, the wounds of the defeat in 1917 were reopened in the long Caporetto Inquest of 1918–19, which blamed the invasion largely on various top military leaders.

The war was deeply unpopular both among the troops—mostly conscripted peasants who were undernourished and fighting for a cause few could understand—and among the civilian population back home, which included almost one million workers in arms factories who were also subject to military discipline. Many rebelled within the army. (It has been estimated that some 470,000 conscripts resisted call-up, 310,000 committed acts of indiscipline under arms, and 300,000 deserted.) More than one million soldiers came before military tribunals before a postwar amnesty was granted. Many once again saw the Italian state only as a repressive institution. Antiwar disturbances struck Milan in May 1917, and serious bread riots took place among the industrial workers of Turin in August 1917. Troops occupied Turin and took four days to restore order; some 50 demonstrators and 10 soldiers were killed in the clashes. After November 1917 a more liberal government under Vittorio Emanuele Orlando rallied the country to defend its frontiers. Diaz made welfare concessions to the troops and fought a far more defensive campaign until October 1918, when, in the closing stages of the war, the Italians won a final, decisive victory at the Battle of Vittorio Veneto. In reality, Italy's victory was as much the result of the internal collapse of the Austro-Hungarian Empire and Germany as of any radical transformation in the capacities and motivations of the Italian army.

Italy won the war, therefore, but at a huge cost: some 600,000 dead, 950,000 wounded, and a legacy of bitterness and division. The victorious patriots and nationalists now detested parliament, where the Giolittian majority had never supported the war, although they defended the idea of the nation and the war record of the Italian army. Many workers, peasants, Socialists, and trade unionists were disgusted by the costs of the conflict and were inspired by the revolutions in Russia and Germany. Returning veterans expected the land that they had been promised in 1917–18. The Italian flag became a powerful focus of division and hatred. War memorials were contested all over the peninsula. These divisions greatly weakened the postwar political regime and fractured elements of society.

Furthermore, the pro-war groups were themselves bitterly divided when the war ended. Should Italy, at the Paris Peace Conference (1919–20), try to secure the terms of the Treaty of London, as Foreign Minister Sonnino urged, or should it support U.S. President Woodrow Wilson and adhere to the "principle of nationality"—that is, be willing to accept less territory in the Adriatic region, as the Left Liberals and Republicans advocated? In the Treaty of Saint-Germain (1919), Italy gained Trentino, part of Slovene-speaking

Gorizia, Trieste, the German-speaking South Tirol, and partly Croatian-speaking Istria. But Dalmatia was excluded, despite the Treaty of London, as was Fiume (now Rijeka, Croatia), a Yugoslav port largely inhabited by Italian speakers, which Sonnino had also decided to claim; so, too, were any colonial territories in Africa or Asia and any claim on Albania. Nationalists therefore argued that Italy had been robbed of its rightful gains ("a mutilated victory").

Orlando resigned in June 1919. When the new government of the Radical leader Francesco Saverio Nitti was also unsuccessful in foreign affairs, the flamboyant poet Gabriele D'Annunzio led a group of volunteers to Fiume in September and captured the city himself. Fiume became a centre of nationalist agitation for more than a year, and D'Annunzio was dislodged (by Italian forces) only in December 1920 when Fiume became, briefly, an independent republic. Fiume became a symbol of heroic nationalism for those Italians who had supported the war and felt betrayed by the postwar settlement.

ECONOMIC AND POLITICAL CRISIS: THE "TWO RED YEARS"

Italy faced serious postwar economic problems. Wartime governments had printed money to pay for arms, and inflation intensified. By the end of 1920 the lira was worth only one-sixth of its 1913 value. Savings became nearly worthless, and rents collected by landowners plummeted in value. Meanwhile, the major arms and shipbuilding firms went bankrupt after the war for lack of government orders. Unemployment rose to two million as returning soldiers searched for work. Peasants, organized by trade unions, ex-servicemen's groups, or Catholic leagues, seized land for themselves, especially in the south; agricultural labourers went on strike at harvest time. Trade unions, now operating again, pressed for higher wages, and strikes, including those in the public services, became routine. A series of stoppages paralyzed the railroads, as well as postal and telegraph services.

Throughout the *biennio rosso* ("two red years"; 1919–20), revolution appeared imminent. While spontaneous land occupations swept through the south, riots and lootings hit shopkeepers in the north and centre in the summer of 1919, and prices were cut by half throughout the country. Socialist deputies walked out of parliament in December 1919 to protest the presence of the king. They were attacked by nationalists, and widespread general strikes followed. In April 1920 the Piedmontese General Strike blocked work throughout Piedmont. The Socialist Party and the trade unions met in Milan to decide, absurdly, whether or not to call a revolution. They voted against, and Piedmont was isolated. In June 1920, mutinies, riots, and strikes hit the Ancona region and threatened to become an insurrection. Massive rural-worker agitation swept the whole of the Po valley and threatened the harvest during the summer of 1920. The Catholic "white" (as opposed to the Socialist "red") union federation, the CIL (Confederazione Italiana Lavoratori), formed in 1918, grew massively throughout the *biennio rosso*, above all in the agricultural regions of the north and especially around Bergamo, Brescia, and Cremona. A Catholic left even emerged in the north that preached revolution and led long strikes in Lombardy and the Veneto. Yet this mass movement never linked up with the Socialists, whose ideological anticlericalism alienated them from all wings of the Catholic movement.

The *biennio rosso* concluded with sit-down strikes in which workers occupied most of the factories of the north in August and September 1920. For three weeks workers attempted to continue production, seeking to promote the idea that they could "replace the ruling class" in thousands of factories across Italy. Meanwhile, the government (led again by the wily Giolitti) and the industrialists waited for the occupations to fizzle out, which they eventually did. The factory occupations marked not the beginning but the end of the mass movements of the *biennio rosso*.

The Socialist Party was dominated by its maximalist wing, a faction led by Giacinto Serrati that abandoned the Socialists' prewar and wartime reformist policy for a more radical approach, and by the New Order (Ordine Nuovo) group of intellectuals based in Turin around Antonio Gramsci. These Socialists continually proclaimed the need for revolution and their desire to "do as in Russia." Reformist leaders, such as Turati, were isolated and vilified. However, the party did little to actually prepare for revolution, and its working-class base, as well as most trade union leaders, remained largely moderate and reformist. Only in Turin, where the factory council movement undermined both union and employer power, did revolutionary practice go beyond the empty rhetoric of the maximalists. As Serrati put it, the maximalists based their strategy on the view that "We Marxists interpret history, we do not make it." Very little attempt was made to link up the two great classes of Italian society, the workers and the peasants, and the middle classes were either ignored or reviled as "doomed to disappear." "Who does not work shall not eat" was one popular maximalist anti-middle-class slogan. Socialists and unions were extremely hostile to small property and favoured land collectivization, a policy that alienated the new class of small landowners created before and after the war across Italy. Catholic and Socialist unions also fought each other bitterly throughout this period and failed to form alliances to fight the Fascist onslaught against both movements after 1920. Each movement was hamstrung by its deep-rooted, ideological distrust of the other—the Socialists by their anticlericalism, the Catholics by their antisocialism.

The postwar coalition governments of Nitti (1919–20) and his successors Giolitti (1920–21), Ivanoe Bonomi (1921–22), and

Luigi Facta (February–October 1922) were all weak and could do little except repress the strike movements by force or urge industrialists and landowners to make concessions not only on pay but even on "control" of the workplace. Inflation threatened the livelihood of many of those on fixed incomes, especially pensioners, administrative workers, and other groups not able to organize as effectively as industrial workers. These governments were powerless to keep prices from rising or to satisfy the demands of the unions. Nor was there any attempt at serious reform of the state or the economy—a project that Turati outlined in his *Rifare l'Italia!* (1920; "Remake Italy!"). The possibility of a democratic revolution was lost in the violence, bitterness, and fear of the postwar years.

Diplomatic and economic failures undermined middle-class confidence in government, especially when Giolitti also imposed taxes on war profits. In 1919 universal male suffrage and proportional representation were introduced for parliamentary elections. The result, in the new parliament elected in November 1919, was that the Socialists, with 30 percent of the vote, became the largest party, with 156 seats, and the new (Catholic) Italian Popular Party, with more than 20 percent of the vote, won 100 seats. These two parties dominated northern and central Italy. Giolitti had to bring the Popular Party into his government in 1920 and make many concessions to certain peasant interests, including giving guarantees to squatters and giving the Ministry of Agriculture to the Catholics. These reforms did not go far enough to satisfy the landless peasants but managed to terrify landowners. Furthermore, the two "subversive" parties won control of almost half the municipalities in the autumn of 1920, ensuring that Socialist or Catholic cooperatives would be given all local public works contracts. The radical language of the maximalist local campaigns particularly alarmed the urban middle classes.

In January 1921, during a congress in Livorno, the left wing of the Socialists split away to found the Italian Communist Party (Partito Communista d'Italia, later Partito Communista Italiano [PCI]; now Democrats of the Left [Democratici di Sinistra]), which increased middle-class alarm. In reality, this split was a sign of defeat and weakened the left. The Communist Party—led by Amadeo Bordiga (until 1924), who advocated abstention from elections, and then by Palmiro Togliatti—pursued a sectarian policy of eschewing anti-Fascist alliances, which made the victory of the right far easier than it might have been. The PCI began to depend heavily on support and orders from Moscow, a close relationship that was to last well into the 1970s.

THE FASCIST ERA

The political crisis of the postwar years provided an opportunity for militant, patriotic movements, including those of ex-servicemen and former assault troops, students, ex-syndicalists, and former pro-war agitators. D'Annunzio in Fiume led one such movement, but the ex-Socialist journalist Benito Mussolini soon became even more prominent, founding his *fasci di combattimento* ("fighting leagues"), better known as Fascists, in Milan in March 1919. The group's first program was a mishmash of radical nationalist ideas, with strong doses of anticlericalism and republicanism. Proposals included the confiscation of war profits, the eight-hour day, and the vote for women.

Mussolini's movement was initially unsuccessful, but Fascists soon began to agitate in the streets and against the left. In April 1919 Fascists and nationalists burned down the offices of the national Socialist daily, *L'Avanti!*, in Milan. Four people were killed, and the paper shut down for several days. This was the first demonstration of the ability of the Fascists to attack Socialist institutions. The offices of *L'Avanti!* were attacked twice more between 1920 and 1922. Organized militias began to attract support across Italy in an anti-Bolshevik crusade that united various social and political sectors and organizations. Local Fascist groups were soon founded in Emilia, Tuscany, and Puglia and by autumn 1920 were busy not only breaking up strikes but also dismantling Socialist and Catholic labour unions and peasants' cooperatives and—often with police collusion—overthrowing newly elected local councils. Fascist squads, dressed in black-shirted uniforms and often financed by landowners or industrialists, used systematic violence to destroy these organizations. Thousands of people were beaten, killed, or forced to drink castor oil and run out of town. Hundreds of union offices, employment centres, and party newspapers were looted or burnt down. In October 1920, after the election of a left administration in Bologna, Fascists invaded the council chamber, causing mayhem and nine deaths. The council was suspended by the government. Later, Socialist and Catholic deputies were run out of parliament or had their houses destroyed. The *biennio nero* ("two black years"; 1921–22) destroyed opposition to the Fascists. Union organizations were crushed. The Federterra shrank from some one million members to fewer than 6,000 in less than five years. Unable to defend basic democratic rights or to prevent the criminal activities of a private militia that operated openly and nation-wide, the state had lost all credibility.

Within a few months, paramilitary Fascist squad leaders controlled many rural areas of central Italy. Local bosses built power bases in various areas—e.g., Italo Balbo in Ferrara, Roberto Farinacci in Cremona, and Leandro Arpinati in Bologna. These men became known as *ras* (meaning "provincial viceroy" in Ethiopia's Amharic language) and exercised considerable local power throughout the Fascist period. The Fascists had become a major political force, backed not only by landowners but also by many members of the urban middle class, including students, shop-keepers, and clerical workers. In May 1921, when Prime Minister Giolitti called new elections, 35 Fascists were elected to parliament as part of a government bloc of 275 deputies. In October Mussolini abandoned republicanism, and in November he formed his movement into a proper political party, the National Fascist Party (Partito Nazionale Fascista; PNF), which by this time was well-financed if ill-disciplined and extremely disparate. Local bosses remained paramount in their areas. The Fascists also organized their own trade unions, the Fascist "syndicates," among strategic groups such as postal administrative workers and taxi drivers, to replace Socialist or Catholic organizations, to provide mass membership, and to control labour. These unions never managed to penetrate the organized working class but did have some support among the lower middle class and small landowners.

Mussolini manipulated this volatile situation in the next few months to his advantage, and the Liberal political establishment sought to conciliate him and the

Benito Mussolini (centre) *leading the March on Rome in 1922 that first brought the Fascist dictator to power.* BIPS/Hulton Archive/Getty Images

Fascist thugs. The police, the army, and much of the middle class sympathized with Fascist destruction of Socialist unions. Mussolini, as *duce* (leader) of Fascism, gradually made himself indispensable in Rome, and the squads took over more cities in the provinces. Only a very few areas were able to resist the "Blackshirts" in street fighting, including Parma and Bari in 1922. Attempts by the left to organize defense squads against the Fascists were, in general, a failure. A major anti-Fascist protest strike, called by the Socialist-led Confederation of Labour in August 1922, quickly collapsed, strengthening Mussolini's bargaining position even further. Fascists used the opportunity to inflict further damage on the left and union institutions, and the offices of *L'Avanti!* were again attacked and razed. In October 1922 Mussolini organized a "March on Rome" by Fascist supporters. Fascist squads, numbering about 25,000 men altogether, began to converge on the capital from all over Italy on October 26, occupying railway stations and government offices. Prime Minister Facta asked the king to declare martial law, but Victor Emmanuel III eventually refused in order to avoid possible army disloyalty or even a possible civil war. Instead, he asked Mussolini to form a government on October 29, hoping to tame him by constitutional means.

Mussolini became prime minister, therefore, in a more or less constitutional manner, but only after three years of near civil war in the country and an armed invasion of Rome. He was appointed by the king, and he headed a coalition government that included nationalists, two Fascist ministers, Liberals, and even (until April 1923) two Catholic ministers from the Popular Party. For 18 months he ruled through the usual government machinery, pursued a policy of "normalization," and gradually concentrated power in his own hands. The Fascist squads were incorporated into an official Voluntary Militia for National Security. Ordinary middle-class job seekers flooded into the Fascist Party, making it more respectable and amenable; the nationalists also merged their organization into it, bringing with them much respectable backing in the south. In 1923 the electoral law was changed once more, so that a group of parties with the largest vote—even if only 25 percent of the total—would receive an absolute majority of the seats. This enabled the Fascists to attract most of the old Liberal deputies into a "national alliance." In April 1924 elections were held under this system. In a climate of violence and threats, the Fascist-dominated bloc won 64 percent of the votes and 374 seats, doing particularly well in the south. The opposition parties—by now including the Popular Party—remained divided but won a majority of the votes in northern Italy. The Socialists, indeed, had by this time split again, and the left now consisted of three rival parties, which spent much time criticizing one another: the Communists, the Socialists, and the reformist Socialists. The Popular Party was disowned by the Vatican, and its leader, Luigi Sturzo, resigned at the Vatican's request.

THE END OF CONSTITUTIONAL RULE

Mussolini's relative success as leader of a "normalizing" constitutional government did not last long. When the new parliament met, Giacomo Matteotti, leader of the reformist Socialists, denounced the recent elections as a sham and claimed there had been widespread intimidation of opposition voters. On June 10, 1924, Matteotti disappeared. His body was recovered on July 16, and he was later found to have been murdered by Fascist thugs led by the assistant to Mussolini's press office, Amerigo Dumini. The "Matteotti crisis" aroused public distrust in Mussolini and the Fascists. Mussolini was suspected of personal complicity in ordering the murder to eliminate a troublesome opponent. The press denounced the government, and the opposition parties walked out of parliament. However, Mussolini still had a majority in parliament, and the king backed him. For some time Mussolini hung on, but by autumn his Liberal supporters were drifting away, and in any case the "normalization" policy infuriated Fascist extremists in the country—especially the local bosses who were threatened with dismissal by the new militia commander, an army general. They demanded a showdown, and Mussolini—who was too weak by this time to rule by constitutional means—had to agree. On January 3, 1925, he made a famous speech in the Chamber of Deputies accepting "political, moral, and historical responsibility" for Fascist rule and Matteotti's death and promising a tough crackdown on dissenters. The king made no move. On January 4, orders were given to prefects throughout Italy to control all "suspect" political organizations. Searches, arrests, and the elimination of several offices and organizations followed.

During the next two years, which included several failed assassination attempts, Mussolini disbanded most of Italy's constitutional and conventional safeguards against government autocracy. Elections were abolished. Free speech and free association disappeared, and the Fascist government dissolved opposition parties and unions. At the local level, appointed podestas replaced elected mayors and councils. Freemasonry was outlawed—a real blow to most non-Catholic anti-Fascists. A Special Tribunal for the Defense of the State, run by militia and army officers, was set up to try anti-Fascist "subversives"; it imprisoned or sent to exile on remote islands thousands of political opponents, including the Communist leader Antonio Gramsci, and it imposed 31 death penalties. Other opposition leaders, such as the Liberals Piero Gobetti and Giovanni Amendola, died at the hands of Fascist thugs. Severe controls were imposed on movement into and out of Italy. Although the repression was carried out essentially by old state institutions such as the police and the army and not by Fascist bodies, in 1927 Mussolini established the main information network of spies, the Organizzazione di Vigilanza Repressione dell'Antifascismo

ANTONIO GRAMSCI

One of the founders of the Italian Communist Party, Antonio Gramsci (born January 23, 1891, Ales, Sardinia, Italy—died April 27, 1937, Rome, Italy) was an intellectual and politician whose ideas greatly influenced Italian communism. In 1911 Gramsci began a brilliant scholastic career at the University of Turin, where he came in contact with the Socialist Youth Federation and joined the Socialist Party (1914). During World War I he studied Marxist thought and became a leading theoretician. He formed a leftist group within the Socialist Party and founded the newspaper *L'Ordine Nuovo* (May 1919; "The New Order"). Gramsci encouraged the development of factory councils (democratic bodies elected directly by industrial workers), which undercut the control of trade unions. The councils participated in a general strike in Turin (1920), in which Gramsci played a key role.

Gramsci led a leftist walkout at the Socialist congress at Livorno (January 1921) to found the Italian Communist Party and then spent two years in the Soviet Union. Back in Italy, he became head of his party (April 1924) and was elected to the country's Chamber of Deputies. After his party was outlawed by Benito Mussolini's Fascists, Gramsci was arrested and imprisoned (1926). At his trial the Fascist prosecutor argued, "We must stop his brain from working for 20 years." In prison, despite rigorous censorship, Gramsci carried out an extraordinary and wide-ranging historical and theoretical study of Italian society and possible strategies for change. Plagued with poor health in the 1930s, he died not long after being released from prison for medical care.

Extracts of Gramsci's prison writings were published for the first time in the mid-20th century; the complete *Quaderni del carcere* (*Prison Notebooks*) appeared in 1975. Many of his propositions became a fundamental part of Western Marxist thought and influenced the post–World War II strategies of communist parties in the West. His reflections on the cultural and political concept of hegemony (notably in southern Italy), on the Italian Communist Party itself, and on the Roman Catholic Church were particularly important. The letters he wrote from prison also were published posthumously as *Lettere dal carcere* (1947; *Letters from Prison*).

(Organization for the Vigilant Repression of Anti-Fascism; OVRA). This network extended abroad, where the OVRA organized assassinations of those hostile to the regime—such as the brothers Nello and Carlo Rosselli, anti-Fascist intellectuals, in France in 1937.

The prefects—mostly still career civil servants—retained their traditional dominance over local government, and the new podestas were nearly always landowners or retired army officers rather than Fascist enthusiasts. The Fascist Party itself was soon swamped by more than a million job seekers and clerical workers, and thousands of the original Fascists were purged. The party, and the militia, soon had little to do except engage in propaganda and parades. The Fascist regime was mostly run by the traditional elites

GIOVANNI AMENDOLA

The journalist and politician Giovanni Amendola (born April 15, 1882, Rome, Italy—died April 7, 1926, Cannes, France) was the foremost opponent of the Italian Fascists in the early 1920s. As a young journalist, Amendola expressed his philosophical and ideological views in articles appearing first in *La Voce* ("The Voice") and then in the newspapers *Resto di Carlino* and *Corriere della Sera*. He urged Italy's entry into World War I in 1915 and fought as a volunteer, reaching the rank of captain and winning a medal of valour.

After the war Amendola devoted himself entirely to politics as a Democratic Liberal in favour of a policy of rapprochement with the Slavs. First elected to parliament in 1919, he was in 1922 minister for the colonies in Luigi Facta's cabinet. With Benito Mussolini's advent to power, Amendola became a leader of the opposition and attacked the new regime through the columns of his newspaper *Il Mondo*. After the murder of the socialist leader Giacomo Matteotti, Amendola was one of the deputies who withdrew from the chamber in protest. In spite of threats against his life during the election campaign of 1924, he declared the Fascist electoral law to be unconstitutional. He died as a result of injuries received when a gang of Fascists attacked him in the Italian spa of Montecatini.

in the military and civilian bureaucracy, which were linked, as previously, to land-owners and the court. That said, it was much more authoritarian and also much more nationalistic and interventionist than the Liberal governments had been. By the 1930s the Fascist Party dominated all aspects of daily life, from the workplace to the schools to leisure activities. However, many of the regime's opponents merely went along with its formal elements to procure space for protest and underground activity.

Fascist indoctrination was never really successful, but the press was tightly censored, motion picture newsreels were largely government propaganda, and the regime controlled the new radio broadcasting. It also ran semi-compulsory Fascist youth movements, and new textbooks were imposed on the schools. Moreover, the government provided mass leisure activities, such as sports, concerts, and seaside holidays, which were genuinely popular. These attempts to create consent went hand in hand with the coercion imposed by the regime through the OVRA and its enormous network of spies. The fear of arrest, imprisonment, or economic marginalization hung over thousands of anti-Fascists and former oppositionists, and silence replaced the propaganda of the *biennio rosso*. Fascist control of daily life reached right down to the most basic levels. In 1938 the government imposed the use of

Voi as the formal pronoun instead of *Lei* and banned handshakes in all places of public work. Foreign words and names were replaced. *Bordeaux* became *Barolo*, *film* became *pellicola*, and German place-names were Italianized. The walls of offices, schools, and public buildings were covered with slogans and murals paying homage to Mussolini and Fascism, such as "Mussolini is always right" or "Better to live one day as a lion than 100 years as a sheep."

ANTI-FASCIST MOVEMENTS

For a long time, organized anti-Fascist movements remained weak, divided, and illegal and had no access to press or radio. The Communists were soon the most significant of these movements, as they had an underground organization and some Russian support and finance, but even they had only 7,000 members at most and had great difficulty in spreading their propaganda in Italy. Spies within the movement exposed many of the underground networks before they even had a chance to put down roots. New anti-Fascist groups were founded occasionally, but the secret police soon cracked down on them. Apart from the Communists, only Justice and Liberty, an alliance of republicans, democrats, and reformist Socialists founded by Carlo Rosselli and others in 1929, managed to build up a clandestine organization in Italy and a strong organization abroad, above all in France and Switzerland. Most

prominent anti-Fascists were in prison, in "confinement" on remote islands, or in exile and had little contact with Italian reality. Mussolini had disbanded unions and replaced them with new syndicates with little bargaining power. Strikes were illegal and more or less ceased to occur. Employer power was reimposed in both the countryside and the city after the union victories of the postwar years, although the welfare corporatism of the Fascist regime allowed workers important economic benefits.

The only strong non-Fascist organization in the country was the Roman Catholic Church. The Vatican implicitly supported Mussolini in the early years and was rewarded in February 1929 by the Lateran Treaty, which settled the "Roman Question" at last. Vatican City became an independent state, Italy paid a large financial indemnity to the pope for taking over his pre-1870 lands, and a concordat granted the church many privileges in Italy, including recognition of church weddings as valid in civil law, religious education in secondary as well as primary schools, and freedom for the lay Catholic organizations in Catholic Action. However, the government soon began curbing Catholic Action, seeing it as a front for anti-Fascist activity by former members of the Popular Party. The Catholic youth organizations were closed for a time in 1931. When they reopened, they had to avoid sports, but, even so, they grew considerably in the 1930s. They were a serious rival to the

Fascist youth bodies and trained a new generation that often managed to avoid Fascist indoctrination. The 1929 concordat remained in force until the 1980s and was the legal basis for continued church dominance of Italian society after World War II. The Fascist regime could easily enough repress forms of local opposition such as demonstrations and strikes, but anti-Fascist feeling became more widespread after the mid-1930s.

Nonetheless, Italy sent some 60,000 "volunteer" militiamen, as well as about 800 warplanes, 90 ships, and 8,000 jeeps, to fight on the side of Mussolini's ideological cohort, Francisco Franco, in the Spanish Civil War (1936–39). This Italian force was defeated in 1937 at the Battle of Guadalajara. By the end of the war, some 4,000 Italian troops were killed and 11,000 injured. Italian anti-Fascists also fought Mussolini's troops in Spain, a rehearsal for the civil war in Italy after 1943. Many of these Italian anti-Fascists joined the Spanish Republican armies (notably, four Italian companies in 1936), inspired by Carlo Rosselli's cry "Today in Spain, tomorrow in Italy." In all, at least 3,000 Italians fought on the anti-Fascist side, about 200 of whom had traveled directly from Italy. Some 500 Italian anti-Fascists were killed and 2,000 injured in the war. Leading Italian Communists and Socialists were Togliatti and Pietro Nenni.

Italy's increasingly close alliance with Adolf Hitler's Nazi Germany was resented and feared, even by many Fascists. So, too, was the shocking decision to impose sweeping Nazi-like anti-Semitic laws in 1938. These laws followed a long racist campaign organized by the Fascist press and media. Under these laws and decrees, signed by the king, Jews were condemned as unpatriotic, excluded from government jobs and the army, banned from entering Italy, and banned from attending or teaching school. In addition, all Jews had to register with the authorities, limits were placed on their economic activities, and they were forbidden to marry "Aryans." In 1939 all books by Jewish authors were removed from the shops. Many Jews left Italy, while others were marginalized within Italian society. It had become clear that the Fascist government was likely to involve Italy in a disastrous European war, as indeed it did in 1940.

ECONOMIC POLICY

Fascist intervention in the economy was designed to boost prestige and military strength. In the early years the Fascists compromised with the business establishment and rescued failing banks. However, in 1926 the lira was suddenly revalued for political reasons, and Italy suffered all the usual consequences of an overvalued currency. Exports fell sharply, unemployment rose, wages were frozen or even cut, and prices fell. The steel, electricity, and chemical industries expanded, for their markets were domestic, and they were helped by cheaper raw material imports;

industries producing textiles, food, and vehicles, which depended on foreign markets, declined.

When the Great Depression came after 1929, these deflationary processes were accentuated, although the government increased spending on building roads and on welfare in order to provide employment. The leading banks, which had lent heavily to industry, had to be rescued in the early 1930s, as did many large industrial companies. Two new state-run holding companies, the Italian Industrial Finance Institute (Istituto Mobiliare Italiano) and the Institute for Industrial Reconstruction (Istituto per la Ricostruzione Industriale; IRI), were set up to bail out failing firms and to provide capital for new industrial investment; they also provided trained managers and effective financial supervision. Italy thus acquired a huge, state-led industrial sector, which was especially important in banking, steel, shipping, armaments, and the supply of hydroelectricity. However, these firms were not nationalized. Instead, they operated in the market as private companies and still had many private shareholders. In the long term they gave Italy a modern infrastructure—including roads and cheap energy—a sounder financial sector, and some efficient modern industries in expanding sectors such as chemicals and synthetic fibres. Most industrial development, and most workers, remained in northern Italy, although by this time large steelmaking and shipbuilding plants had been started at Naples and Taranto. After 1931 vast

tracts of land were reclaimed through the draining of marshes in the Lazio region, where gleaming new towns were created with Fascist architecture and names—Littoria (now Latina) in 1932, Sabaudia in 1934, Pontinia in 1935, Aprilia in 1937, and Pomezia in 1938. Peasants were brought from the regions of Emilia and the Veneto to populate these towns. New towns, such as Carbonia, were also built in Sardinia to house miners for the revamped coal industry.

After October 1925 the Fascist syndicates, or trade unions, were the sole recognized negotiators for workers' interests. Strikes and lockouts became illegal, and wages fell between 1927 and 1934, but the syndicates had considerable political influence. They secured a shorter workweek (40 hours in November 1934), higher welfare benefits (such as family allowances, also introduced in 1934), and public works schemes, and they also helped run leisure and social activities. In 1934 the Fascists also set up "corporations"—mixed bodies of workers and employers—to resolve labour disputes and supervise wage settlements. Despite much rhetoric and propaganda about them, they had little impact in practice and virtually none on industrial management or economic policy making.

In agricultural policy, the government aimed at self-sufficiency by encouraging grain production after 1925 ("the battle for wheat"). Mussolini was filmed and photographed as he cut grain, bare-chested, in fields throughout Italy. Grain was grown for symbolic reasons in city centres such as Milan's Piazza del Duomo (Cathedral Square). A high tariff was reimposed on imported wheat, and grain prices were kept artificially high. Production rose sharply as northern farmers used more chemical fertilizers. In much of the south the climate was less favourable for growing wheat, but vineyards and olive groves were nonetheless plowed up, especially after 1929 when the world price of olive oil halved. The real beneficiaries of this policy were the large farmers of the Po valley and of the southern latifundia. These men also benefited most from the government's land-reclamation schemes, forming their own consortia and receiving government money to drain or irrigate their own land. Moreover, during the Depression they could buy land cheaply from the smaller landowners because many of the peasants who had acquired land during and after World War I were forced to sell after 1926.

After Italy's invasion of Ethiopia in 1935–36, the League of Nations subjected

A shirtless Mussolini takes advantage of a photo opportunity while working in the wheat fields with peasants. Keystone-France/Gamma-Keystone/Getty Images

the Italian economy to sanctions. This led to a more extensive drive for national self-sufficiency, or autarky; imports were replaced where possible by native products, and most exports were diverted to Germany and Switzerland or to Africa. Ethiopia, once conquered, became a vast drain on resources. The government expanded its intervention and licensing role, encouraged official cartels and quasi monopolies, and shifted resources from above to heavy industry and armaments. All this led to budget deficits, big tax increases, and capital levies, which were hugely resented because they mainly went to pay for wars in Africa and Spain. Resented, too, was the obvious corruption of the Fascist governing clique, without whose permits—available at a price—nothing could be done. Among the members of the various conservative groups, including those in the army, the civil service, the law, and the church, that in the mid-1920s had looked to Fascism to protect their interests, some had realized by the late 1930s that Fascism was unreliable and began to withdraw their support.

American restrictions, European recession, and Fascist economic nationalism combined to curtail emigration drastically in the 1930s, from more than 600,000 people per annum before 1914 to fewer than 50,000 per annum. The closing of emigration outlets hit the south particularly badly. Because they could not go abroad, rural Italians moved to the cities. Rome doubled in size between 1921 and 1940, and northern cities attracted many rural emigrants, especially from the south. Fascism attempted to halt these movements through an anti-migration law in 1938. This measure banned migrants from moving within Italy without a job at their intended destination, and made many Italians "clandestine" in their own country. However, the law had little practical effect in preventing migration. Meanwhile, government policy encouraged population growth by providing tax incentives to have children and excluding the childless from public jobs. Admittedly, all this had little effect before 1937. Italians married later than ever and had fewer children than previously, so much so that in several northern and central regions the birth rate dropped below replacement level in the 1930s.

FOREIGN POLICY

As time passed, Fascist foreign policy became more expansionist. In particular, Mussolini aimed at acquiring territory in Africa and in the Mediterranean, for which he adopted the ancient Roman term *mare nostrum* ("our sea"). Even in 1923, in his first year in office, he briefly invaded the Greek island of Corfu to avenge the murder of four Italian nationals forming part of an international boundary delegation. During the next decade he played the European statesman, and in 1924 he reached an agreement with Yugoslavia that gave Fiume to Italy. He also continued to strengthen the Italian hold on Libya, to build up the armed forces, and to plan further expansion in Africa—particularly in Ethiopia, where he believed the defeat at Adwa in 1896 still needed to be avenged. In October 1935 Italy finally invaded Ethiopia—one of the first conquests was Adwa—and by May 1936 had conquered the country and proclaimed the Italian king, Victor Emmanuel III, emperor of Ethiopia. Ethiopia had been the only remaining country in Africa to escape colonization. Nearly 400,000 Italian troops took part in the conflict. The army employed brutal methods, including massacres and poison gas bombs. After an attempt in February 1937 on the life of the "viceroy" of Ethiopia, General Rodolfo Graziani, Italian forces arrested and shot hundreds of Ethiopians. However, the war was popular at home and among Italians abroad, especially in the Italian American community. Racist propaganda depicted the Ethiopians as backward barbarians "civilized" by the Italian army. The colonial wars coincided, not by chance, with the period when the regime enjoyed its maximum popularity.

Italy made further colonial gains in April 1939 with the invasion of Albania.

ITALO-ETHIOPIAN WAR

Often seen as one of the episodes that prepared the way for World War II, the Italo-Ethiopian War (1935–36) resulted in Ethiopia's subjection to Italy. It also demonstrated the ineffectiveness of the League of Nations when League decisions were not supported by the great powers.

Ethiopia (Abyssinia), which Italy had unsuccessfully tried to conquer in the 1890s, was in 1934 one of the few independent states in a European dominated Africa. A border incident between Ethiopia and Italian Somaliland that December gave Mussolini an excuse to intervene. Rejecting all arbitration offers, the Italians invaded Ethiopia on October 3, 1935.

Under Generals Rodolfo Graziani and Pietro Badoglio, the invading forces steadily pushed back the ill-armed and poorly trained Ethiopian army, winning a major victory near Lake Ascianghi (Ashangi) on April 9, 1936, and taking the capital, Addis Ababa, on May 5. The nation's leader, Emperor Haile Selassie, went into exile. In Rome, Mussolini proclaimed Italy's king Victor Emmanuel III emperor of Ethiopia and appointed Badoglio to rule as viceroy.

In response to Ethiopian appeals, the League of Nations condemned the Italian invasion in 1935 and voted to impose economic sanctions on the aggressor. The sanctions remained ineffective because of general lack of support. Although Mussolini's aggression was viewed with disfavour by the British, who had a stake in East Africa, the other major powers had no real interest in opposing him. The war, by giving substance to Italian imperialist claims, contributed to international tensions between the fascist states and the Western democracies. It also served as a rallying point, especially after World War II, for developing African nationalist movements.

Italian control over Albania already had been growing throughout the 1920s through agreements with the Albanian regime. Moreover, in 1933 Italian had been made obligatory in Albanian schools. When Albania's King Zog refused to accept a trade agreement, however, the Italian army took control of the main strategic centres of the country and installed Italian loyalists in the civil service. Victor Emmanuel was made king of Albania. King Zog escaped to Greece.

The Italo-Ethiopian War antagonized the British and French governments, led to sanctions by the League of Nations, and isolated Italy diplomatically. Mussolini moved into Hitler's orbit, hoping that German backing would frighten the British and French into granting further concessions to Italy. However, the policy failed to bring further territorial gains in Africa. Furthermore, Italy became the junior partner in the "Rome-Berlin Axis," and in 1938 Mussolini had to accept Hitler's annexation of Austria, bringing the German Reich right up to the Italian border. In May 1939 Mussolini entered a formal military alliance with Hitler, the "Pact of Steel," which further reduced his scope for maneuver. Not only was each country committed to take part in any conflict involving the other, defensive or otherwise, but each leader was to consult the other before taking any military action. Even so, when the Germans unexpectedly invaded Poland in September 1939, Mussolini insisted on remaining neutral.

ITALY DURING WORLD WAR II

Only in June 1940, when France was about to fall and World War II seemed virtually over, did Italy join the war on Germany's side, still hoping for territorial spoils. Mussolini announced his decision—one bitterly opposed by his foreign minister, Galeazzo Ciano—to huge crowds across Italy on June 10. Italy's initial attack on the French Alps in June 1940 was quickly cut short by the Franco-German armistice. The real war for Italy began only in October, when Mussolini attacked Greece from Albania in a disastrous campaign that obliged the Germans, in 1941, to rescue the Italian forces and take over Greece themselves. The Germans also had to lend support in the hard-fought campaigns of North Africa, where eventually the decisive second battle of El-Alamein (October 1942) destroyed the Italian position and led to the surrender of all of Italy's North African forces in May 1943. Meanwhile, the Italians had lost their extensive empire in eastern Africa, including Ethiopia, early in 1941; and 250,000 Italian troops in Russia, sent to help the German invaders, suffered untold hardships. The epic winter retreat of the Alpine division left thousands dead. In all, nearly 85,000 Italian troops failed to make it home from Russia.

In short, the war was an almost unrelieved succession of military disasters. Poor generals and low morale contributed much to this outcome—the Italian conscripts were fighting far from home for causes in which few of them believed. In addition, Italy had few tanks or anti-tank guns; clothing, food, vehicles, and fuel were all scarce; and supplies could not safely be transported to North Africa or Russia. Italian factories could not produce weapons without steel, coal, or oil, and, even when raw materials were available, production was limited because the northern Italian factories were subject to heavy Allied bombing, especially in 1942–43. Heavy attacks destroyed the iron ore production capacities on Elba, off the Tuscan coast, and damaged several industrial zones, particularly in northern Italian cities such as Genoa, La Spezia, Turin, and Milan. Naples and other southern cities also were bombed, as was the San Lorenzo district of Rome. (The San Lorenzo air raid, carried out by U.S. forces in July 1943, killed more than 3,000 people.)

Bombing indeed was one of the causes of the first major strikes since 1925. In March 1943 the leading factories in Milan and Turin stopped work in order to secure evacuation allowances for workers' families. By this time civilian morale was clearly very low, food shortages were endemic, and hundreds of thousands of people had fled to the countryside. Government propaganda was ineffective, and Italians could easily hear more-accurate news on Radio Vatican or even Radio London. In Friuli-Venezia Giulia, as in Italian-occupied Slovenia and Croatia, the local Slavic population supported armed Resistance movements, and anti-Italian terrorism was widespread. In Sicily landowners formed armed bands for possible use against mainland interference. On the mainland itself the anti-Fascist movements cautiously revived in 1942 and 1943. The Communists helped to organize strikes, the leading Roman Catholics formed the Christian Democratic Party (now the Italian Popular Party) in 1943, and the new Party of Action was founded in January 1943, mainly by republicans and Radicals. Leading Communists began to reenter Italy, and their party began to put down deep roots across the country. By this time most of the leading clandestine parties were more willing to work together to overthrow Fascism. In March 1943 they signed an agreement to do so.

A further consequence of the war was the internment of hundreds of thousands of Italian emigrants across the world, especially in Britain and the United States. Italians, even with strong anti-Fascist credentials, were rounded up and sometimes stripped of their citizenship. This draconian policy left a legacy of bitterness and recrimination which lasted for years on both sides.

END OF THE REGIME

By the summer of 1943 the Italian position was hopeless. Northern and eastern Africa had been lost, the northern Italian cities were being regularly bombed, war production was minimal, and morale had collapsed. So, too, had the Fascist regime, which could no longer command any obedience. Court circles began sounding out Allied terms, which of course included the removal of Mussolini. In July 1943 the Allies invaded Sicily, and within a few weeks they controlled the island. On July 24–25 the Fascist Grand Council met in Rome for the first time since the beginning of the war and passed a motion asking the king to resume his full constitutional powers—that is, to dismiss Mussolini. In a dramatic decision, a substantial majority of the members voted against the duce. The king dismissed Mussolini the same day and installed Marshal Pietro Badoglio, an elderly World War I veteran who had fought in Ethiopia, as prime minister. Spontaneous demonstrations followed throughout the country, in which statues of Mussolini were torn down, Fascist symbols removed, and political prisoners released. At first the authorities did not react, but, in the five days after July 25, troops shot dead 83 demonstrators. The army took over the key positions in Rome, the duce was arrested, and the main Fascist institutions, including the Fascist Party, were dissolved. On July 27 Badoglio formed an interim government that consisted mostly of ex-Fascists.

Badoglio assured Germany and the Italian people that the war would continue, but he also attempted, rather feebly, to reach armistice terms with the Allies. German troops began pouring into Italy. Heavy Allied bombing continued over most Italian cities. Strikes broke out throughout the country. Allied troops arrived on the Italian mainland in early September but met heavy resistance from the Germans at Salerno. The Badoglio government agreed to an armistice with the Allies, and U.S. General Dwight D. Eisenhower, the Allied commander in chief in the Mediterranean, announced it on September 8, 1943. Under this agreement (the so-called Short Armistice), the Italian government promised to cease hostilities against the Allies and end its alliance with Germany.

The Germans immediately took over Rome. In the previous few weeks, they had already taken over most of central and northern Italy. The Italian army, left without orders even to defend Rome, was disintegrating despite some brave spontaneous fighting (the official beginning of the Resistance) at Porta San Paolo. The king and his government fled south to Brindisi, leaving Rome to the Germans. Chaos reigned among Italian troops, and thousands deserted, while others joined the Resistance forces. At Cephallenia, a Greek island, Italian troops refused to obey German orders to give up their arms, and thousands of them were shot or deported. In late September the Badoglio government signed a "Long Armistice," which virtually gave up military and political control over Italy, as well as control of the mass media and financial institutions, to the Allies. This agreement was not made public during the conflict.

Badoglio officially declared war on Germany on October 13. Italy became a war zone. For 18 months the Allies fought

German troops in southern Italy driving an Italian tank in 1943, during World War II. Italy declared war on their former German allies that same year. Keystone-France/Gamma-Keystone/Getty Images the Germans up the peninsula, wreaking untold devastation throughout the land. The Allies took Naples in October 1943 but reached Rome only in June 1944, Florence in August, and the northern cities in April 1945.

The Allies ruled the south after September 1943, and Badoglio's government had very little influence on events. The anti-Fascist parties, which detested Badoglio and wanted the king to abdicate, refused to join the government until April 1944, when the Communist Party leader Palmiro Togliatti agreed to do so. Scholars disagree on whether this decision was autonomous or came in response to orders from Moscow. When Rome was liberated, Victor Emmanuel was replaced by his son, Umberto, as "lieutenant general of the realm," and the leading anti-Fascist parties formed a nominal government led by the reformist Socialist Ivanoe Bonomi, who had been prime minister from 1921 to 1922.

THE REPUBLIC OF SALÒ AND THE GERMAN OCCUPATION

In the meantime the Germans had rescued Mussolini from his mountain prison and restored him in the north as ruler of the "Italian Social Republic," a last-ditch puppet Fascist regime based in Salò on Lake Garda. The republic tried to induct those born in 1923, 1924, and 1925 into its army, but only 40 percent of young men responded. Many others deserted soon after the call-up. In a congress held in Verona in November 1943, the "republic

of Salò" seemed to take a leftward turn, calling for an end to the monarchy and a more worker-oriented ideology, but this program never went into practice. Some of the leading Fascists who had voted out the duce in July 1943, including Mussolini's son-in-law, the former foreign minister Galeazzo Ciano, were tried by a Fascist court and shot. Meanwhile, Fascist officials collaborated with the German army and essentially followed Hitler's orders as the war continued in the north and centre. Official and unofficial armed bands roamed the big cities arresting suspected partisans (members of the Resistance) and terrorizing the local population.

The German occupiers ruled through violence and the aid of the local Fascists. Throughout German-occupied Italy, Jews and oppositionists were rounded up and sent to detention camps or prisons. Many Jews were sent straight from Italy on trains to concentration and extermination camps in Poland and Germany. In all, nearly 9,000 Jews were deported under the Germans. Only 980 returned. The biggest deportation occurred in Rome in October 1943, when the Germans gathered more than 1,000 Jews from the city's ghetto and sent them to death camps. The Jewish community had been forced early on to hand over gold and money to the German army. One concentration camp on Italian soil, near Trieste, also had an oven for burning bodies. Some 8,000 Italians (of whom 300 were Jews) were deported to Mauthausen in Austria. Only 850 came back alive.

The German army responded to partisan activity with violence and reprisals. A series of massacres of civilians and partisans accompanied the German occupation and gradual retreat up the peninsula. In March 1944, after a partisan bomb attack killed 33 members of the occupying forces in Rome, the German army shot 335 people (Jews, Communists, and others) in the Fosse Ardeatine, caves located outside the city. This massacre was one of the biggest of the war in Italy and has inspired controversy ever since.

(In the 1990s a former Nazi captain, Erich Priebke, was arrested in Argentina and, after two dramatic trials, was convicted in Rome for his role in the massacre.) Elsewhere the German army carried out frequent brutal and random massacres of civilians as they retreated northward, above all in Tuscany and Emilia, where German troops destroyed an entire village of some 1,800 people at Marzabotto in 1944. In addition, the Germans deported hundreds of thousands of young men to work as forced labourers in Germany and

Pope Benedict XVI (left, in white) during a March 2011 visit to the site of the March 1944 Ardeatine cave massacre, where hundreds of Italian civilians were shot in retaliation for the killing of 33 German military officers by Italian partisans. Vincenzo Pinto/AFP/Getty Images

elsewhere. Fiat workers struck against these deportations in March 1944. Many of those deported died en route.

Mussolini faded from view and appeared less and less in public, making his last speech in Milan in December 1944. As defeat became more and more likely, he made plans for his escape and tried to negotiate a deal with the Allies. In April 1945 Mussolini and his government fled to Milan, and later, disguised as a German soldier, he attempted to cross the border to Switzerland. Discovered by Communist partisans, he was shot in a small town on Lake Como. His body was taken to Milan and displayed for a time in Piazzale Loreto, along with the bodies of several other Fascist ministers and leaders, hung by their feet at a service station in front of huge festive crowds. These events have generated controversy and debate ever since. Other leading Fascists were executed across Italy during the days of liberation. Mussolini's remains, after being interred in various places, were finally buried in 1957 at his birthplace in Predappio, in the Romagna.

THE PARTISANS AND THE RESISTANCE

After September 1943, partisan Resistance groups were active throughout northern and much of central Italy. Often they were former soldiers cut off from home and still in possession of their weapons. Many were young men fleeing Mussolini's attempts to conscript them. Others were urban evacuees or released prisoners of war. Many were recruited, organized, and armed by the anti-Fascist parties or at least owed vague allegiance to one of them. They were most active in summer in the hills and mountains, where they were usually supported by the peasants, and they tied down thousands of German troops. In some areas they were a virtual armed uprising against not only the Germans and Fascists but also against the local landowners. Partisans were fighting three types of war: a civil war against Italian Fascists, a war of national liberation against German occupation, and a class war against the ruling elites. Communist Party groups fought all three types. Catholic or monarchist partisans, on the other hand, fought only one or two of these. There were also terrorist groups operating in the cities, and major strikes in industrial areas sabotaged war production. Sometimes, different partisan groups came into conflict with each other, but in general the Resistance was united. Nonetheless, those who actually fought as partisans were a small minority of Italians, and most civilians and ex-soldiers simply waited for the war to end. In all, about 200,000 partisans took part in the Resistance, and German or Fascist forces killed some 70,000 Italians (including both partisans and civilians) for Resistance activities. Ultimately, however, these figures do not indicate the extent of civilian participation in the Resistance, which scholars continue to debate.

The various political parties organized most of the partisan units, but they also cooperated with one another and the Allies. The Communist Party, although still very small in 1943 (about 5,000 members), led the largest group of partisans (at least 50,000 by summer 1944), drawing on years of experience in underground organization and on Yugoslav support. Success in the Resistance transformed the Communists into a major force in postwar Italian politics. The new Party of Action was also very active in the Resistance, constituting about one-fourth of all partisan units. It had a strong commitment to radical political change (including the change to a republic and a purge of officials) as well as to military victory. The Christian Democrats included roughly 20,000 partisans, and both Socialists and Liberals had significant armed bands in some areas. Partisans of different political persuasions normally worked together in local Committees of National Liberation (CLNs), which coordinated strategy, cooperated with the Allies, administered liberated areas, and appointed new officials. Above all, they organized the uprisings in the northern and central cities, including Milan in April 1945, which fell to the partisans before Allied troops arrived. In some cities the partisan liberation appeared to be a revolution—as in Genoa, Turin (where the Fiat factories were occupied), and Bologna—and red flags, Italian flags, and American flags greeted the "liberating" Allied troops. Some smaller zones

actually became "republics" for weeks or even months, such as Alba and Val d'Ossola in Piedmont. Many radical partisans expected there to be a revolution in postwar Italy and failed to hand in their arms at the bidding of the Allies in 1945. Still, the partisans' cooperation in the CLNs had laid the foundation for postwar political collaboration.

ITALY IN THE DECADES AFTER WORLD WAR II

When World War II ended in Europe in May 1945, all the anti-Fascist parties formed a predominantly northern government led by the Resistance hero and Party of Action leader Ferruccio Parri. The CLNs continued to administer the northern regions and the larger northern factories for a short time. Up to 15,000 Fascists were purged or killed, and in some areas (such as Emilia and Tuscany) reprisals continued through 1946. Women "collaborators" had their heads shaved and were paraded through the streets. A commission was set up to purge Fascists throughout the country. (A similar body had been operating in the south since 1943.) The purges caused much alarm, as virtually anybody with a job in the public sector had had to be a member of the Fascist Party. Soon there was an anti-purge backlash, supported by the Liberals. In reality, the purges were short-lived and superficial, and even leading Fascists were able to benefit from a series of amnesties, the most important of which was backed by the Communist minister of justice, Togliatti. In November 1945 Parri was forced to resign and was replaced by the Christian Democratic leader, Alcide De Gasperi, who formed a more moderate—and "Roman," or southern—interparty government. It soon gave up attempts at a purge, returned the large industrial firms to their previous owners, and replaced the partisan administrators in the north with ordinary state officials. In general, the Italian purges went much less far than those in Germany, and there was considerable continuity in many areas, including the judiciary, the police force, and the body of legislation created in the 1920s and '30s.

In May 1946 King Victor Emmanuel III finally formally abdicated. His son briefly became King Umberto II, but the royal family was forced to leave the country a month later when a referendum decided in favour of a republic by 54 percent of the votes cast. (When the new constitution was adopted the following year, it stated that no male members of the Savoy family could live in Italy; the rule was rescinded in 2002.) Many southerners, including 80 percent of Neapolitans, voted for the monarchy, but the centre and north opted overwhelmingly for the republic. The "May king," his father, and the monarchy in general had been punished not only for supporting Mussolini but also for their cowardly behaviour in the face of German occupation.

At the same time, a Constituent Assembly was elected by universal suffrage—including women for the first time—to draw up a new constitution. The three largest parties—the Christian Democrats, Socialists, and Communists—took three-fourths of the votes and seats and dominated the assembly. The Christian Democrats, with more than one-third of the votes and seats, began their postwar dominance as the most powerful party, although the Liberals, whose deputies included several constitutional lawyers, had a major impact on the new constitution, as did the Communists and Socialists. Over the next three years, the assembly discussed (in 170 sessions) what form the new Italian state should take, in a climate of democratic debate and collaboration. The constitution was finally ready and signed in December 1947 and took effect on January 1, 1948.

BIRTH OF THE ITALIAN REPUBLIC

The Constitution of the Republic of Italy established a parliamentary system of government with two elected houses (Chamber of Deputies and Senate). It also guaranteed civil and political rights and established an independent judiciary, a constitutional court with powers of judicial review, and the right of citizens' referendum. Many of these measures, however, were not implemented for several years. The Constitutional Court was not set up until 1955, and the first abrogative referendum was held only in 1974. The president was to be elected by parliament and had few real powers. The electoral system had a high level of proportional representation. Legislation had to pass through both elected chambers, but decrees could be issued by the Council of Ministers. The 1929 Lateran Treaty with the church was recognized in a Communist-inspired compromise. Autonomous regional governments were promised and were soon operating in the outlying zones—Sicily, Sardinia, Valle d'Aosta, Trentino–Alto Adige (including South Tirol), and (after 1963) Friuli–Venezia Giulia—inhabited by populations with linguistic or ethnic differences from those in the rest of Italy. In short, the constitution was an "anti-Fascist" document, providing for weak governments and individual liberty—exactly the opposite of what Mussolini had attempted.

THE COLD WAR POLITICAL ORDER

In 1947 the Cold War began to influence Italian politics. De Gasperi visited the United States in January 1947 and returned with $150 million in aid. He had excluded the Communists and their allies, the Socialists, from his government the previous May both to placate the Vatican and the conservative south and to ensure that much-needed U.S. aid continued. As parliamentary elections approached, U.S. Secretary of State George C. Marshall threatened that aid would be cancelled if the Communists and Socialists came to power.

In the campaign leading up to the first parliamentary elections of the new republic in April 1948, the United States provided huge backing for the Christian Democrats and their Liberal, Social Democratic, and Republican partners, including funding for party propaganda. Anti-Communist and anti-Catholic propaganda dominated the Christian Democrat campaign. Numerous civic committees were formed throughout Italy to get out the anti-Communist vote. The Christian Democrats, also backed by the church, won more than 48 percent of the vote and more than half the seats. The Communist-Socialist alliance won 31 percent of the overall vote and was the biggest vote-getter only in the "Red Belt" central regions of Emilia-Romagna, Tuscany, and Umbria. An extraordinary 92 percent of Italians who were qualified to vote did so.

The election dashed the hopes of many former Resistance fighters for radical change. One more key event was to follow in 1948. In July the popular Communist Party leader, Togliatti, was shot by an isolated right-winger on the steps of parliament. Togliatti survived, but the assassination attempt sparked off strikes and demonstrations all over Italy. In some areas, such as Genoa and Tuscany, Communist supporters seemed to put into practice a plan for revolution, taking over tram lines and occupying key communication centres. Togliatti and Communist leaders called for calm, and after a week the movement petered out.

The Christian Democrats accused the Communists of preparing an insurrection to overthrow a democratic government, and the spectre of a Communist coup d'état hung over Italian politics for years to come. Those who had kept their arms after the war saw their hopes of revolution disappear. The Communists continued to elaborate an "Italian road to socialism" that ruled out violent insurrection and called for progressive reforms.

Another effect of the 1948 election was the division of the trade union movement into three competing federations, the "red" (Communist and Socialist) Italian General Confederation of Labour, the "white" (Catholic and Christian Democratic) Italian Confederation of Workers' Trade Unions, and the moderate Italian Labour Union. These divisions were to be overcome only briefly in the waves of strikes after 1969.

Italian politics set for the next 40 years into its "Cold War" mold. The Christian Democrats, backed by U.S. military and financial muscle, shared power and patronage with their smaller pro-Western coalition partners. They had a strong social and religious base in northern regions, could count on anti-Communist sentiment in the south, appealed to peasant landowners and women voters everywhere, won about 40 percent of the vote at successive elections, and held the key posts in government, including that of prime minister. The Socialist Party broke off its alliance with the Communists in the late 1950s and began to cooperate with the Christian Democrats. Vested interests blocked the ambitious reform programs promised by the Socialists time and again, but the centre-left administrations under Amintore Fanfani in the late 1950s and early 1960s managed to pass important measures in the fields of education reform, nationalization, and public housing. Beginning in 1963, under Nenni, the Socialists joined centre-left coalition governments, acquiring control of some of the key ministries and public-sector enterprises. The Christian Democrat Aldo Moro led several such coalition governments during the mid-1960s.

The Communists, excluded from central government, gradually made themselves more respectable but never quite shook off their Soviet links. They won 25 to 30 percent of the vote (reaching a peak of 34 percent in 1976), were particularly strong among industrial workers, agricultural labourers, and sharecroppers, ran local (and, from the 1970s, regional) governments in central Italy, and controlled the major trade unions. Even so, international factors dominated domestic politics and outweighed the old Resistance anti-Fascist alliance in a system known as blocked pluralism or polarized pluralism.

PARTIES AND PARTY FACTIONS

All the major Italian parties had large memberships (the Communists had more than two million until 1956, the Christian Democrats almost the same by the early 1970s), recruited from organizations such as Catholic Action, cooperatives, and trade unions. These organizations often provided tangible benefits—jobs, disability pensions, and cheap holidays—to their members. Distinct subcultures—based on a wide range of institutions, including newspapers, bars, theatres, and schools—grew up around each major party. The "white" subculture dominated parts of the south and northeast; the "red" subculture prevailed in Emilia, Tuscany, and Umbria, as well as the industrial heartlands of working-class Turin, Milan, and Genoa. Every city had its "red," "white," and "black" (neofascist) zones.

Most parties were groupings of organized factions, each with its own leaders, deputies, regional or ideological base, sources of finance, and journals. Within each party, and in particular within the Christian Democratic Party, these factions contended for power and for control of lucrative firms and agencies in the public sector to secure financial backing and jobs for supporters. One of the key reasons why governments between 1945 and 1994 were short-lived, with an average life of 11 months, was that governments had to be reshuffled regularly in order to allow different faction leaders to obtain posts, partly due to an electoral system that was so highly proportional. Another reason for the frequent changes was the need to form new coalitions excluding the neofascists and the Communists, who could never be allowed to govern in the Cold War world. The constitution also allowed for frequent and often inexplicable government "crises" that often ended with very similar governments forming and reforming. Giulio Andreotti alone presided over seven governments.

Government instability also stemmed from secret voting in parliament, which enabled deputies from dissatisfied factions within the coalition parties to bring down governments without attracting blame. However, instability was more apparent than real—top politicians often held the key government posts semipermanently—and it was mitigated by the secretaries of the leading parties, whose role it was to negotiate acceptable deals among faction leaders. Indeed, the party secretary was sometimes more significant than the prime minister, since the latter had no direct mandate from the electorate and was often not even the most prominent member of a party. Despite periodic shifts in the composition of the government, the same group of parties, dominated by the Christian Democrats, remained in power in the postwar period.

The Christian Democrats had to find coalition partners after 1953, when they lost their absolute majority in parliament. The need for coalition government gave exaggerated power to the smaller coalition parties, who could demand key ministries and benefits. In addition, the option of allying with the monarchists or the small but stable neofascist party, the Italian Social Movement (Movimento Sociale Italiano; MSI), was blocked by the anti-Fascist consensus among the major parties and in the country at large. When the Christian Democrats tried to bring the MSI into the coalition, they faced mass demonstrations, as at Genoa in 1960. The neofascists remained "untouchable" until the 1990s.

At parliamentary elections voters could select not only a party but also particular candidates from that party. Deputies therefore needed to win favours for constituents, which could include suitable pieces of legislation or pressuring ministers or managers of state enterprises—themselves often political appointees. The state sector of the economy, already large in 1945, and the welfare services were both expanded after the war, and the new jobs were often given to party members or sympathizers. In turn, state firms financed the parties or particular factions of the parties. In many areas, especially in the south, party-controlled agencies came to dominate economic and social activity. The leading politicians used patronage to build power bases in particular regions, such as Fanfani did in Tuscany and Andreotti in Sicily. Local government could rarely operate without favours and finance from central, party-controlled agencies. The civil service, never very prestigious, was bypassed by politicians and government agencies and became increasingly demoralized.

Clientelism and patronage penetrated all areas of political, social, and cultural life. These features were strongest in the south, in part because of the domination of the Christian Democratic Party in that part of the country. As a result, southerners increasingly predominated in government posts, even in the north. State employees received generous benefits, often without real controls, and some public pensions allowed for retirement after only 20 years of service. This proved a huge drain on public finances. A series of little laws, or *leggine*, determined the precise distribution of state resources, jobs, and taxes among parties and factions, including those in the opposition, in a system known as *partitocrazia* ("partyocracy"). Although this system was obviously corrupt, it commanded a broad public consensus, and there were few Italians who did not participate in some way in the system. In the worst cases, in parts of the south, the links between organized crime, political patronage, and government contracts were built up and maintained throughout the postwar period. This brought the destruction of many of the most beautiful cities of Italy through the construction of vast swaths of ugly cement housing. The so-called "rape of Palermo," under Mafia–Christian Democratic control in the 1960s, was one of the most tragic examples. Parties and their clients also siphoned money and resources meant to aid victims of natural disasters, such as earthquakes.

FOREIGN POLICY

The Cold War political system had one major advantage. Italian foreign policy ceased to be adventurous. De Gasperi had to accept the harsh Treaty of Paris in 1947, in which Italy gave up all African colonies and relinquished some Alpine territories to France and the Dodecanese islands to Greece. But thereafter Italy joined the North Atlantic Treaty Organization (NATO) and became a respectable member of the Western alliance. NATO—in effect, the United States—guaranteed Italy's political stability and security. Italy also joined the European Coal and Steel Community (1952) and in 1957 was a founding member of the European Economic Community (EEC; later succeeded by the European Union).

The Paris treaty left unresolved the most thorny and difficult territorial question, that of Trieste. Yugoslav troops had taken the city and its surroundings from the Germans in 1945, claimed the region (which was populated by both Italians and Slovenes) for Yugoslavia, and embarked on a large-scale purge in which thousands of Italians were killed and then dumped into deep caves. The Paris treaty divided the region into two zones: one, including the mostly Italian-speaking city of Trieste, administered by the Western Allies and the other by Yugoslavia. The divided region became a focus of Cold War tensions. Finally, in 1954, the city of Trieste and a narrow coastal strip to its north came under direct Italian rule, while the remainder of the region was ceded to Yugoslavia.

THE ECONOMIC MIRACLE

The republic enjoyed economic success for many years. Initial U.S. support, especially food, oil, and Marshall Plan aid, helped to rebuild basic industries, including steel. The government abandoned the controls that had existed under the Fascists and the attempts at autarky, and all parties and trade unions approved the "reconstruction" program of 1945-47. Prewar industrial production levels were regained by 1948, and production for the Korean War (1950-53) provided further stimulus to growth. Italy became fully integrated into European trade and took an increasingly active part in Middle Eastern oil exploration and engineering development. Until 1964 (and in particular in the boom years of 1958-63) the country enjoyed an "economic miracle," with industrial growth rates of more than 8 percent per year. Its most prominent industries, still in the northwestern industrial triangle, produced fashionable clothing (especially shoes), typewriters, refrigerators, washing machines, furniture, plastics, artificial fibres, sewing machines, inexpensive motor scooters (the Vespa and the Lambretta), and cars (from economical Fiats to luxury makes such as Maserati, Lamborghini, and Alfa Romeo). Italian firms became famous for their combination of elegant design and inexpensive production techniques. An extraordinary network of superhighways was constructed across Italy. The country was transformed in less than two decades from a largely agricultural backwater into one of the world's most dynamic industrial nations. Economic success gave politicians additional resources to maintain their political support.

The postwar recovery and subsequent expansion benefited from a stable currency from 1948 onward and from Italy's cheap access to raw materials, especially Middle Eastern oil. The dynamic policies of Enrico Mattei, president of ENI (Ente Nazionale Idrocarburi, the state-owned energy group), were central to this development. The petroleum company AGIP (Azienda Generale Italiana Petroli), which became a division of ENI in 1953, discovered natural gas in the Po valley and sold it at low prices to industry. Labour was inexpensive, as rural migrants flooded into the cities, trade unions were weak and politically divided until the late 1960s, regulatory agencies were even weaker, and taxes were low and easily avoidable. All this encouraged investment, especially as businessmen could borrow cheaply from state-owned banks and credit institutes. The IRI, founded under Mussolini in 1933, continued to dominate much of the economy, including not only heavy industry but also telephone service, air transport, and highway construction. The "economic miracle," therefore, did not rest on market principles alone; government agencies played a vital role in it.

In agriculture the major postwar change was the land reform laws of 1950, which made it possible for land reform agencies to expropriate large, badly cultivated estates, mostly in southern or central Italy, improve them, and sell them off to new peasant owners. The aim was to create a settled society of peasant cultivators, but this was achieved only in a few areas, because normally there was not enough land to go around: only 117,000 families actually acquired farms.

Landless peasants moved abroad or to the cities instead. A major consequence of land reform, however, was that the reform agencies—run by central politicians in Rome—became economically dominant in many rural areas, controlling, among other things, land allocation, loans, and improvement grants. They thus undermined the traditional power of local landowners and became transmission belts for the political patronage of the Christian Democrats, especially in the south. Mechanization and modernization gradually replaced many of the traditional jobs in the Italian countryside. Seasonal women rice workers disappeared from the north, as did most day labourers and sharecroppers. Smaller, well-managed farms prospered, in part through EEC subsidies, and rural towns grew.

The major economic problem was still the relatively underdeveloped south, where there was little industry and where per capita income in 1950 was half that of northern Italy. Initial policy stressed land reform and irrigation. For a while it seemed as if southerners were taking control of their own destiny for the first time since the Risorgimento. The huge, organized land occupation movements that swept across the south in 1949 and 1950 involved hundreds of thousands of landless peasants and politicized a whole generation. But the state intervened, sometimes lethally, to end the occupations on behalf of the powerful landowners. Because the land reforms that followed the occupations actually transferred little land to the peasantry and left many of the south's inequities intact, millions of young men and women decided to migrate to the north.

The special Southern Development Fund (Cassa per il Mezzogiorno), established in 1950, financed roads, schools, electrification, water provision, and land reclamation. After 1957 it began to invest in industrial development as well, helped by a government policy that directed the expansion of state firms southward and by credit and tax breaks for private investors. Other agencies were founded to develop specific sectors. Promising areas of the south were selected for industrial development, and key plants were built there, together with the necessary infrastructure. The result was the establishment of a number of large, capital-intensive plants—for example, steelworks and heavy engineering at Taranto and oil refineries at Porto Torres—that were hugely expensive, often produced nonmarketable goods, and employed little local labour. These factories quickly became known as "cathedrals in the desert." Although a few areas did take off (notably the Puglian coast north of Bari), the industrialization policy soon faced widespread criticism. Northerners resented having to pay for it, and southerners could see little benefit, especially as small firms received few incentives. The environmental costs were also enormous. Funding was gradually shifted, therefore, to subsidizing labour costs—especially social security contributions—and training and, by the 1980s,

to making selective grants available for small and medium projects. The fund spent $20 billion between 1950 and 1980, but it did not industrialize southern Italy. Southern unemployment remained at three times the northern rate, and wages were still 40 percent below the national average.

The south did benefit, however, from some of the fund's original activities, such as providing decent roads, clean water, much improved health services, and secondary schools, as well as eradicating malaria. It also received many state welfare benefits—often derived from friendly politicians in need of votes—and subsidies to agriculture. The social impact of automobiles, television, and processed foods was as great in southern Italy as elsewhere. The south also benefited from emigrants' remittances as large-scale migration to western Europe and the northern cities resumed from 1950 onward. More than three million people, mostly able-bodied young men, left the south between 1955 and 1970. Some rural areas became seriously depopulated, whereas Rome and many of the northern cities virtually doubled in size, with the immigrants being crowded into bleak housing estates on the outskirts or into improvised shantytowns.

ITALY IN THE LATE 20TH CENTURY

Beginning in the 1960s, Italy completed its postwar transformation from a largely agrarian, relatively poor country into one of the most economically and socially advanced countries of the world. One consequence of these changes was that migration from the south slowed after 1970 and, by the 1980s, even reversed, as jobs became scarcer in northern Italy and northern Europe. Other demographic, economic, technological, and cultural changes transformed Italian daily life and fueled social unrest. After the Cold War ended in 1989, pressures for political and economic reform, European economic unification, and globalization exposed Italy to a new range of challenges.

DEMOGRAPHIC AND SOCIAL CHANGE

In general, population growth in Italy had slowed dramatically by the 1960s. The birth rate in the north had already been low in the postwar years and dropped below replacement level in the 1970s in most northern and central regions. Even in the south, birth rates fell sharply after 1964. By 1979 there were only 670,000 live births in all of Italy and by 1987 some 560,000. Italians had one of the lowest birth rates of any industrial country by the 1990s, and there was a growing tendency toward families having only one child and adults remaining single.

The reasons for the dramatic decline in births are complex. Contraception became readily available after 1971, and

most Italians were now urbanites living in apartments and thus not in need of a large number of children to help till the soil. Women were now better-educated. Girls in general began going to secondary schools only in the 1960s, and by 1972 there were a quarter-million female graduates. They could now pursue satisfying careers or at least readily find gainful employment that gave them financial independence from men and alternatives to lives as homemakers and mothers. In 1970, following a campaign led by the Radical Party and opposed by the church and Christian Democrats, Italy's first divorce law was passed. It was confirmed in a nationwide referendum (called by the Christian Democrats) in May 1974 by 59.1 percent of the voters—a real victory for secular groups against church and Christian Democratic dominance of society. In 1975 many antiquated provisions in family law were altered or abolished, and in 1981 another referendum confirmed by 67.9 percent of the vote the 1978 law permitting abortion. Meanwhile, civil marriage became more common (almost 12 percent of all marriages by 1979), as did unmarried cohabitation.

Legal contraception, divorce, and abortion provided dramatic evidence of a more secularized society. Regular church attendance fell sharply, from about 70 percent in the mid-1950s to about 30 percent in the 1980s. The membership of Catholic Action fell to about 650,000 by 1978, about one-fourth of its figure in 1966, and in the late 1960s Catholic trade unions allied with their erstwhile Communist rivals. Broadcasting in 1976 ceased to be a state monopoly dominated by the Christian Democrats. Furthermore, many church-controlled charities, especially at the local level, were taken over by regional governments in 1977 and 1978 and run as part of the state welfare system by political appointees. Although the Christian Democrats still held most government posts, Italy by the 1980s was indeed markedly "de-Christianized," as Pope John Paul II said. In 1985 a new concordat that recognized many of these changes was ratified by the Vatican and (significantly) a government led by the Socialist Bettino Craxi. Roman Catholicism ceased to be the state religion, religious instruction in schools became voluntary, and the state stopped funding priests' salaries.

ECONOMIC STAGNATION AND LABOUR MILITANCY

After 1963, when the Socialist Party entered government, an increasing number of political appointments were made in the firms and agencies of the public sector, and trade unions became more powerful. Soon inflation began creeping up once again, as governments printed money to pay for higher wages and welfare. Many firms had to be rescued by the IRI at public expense, the balance of payments deteriorated, and the official economy began to slow down, although the black-market economy of domestic textile workers and self-employed artisans, among others, continued to flourish.

This economic slump led to the "hot autumn" of 1969, a season of strikes, factory occupations, and mass demonstrations throughout northern Italy, with its epicentre at Fiat in Turin. Most stoppages were unofficial, led by workers' factory committees or militant leftist groups rather than by the (party-linked) trade unions. The protests were not only about pay and work-related matters but also about conditions outside the factory, such as housing, transport, and pensions, and they formed part of a more general wave of political and student protest, including opposition to the Vietnam War.

The stoppages forced employers to grant large pay raises—at least 15 percent—and factory councils were set up in nearly all major plants. Often, migrant urban newcomers were at the head of the struggles. In 1970, legislation—the Statute of the Workers—ratified these developments and established rights never before codified in law. In 1975 most pay scales were indexed to inflation on a quarterly basis for wage and salary earners, thus guaranteeing the big pay raises of the previous few years. Jobs, too, were virtually guaranteed in the official economy, and trade unions became influential on a host of planning bodies. The firing

Workers demonstrating against the Pirelli tire factory in Milan during a season of strike in Italy, in the fall of 1969. Mondadori/Getty Images

of workers became extremely difficult in many sectors.

Labour militancy continued throughout most of the 1970s, often led by unofficial "autonomous" unions. Many firms therefore chose to restructure themselves into smaller units employing part-time or unofficial workers on piece rates, who could be dismissed easily and did not enjoy guaranteed wages. This was particularly true in the areas of textile production and light engineering. Unemployment rose sharply, especially among the young. By 1977 there were one million unemployed people under age 24. Inflation continued, aggravated by the increases in the price of oil in 1973 and 1979. The budget deficit became permanent and intractable, averaging about 10 percent of the gross domestic product (GDP), higher than any other industrial country. The lira fell steadily, from 560 lire to the U.S. dollar in 1973 to 1,400 lire in 1982.

STUDENT PROTEST AND SOCIAL MOVEMENTS

Student protests in Italy had also begun to take off in 1967, and the movement continued right through the 1970s. Universities, from Pisa to Turin to Trento, were occupied, lecturers and schoolteachers were challenged in the classroom, and alternative lifestyles began to dominate youth culture. A whole generation was radicalized.

Students challenged both the church and the Communist Party, as well as the ubiquitous consumer society and the traditional power of the family. One of the slogans of the movement was "I want to be an orphan." However, after an initial phase of creativity and democratization, the movement fell under the shadow of various small and ideological groupings who often used violence to communicate their message.

A new group of student movements emerged in 1977, known collectively as *autonomia* ("autonomy"). The best-known of these, Autonomia Operaia ("Worker Autonomy"), took a more violent approach. Other branches of the movement, such as those calling themselves "Metropolitan Indians," were more creative and interesting. This time, the movement saw the traditional left as an enemy. Trade union leaders were shouted down and attacked. Ritualistic and violent demonstrations occurred in 1977, and some of the followers of the movement carried guns. The state arrested most of the leaders of the movement in 1979, while others fled abroad to escape trial. The *autonomia* reemerged in the 1980s and addressed environmental issues; squatted in vacant buildings, partly to protest the shortage of affordable housing; and set up alternative spaces known as "social centres."

The feminist movement also invigorated society in the mid-1970s, making its arrival in Italy later than in most other

SECOND VATICAN COUNCIL

The 21st ecumenical council of the Roman Catholic Church, known as the Second Vatican Council or Vatican II, was announced by Pope John XXIII on Jan. 25, 1959, as a means of spiritual renewal for the church and as an occasion for Christians separated from Rome to join in search for reunion.

The work of the council continued under Pope John's successor, Paul VI, and sessions were convened each autumn until the work of the council was completed on Dec. 8, 1965. Sixteen documents were enacted by the council fathers.

The "Dogmatic Constitution on the Church" reflects the attempt of the council fathers to utilize biblical terms rather than juridical categories to describe the church. The treatment of the hierarchical structure of the church counterbalances somewhat the monarchical emphasis of the first Vatican Council's teaching on the papacy by giving weight to the role of the bishops. The teaching of the constitution on the nature of the laity (those not in holy orders) was intended to provide the basis for the call of lay people to holiness and to share in the missionary vocation of the church. By describing the church as the people of God, a pilgrim people, the council fathers provided the theological justification for changing the defensive and inflexible stance that had characterized much of Catholic thought and practice since the Protestant Reformation.

The "Dogmatic Constitution on Divine Revelation" attempts to relate the role of Scripture and tradition (the postbiblical teaching of the church) to their common origin in the Word of God that has been committed to the church. The document affirms the value of Scripture for the salvation of men while maintaining an open attitude toward the scholarly study of the Bible.

The "Constitution on the Sacred Liturgy" establishes the principle of greater participation by the laity in the celebration of mass and authorizes significant changes in the texts, forms, and language used in the celebration of mass and the administration of the sacraments.

The "Pastoral Constitution on the Church in the World of Today" acknowledges the profound changes humanity is experiencing and attempts to relate the church's concept of itself and of revelation to the needs and values of contemporary culture.

The council also promulgated decrees (documents on practical questions) on the pastoral duties of bishops, ecumenism, the Eastern-rite churches, the ministry and life of priests, the education for the priesthood, the religious life, the missionary activity of the church, the apostolate of the laity, and the media of social communication. Furthermore, declarations (documents on particular issues) on religious freedom, the church's attitude toward non-Christian religions, and on Christian education were produced. These documents reflected the renewal in various areas of church life begun decades before Pope John—biblical, ecumenical, liturgical, lay apostolate. The impulse of the documents and the council deliberations in general had by the early 1970s been felt in nearly every area of church life and had set in motion many changes that may not have been foreseen by the council fathers.

Western countries. Feminists challenged the rigid Catholic morals of society and a legal system that gave women little defense against male oppression, rape, or even murder. The feminists also challenged the male dominance of politics right across the spectrum and even within the far-left political movements. The great victories in the referendums of the 1970s and '80s on divorce and abortion would have been impossible without the agitation of the feminist movement.

Even the church began to open up to social and cultural change. The Second Vatican Council (1962–65), called by the reformist Pope John XXIII and implemented by his successor Pope Paul VI, provided a framework for the partial liberalization and democratization of the church. This process of liberal reform and the hopes that it raised for a transformation of the church declined, however, with the succession of the more conservative Pope John Paul II in 1978.

TERRORISM

When economic, social, and political stability suddenly collapsed after 1969, one of the most alarming results was terrorism. Initially, neofascist groups backed and armed by some members of the security services carried out most acts of violence. They began planting bombs and derailing trains as part of a "strategy of tension" to undermine the labour advances of 1969–72 and encourage a right-wing coup. The "strategy of tension" began in earnest with a series of bombings in Milan and Rome in December 1969. In a Milan bank, a bomb killed 16 people and wounded more than 90. Initial police suspicion fell upon the far left, especially the anarchists. One anarchist, Giuseppe Pinelli, died in mysterious circumstances after "falling" from a fourth-floor window of Milan's central police station. Another anarchist, Pietro Valpreda, was arrested and charged with the Milan bomb attack. The Valpreda and Pinelli cases split Italy and radicalized large sectors of the student and workers movements. Many on the right continued to believe the version put out by the police and the state, while vast swathes of liberal opinion saw the affair as a mixture of conspiracy and cover-up. The inability of the state to find or prosecute those responsible (the eighth trial relating to the case began in 2000 and eventually ended in acquittal) only increased the disaffection with the authorities. Meanwhile, evidence emerged—which the police had ignored—that suggested that neofascists had planted the bombs with the active support of sectors of the Italian secret services. Valpreda was not acquitted until the 1980s and spent three years in jail awaiting trial. The Pinelli case was never resolved. The "strategy of tension" continued until 1984. The most deadly incident occurred in August 1980, when a bomb

RED BRIGADES

In the 1970s an Italian militant left-wing organization known as the Red Brigades (Italian: Brigate Rosse) gained notoriety for kidnappings, murders, and sabotage. Its self-proclaimed aim was to undermine the Italian state and pave the way for a Marxist upheaval led by a "revolutionary proletariat."

The reputed founder of the Red Brigades was Renato Curcio, who in 1967 set up a leftist study group at the University of Trento dedicated to figures such as Karl Marx, Mao Zedong, and Che Guevara. In 1969 Curcio married a fellow radical, Margherita Cagol, and moved with her to Milan, where they attracted a coterie of followers. Proclaiming the existence of the Red Brigades in November 1970 through the firebombing of various factories and warehouses in Milan, the group began kidnapping the following year and in 1974 committed its first assassination; among its victims that year was the chief inspector of Turin's antiterrorist squad.

Despite the arrest and imprisonment of hundreds of alleged terrorists throughout the country—including Curcio himself in 1976—the random assassinations continued. In 1978 the Red Brigades kidnapped and murdered former prime minister Aldo Moro. In December 1981 a U.S. Army officer with the North Atlantic Treaty Organization (NATO), Brigadier General James Dozier, was abducted and held captive by the Red Brigades for 42 days before Italian police rescued him unharmed from a hideout in Padua. Between 1974 and 1988, the Red Brigades carried out about 50 attacks, in which nearly 50 people were killed. A common nonlethal tactic employed by the group was "kneecapping," in which a victim was shot in the knees so that he could not walk again.

At its height in the 1970s, the Red Brigades was believed to comprise 400 to 500 full-time members, 1,000 members who helped periodically, and a few thousand supporters who provided funds and shelter. Careful, systematic police work led to the arrest and imprisonment of many of the Red Brigades' leaders and ordinary members from the mid-1970s onward, and by the late 1980s the organization was all but destroyed. However, a group claiming to be the Red Brigades took responsibility in the 1990s for various violent attacks, including those against a senior Italian government adviser, a U.S. base in Aviano, and the NATO Defense College.

placed in a crowded waiting room at a Bologna railway station killed 85 people. Neofascists were later convicted of planting the bomb.

By the mid-1970s left-wing terrorism had begun to attract many young people unhappy with U.S. foreign policy, the failures of centre-left governments, and the Communists' recent collaboration with the Christian Democrats. It was carried on by hundreds of former militant students and unemployed workers in a host of small groups. The "red" terrorists began by kidnapping factory supervisors for brief periods of time. Soon they began kidnapping and killing politicians, judges, and journalists. The "red" terrorists were relatively popular on the far left at first, but after 1977–78 the extra-parliamentary movement began to distance itself from them. The best-known organization, the Red Brigades, kidnapped and murdered former prime minister Aldo Moro in 1978; for 55 days the Red Brigades held him in Rome as Italy held its breath. Since then a series of mysteries have emerged over secret service blunders and possible complicity with the Red Brigades. After Moro's murder the police were reorganized and given special powers, the courts gave captured terrorists every incentive to provide evidence, and by 1981–82 the terrorist threat was greatly reduced.

POLITICS IN THE 1970S AND '80S

The political system survived with the assistance of the Communists, whose trade unions had helped to restrain wage claims after 1972 and who took a firm line against terrorism. In the face of the twin crises of the economy and terrorism, as well as the example of the recent military coup d'état in Chile that had toppled a Marxist government, the Communist Party, led by Enrico Berlinguer, adopted a policy in 1973 that he called the "historic compromise." It entailed more or less formal alliances between the Christian Democrats and the Communists for the good of the country. The Communist Party won 34.4

percent of the vote and 228 seats in the Chamber of Deputies in 1976. However, Berlinguer's "historic compromise" alienated many Communist supporters. Although the Communists never actually joined a coalition government, they supported (mainly by abstaining during votes of no confidence) ones led by the Christian Democrats from 1976 to 1979 and were given several key institutional posts, including speaker of the Chamber of Deputies. The Communists also accepted Italy's membership in NATO. This period saw the elaboration of networks that spread patronage across the political system. It was these corrupt networks that were to cause a political crisis when they were exposed in the 1990s. Communist cooperation ended, however, in 1979 as international tensions increased, and in the elections of that year the party's vote declined to 30.4 percent. After 1979 the Communists went into opposition again. By 1987 their share of the national vote had declined to about one-fourth.

Governments in the 1980s were usually four- or five-party coalitions in which the smaller parties played a more significant role than hitherto. The Christian Democrats, weakened by secularization, factional disputes, and successive scandals, also saw their vote decline from 38.3 percent in 1979 to 32.9 percent in 1983. In 1981–82 the Christian Democrats had to give up the prime ministry temporarily, for the first time since 1945. The forceful

Socialist leader, Craxi, was prime minister from 1983 to 1987.

Socialists, in fact, secured many key posts in the 1980s, not only in government but also in economic agencies, broadcasting, and health services. The Socialist vote rose, but only to 11.4 percent in 1983 and to 14.3 percent in 1987. Disputes among and within the leading parties over the allocation of jobs and resources became more prolonged and often paralyzed effective government. Public debt rose to unsustainable levels. All this fueled popular resentment of *partitocrazia*, increasingly frequent corruption scandals, and the clandestine influence of Masonic or other shadowy pressure groups. The system could no longer deliver the patronage that once sustained it, and the state-dominated economy was falling behind those of other European countries.

The 1980s were also a decade of a general "withdrawal" (*il riflusso*) from politics and political activism after the upheavals of the 1960s and '70s. All the parties and unions began to lose members, and election turnouts dropped. Protest movements attracted far fewer people than in the previous two decades. The ideologies that had held the Cold War system together—communism and anticommunism, fascism and antifascism—began to lose their appeal.

While even the Communists had accepted Italian membership in NATO in the 1970s, Italy frequently stood apart from U.S. overseas military actions from the Vietnam War onward. The continuing strength of the Roman Catholic Church in Italian society and the power of the Communist Party made active participation in "American" wars a political impossibility. Only after the Cold War did the Italian army actually participate in a NATO military intervention, with its involvement in the conflict in Kosovo in 1999.

REGIONAL GOVERNMENT

During the 1970s, elected regional assemblies and governments, which had previously existed only in the five outlying regions given special powers at various times (Sicily, Sardinia, Friuli–Venezia Giulia, Trentino–Alto Adige, and Valle d'Aosta), were finally set up throughout Italy, as the constitution had required. They acquired extensive devolved powers of legislation and administration, especially over agriculture, health, social welfare, and the environment. Many national agencies were dissolved in 1978, and their powers were allocated to the regions. In 1984 even the Southern Development Fund was abolished and its planning and investment powers transferred to a complex set of institutions, including the southern regional governments. Elections were held at five-year intervals, and after 2000 the president of each region was elected directly under a new law.

The effects of regionalism were profound. The regions became the main bodies responsible for welfare and for organizing the health services, which, in turn, decreased the influence of central politicians. (The political nature of appointments to these services in the regions, however, often drew much criticism.) In the north politicians became more conscious of regional interests and more intent on running their own affairs without interference from Rome. This was less true in the south, where continuing poverty ensured a steady need for subsidies from the central government. Conflicts began to emerge between local and national interests, especially in the large and rich regions of the north.

THE ECONOMY IN THE 1980s

Economic growth revived in the mid-1980s, once terrorism had ended and the 1979 oil crisis had subsided. In autumn 1980 Fiat laid off more than 20,000 workers in Turin, and the unions' protest strike quickly collapsed. The long season of protest that began in 1969 was finally at an end. Other employers followed Fiat's example, and the power of trade unions went into decline. Big industry began to slump all over Italy but especially in the industrial northwest. Historic factories, linked to mass production and class struggle, closed or scaled down their operations. A 1985 referendum markedly reduced the indexation of wages, despite a strong Communist campaign against this action. However, northern Italy prospered in the financial boom years of the

middle and late 1980s, helped by the low price of oil, and people spoke of a "new economic miracle."

The Italian economy began to develop along new lines. In central and northeastern Italy—collectively known as the "third Italy," alongside the less-developed south and the northwest, with its older industries and financial centres—small businesses flourished. These firms mainly produced quality goods for export and were often family-run. New industrial districts in these regions specialized in particular products, from taps to ties. New industries, such as fashion, began to replace traditional businesses in the northern cities. Milan became one of the world's fashion capitals during the 1980s, bringing in billions of lire in business and advertising. With the diversification of the media at the end of the 1970s, private television took off under the influence of a dynamic entrepreneur, Silvio Berlusconi.

However, serious problems persisted. Budget deficits remained large and, given the political system, untackled. By 1989 the accumulated national debt exceeded the annual GDP. The economy continued to depend heavily on decentralized, "unofficial" work done by casual workers in small firms and service industries (the so-called black-market economy), as well as on a handful of successful international entrepreneurs. The south, moreover, did not participate fully in the country's economic recovery, aside from pockets of growth in Puglia and

Abruzzi. The rise in oil prices in the 1970s and the world steel glut devastated industry in the south except for a few areas of light engineering and textile production. In December 1992 the system of "extraordinary incentives" was abolished, just as welfare payments were being reduced and state industries privatized. The south, however, maintained a thriving black-market economy supported partly by organized crime activity. As emigration diminished and mass education expanded, living standards began to rise in line with, but always well behind, the more affluent north. The most worrying aspect of the southern economy was, as ever, youth unemployment, particularly in poverty-stricken cities such as Naples, Palermo, and Reggio di Calabria.

Public services remained an economic and political quagmire and a target of growing public resentment. Despite centres of excellence, the state's postal, transport, health, legal, and financial services were top-heavy with bureaucracy, inefficient, and corrupt, and they cost Italy's citizens hundreds of hours each year in (often pointless) queuing and interminable document collection. Most attempts to reform the system confronted massive resistance from well-organized trade unions armed with contracts protecting their members. It was almost impossible to dismiss a civil servant, and the role of political patronage in public hiring only complicated matters.

Italy had some of the best state nurseries in the world and some of the worst secondary schools. Its universities were full of students who rarely saw their lecturers or actually finished their courses. Not only did Italians pay more taxes than most other western Europeans, but the services they received in return were often comparable to those of eastern Europe or the world's less-developed countries. Still, some benefited from this system—above all, those working within it or those able to avoid tax through corruption or inefficiency. For the vast majority of ordinary Italians, however, their daily dealings with the state brought frustration and anger. Some of this anger was to explode in the crisis of the 1990s.

THE FIGHT AGAINST ORGANIZED CRIME

Organized crime dominated whole regions politically, socially, and economically by the 1980s. In Campania and Naples the Camorra controlled whole swaths of the urban landscape and the underground economy. Several politicians were linked to the Camorra when it siphoned off huge sums of state relief funding after the 1980 earthquake. The 'Ndranghetta organization in Calabria specialized in kidnappings and drug smuggling. In Puglia the Nuova Sacra Corona held sway, while the Mafia dominated Sicily. In Sardinia, bandits continued to operate in some regions, and, although anti-kidnapping laws had been somewhat effective, high-profile kidnappings dominated the news for months.

MAFIA

The society of criminals known as the Mafia arose in Sicily in the late Middle Ages, possibly as a secret organization to overthrow the rule of foreign conquerors. It drew its members from the small private armies, or *mafie*, hired by landlords to protect their estates. By 1900 the Mafia "families" of western Sicily controlled their local economies. In the 1920s Mussolini jailed most of the members, but they were released by the Allies after World War II and resumed their activities. In the 1970s their control of the heroin trade led to fierce rivalry among the clans, followed in the 1980s by renewed governmental efforts to imprison the Mafia leadership. In the U.S., Sicilian immigrants included former Mafia members who set up similar criminal operations. Their operations expanded from bootlegging in the 1920s to gambling, narcotics, and prostitution, and the Mafia, or Cosa Nostra, became the largest U.S. syndicated crime organization. About 24 Mafia groups or "families" controlled operations in the U.S.; the heads (or "dons") of the largest families formed a commission whose main function was judicial and could override a don's authority. At the beginning of the 21st century the Mafia's power was greatly diminished through convictions of top officials, defections, and murderous internal disputes.

In addition, organized crime used violence to block enforcement of environmental protection laws and the establishment of public parks (which reduced opportunities for illegal construction) in Sicily and Sardinia in particular. Throughout the south, illegal construction was rife, and successive government amnesties—the last in 1994—further encouraged these builders. It was only after 1996 that the state began to act seriously against illegal construction, and it demolished houses and villas in natural parks in Sicily and Rome.

During the mid-1980s the state and civil society began to move, finally, against the hegemonic control of organized crime. After a series of high-profile Mafia assassinations of major political and institutional figures, above all prefect-general Carlo Alberto Dalla Chiesa (and his wife) in Palermo in 1982, local elites began to evolve a strategy for combating the Mafia. A key Mafia figure, Tommaso Buscetta, turned state's evidence in 1984 in defiance of the organization's code of silence. Buscetta was the first to provide detailed information on the workings and plans of the Mafia. His testimony led to hundreds of arrests of key Mafia leaders and henchmen. Soon other mafiosi turned state's evidence that helped prosecutors win convictions of important Mafia bosses. In addition, the Mafia families became involved in a damaging internal war in the 1980s that left more than 1,000 dead. Finally, there were moves from within the Christian Democratic Party itself against the Mafia after the murder in 1980 of the

Christian Democratic Sicilian regional president Piersanti Mattarella, a traditional politician who had decided to lead a campaign against corruption in Sicily. The state passed strong anti-Mafia laws for the first time, and several trials in 1986 condemned hundreds of mafiosi to long prison sentences.

The Mafia took its revenge in devastating yet counterproductive fashion. In 1992 Judges Giovanni Falcone and Paolo Borsellino, who had both presided over anti-Mafia trials, were killed in horrific bomb attacks that left another nine people (bodyguards and relatives) dead. These murders galvanized the anti-Mafia movement. Even parliament—which had been stalled on the election of a new president, leaving Italy in a sort of power vacuum—came out of its stupor to elect Oscar Luigi Scalfaro in the aftermath of the Falcone bombing.

Beginning in 1993, authorities arrested several remaining key Mafia figures. Corruption investigations in the early 1990s permitted the prosecution of previously immune political figures who had links to the Mafia. In 1993 seven-time prime minister Guilio Andreotti was charged with collusion with the Mafia, a move that shook the political system to its foundations, although Andreotti was later absolved after a long and dramatic trial. Giancarlo Caselli continued the work of Falcone and Borsellino. Leoluca Orlando, an anti-Mafia campaigner, was elected mayor of Palermo in 1993 and 1997 with huge majorities. The city and

the region began to stabilize, although no one believed that the Mafia had been entirely defeated. In Naples as well, the judges began to break down the powerful Camorra organizations, which were engaged in a bloody internal civil war that had left hundreds of young people dead. Leading politicians and Camorra bosses were arrested and charged.

In the late 1990s, however, the Mafia appeared to be making something of a comeback, although it seemed to have abandoned the tactics of direct confrontation with the state. The right—and in particular the new party called Forza Italia ("Go Italy"), led by Silvio Berlusconi—made continual attacks on anti-Mafia judges and the use of supergrass evidence (ex-mafiosi who turn state's evidence), especially after leading members of Forza Italia itself were implicated in Mafia corruption. These attacks resulted in the ouster of one of the most prominent anti-Mafia judges, Giancarlo Caselli, in 1999. These events suggested a return to previous patterns of government noninterference, albeit much less overt than in the past.

ITALY AT THE TURN OF THE 21ST CENTURY

The fall of the Berlin Wall in 1989 ended the Cold War pattern that had marked Italian politics since the 1940s. Meanwhile, in the wake of growing economic prosperity and the challenges of globalization, most Italians had come to resent the corrupt and costly system of patronage and the large state economic sector that hampered Italy's competitiveness and tarnished its political culture. With the bankruptcy of Cold War ideologies and *partitocrazia*, the party system itself began to appear outdated, politicians experimented with new forms of organization and communication, and shifting alliances replaced the solid blocs of the Cold War world.

The end of the Cold War had an immediate impact on Italy's two biggest parties. Ongoing scandals and the loss of anticommunist appeal brought a further decline in the popularity of the Christian Democrats, who won only 29.7 percent of the vote in the 1992 elections. Under its new leader, Achille Occhetto, the Communist Party adopted a more moderate program and, in 1991, even took a new name: the Democratic Party of the Left (Partito Democratico della Sinistra; PDS). In the same year, a small group of die hard Communists split off to form the Communist Refoundation Party (Partito della Rifondazione Comunista; PRC), which became one of the more important small parties, gaining about 5 percent of the vote in the national elections of 1994 and 1996. The collapse of communism in eastern Europe after 1989 undermined the communist subculture in Italy, and the PDS vote declined further to 16.1 percent in the 1992 elections. Nonetheless, the PDS remained the most important centre-left party.

Public protests against political corruption had little effect until 1992, when investigating magistrates in Milan began uncovering a series of bribery scandals. The city soon became known as "Bribesville" (Tangentopoli), and under "Operation Clean Hands" many leading politicians, civil servants, and prominent businessmen were arrested and imprisoned. Nearly all of Italy's political parties were involved, but the Christian Democrats and the Socialists were the heart of the system. Craxi, the former prime minister, was eventually convicted on multiple charges and escaped imprisonment only by fleeing to Tunisia, where he died in 2000. By mid-1993 more than 200 deputies were under investigation, as were several former ministers, in a series of televised and closely followed trials. Protests about irregularities in the investigations fell on deaf ears at first but gradually began to pick up support.

Apart from the PDS, whose role in the corruption was limited, the main political parties dissolved in disgrace in 1993 and 1994, some to reappear under new names and with new leaders. The Christian Democrats became the Italian Popular Party (Partito Popolare Italiano; PPI), although some former Christian Democrats left the party to form several smaller Catholic-inspired political groupings. Members of the neofascist MSI (which had remained largely outside of the system of corruption) formed the new National Alliance (Alleanza Nazionale; AN). The Socialists, so important to the political system since the 1960s, became irrelevant. It was an extraordinary, unprecedented reshaping of an entire political system.

In 1993 voters approved several referenda, later ratified by parliament, to alter the electoral law so that thenceforth three-fourths of deputies and senators would be elected from single-member constituencies rather than proportionally. Socialist Prime Minister Giuliano Amato (1992–93), whose government had been rocked by the corruption scandal, resigned shortly after the passage of the referendum, and President Scalfaro asked Carlo Azeglio Ciampi to step in and form a government to implement the electoral reforms and stabilize the economy. The collapse of the existing party system and national elections under the new law the following year marked the end of *partitocrazia* and the beginning of a new political order.

ECONOMIC STRENGTH

Economic problems increased sharply after 1991, as Italy felt the effects of a global recession that hit most European economies. In 1992 the budget deficit rose to more than 10 percent of GDP, and industrial production fell by 4 percent from 1992 to 1993. In September 1992 the lira was temporarily forced out of the European Monetary System, in which several nations had linked their currencies. In an effort to reduce the budget deficit, Amato's government abolished the indexation of wages, rapidly decreased welfare spending (especially on health and pensions), and drew up a program to privatize leading state firms, although the privatizations were to occur only very gradually. Amato's successor in 1993 as prime minister, Ciampi, was not a politician at all but a former governor of the Bank of Italy. Committed to privatization and continued government austerity, Ciampi was chosen to reassure investors and to prevent a disastrous flight from the lira. Although a prosperous country, Italy was still a junior partner in the new Europe and could no longer resist northern European pressure for financial prudence. Furthermore, Italy's voters strongly supported the common European currency outlined in the 1991 Maastricht Treaty on the European Union, and Italy needed to implement a program of fiscal discipline to qualify for inclusion in the common currency zone. One facet of the new rigour was that the country's deficit could not breach more than 3 percent of GDP.

During the late 1990s the economy resumed the strong growth of the previous decade, led by the flourishing design and manufacturing small-business networks of the centre and north. Living standards throughout Italy rose to the levels of the most advanced economies, although large pockets of youth unemployment and poverty remained, particularly in parts of the south and on the bleak peripheries of the northern cities. Immigrants from outside Italy also tended to have much lower living standards than Italians.

Italy participated in the Maastricht Treaty and all subsequent agreements on European political and economic union. The European Union remained far more popular in Italy than in many other European countries. Moreover, the strong desire of many Italians to participate in the common European currency enabled the centre-left government of Romano Prodi (1996–98) to pass a series of austerity budgets that dramatically reduced Italy's chronic budget deficits. Under the Prodi government, privatizations began in earnest, and inflation was reduced to record lows. This fiscal discipline allowed Italy to meet the strict requirements for adoption of the common European currency, the euro, which replaced the lira as Italy's unit of exchange on January 1, 1999.

A NEW POLITICAL LANDSCAPE

While electoral reforms failed to produce the desired political stability after 1993, they nevertheless helped transform Italy's political landscape from one of multiple national parties that formed shifting parliamentary coalitions to one of parties, often with a distinct regional basis, that formed electoral coalitions, which then often failed to withstand the rigours of parliamentary cooperation.

In the north, and especially in the Veneto and Lombardy, local or regional "leagues" had developed in the early 1980s to protest corrupt party rule by the central government in Rome, as well as high taxes, poor public services, organized crime (which they often blamed on southerners), and immigration (especially from Africa but later from Albania). These leagues united in 1991 to form a federation, the Northern League (Lega Nord). In 1992, when numerous Socialist and Christian Democratic leaders were being arrested and the Communists were seeking a new identity after the failure of state socialism in eastern Europe, the Northern League secured almost 20 percent of the northern vote in the parliamentary elections. Later it advocated a new constitution with a federal Italy divided into three autonomous republics that would have separate responsibility for everything except defense, foreign affairs, and monetary policy. The northern part of this system was to be known as "Padania."

THE RISE OF BERLUSCONI

The decline of Italy's major political parties as a result of the corruption scandals of the early 1990s created a political vacuum. The Northern League filled part of this vacuum, as did the "post-Fascist" National Alliance led by Gianfranco Fini, which in Rome and the mainland south became the party of continuing Italian patriotism as well as of continuing state subsidies and economic interventionism. Above all, the political vacuum was filled early in 1994 by media entrepreneur Silvio Berlusconi, who controlled three national commercial television channels, much of the press, and the highly successful A.C. Milan football (soccer) club. Berlusconi

Forza Italia party leader Silvio Berlusconi celebrating election results in 1994 that gave his right-wing coalition a majority of seats in the lower house of Italy's parliament. AFP/Getty Images

hastily founded an ad hoc political association, Forza Italia, with a message of populist anticommunism, and formed an equally ad hoc electoral alliance with the Northern League (in the north) and the AN (in the south). This loose right-wing coalition won a majority of about 50 seats in the Chamber of Deputies (although not in the Senate) in the March 1994 parliamentary election, the first held under the new electoral law.

Berlusconi, who became prime minister, had pledged to cut taxes, lower public spending, decentralize government, and generate a million new jobs. However, the new government—which had neofascist ministers for the first time since World War II, as well as a Northern League interior minister—was just as faction-ridden as previous governments.

During huge protests against AN-led inheritance and pension reforms, the trade unions managed to mobilize more than a million people onto the streets of Rome. In July 1994 Berlusconi himself became the subject of anticorruption investigations that he was unable to halt. The allegations weakened Berlusconi's government, as did his attempts to control the state-owned media, which not only had criticized the government but also competed directly with his privately owned media outlets. Berlusconi promised at various times to sell his television stations or leave them to be managed by a "blind trust," but they continued to broadcast propaganda in his favour. Finally, in December 1994 the Northern League ended its alliance with Berlusconi, and his government fell.

SHIFTING POWER

Once again, President Scalfaro invited a banker to head the government, this time Lamberto Dini, the former chief executive of the Bank of Italy and previously Berlusconi's treasury minister. In January 1995 Dini formed a government of nonpolitical "technocrats," supported by the Northern League and by the left-wing parties in parliament (the losers in the 1994 elections). This new government, known on the right as the "turnabout" (*ribaltone*), reached a long-term agreement on pensions and limited the budget deficit. Dini's government lasted until the spring of 1996, when

President Scalfaro called for new parliamentary elections.

In the period of electoral alliances and unstable governments that followed the collapse of Italy's party system—a period that became known as the "second republic"—the president assumed a more powerful role. Powers that the parties had previously exercised—such as the decision to dissolve parliament—rested increasingly with the president. Scalfaro adhered to his constitutional responsibilities in times of crisis, but his disquiet with aspects of the new populist right was clear, and he was often accused of favouring the centre-left at key moments.

Like the right-wing parties, a group of left-wing parties including the PDS had formed an electoral alliance. After the failure of this alliance in the 1994 elections, Massimo d'Alema assumed leadership of the PDS and began to build alliances with the centre. In 1995 Romano Prodi, a former Christian Democratic minister and former head of IRI, proposed to lead a new centre-left alliance known as L'Ulivo ("the Olive Tree"). Promising to enable Italy to adopt the euro and to reform the bureaucracy and civil service, Prodi won the support of the PDS and the other major left and centre parties. With a few exceptions, such as Milan, the left managed to take control of most important city governments in the 1990s. Some of these cities proved to be important laboratories of stable government and reform, including Venice under Massimo Cacciari, Rome under the Green Party's Francesco Rutelli, and Naples under Antonio Bassolino.

Meanwhile, the bitterness inspired by Northern League leader Umberto Bossi's "betrayal" of Berlusconi in 1994 kept the right divided in the north. Berlusconi went into the 1996 elections supported by some smaller Catholic parties and the AN but without the support of the Northern League, which did better than expected in the north. Encouraged by these results, the Northern League issued a symbolic declaration of independence for the northern "Republic of Padania." However, polls showed that the vast majority of the league's voters did not want complete separation, and the league, without the media power of Berlusconi behind it, began to lose ground.

At the same time, the division on the right in 1996 allowed the Olive Tree to win a surprise victory, and Prodi assumed the premiership. However, the Olive Tree coalition's small majority in the lower house made it dependent on the cooperation of the Refounded Communists (the PRC). In October 1998 PRC dissatisfaction led to a narrow defeat in a confidence vote that forced Prodi to resign. D'Alema, leader of the Democrats of the Left (Democratici di Sinistra; DS), as the PDS had renamed itself, assembled a working majority and became prime minister.

D'Alema's government continued the fiscal discipline of Prodi's administration but with less conviction and under continual pressure from various allies. It remained unpopular in the country, while on the right the division and resentments of 1994 were beginning to subside. A new law regulated television time for all parties, but nothing was done about opposition leader Berlusconi's huge media advantage. The left began to hemorrhage votes and, in a highly symbolic defeat, even lost "red Bologna" in 1999 to the centre-right after 50 years of communist city governments. Another heavy defeat followed in the European elections. D'Alema limped on until April 2000, when a new electoral alliance between Berlusconi, the Northern League, and the AN crushed the centre-left in regional elections. D'Alema resigned, and Giuliano Amato assumed leadership of a further weakened centre-left government, which fell in 2001 when Berlusconi led his centre-right coalition back into power and began his second tenure as prime minister, one of the longest in recent history.

In the contentious and close elections of 2006, Prodi returned to the national spotlight to lead his centre-left coalition against Berlusconi, whom he replaced as prime minister. Just 20 months later, in January 2008, Prodi lost a vote of confidence in the Senate and resigned once again. Italian Pres. Giorgio Napolitano called for the formation of an interim government, charged with revising the country's problematic electoral law that had been pushed through parliament by Berlusconi just months before the 2006 elections. Many cited the law, which overturned changes to the electoral system made in the 1990s, as the reason for Prodi's downfall. Attempts to form an interim government failed, however, and Napolitano dissolved parliament in February. In the national elections held in April, Berlusconi—heading a new party known as the People of Freedom (Popolo della Libertà; PdL)—clinched a third term as prime minister.

SCANDAL AND THE STRUGGLING ECONOMY

When an earthquake devastated the historic town of L'Aquila in April 2009, Berlusconi focused attention on the area by visiting victims of the temblor and relocating a Group of Eight summit to the city. His popularity suffered, however, as he became embroiled in a sex scandal involving a teenage model. Berlusconi took another hit in October 2009, when Italy's Constitutional Court struck down a law that protected the prime minister from prosecution while in office. The ruling meant that Berlusconi could be tried on outstanding corruption and fraud charges, as well as other unrelated charges that would accrue over the following years. Italy's economy sagged in 2009 as the global economic crisis drew the country into recession. The unemployment rate approached double digits throughout 2010, and disagreements between Berlusconi and former AN leader Gianfranco Fini triggered the departure of Fini and dozens of supporters from the PdL.

Fini retained his position as leader of the Chamber of Deputies, and, despite his differences with Berlusconi, Future and Freedom (Futuro e Libertà per l'Italia; FLI), the breakaway party that Fini formed, proved instrumental to Berlusconi's political survival, as the embattled prime minister faced three votes of confidence in the latter half of 2010. In February 2011 Berlusconi was mired in yet another scandal when prosecutors alleged that he had solicited sex from an underage prostitute and had abused the powers of his office in the subsequent cover-up. That case was adjourned in April 2011, pending a review by Italy's Constitutional Court. Berlusconi faced another confidence vote in June 2011 following crushing losses for the PdL in local elections. He survived that test, but the country's ongoing political uncertainty, along with a host of economic factors, caused euro zone economic ministers to turn their attention to Italy's public debt market.

For more than a year, financial markets had responded with trepidation to the debt crisis that had escalated for the so-called "PIGS" (Portugal, Ireland, Greece, and Spain) countries, as the EU and IMF called for the enactment of austerity measures in those countries and provided financial bailouts for Greece and Ireland, primarily to preserve the stability of the euro. Italy's outstanding public debt, which approached €2 trillion, amounted to more than that of the four PIGS combined, causing some economists to label the country as "too big to fail." In July 2011 the Italian legislature approved a basket of austerity measures, including massive budget cuts, in an attempt to calm markets and restore confidence in the Italian economy. Investors judged these efforts to be insufficient, however, and a public feud between Berlusconi and finance minister Giulio Tremonti put additional pressure on the Italian bond market. Interest rates on benchmark 10-year government bonds surpassed 6 percent, and in September 2011 labour unions responded to the proposal of an additional round of austerity measures with a one-day general strike that paralyzed the country. The ratings agency Standard & Poor's downgraded Italy's sovereign credit score, and Berlusconi narrowly survived a vote of confidence in parliament, as even his allies began to question the viability of his administration.

On November 8, 2011, Berlusconi effectively lost his parliamentary majority on a key budget vote, and he announced his intention to resign after the passage of his proposed budget reforms. Italian bond yields topped 7.5 percent before the market began to respond to the news. The Italian parliament sped the approval of Berlusconi's austerity measures, and he resigned within hours of their passage on November 12, 2011. Italian Pres. Giorgio Napolitano selected former European commissioner Mario Monti as Berlusconi's replacement, and Monti began to assemble a government with the intention of assuaging fears about the Italian economy.

IMMIGRATION AND FOREIGN POLICY

The economic growth that had begun in the 1980s transformed Italy by the 1990s into a host country for immigration. Emigration from Italy and south-north internal migration had all but disappeared by the 1980s. From the mid-1970s onward, immigrants from all over the world, but in particular from North Africa, the Philippines, and eastern Europe, had begun to appear in the big cities. Most worked in the service sector or in small-time street trading. Italy took a long time to react to this trend, and immigration became a national crisis. By 2000 Italy had more than one million immigrants, many of whom found it difficult to procure documents for legal residence. Racism emerged in Italian society and politics, and immigrants were stereotyped as criminals, just as southern Italians had been in the 1960s. However, this cheap labour was essential to the Italian economy.

In 1993 Italy ratified the Schengen Treaty, which eliminated passport controls between its European member states and mandated rigorous controls for persons arriving from nonmember states. Italy implemented these controls and joined the Schengen zone in 1997. Because of its position at the edge of prosperous western Europe and, after 1997, of the exclusive Schengen zone, Italy played a frontier role in immigration, with immigrants every day attempting the perilous sea crossings from Albania and North Africa despite Italian authorities trying to stop them.

Economic dislocations after the Cold War brought massive immigration from Albania in particular, especially in 1990 and 1991. Italy sent troops to Albania twice at times of crisis, and the huge boatloads of Albanians arriving on the coast of Puglia became symbols of pressures that some Italians perceived as a threat. Only the first Albanians were welcomed. Thereafter Italy adopted a policy of expulsion and began nightly patrols up and down the coast. The end of the Cold War and growing European political and economic integration also had combined to erode Italy's long-standing resistance to overseas military action, as the interventions in Albania demonstrated. In 1999 D'Alema faced the Kosovo crisis on his doorstep, and, in contrast with Italy's complete inaction during the four preceding years of war in the Balkans, Italy permitted the use of its bases to bomb targets in Yugoslavia. This intervention, however, proved unpopular in Italy, both on the left and among Catholics.

Italy entered the 21st century far richer and more developed than it had been a hundred years previously. Many problems remained, however, including continuing political instability and corruption, the historic but persistent economic and cultural divisions between the north and the south, and the new challenges of immigration and European economic and political unification. These challenges dominated Italy's political and economic agenda early in the new century.

CONCLUSION

The contributions of Italy and its people to the world's cultural heritage and history—both ancient and modern—are nearly without parallel. As the centre of the Roman Empire, Italy had an enormous influence on the course of world history. During the modern era of colonialism, the country wielded less power and colonized fewer countries than some of its European peers such as England, France, and Belgium, but Italy owes much of its significance today to a more benevolent and perhaps more enduring kind of colonialism. It holds a place of prominence through its great works of art and music, its design sensibility and style, its cuisine, and even its automobiles. Indeed, Italy's very geography—from the Alps to the Italian Riviera and the Adriatic coast, over rolling olive-green hills, down the rugged Apennines, and through the Mezzogiorno to sun-beaten Sicily—occupies a significant place in the world's imagination.

Italy's heritage and accomplishments are accepted as a leading part of the world's patrimony. Its most significant native sons and daughters in the realms of politics, exploration, culture, and thought are countless and range across many centuries. Dante, Petrarch, Machiavelli, Leonardo da Vinci, Michelangelo, Bernini, Scarlatti, Puccini, Verdi: a thorough list, even restricted to Italy's acknowledged geniuses, would be lengthy.

Italy has journeyed through many centuries to create itself as a unified country. After the fall of the Roman Empire, portions of Italy were at times subject to rule by a succession of powers from elsewhere in Europe and to the east: the Byzantine Empire, Saxony, Spain, France, Germany. Its disparate collection of kingdoms, principates, and republics flourished during the Renaissance and, after the collapse of the Napoleonic empire, coalesced finally, deliberately, during the unification in the late 19th century.

Even so, the formation of a single Italian identity, according to many, is still incomplete and is likely to remain so. Although globalization is one of the watchwords of the 21st century and Italy is among the world's most highly developed and industrialized countries, relatively strong regional identities remain a part of the country's cultural landscape. Much like the regions whose contributions collectively define the country itself, Italy brings its unique character and defining history to bear as a member of the European Union.

GLOSSARY

ALLUVIAL Composed of clay, silt, sand, gravel, or similar material deposited by running water.

AUTONOMY The state of being self-governing.

BICAMERAL Consisting of two legislative chambers.

BRIGANDAGE Raiding and plundering, usually as a member of a band.

CODIFIED Made into law; made systematic.

DEBOUCH To emerge or issue forth, as a river.

DORMANT Marked by a suspension of activity.

EXARCHATE An Eastern bishop; the head of a Byzantine independent church.

FIEFDOM An area of land over which one has rights or exercises control.

HEGEMONY The social, cultural, ideological, or economic influence exerted by a dominant group.

OLIGARCHY A government in which a small group exercises control, especially for corrupt and selfish purpose.

PROMULGATE To put into action through public declaration, as for laws.

PROTECTIONISM A governmental policy of economic protection for domestic producers through placing restrictions on foreign competitors.

QUIESCENT Marked by inactivity or causing no symptoms.

RISORGIMENTO The 19th-century movement for Italian political unity.

SYNOD An official gathering of an ecclesiastical (religious) governing body or advisory council.

VITICULTURE The cultivation or culture of grapes, especially for wine making.

BIBLIOGRAPHY

ITALY: THE LAND AND ITS PEOPLE

GENERAL WORKS

Comprehensive description of many geographic aspects of the country is found in Mario Pinna and Domenico Ruocco (eds.), *Italy: A Geographical Survey* (1980). Rinn S. Shinn (ed.), *Italy: A Country Study*, 2nd ed. (1987), surveys both the geography and the history of the country.

PEOPLE

Anna Laura Lepschy and Giulio Lepschy, *The Italian Language Today*, 2nd ed. (1988, reissued 1992), offers a survey of modern Italian and its dialects. National, social, and demographic characteristics of the country, with a look at regional differences, are discussed in David Willey, *Italians* (1984); and David I. Kertzer and Richard P. Saller (eds.), *The Family in Italy from Antiquity to the Present* (1991). Other works include John Agnew, *Place and Politics in Modern Italy* (2002); and Tobias Jones, *The Dark Heart of Italy*, rev. ed. (2007).

THE ITALIAN ECONOMY

Broad surveys are offered in Peter Groenewegen and Joseph Halevi (eds.), *Italian Economics Past and Present* (1983); and Russell King, *Italy* (1987). Russell King, *The Industrial Geography of Italy* (1985) analyzes the location of industries. Raffaella Y. Nanetti, *Growth and Territorial Policies: The Italian Model of Social Capitalism* (1988), focuses on regional disparities and the role of local government in economic development. Special studies include Alan B. Mountjoy, *The Mezzogiorno*, 2nd ed. (1982), a brief review of economic conditions in southern Italy; and Vera Zamagni, *The Economic History of Italy, 1860–1990* (1993).

ITALIAN GOVERNMENT AND SOCIETY

Comprehensive historical introductions to political institutions and processes are presented in Paul Ginsborg, *A History of Contemporary Italy: Society and Politics, 1943–1988* (1990, reissued 2003); Frederic Spotts and Theodor Wieser, *Italy: A Difficult Democracy* (1986); and Joseph LaPalombara, *Democracy, Italian Style* (1987). Useful insights into the machinations of the power system are provided in Alan Friedman, *Agnelli and the Network of Italian Power* (1988). The dynamics of various political forces are the subject of Paolo Farneti, *The Italian Party System (1945–1980)*, ed. by S.E. Finer and Alfio Mastropaolo (1985). A full analysis of the political, social, and economic crisis of the 1970s and the radical transformations that resulted from it is found in Sidney Tarrow, *Democracy and Disorder: Protest and Politics in Italy, 1965–1975* (1989).

CULTURAL LIFE IN ITALY

A well-illustrated discussion of popular culture and social customs, with a look at rustic decoration and ornament, is found in Catherine Sabino, *Italian Country*, rev. ed. (1995). David Forgacs, *Italian Culture in the Industrial Era, 1880–1980: Cultural Industries, Politics, and the Public* (1990), is a history of popular culture and politico-cultural dynamics. John Julius Norwich (ed.), *The Italians: History, Art, and the Genius of a People* (also published as *The Italian World*, 1983, reprinted 1989), sur-veys developments from Roman times to the 20th century. James Hall, *A History of Ideas and Images in Italian Art* (1983, reissued 1995), traces the inspiration behind Italian art from Etruscan times. Italy's contribution to modern motion pictures is examined in Peter Bondanella, *Italian Cinema: From Neorealism to the Present*, 3rd ed. (2001).

HISTORY

GENERAL WORKS

A comprehensive survey of Italian history is Reinhold Schumann, *Italy in the Last Fifteen Hundred Years: A Concise History*, 2nd ed. (1992). A good compendium is George Holmes, *The Oxford Illustrated History of Italy* (2001).

EARLY MIDDLE AGES THROUGH THE 13TH CENTURY

Comprehensive discussions of medi-eval Italy are provided in the first three volumes of *The Cambridge Medieval History*: *The Christian Roman Empire and the Foundation of the Teutonic Kingdoms*, 2nd ed., vol. 1 (1924, reprinted 1967); *The Rise of the Saracens and the Foundation of the Western Empire*, 2nd ed., vol. 2 (1924, reissued 1967); and *Germany and the Western Empire*, 2nd ed., vol. 3 (1924, reissued 1968).

Specific political and social top-ics of early periods are studied in T.S. Brown, *Gentlemen and Officers: Imperial Administration and Aristocratic Power in Byzantine Italy, A.D. 554–800* (1984); Thomas F.X. Noble, *The Republic of St. Peter: The Birth of the Papal State, 680–825* (1984); and Barbara M. Kreutz, *Before the Normans: Southern Italy in the Ninth and Tenth Centuries* (1991). Chris Wickham, *The Mountains and the City: The Tuscan Appennines in the Early Middle Ages* (1988), is a regional study.

Works embracing the whole period include *Contest of Empire and Papacy*, 2nd ed. (1924, reissued 1968), vol. 5 of *The Cambridge Medieval History*; and Chiara Frugoni, *A Distant City: Images of Urban Experience in the Medieval World*, trans. by William McCuaig (1991; originally published in Italian, 1983).

ITALY IN THE 14TH AND 15TH CENTURIES

General outlines of the period, together with references to important works in Italian and other languages, are to be found in Denys Hay and John Law, *Italy in the Age of the Renaissance, 1380–1530* (1989). An excellent work of reference is J.R. Hale (ed.), *A Concise Encyclopaedia of the Italian Renaissance* (1981).

Most writings in English have concentrated on the republics. Valuable works on the great Tuscan city of Florence are Gene A. Brucker, *Renaissance Florence* (1969, reissued 1994); and, on the great ruling family, J.R. Hale, *Florence and the Medici: The Pattern of Control*, new ed. (2001). An interesting contribution on the Serenissima is Robert Finlay, *Politics in Renaissance Venice* (1980).

The Papal States are treated in Peter Partner, *The Lands of St. Peter: The Papal State in the Middle Ages and the Early Renaissance* (1972); and studies of its *signori* include Trevor Dean, *Land and Power in Late Medieval Ferrara: The Rule of the Este, 1350–1450* (1988, reissued 2002). Works on the southern kingdoms include Denis Mack Smith, *Medieval Sicily, 800–1713* (1968, reprinted 1988), vol. 1 of *A History of Sicily*.

EARLY MODERN ITALY THROUGH UNIFICATION

General surveys of the early modern period include Eric Cochrane, *Italy 1530–1630*, ed. by Julius Kirshner (1988); and Dino Carpanetto and Giuseppe Ricuperati, *Italy in the Age of Reason, 1685–1789*, translated from Italian by Caroline Higgitt (1987).

Works covering the periods up to and including unification include David Laven and Lucy Riall (eds.), *Napoleon's Legacy: Problems of Government in Restoration Europe* (2000); John A. Davis and Paul Ginsborg (eds.), *Society and Politics in the Age of the Risorgimento* (1991), a collection of essays; Frank J. Coppa, *The Origins of the Italian Wars of Independence* (1992); and Benedict S. LiPira, *Giuseppe Garibaldi: A Biography of the Father of Modern Italy* (1998). An essential work on Garibaldi is Lucy Riall, *Garibaldi: Invention of a Hero* (2007).

ITALY FROM 1870 TO THE PRESENT

The fullest one-volume studies in English include Denis Mack Smith, *Modern Italy: A Political History* (1997); and Jonathan Dunnage, *Twentieth Century Italy: A Social History* (2002).

The early socialist movement is discussed well in Richard Hostetter, *The Italian Socialist Movement* (1958). On Giolitti, A. William Salomone, *Italy in the Giolittian Era: Italian Democracy in the Making, 1900–1914* (1960), is still very useful. Denis Mack Smith, *Mussolini* (1981, reissued 1994), is indispensable. The rise of fascism is examined by Adrian Lyttelton, *The Seizure of Power: Fascism in Italy, 1919–1929*, 3rd ed. (2004). The impact of fascism is discussed in Doug Thompson, *State Control in Fascist Italy: Culture and Conformity, 1925–43* (1991).

The history of Italian communism is treated in Alexander De Grand, *The Italian Left in the Twentieth Century* (1989). For the "two red years," Gwyn A. Williams, *Proletarian Order: Antonio Gramsci, Factory Councils, and the Origins of Italian Communism, 1911–1921* (1975) remains useful.

The best study of postwar Italy is without doubt Paul Ginsborg, *A History of Contemporary Italy: Society and Politics, 1943–1988* (1990; originally published in Italian, 1989). One of the best accounts of the postwar political system is Donald Sassoon, *Contemporary Italy*, 2nd ed. (1997).

On the Mafia and organized crime, particularly noteworthy are Diego Gambetta, *The Sicilian Mafia: The Business of Private Protection*, (1993; originally published in Italian, 1992); and Peter Robb, *Midnight in Sicily* (1996).

The student and worker movements of recent decades are discussed in Sidney Tarrow, *Democracy and Disorder: Protest and Politics in Italy, 1965–1975* (1989). The feminist perspective may be seen in Judith Adler Hellman, *Journeys Among Women: Feminism in Five Italian Cities* (1987). Trade unions and labour problems are discussed in Miriam Golden, *Labor Divided: Austerity and Working-Class Politics in Contemporary Italy* (1988).

The best studies of terrorism in the 1970s are David Moss, *The Politics of Left-Wing Violence in Italy, 1969–85* (1989); and Raimondo Catanzaro (ed.), *The Red Brigades and Left-Wing Terrorism in Italy* (1991).

Coverage of the 1980s and '90s is in Stephen Gundle and Simon Parker (eds.), *The New Italian Republic: From the Fall of the Berlin Wall to Berlusconi* (1996); and Vittorio Bufacchi and Simon Burgess, *Italy Since 1989: Events and Interpretations* (1998). Works on the Berlusconi government are Paul Ginsborg, *Silvio Berlusconi: Television, Power, and Patrimony*, 2nd ed. (2005); and David Lane, *Berlusconi's Shadow: Crime, Justice, and the Pursuit of Power* (2005).

INDEX